Divorce, American Style

POLITICS AND CULTURE
IN MODERN AMERICA

Series Editors:
Keisha N. Blain, Margot Canaday,
Matthew Lassiter, Stephen Pitti, Thomas J. Sugrue

Volumes in the series narrate and analyze political and social change in the broadest dimensions from 1865 to the present, including ideas about the ways people have sought and wielded power in the public sphere and the language and institutions of politics at all levels—local, national, and transnational. The series is motivated by a desire to reverse the fragmentation of modern U.S. history and to encourage synthetic perspectives on social movements and the state, on gender, race, and labor, and on intellectual history and popular culture.

Divorce, American Style

Fighting for Women's Economic Citizenship in the Neoliberal Era

Suzanne Kahn

PENN

UNIVERSITY OF PENNSYLVANIA PRESS

PHILADELPHIA

Published by
University of Pennsylvania Press
Philadelphia, Pennsylvania 19104-4112
www.upenn.edu/pennpress

Printed in the United States of America
on acid-free paper
1 3 5 7 9 10 8 6 4 2

A Cataloging-in-Publication record is available from the Library of Congress
ISBN 978-0-8122-5290-3

For my parents, Paul Kahn and Catherine Iino,
who always knew I would write a book.

And for Noah, who made sure I could.

CONTENTS

INTRODUCTION

Divorce, 1970s Style

The first woman to run for vice president of the United States on a major party ticket, Geraldine Ferraro, did not start her political career as a feminist. "When I ran for Congress in 1978, I did not consider myself a feminist. I ran as a tough, no-nonsense prosecutor. My campaign slogan was 'Finally, a Tough Democrat,'" the New York congresswoman told an audience in 1983. In Washington, however, she began hearing from constituents. "I learned by listening," she explained. "I listened to a woman whose husband divorced her while she was in the hospital having cancer surgery. Her husband's former employer is refusing to pay her part of his pension. The company claims he earned it all by himself during 30 years of marriage."[1] Stories like this one convinced Ferraro to adopt a feminist agenda.

Ferraro's narrative of feminist awakening rooted in the particular experiences of divorced women would have sounded familiar to her audience in the 1980s. Between 1967 and 1979 the divorce rate in the United States doubled.[2] When it reached its all-time high in 1979, the divorce rate was two and a half times what it had been in the 1950s.[3] Ultimately, close to half of marriages formed in the 1970s ended in divorce.[4] For many women, divorce led to a political awakening and brought them into the feminist movement. There they articulated a political agenda that sought to directly address issues women faced after divorce like the loss of retirement security Ferraro described. This book tells the story of these women—whom I call "feminist divorce reformers"—women specifically politicized by their divorces who turned to the feminist movement for answers and molded their corner of the movement to fit their needs.

In 1976, the popular women's magazine *McCall's* ran an article about these women titled "Divorcees: The New Poor." It announced, "America's four million divorcees are the new poor of our society. If last year's divorce rate holds steady they will be joined by at least another million in 1976, swelling the ranks of women and children who once lived in middle-class comfort who now live in or near hardship and poverty."[5] The article explained what divorce did to a homemaker: "Divorce wipes out her job, her health insurance pension rights, and often old-age benefits. Many men have low-cost group health insurance as a fringe benefit of their employment. When divorce comes, it continues to cover the children but not the ex-wife. To purchase a health policy on her own she often has to pass a physical exam and many women can't qualify."[6] At divorce, the article showed, women discovered that they not only depended on their husbands for their incomes but also for myriad other economic rights and resources that by law and custom flowed to women through their husbands.

The *McCall's* story ended on a hopeful note, reporting on divorced women's efforts to address their economic situation through activism. One woman told the magazine, "Women are getting together out of frustration and despair. . . . It's a fragmented grass-roots kind of ferment."[7] This grass-roots ferment was led by women who had been in their marriages and out of the workforce for years. When divorced women tried to reenter the workforce to regain access to the resources they had lost, they found that getting a job was difficult, to say the least, especially when balancing ongoing childcare responsibilities. For this reason, the divorced women who managed to also add activism to their full plates skewed older with children out of the home. Often self-conscious of the fact that they did not fit the popular image of radical young feminists, feminist divorce reformers frequently disagreed with some of the analysis offered by their younger colleagues in the movement. Nevertheless, they found that, overall, the feminist movement offered a compelling explanation for their experience and its organizations provided a useful home for their work.

The large number of divorced women who responded to their suddenly precarious economic lives by joining the feminist movement tells us much about the formation of political identity and sheds new light on the history of feminism and how it intersected with the conservative backlash of the late twentieth century. From the start, feminist divorce reformers had a complex relationship with other feminists not just because of demographic differences but also because of their agenda. More focused on creating equality in marriage and the home than in the workforce, their agenda often did not look like the 1970s feminist agenda with which historians are most familiar. Furthermore, the timeline on which feminist divorce reformers campaigned and succeeded forces us to look beyond the time frame historians have typically applied to the "Second Wave" feminist movement. Acting from within the most prominent feminist organizations of the 1970s (for example, the National Organization for Women and the Women's Equity Action League), divorced women activists won important victories well into the 1980s.

From the late 1960s through the 1980s, feminist divorce reformers struggled to articulate to their fellow feminists and to policymakers how the state should conceptualize marriage. They experimented with a wide range of theories of marriage and policy solutions, but throughout remained committed to the idea that women's economic relationship to the state—their economic citizenship—need not be mediated through their husbands. The many understandings of marriage that activists and policymakers considered as they tried to respond to the problems caused by the rising divorce rate provide new insights into how marriage has operated as both a political and politicizing institution in the late twentieth century.

Feminist divorce reformers fought for new economic protections from the state. They claimed this support both on the basis of the economic and social value of the care work they performed in the home and on the basis of the moral value of their marriages. In the former argument, divorced women's claim to economic resources was rooted in an understanding of marriage as a sort of economic contract; in the latter argument, marriage was understood as conferring a privileged status on women, one that should outlast the length of any specific marriage. Feminist policy debates about divorced women's rights thus made concrete a century-long debate among legal theorists about whether marriage is best conceptualized as a public status because by entering a marriage individuals gain a predetermined set of rights and obligations enforceable by the state or as a private contract whereby two individuals make enforceable economic commitments to each other.[8] Throughout the 1970s and 1980s these two lines of argument led to conflict among divorced women and between feminist divorce reformers and other feminists.

By the late 1980s, the legislative agenda most feminist divorce reformers favored, an agenda that proposed that public social insurance programs see marriage as a contract, had failed almost entirely. Feminist divorce reformers and their allies had compromised it away even as they won legislative victories. By the end of the 1970s, feminist divorce reformers had tacitly agreed to focus on state-ensured access to private and work-based social insurance rather than public or universal programs. Even as they put their energy into these programs, they understood that a move away from an agenda focused on public programs meant abandoning low-income women. As they made this compromise, feminist divorce reformers continued to insist that such policies recognize marriage as a contract. Over the first half of the 1980s, the rise of social conservatism alongside neoliberalism led to further concessions. In the end, Congress agreed to expand access to private insurance benefits to divorced women on the basis of a moral claim rooted in their relationships to their former husbands rather than on the basis of an implied economic contract.

Policymakers showed a deep and lasting commitment to using social insurance benefits to encourage and reward the breadwinner-homemaker model of marriage. Despite women's growing economic independence and changing popular understandings of marriage, throughout the 1970s and 1980s policymakers clung to a model of marriage that had its roots in the common-law concept of coverture and suggested that marriage was above all a status. The activism of feminist divorce reformers had the ironic result of deepening the state's use of marriage to distribute economic resources by creating new marital statuses through which an individual could become eligible for benefits.

Divorce, American Style examines feminist divorce reformers, their relationship with the broader feminist movement, and their lasting effects on the American social welfare regime. It shows how two distinctive qualities of the American welfare state—its gendered nature and its public/private nature—combined to encourage the breadwinner-homemaker model of marriage's use as policy tool. The linking of access to economic benefits to marriage, begun early in the development of the American social insurance system, shaped political identity and activism in the 1970s and has continued to do so into our current political moment. The result has not only affected policy questions directly relating to marriage but also limited the possibilities for expanding America's social welfare provisions. As a gateway to full economic citizenship, marriage has always served as an institution that protects and perpetuates class privilege.

An Era of Instability

American marriages started to fall apart at a moment when many Americans believed that social traditions all around them were crumbling. The social and political assumptions that had shaped the decades immediately after World War II fell one by one in the 1960s and 1970s. New social movements, such as the civil rights movement, the women's rights movement, and the antiwar movement, challenged long-held beliefs about Americans' rights and duties. African Americans moved slowly into the voting booth and an unprecedented number of women entered the paid workforce. The 1970s began hopefully for many Americans who had previously been excluded from basic social, political, civil, and economic rights. Then, as questioning of and challenges to traditional authority spread, a backlash formed. The rising divorce rate contributed to the sense of a widespread and dangerous—if potentially also liberating—social instability. Women's responses to their divorces carried both feminist social movements and the backlash to them forward into the 1980s in new and unexpected directions.

Second Wave feminism has many origin stories. Some date it to 1963 when Betty Friedan published *The Feminine Mystique*, which exposed the simmering discontent of suburban housewives throughout the United States. The postwar baby boom and drive toward suburbanization had led a remarkable number of women out of the workforce and into suburban subdivisions full of children. Friedan's book allowed millions of women to realize that the lack of fulfillment they found in the home was a shared experience—a widespread "problem with no name." They came together and began to organize.[9] Others argue that the feminist revival of the 1960s began in 1964 with segregationist senator Howard Smith's addition of legislation banning sex discrimination in employment to the Civil Rights Act in an attempt to stop the act from passing. In spite of Smith's intentions, Congresswoman Martha Griffiths (D-MI) seized on the addition and pushed the bill through. In the following years, this new legal ban on sex discrimination was weakly enforced. Anger over the government's failure to stop employers from discriminating on the basis of sex led a group of women, including Friedan, to found the National Organization for Women (NOW) in 1968.[10] Still others trace the Second Wave feminist movement to the meeting rooms of the social movements that predated it. Women in the civil rights movement and on the student left would later describe being pushed into secretarial and other support roles by the men leading these efforts. Eventually, women decided they needed a movement of their own.[11]

The truth, of course, is that the revival of feminist activism in the 1960s had many mothers. Indeed, historians today are likely to refer to feminist movements, plural, to describe this outpouring of activism. The activism of the African American women's movement looked different from the efforts of legalist feminists to pass anti-sex-discrimination laws, and the legalists, in turn, had a different agenda than lesbian separatist feminists. This book argues that feminist divorce reformers also crafted their own form of feminism within the movement and are just as important to understanding the late twentieth-century feminism as other, more frequently discussed, branches of the feminist movement(s).

Despite the tremendous variety encompassed within the umbrella category of Second Wave feminism, for the wider public, feminism quickly became associated with a few specific demands. The National Organization for Women made passing the Equal Rights Amendment (ERA), which had first been proposed by feminist activists in the 1920s, its legislative priority. After the ERA passed quickly in both houses of Congress in 1972, ratification by the states became the recognized priority of feminists. Then, only a year later, the Supreme Court ruled on the legality of abortion in *Roe v. Wade*. Both the ERA and abortion received a tremendous amount of attention, in part because they inspired a backlash that took the form of vocal opposition to the entire feminist agenda. Although feminist organizations addressed a broad range of issues—including, but not limited to, equal pay, women's representation in the media, gender-based violence, and federal child care legislation—the ERA and abortion became the iconic centers of the feminist movement.

Historians often divide the 1970s in half, arguing that the first half of the decade was a continuation of the 1960s social rights movements and liberal politics, while the second half saw the rise of a conservative backlash and the start of the economic contraction that would define the 1980s.[12] This framework papers over some of the decade's complexities. Progressive social movements may have continued to blossom in the first half of the 1970s, but they did so in the context of the conservative Nixon presidency, the ongoing Vietnam War, and eventually the Watergate scandal—a political moment that suggested instability and a crisis of traditional lines of authority perhaps more than any other. Just as the ERA and abortion came to infuse all feminist politics, Watergate and Vietnam infused all politics in the first half of the decade.

For political activists, policymakers, and the general public, instability defined the 1970s. Even the social movements that had challenged old structures of authority in the 1960s began, themselves, to fracture. Women on the student left and working in the civil rights movement began to rebel against the service roles they were pushed into; within the feminist movement, lesbian activists demanded their own voice.[13] Authority figures as big as the president and as small as people's own fathers and husbands fell. This instability was exacerbated by a weakening economy. Starting in the middle of the decade, rampant inflation and deindustrialization undermined the earning power of the American middle class. The inflation rate in 1974 was 11 percent; it hit 18 percent in the summer of 1980.[14]

In the face of this instability, some people saw social movements like feminism as offering a way to understand why old lines of authority should fall. But others turned to religion and conservative political movements to push back against the rapidly changing world. At the heart of this new conservatism was a coalition that defined itself around "family values." Their agenda included a wholesale rejection of feminist demands, an effort to increase parental control in schools, and a general belief that families, not government, should serve as the social safety net. In 1972, the best-known leader of the "pro-family" antifeminists, Phyllis Schlafly, founded her first antifeminist organization, STOP ERA; three years later she founded the Eagle Forum. Both organizations were devoted to fighting the ERA and by extension the rest of the feminist agenda.

Whether they were attacking or defending old structures of authority, political activists and elected officials on the Right and Left paid increasing attention to the family. When they turned their attention in this direction, activists—no matter their political persuasion—could not help but notice the rising divorce rate. In a 1973 report calling for legislative reforms, the National Organization for Women's Marriage and Divorce Task Force informed readers that, "For the 12 months ending August 1972, there were 72,000 more [divorce] decrees than in 1971."[15] And in testimony on behalf of support of Social Security reform in 1978, the executive director of President Carter's Interdepartmental Task Force on Women argued that the rising divorce rate was one of the most "important aspect(s) of the change in the American family."[16]

Many factors drove the rapid rise in the divorce rate. Some contemporaries blamed the feminist and sexual liberation movements and the attendant combination of new contraceptive technologies and shifting morals that made it possible for women not to marry. Shifting morals also lifted the stigma of divorce and encouraged individuals to seek self-fulfillment through divorce and remarriage when their current spouses did not meet all their wants and needs. Others argued that increasing career opportunities for women allowed women to leave husbands they had relied on for support.[17] Crucially, changing laws made getting a divorce significantly easier.

In the five years between 1969, when California adopted the nation's first no-fault divorce law, and 1974 almost every state modified its divorce laws so that they no longer required couples to prove that adultery, abuse, or other specific violations of the code of marital conduct had occurred. In place of these rigid requirements, reformed laws allowed couples to receive a divorce on the basis of "irreconcilable differences," with no party at fault.[18] Since couples knew that a loosening of divorce laws was in the works, part of the rise in divorce rate in the 1970s came from a pent-up demand from couples that waited to divorce under the new laws.[19] Between 1970 and 1975 alone, the divorce rate rose from fifteen divorces per thousand married women to twenty.[20] Once the backlog of divorces had resolved itself, after 1979, the divorce rate leveled off with around 50 percent of marriages formed in the 1970s ending in divorce within twenty-five years.[21]

Even as the divorce rate found a new equilibrium, the number of divorced women remained high. The remarriage rate for divorced women dropped 38 percent between 1970 and 1990.[22] But women's chances of remarriage also dropped dramatically as they aged. Three quarters of women who divorced under thirty remarried and half of women who divorced in their thirties, but only one quarter of women who divorced after forty, would remarry.[23] (Remarriage rates also differed by sex. Of the cohort born between 1950 and 1955, 71.3 percent of divorced men remarried, while only 66.8 percent of women remarried.) All of this meant that in the 1970s and 1980s there were not only increasing numbers of divorced women but also increasing numbers of divorced women who could expect that "divorced" would be their marital status for, if not the rest of their life, then a substantial portion of it. By 1973 there were 3.25 million divorced women in the United States, a political identity group ready to act.[24]

Political Identity, Social Insurance, and the Feminist Divorce Reform Movement

Divorce was often a politicizing moment for women because, through divorce, middle-class, white, formerly married women lost their membership in the mainstream political, economic, and social culture. Divorced women organized around their sudden loss of status, which, not incidentally, generally came with the literal loss of credit, health insurance, Social Security, and pension rights. This loss forced divorced women to reckon not only with the new no-fault divorce laws but also with the gendered structure of the American social insurance system and the many ways the federal government used marriage to regulate access to economic benefits.

Women in the 1970s divorced at a moment when they could not help but be aware of how the law shaped their divorces. Because almost every state had adopted new no-fault divorce laws, women divorced under a different legal regime from the one they had married under. New state divorce laws not only loosened the grounds on which a couple could divorce but also changed how property was divided and ended the assumption that alimony would be awarded at a marriage's end. Instead, judges were told to award continuing support payments on the basis of need. *McCall's* summed up the effect of the new laws this way: "With a dramatic shift to no-fault divorce in recent years, the battle over money is now what divorce is all about."[25] When a couple went to court, the question was no longer whether they would get a divorce but what its financial consequences would be.

By the early 1980s, only about 15 percent of divorced women were awarded alimony and only about 4 percent of those women regularly collected it.[26] Not only did men fail to pay alimony, support payments specifically for the ex-wife, but women had difficulty even collecting child support.[27] By 1976, 44 percent of divorced women were awarded child support, but only 20 percent of divorced mothers collected regularly.[28] Providing support to children and women from multiple marriages was outside the financial capacity of many men. These were not new problems, but the increasing prevalence of divorce and prominent public debates about efforts to reform divorce law increased women's awareness of divorce's financial dangers.[29]

With support payments so rarely awarded and even more rarely complied with, women's post-divorce financial security rested increasingly on how property was divided in a divorce. Here, too, women encountered problems. Courts were familiar with dividing traditional forms of property—real estate holdings, savings, and personal belongings. Increasingly, however, families—especially poor and middle-class families—held their wealth not in these forms of property but in income streams embedded in the American social insurance system such as Social Security benefits and veterans' benefits. Even the better-off depended on economic resources such as occupational licenses, housing subsidies, and government-regulated services such as insurance. In a 1964 *Yale Law Journal* article, the legal scholar Charles

Reich dubbed these sources of income "the new property" and argued, "The wealth of more and more Americans depends upon a relationship to the government."[30]

Though "new," these forms of property had developed using the breadwinner-homemaker model of marriage as their spine, the very same spine as traditional forms of property. From its earliest days, the American social insurance system was designed to treat men and women and married and unmarried women differently. Beginning in the aftermath of the Revolutionary War, certain categories of women—defined by marriage or motherhood—have always been able to make special claims on the American state.[31]

The system of distinct entitlements for women—especially widows and single mothers—that developed over the course of the nineteenth century became firmly entrenched in American law and began to touch the lives of the majority of Americans during the 1930s with the rise of the New Deal. The architects of the New Deal, the basis of the modern American welfare state, built the country's new Social Security system on the assumption that married women would not, or at least should not, work outside the home, and designed policies to encourage this pattern of family labor.[32] Under this system, for example, most married women, even those who worked outside the home, received access to Social Security as their husbands' dependents instead of earning Social Security credits on their own.[33] Many women never worked outside the home, and among those who did, the majority held jobs that were not covered by the original Social Security law, such as domestic service jobs. Moreover, married women employed outside the home tended to move in and out of the workforce as their family situations changed, and they generally received lower wages than men. As a result, even when they accumulated Social Security benefits through their own employment record, women did so more slowly and at lower rates than men. When it came time to claim benefits, married women had to choose between their own benefits and the benefits they were eligible for as their husbands' dependents. The latter almost always amounted to more money. When married women chose to collect Social Security through their husbands' record, any contributions they had made to Social Security through their own work record over the years went into a general fund. From the start, the Social Security system was designed to support and reward families with breadwinner fathers and homemaker mothers.[34]

The Social Security system could not completely ignore the fact that not all women were married. The same law that created Social Security retirement benefits created Aid to Dependent Children (ADC) (later Aid to Families with Dependent Children [AFDC], which we colloquially know as "welfare"). ADC was a program designed for poor, single women with children. Unlike Social Security's retirement pension programs, it was a means-tested program, which meant that it offered support payments to qualifying women with children and no male provider. These support payments were less generous than other payments created under the Social Security Act. Receipt of ADC payments also came with far more social disapprobation than participation in other Social Security programs.[35]

After the 1930s, whenever the government expanded the social insurance benefits it offered—especially during the Great Society reforms of the 1960s—it took Social Security's distributive mechanisms as its model. So, too, did the private benefits—such as pensions and health insurance—that were layered onto government-sponsored programs as the United States built a unique social insurance system that combined benefits sponsored by both public and private entities to ensure most people a basic standard of living. In the hybrid American social welfare regime, in addition to directly administering some benefits to some populations, the government promotes and regulates privately offered economic resources to help ensure their availability.[36] For example, since 1954, the government has encouraged and regulated employer-sponsored health insurance through beneficial tax treatments.[37] These private, employment-based benefits often include dependent benefits just as Social Security does. By positioning employers as the source of health insurance for most Americans, the federal government encouraged private benefits to become part of what breadwinner men expected to provide for their families.

By the time no-fault divorce laws swept across the country, America's hybrid social insurance system built on a breadwinner-homemaker model of the family was solidly entrenched, yet invisible to most Americans. Historians and political scientists have spent the last thirty years carefully documenting each strand of this system's development: they have progressively pushed back our understanding of when the government began to offer welfare benefits; deepened our understanding of how gender has shaped those benefits; and woven in the parallel and linked history of the private, government-regulated social insurance benefits that are unique to the American social insurance system. Until now, however, scholars have not asked what happened to this system when the nature of marriage shifted in the public consciousness. When no-fault divorce laws emerged at the end of the

1960s, social insurance programs had only barely begun to consider how divorced women might access benefits. This is the point at which this book picks up the story of the gendered, hybrid welfare state. It asks what a dramatic shift in the assumptions about marriage meant for a social insurance system organized around the logic of marriage and, reciprocally, what the social insurance system meant to women whose place within it suddenly changed when their marriages ended.

After divorce many women faced a precipitous decline in standard of living. Studies suggested a woman's standard of living, measured as income compared to need, fell by anywhere from 29 to 73 percent immediately after a divorce.[38] Many newly divorced women facing this loss were pulled toward the revived feminist movement. As Geraldine Ferraro explained when describing her own feminist awakening, through the experience of divorce women learned that "our laws and our budgets and our federal regulations—all neutral and fair sounding on the their face—are simply not working for women the same way they work for men."[39] Even many divorced women who had never before identified as feminists turned to the burgeoning women's movement for an explanation for the situation in which they found themselves and for the tools with which to deal with it.

As divorced women reached out to them for help, national feminist organizations quickly set up committees to address their needs and feminist elected officials had their staff begin to look for solutions. NOW, the Women's Equity Action League (WEAL), 9to5, and the 1975 International Women's Year (IWY) Committee all worked on the rights of divorced women. By 1975, the NOW Marriage and Divorce Task Force had the fifth largest national membership of any of the organization's twenty-four issue-based task forces.[40] By the mid-1970s, WEAL, which devoted much of its time to homemakers' economic rights, had several thousand members.[41] An array of regional divorced women's membership organizations emerged as well, as did groups devoted to specific constituencies of divorced women like ex-military wives.

The women activists I group together under the term "feminist divorce reformers" share two key traits: they joined feminist organizations specifically to advocate for the state to take on an expanded role providing divorced women with economic security, and their politics flowed directly from their experience of divorce.[42] Both sides of this definition are critical to understanding these women as a distinct ideological group. Many different women engaged with issues surrounding divorce. Social Security reform, child support, and marital property rights were issues of concern for socialist feminists, welfare rights activists, and other women working under the big tent of feminism, including some of the larger movement's most prominent leaders, such as Betty Friedan and Bella Abzug. Moreover, antifeminists and conservative women also spent time on these issues. The women I term "feminist divorce reformers," however, specifically joined the feminist movement because of their experience of divorce. Unlike antifeminists and conservatives concerned with the problems of divorce, feminist divorce reformers wanted to create more equal marriages and divorces and believed that a more active presence of women throughout the legal and political process would help bring this about. Their divorces led them to believe (or confirmed their belief) that men's control over the law had created the problems they now faced.

As feminist divorce reformers worked through the 1970s and into the 1980s, they encountered an increasingly hostile social and political response. A great deal of work has been done on the rise of a conservative backlash against feminism and the welfare state in the 1970s and the rise of neoliberalism.[43] The history of feminist divorce reformers' work allows us to see how one group of feminists sought to adapt in real time to conservative and neoliberal challenges to the New Deal order. As the 1970s progress we see divorced women pivoting their agenda away from building more expansive social insurance programs and toward gaining access to their husbands' existing benefits. By the 1980 these concessions to fiscal conservatism were joined by concessions to increasingly powerful social conservatives. In order to continue to enact some form of their agenda, feminist divorce reformers were obliged to agree to reforms that upheld marriage as a status rather than a contract and understood wives as dependents, not partners.

It is in understanding when feminist organizations made decisions to compromise and how and why certain women got left out of reform packages as a result that the origins of activists' feminism become most relevant. The problems divorced women faced were in many ways the problems of all low- and middle-income single women in a political and economic system designed around men. As a result, feminists of many different stripes with many different marital statuses advocated legislation that supported the feminist divorce reform agenda. But the vocal and organized women whose agenda grew specifically out of their experience of divorce were remarkably white, and when they had to make difficult choices this showed.

The rise in the divorce rate and decline in standard of living after divorce reached across classes and touched both black and white women; however, it was not equally politicizing.[44] Although black women and women from other minority groups suffered economically and emotionally in a divorce, they did not experience the same sudden transition to outsider status in relationship to their citizenship rights.[45] Already too familiar with the inequities of the American social welfare system, women of color did not, for the most part, experience divorce as a reason to enter politics. At a moment when race- and ethnicity-based social movements flourished, women of color were far more likely to connect limitations on their citizenship rights to racism than to divorce. Although there were black, Latino, lesbian, and poor divorced women, it was middle-class white women for whom divorce served as a primary politicizing catalyst and whose needs dominated feminist divorce reformers' political agenda. Thus, when feminist divorce reformers struck compromises, they often chose legislation narrowly tailored to address the needs of women who could access middle-class status through their ex-husbands. These choices understandably provoked frequent conflict with women of color and feminists whose analysis was rooted in race or class.

The following chapters reconstruct the ideologies and agendas of feminist divorce reformers in order to understand how these activists came into conflict with each other and with other sectors of the feminist movement in ways that transformed not only the movement but also the social insurance system. Many scholars have argued that, in the late 1970s and early 1980s, feminists moved away from a "formal equality" agenda to demand "equality in fact," or laws that accounted for men's and women's different life patterns in order to create more equal outcomes.[46] But feminist divorce reformers offered an alternative to the formal equality agenda from the earliest years of the Second Wave feminist movement, when they began advocating for divorce, pension, and equal credit legislation that accommodated women's roles as mothers and wives instead of treating them exactly like men.

Though focused on the home, not the workplace, feminist divorce reformers, like earlier difference feminists, sought policies that recognized and compensated women for their different social and legal position instead of policies that tried to change that position. In this respect, they shared much with welfare rights activists working at the same time. Yet, despite their shared focus on compensation for women's work in the home, feminist divorce reformers and welfare rights activists clashed frequently. Most (but not all) feminist divorce reformers maintained their distance from women receiving welfare payments by refusing to organize as mothers. Welfare rights activists, in their campaigns, drew on a long history of maternalist politics, arguing that women deserved robust economic support from the state in recognition of the important work they did caring for their children.[47] In contrast, divorced women consistently emphasized their connection to their husbands rather than their children when demanding economic support. Feminist divorce reformers organized not as single mothers but as single wives. This failure to find common ground—even among women who shared an emphasis on the value of care work in the home—reinforced class and racial divisions within the feminist movement.

By organizing around the status of single wife, feminist divorce reformers accepted and perpetuated two defining aspects of the American social insurance system: its ideology of "breadwinner liberalism" and its structure of "selective entitlements." Historian Robert Self has argued that "breadwinner liberalism" drove the expansion of public social insurance benefits over the course of the twentieth century. As a political ideology, "breadwinner liberalism" sought to make the "idealized nuclear family" with a breadwinner father and homemaker mother "attainable to more Americans than ever before."[48] Programs built around this ideology consistently created and affirmed a privileged place for married women within the social insurance system. By their very nature these programs insisted that married women were worthy of what historian Kristin Collins has called "the selective entitlement," not broad, citizenship-based economic rights but rather specific entitlements for constituencies considered especially deserving[49]

Although they accepted and worked within many of the confines of the American social insurance system's structures, feminist divorce reformers did demand a radical shift in the legal understanding of women's economic citizenship. Scholars of the welfare state often talk about four types of citizenship: political, social, civil, and economic.[50] The final category, economic citizenship, refers to the access to economic resources that allows full participation in the polity.[51] In the early twentieth century, women's rights activists won full political citizenship through the vote. Their political rights no longer flowed through their husbands. But in the ensuing years, as the state apparatus around economic citizenship was built out, in almost every case public policy ensured that access to economic resources flowed to married women through their husbands. Feminist divorce reformers sought to change that and bring married women into a direct economic relationship with the state.

The history of divorced women's activism shows how the selective entitlement system creates a set of specific political incentives for constituencies trying to win new benefits. It encourages individuals to make claims on the state on the basis of their moral deservingness. Moreover, it raises the stakes of such claims by not only deciding whether or not to provide benefits to each group on the basis of subjective judgments about the morality and righteousness of their need, but also deciding the size of the benefits, their administrative structure, and the stigma attached to them on the basis of these judgments. Feminist divorce reformers proved ready and willing to position themselves as a particularly deserving group.

Between 1974 and 1986, in response to the demands of feminist divorce reformers, Congress passed ten national laws expressly designed to improve divorced women's access to economic resources. This wave of legislation is almost entirely missing not only from our histories of the welfare state and feminism, but also from the historiography of marriage and divorce.[52] Yet, this legislation and its history provide a key to understanding the marriage equality movement and, more generally, how marriage functions to distribute rights, resources, and economic power in the contemporary United States. Rather than limiting marriage's distributive role, each of these laws tied divorced women's new access to benefits to their former marriages. The new laws actually deepened the social insurance system's use of marriage to distribute resources and mediate women's economic citizenship rights and strengthened the idea that marriages were comprised of breadwinners and homemakers instead of equal partners.

The new laws did more than entrench breadwinner-homemaker marriages in the American social insurance system; they also changed how the law understood marriage. When Congress created rights to benefits that continued after a marriage ended, it did so on the basis of the number of years a woman had spent in her marriage. Women who divorced after a certain number of years of marriage won new status-based rights to economic resources. These new laws pushed marriage in the opposite direction from the one many legal historians have seen courts taking the institution in the nineteenth and twentieth centuries: they did not make marriage more contract-like, but rather affirmed its status-creating function. Indeed, the new laws transformed marriage from a unitary status that came with a specific menu of benefits to a series of statuses. The benefits to which a marriage entitled a woman increased with the years spent in it.

The chapters that follow explore how falling outside the family structures and statuses recognized by public policy politicized women. In the book's first section, the spotlight is on the no-fault divorce "revolution" and the myriad ways changing divorce laws brought women into and thus, ultimately, shaped the feminist movement. The second section, "A Galaxy of Laws," looks at a range of economic resources—consumer credit, health insurance, Social Security, and private pensions—that provided the underpinnings of economic citizenship in postwar America.[53]

Across the board, feminist divorce reformers found that the federal government was far more willing to order private companies and employers (e.g., banks) to treat marriage as a partnership than it was to remove the breadwinner-dependency model of marriage from federally managed social insurance programs. This runs contrary to most theories of inequality in public and private benefits. Jacob Hacker, one of the chief theorists of the public-private welfare state, argues that the public has tolerated inequality in private benefits more than they have in public benefits.[54] While this is true of explicitly discriminatory policies in social insurance programs, it is clear that gendered assumptions are more deeply ingrained in the law governing the public insurance system than the law governing the private.

The book's final section takes a step back from detailed legislative policy debates to consider how feminist divorce reformers' work in the 1970s and early 1980s shaped feminists' relationship to state institutions and political activism as the century came to a close. Most histories of feminism end with the collapse of the ERA campaign and the election of Reagan. The history of feminist divorce reformers' work necessarily extends the timeline into the 1980s, when many of the laws feminist divorce reformers advocated for passed. In the 1980s, feminists adapted to a moment of significant political adversity by making difficult choices about what sorts of legislation they could continue to win. When political winds shifted again in the early 1990s, feminist choices in the prior decade not only harmed the women they explicitly abandoned through their 1980s compromises but also created unanticipated constraints on further reform.

As a result of the compromises feminist divorce reformers accepted in order to continue their work, by the end of the 1980s, wealthy, middle-class, and low-income women had radically different experiences of divorce. By compromising on legislation that addressed gender inequities in private benefits and increased judicial control over the division of property, feminist divorce reforms had given an advantage to wealthy women, who could afford to go to court and fight for the award of certain forms of privately

Figure 1. A cartoon from the *Colorado Springs Sun* illustrates the anger many military wives felt when they discovered that they had no individual rights to military benefits. Image from Box 124, Folder: Former Spouses Press, Patricia Schroeder Papers, Archives, University of Colorado Boulder Libraries.

accumulated property. Increasingly, these privileged women found judges willing to treat marriages as contracted partnerships and divide economic resources evenly. On the other hand, when a marriage ended with benefits that were divided according to statute rather than judicial rulings, women were left with fewer resources than men.

At the peak of divorced women's activism, the *Colorado Springs Sun* ran a political cartoon that featured an airplane labeled "military marriage" in a tailspin. Three people fall to earth beside it. A man floats gently down attached to a parachute labeled "government issue retirement benefits." A young boy grips his leg and yells, "Open your parachute Mom!!" The mom, angry, calls back, "I wasn't authorized one!"[55] The cartoon captures how many divorced women—military spouses or not—felt about their rights and the government after going through a divorce. Thrust out of their marriages and the life they expected, divorced women were shocked to learn how few protections the government offered them as individuals. Their political activism in response fundamentally changed the American social safety net—or parachute—often in unexpected ways. By the time the divorce rate stabilized in the 1980s, more women had been authorized parachutes, but many still found themselves in free fall at the end of a marriage, and women who never married still found themselves entirely without support.

PART I

The Divorce Revolution

CHAPTER 1

From Alimony Drones to Breeding Cows

Women and the Divorce Law Revolution

In January 1957, after thirteen years of arguing in court about the end of their marriage and the subsequent divorce settlement, Marguerite and Walter Doyle ended up in New York County's Supreme Court before Judge Samuel Hofstadter. Because the case was really a routine matter, Judge Hofstadter dispensed with his ruling in three sentences and upheld an increase in weekly alimony for Marguerite as awarded by the lower court. But he was not pleased about the decision. Even as he increased Marguerite's monthly allowance, Hofstadter expressed his dislike of the entire legal system under which the case was decided. "Alimony was originally devised by society to protect those without power of ownership or earning resources," he wrote. "It was never intended to assure a perpetual state of indolence. It should not be suffered to convert a host of physically and mentally competent women into an army of alimony drones."[1]

The rest of Judge Hofstadter's opinion reads like a manifesto for the largely lawyer- and judge-led movement to reform divorce law that challenged and fundamentally changed American divorce law over the next twenty years.[2] Hofstadter called for family courts that incorporated social workers alongside lawyers and judges; he suggested standardized tables for determining support awards based on the wife's need and the husband's financial capacity; and he suggested that fault should be removed from the determination of such awards.[3] Over the following decades many different constituencies successfully lobbied for pieces of this agenda such that by the late 1970s, the divorce laws of many states bore little resemblance to the legal framework the Doyles had spent so much time navigating.

The new framework was not an unqualified success. Twenty years after Hofstadter wrote his opinion, another judge addressing a divorcing couple described women transformed by divorce not as drones but as cattle. In that year, Flora and Thomas Brantner ended up in a California appeals court when Flora appealed their original divorce settlement. The Brantners' marriage had lasted twenty-five years. During that time, Thomas had been the family's only breadwinner. The trial court awarded Flora custody of the Brantners' two children. The couple's house was sold and the proceeds used to pay lawyers and debts. The remaining "meager balance" was divided between Flora and Thomas.[4] Thomas was ordered to pay Flora child support of $100 a month per child and $200 a month in alimony for two years. After that, the alimony award would gradually decrease until, twelve years after her divorce, Flora's alimony would terminate entirely.[5] When Flora appealed, Thomas, forty-five, was working at an aircraft company and making $1,578 a month in gross income. Flora, forty-four, had never completed high school and was slowly going blind. She also suffered from arthritis. Flora had made eight efforts to find employment in sales, all of which failed, and was attending a two-year junior college class for women in her situation.[6]

Faced with these facts, in *Brantner*, the court ruled that the original alimony award, with its built-in reductions and automatic termination date, was an abuse of judicial discretion. Its opinion, written by Judge Robert Gardner, explained that the original alimony award was based on a misreading of California's recently reformed divorce law. That law had been "heralded as a Bill of Rights for harried former husbands who have been suffering under prolonged and unreasonable alimony awards"—supporting the women Hofstadter described as "alimony drones." But, wrote Judge Gardner, "The Act may not be used as a handy vehicle for the summary disposal of old and used wives." He continued, "A woman is not a breeding cow to be nurtured during her years of fecundity, then conveniently and economically converted to cheap steaks when past her prime."[7]

While Judge Hofstadter's 1957 opinion put him at the vanguard of the divorce reform movement of the 1960s and 1970s, in *Brantner*, Judge Gardner found himself deciding a case that was enmeshed in a very different legal and political world. Between 1957 and 1977, women's overall workforce participation rate increased by over 10 percent to a point where almost half of women were employed outside the home.[8] Judge Hofstadter was responding to the increasingly visible ability of women to support themselves when he advocated for alimony reform. Over the next two decades, many members of the feminist movement echoed Hofstadter as they responded to women's increasing workforce participation and the myriad problems with existing divorce and alimony laws. Along with Hofstadter and his allies, these feminists argued that women, even married ones, should and could work to support themselves and their families. Yet, in 1977, the majority of married women still worked in the home and even those with paid employment relied on their husbands to maintain their standard of living. This left women vulnerable as divorce laws changed to assume women's ability to support themselves. In the 1970s, newly divorced women often found themselves caught between the expectations embedded in the legal reforms advocated by employment-focused feminists and an economic and cultural system that still expected wives to be supported by their husbands. By the time the Brantners went to court, feminist activists, men's rights activists, legislators, and judges had begun to wrestle with this conundrum.

Before the Revolution: Matrimonial Litigation's Many "Victims"

Part of Judge Hofstadter's horror at the Doyles' case came from his sense that their experience was "typical." According to his account, prior to coming before him, the couple had spent over a decade arguing over alimony in front of "at least twelve judicial officers."[9] "This is, in short," he wrote, "a typical case where the parties have 'shopped' from court to court seeking help. For matrimonial litigation clings to its victims with all the tenacity of the Old Man of the Sea."[10] Hofstadter wrote his scathing opinion at an opportune moment to capture the popular imagination. Only a year before, in 1956, the divorce rate in the United States began to rise after a remarkable decade of decline following World War II.[11] In this face of this increase, divorce pushed its way into the popular consciousness as a new problem at a moment when most states still had outdated divorce laws on the books.

In 1957 the vast majority of the states in the country still operated under common-law divorce regimes that made getting a divorce incredibly difficult. In almost every state, divorce laws required one spouse to prove the other was guilty of a transgression (or fault) from a specific list of grounds for divorce—such as adultery—in order to end their marriage. If it could be shown, however, that both parties were guilty, the divorce would not be granted because the law held "divorce to be a remedy for an innocent party only."[12] Only if these rules could be satisfied, and if the court determined that the couple had not colluded to prove one party's guilt, would a divorce be granted.[13] These requirements led to the unequal treatment of men and women and gave upper-income couples with the means to work around the law better access to divorce than less privileged couples.

Fault-based divorce law regimes not only used fault to establish grounds for divorce, but also to determine alimony, child custody, and property division in divorce settlements. Wives deemed guilty were rarely awarded alimony. They lost rights to marital property, and they could even lose custody of their children. On the other hand, if a husband wanted to divorce a legally innocent wife, she had to consent to bring the case. This gave her bargaining power. In exchange for colluding with her husband to get a divorce, a wife could negotiate a better settlement before the couple ever got to court.[14]

This kind of bargaining was against the law and could lead to a divorce being denied if discovered. Nevertheless, the difficulty of getting a divorce under this system resulted in widespread perjury. Couples that wanted a divorce did collude, almost always claiming that the husband had cheated on the wife (thus preserving both partners' dignity). In some states a healthy industry existed that allowed couples to hire women to pretend to have affairs with husbands and "private detectives" to discover the affair—and take pictures. The pictures could then be presented in court as evidence of the adultery required to receive a divorce.[15] Couples with more resources "moved" to states, like Nevada, which had set themselves up as divorce havens and offered no-fault divorces to new residents. After the move, the divorcing partners perjured themselves when they told a divorce court, as required, that they considered the move permanent.[16] None of these options were cheap. Those who could not afford a divorce often simply went their separate ways and hoped no one had cause to look too closely into their marital status.[17]

The wealthy not only had easier access to divorce under this regime but also were more able to sustain alimony awards. In the early twentieth century, the number of divorced women awarded alimony by a court grew rapidly. According to historian Elaine Tyler May, between 1900 and 1922 the proportion of American divorces granted with alimony doubled. The main determinant of alimony awards was fault, not need.[18] But because establishing fault was a requirement of divorce—and because gender norms dictated that colluding couples portray the divorce as the husband's fault—women could win alimony awards even when both spouses desired a divorce and neither was truly at fault. Men thus came to see alimony as a price extracted by women for a divorce. In contrast, women more often understood alimony as a protection against the vulnerabilities created by the dependent role they were expected to play within their marriage.

Both the belief that alimony was the price of divorce and that idea that it protected women from economic vulnerability in divorce were misguided. When Hofstadter wrote his opinion, only 19 percent of divorced women divorced were legally entitled to alimony.[19] Many of these women did not successfully collect regular payments. Especially if a man remarried and had a second family, the cost of maintaining two families was often out of reach. A 1978 study found that 70 percent of women awarded alimony received some support, but only 40 percent of these women regularly received their full award.[20]

Alimony was only one of many economic decisions that had to be made in a divorce. All the property a couple had shared—from houses and furniture, to retirement savings and investments—would be divided. Here fault mattered less. Before the 1970s, most states divided property based on who held the title. Fault could, but did not always, influence the decision. In community-property states, where married spouses automatically held property jointly, judges were more likely to divide property equally, but fault was still a consideration.[21] In common-law states, which divided property based on which spouse held title, women faced a significant obstacle when trying to claim property acquired during marriage. Sometimes as the result of tradition, sometimes as the result of law, and sometimes simply because men were typically the primary earners, husbands generally held title to most of a couple's property. The award of property to men represented a tremendous loss of wealth for women and created a host of problems for them as they sought to reestablish themselves economically after divorce.

Nobody thought this was an ideal system. Men and women both believed themselves victims of a status quo that exacted too harsh an economic punishment for divorce. In the 1960s both sexes organized to push back against the existing divorce laws. In 1960 two men in California founded a new organization: Divorce Racket Busters in San Francisco. Four years later, the group changed its name to the more professional-sounding United States Divorce Reform, Inc. (USDR).[22] The men in the USDR argued that the fault-based divorce system was ruining marriage. A 1968 publication by the organization explained, "Because of traditional publicity about divorce, it is often assumed that a campaign for divorce reform must be a 'battle of the sexes.' This is not so. Our fight is with the legal profession." It continued, "Everyone loses in the divorce courts, men, women, children, the taxpayer, and the nation as a whole. The only people that gain from our unsuitable method of handling divorce are the judges and lawyers. More divorces mean more judgeships for those lawyers who aspire to be judges, and more divorces mean more profit for those lawyers who handle divorce."[23] In place of this legal system, USDR called for non-adversarial, family arbitration centers.

The men of USDR claimed the courts empowered women to rip their families apart. Historian Deborah Dinner argues the USDR essentially believed that judges usurped men's rightful place of authority in the family. This understanding reflected an actual shift in common law that historian Michael Grossberg argues occurred over the course of the nineteenth century as judges became more and more willing to intervene in the nuclear family over the head of the male patriarch. Grossberg terms this phenomenon "judicial patriarchy."[24] The USDR's message took a stand against not only divorce but also judicial patriarchy and in favor of reestablishing husbands' control over their families and removing judicial intervention. In the 1970s the USDR convinced four states (Pennsylvania, Massachusetts, Maine, and Kansas) to declare June "family preservation month."[25] The family that the USDR was trying to preserve was one with men firmly at the head.[26]

In contrast to the USDR's official message, its members sometimes offered a more disgruntled assessment of marriage as an institution. In a 1970 issue of *Playboy*, a regional leader of the USDR, George Doppler, wrote:

> The divorce-reform movement is spawning a new, more radical anti-marriage movement, led by older males who have learned the hard way that contracting a legal marriage is giving a woman virtual power of attorney over your life from then until death releases you. It is well-known that an enormous number of marriages in America today fail; but what is the price, to the male, of a failed marriage? He loses a large share of his savings; his income is lowered by alimony payments; the car, home and other property will probably go to the wife; and he hasn't a chance of getting custody of the children. . . . And all this can happen to him even if his wife has been frigid, bitchy, Lesbian, lazy and totally no good in every other way throughout the history of the marriage. Why would any man in his right mind sign his name to a contract such as that?[27]

Doppler framed marriage as a financial risk for men. He echoed the USDR's message that divorce courts and lawyers sided with women, allowing women to drain their ex-husbands' resources, but he diverged from the party line on the question of whether the institution of marriage could be saved.[28]

The narrative that men were the true victims of divorce had power. In the decade before no-fault divorce laws swept the country, publications separately aimed at both men and women picked it up. A 1959 article in the women's magazine *Redbook* told readers, "Most divorced women do not suffer as much as we think they do. Most divorced men suffer more than we realize. A divorced woman has lost her husband. A divorced man has lost not only a wife, but very often his children, his home, his possessions, his savings, many of his old friends and much of his self-esteem."[29] The article continued to express sympathy for the hardships created by alimony, explaining that a divorced man's "chances for happiness in any new marriage are constantly threatened by the persistent demands of the old one. His obligation to pay alimony mortgages his future earnings and impedes his ability to make a new life for himself."[30]

Not all women accepted this narrative. Many divorced women matched men's horror stories with their own. They told stories of husbands who relied on their financial support through medical school only to divorce them the minute their education ended and their incomes expanded. Other ex wives described their husbands leaving them in hospital beds without insurance. In 1970, Ann Hirsch wrote her congresswoman, Martha Griffiths, with a story that combined all of these tropes. "Last year my husband and I were divorced after more than twenty years of marriage," she wrote. "He had filed while I was in the hospital and too ill to protect myself."[31] According to Hirsch, although she and her husband "had been married for twelve years before my husband finished his medical training and entered private practice—living with a great deal of poverty and sacrifice throughout this time," and although "his education was financed almost wholly by my two careers—that of a teacher and a fashion model," and although "money I inherited put him into private practice, purchased many items for our home—rather than being used for personal clothing or jewelry," she "received almost none of these items in the final settlement . . . despite the tremendous investment I made."[32]

In the face of this ruling, Hirsch wrote to Griffiths insisting that her economic contributions had played a critical role in supporting her family for years. She understood herself to be trapped by an assumed breadwinner-homemaker model of the family where any of women's work outside the home was for "pin money" not necessary funds to keep a family running.[33] Hirsch may have spent the final eight years of her marriage as a homemaker, but she pointed out that earlier in her marriage she had made substantial investments that eventually allowed for this lifestyle. Nevertheless, despite her investments in her husband's medical practice and home, Hirsch had no rights to either after her divorce. While men demanding divorce reform looked to their post-marriage lives and focused on the ways alimony tied them to their ex-wives in perpetuity, women interested in divorce reform looked back to their old marriages and demanded recognition of their investments.

Griffiths told Hirsch she could not do anything for her personally. The story added to a growing file in her communications with constituents and women throughout the country. These sorts of letters forced Griffiths and others to rethink how a feminist legal regime would treat divorce. In the 1960s, newly awakened feminists joined with men in rejecting alimony. They agreed with the article in *Redbook* that concluded that the entire approach to divorce was based on "obsolete concepts of women's place in society."[34] In 1967, when sociologist Alice Rossi drafted a "guiding ideology" for the newly formed National Organization for Women's Temporary Committee on the Family she called for a "revision of divorce laws and alimony arrangements so that unsuccessful marriages may be terminated without hypocrisy, and new marriages contracted without undue financial hardship to either man or woman."[35] But if marriages were to be terminated with ease and connections between exes severed as completely as possible, what or who would protect the women like Ann Hirsch? This was the question that feminists struggled with throughout the first half of the 1970s.

The Divorce Law Revolution: "Ill-informed, at Best, and at Worse, Irresponsible"

So many judges, lawyers, legislators, and everyday people agreed with Judge Hofstadter's 1957 analysis of the state of marital law that over the next twenty years almost every state amended its divorce laws with relatively little initial conflict. One scholar described this sweeping change as a "silent revolution"—a transformation of policy that was expert-driven and so politically popular that it cost legislators almost nothing while changing everything.[36] This is not an entirely accurate representation of the divorce law reform efforts that took place in the 1960s and 1970s. While it is true that there was widespread agreement that divorce law needed reform, the advocates for reform were hardly silent. Moreover, within the legal profession and among reform advocates there was deep disagreement about the best ways to reform the system that only deepened as states adopted initial reforms. Women and men, judges and lawyers, in states still debating reform began to organize in response to the consequences they saw playing out in the states that had already enacted new divorce laws.

By the mid-1960s the push for divorce reform had become so widespread that multiple organizations began to take on the problem. In 1966, California, which would ultimately pass the country's first no-fault divorce law, created a commission to investigate divorce law reform.[37] That same year the Uniform Law Commission (ULC)—an organization made up of 250 judges, lawyers, and law professors, appointed from all the states of the country—applied for a grant from the Ford Foundation to draft a Uniform Marriage and Divorce Act (UMDA).[38] In its application, the ULC argued that the time was right for this work not only because of changing morals but also because of the ways in which family law affected the administration of welfare benefits. Seizing on the political imperatives of the Lyndon Johnson's War on Poverty, the commission pointed out that because so many welfare programs were administered through the family, lack of clarity in family law posed an obstacle to successfully implementing antipoverty programs.[39] The commission won Ford Foundation funding as well as funds from the United States Department of Health, Education, and Welfare. It quickly hired two law professors to lead its efforts to draft a uniform marriage and divorce law—Robert Levy, of the University of Minnesota, and Herma Hill Kay, a feminist law professor at the University of California at Berkeley who was also involved in the California reform efforts.[40]

Rewriting American family law proved a contentious process.[41] First promulgated by the ULC in 1971, the Uniform Marriage and Divorce Act was only approved by the American Bar Association in 1974, after much debate and with many amendments.[42] Examining the UMDA debate provides a good window into the ideology underpinning the reform of state divorce laws in these years. Chief among these beliefs was the conviction that reforming divorce law could actually save marriages. Thus, the "underlying purpose" of the proposed law was to "strengthen and preserve the integrity of marriage and safeguard family relationships."[43] In support of these grand intentions, the UMDA began by literally renaming divorce cases, replacing the standard title format of *Brantner v. Brantner* with the less adversarial form of *In re the Marriage of Brantner*.[44] The commissioners hoped the new names would signal the more amicable divorce process that the drafters intended the uniform act would create.[45]

Despite its stated intention, the UMDA recognized that some marriages should end. For these marriages, the model law's drafters hoped to provide for easy and final divorce settlements. Under the UMDA, instead of trying to sort out who was at fault for the end of a marriage, a judge could simply declare the marriage "irretrievably broken." In addition, under the model law either spouse could initiate a divorce proceeding. Thus, the UMDA paved the way for unilateral divorces. If one party could convince the court that the marriage was irretrievably broken, even if the other denied it, the marriage could be ended.[46]

Like Judge Hofstadter, the UMDA drafters' desire to allow couples to quickly and easily end their marriages made them suspicious of alimony, which they believed left ex-spouses permanently entangled. In alimony's place, the UMDA encouraged judges to use property division to provide for dependent spouses through one-time settlements.[47] To facilitate this, the UMDA drafters suggested new laws to guide judges in dividing property. The proposals sought to move judges in common-law states away from the title-based assignment of property rights. In fact, the drafters originally suggested that all states adopt the community property model, but many common-law states protested. As an alternative, the drafters proposed a system of equitable property distribution, which left property distribution up to judicial discretion, but urged judges to take into account a host of factors—including the needs of each party and his/her contribution to the marriage, but not including fault—when making their decision.[48] The UMDA also left community property rules as an alternative.[49]

Unfortunately, it was usually impossible to take care of dependent spouses through property division alone. Most couples simply did not own enough property.[50] In these cases, the UMDA encouraged judges to only award support on the basis of need and for limited amounts of time tied to how long the judge thought it would take the dependent spouse to become self-supporting.[51] Such awards were not meant to take fault or desert into consideration. Essentially, new divorce laws imposed means testing on women seeking alimony.[52] This new take on alimony was renamed "maintenance." The concept of need-based maintenance eliminated any notion that ongoing support was an entitlement for formerly married women.

Despite its fairly measured approach to divorce reform, the UMDA sparked controversy within the legal profession. In particular, the Family Law

Section of the American Bar Association—a section whose members were largely family law practitioners—expressed considerable hesitation. In 1971, legal reporter Nina Totenberg remarked in the *National Observer*, "In debating the divorce proposal, the conference members and the ABA section reacted like a couple whose marriage is showing cracks."[53] The Family Law Section's reluctance to endorse the UMDA seems to have been driven both by rank-and-file ABA members who feared the effects the changes would have on their existing legal practices and by personal conflict between the chair of the ABA's Family Law Section and the experts heading up the ULC's process.[54] There were also substantive issues in contention including the definition "irretrievable breakdown" and the rules governing such property divisions.[55] Ultimately, in 1973, the House of Delegates of the ABA adopted the UMDA over the continued objections of the Family Law Section.[56]

By 1978, the Uniform Law Commission recognized only seven states as having fully adopted the UMDA.[57] Nevertheless, the commission's legislative director, John McCabe, believed that the UMDA's influence had gone "far beyond" the list of officially recognized states.[58] By 1974, forty-five states had adopted some form of no-fault procedure; by 1979, fifteen states had eliminated all fault grounds from their divorce procedures.[59] McCabe believed that the ULC should take credit for this "perceived revolution in the law pertaining to marriage and divorce."[60] He argued that along with California, the UMDA had pioneered no-fault, equitable property distribution, and the reform of alimony law—concepts that many states incorporated into their own new laws.[61]

Since most states did not adopt the UMDA in full, what they did with its main concepts varied tremendously. The first states to adopt no-fault laws—California, Iowa, Florida, Oregon, Michigan, and Colorado, which had all passed new divorce laws by 1972—eliminated all fault grounds from divorce proceedings.[62] After that, many states simply added no-fault grounds to the menu of already existing options for divorcing couples.[63] Other states, like New York, adopted a watered-down version of no-fault divorce where couples could divorce without assigning blame to one party only if they had lived apart for a requisite number of years.[64] In an attempt to limit unilateral divorces, other states allowed for a no-fault divorce only if both parties agreed that the marriage was irretrievably broken. Still another set of states, such as Michigan, eliminated fault as a ground for divorce, but explicitly allowed fault to remain a consideration in property division.[65]

Not all states included in their new divorce laws safeguards to protect the dependent spouse after a divorce, like those proposed in the UMDA. For example, in its initial reforms California did not include a provision instructing courts to consider the "contribution of a spouse as a homemaker" or future earnings potential of the parties when dividing property.[66] Without these directives, equal division of property at the time of divorce did not necessarily lead to equal outcomes in the long term. Flora Brantner's original alimony award—the award that a California judge described as based on an understanding of the laws as treating women as "breeding cows"—reveals the effect of these new policies.

Facing this varied legal landscape, organizations concerned with women's post-divorce economic status made the UMDA the standard against which they measured state laws. In 1974 the Citizen's Advisory Council on the Status of Women warned, "Most states adopting the 'irretrievable breakdown' grounds of the [UMDA] have not adopted the economic provisions. . . . These developments pose great danger to children and homemakers."[67] The International Women's Year Committee on the Homemaker recommended, "Organizations concerned with the welfare of children and dependent spouses actively seek amendments in state divorce laws where necessary to assure that as a minimum the economic protections for dependent spouses and children of the Uniform Marriage and Divorce Act are included."[68]

Even before these national organizations got involved, women had begun to protest the enactment of no-fault divorce laws without economic protections on the state level. In Connecticut, a local NOW chapter urged state legislators to vote against a proposed no-fault bill because "divorce is an intricate system. . . . It is our conviction that altering one factor, without a thorough understanding of the entire system, and specifically, without prior knowledge of the effect of such a change would be ill-informed, at best, and at worse, irresponsible."[69] The law passed in spite of this protest.[70] In Virginia, the Women's Lobby pressured the governor to veto a proposed no-fault law. The organization wrote, "While we favor no-fault as the most reasonable divorce procedure, we oppose this bill because no economic provisions for the family have been assured. The bill . . . does not recognize the work in the home as support or give a homemaker some ownership in the property accumulated during the marriage."[71] The governor signed the bill anyway.[72]

As many women's groups celebrated the inclusion of economic protections for dependent spouses in the UMDA, men organized in protest. George Doppler wrote an outraged letter to McCabe demanding, "Who put all these economic provisions in the uniform model? Have you people ever heard of that most obscene four-letter word in the English language: WORK! Were any male rights organizations consulted about this?"[73] Shortly after Illinois passed a version of the UMDA in 1978, a group of men filed a class-action suit challenging the constitutionality of both the child support and equitable property distribution provisions of the law on equal protection, impairment of contract, and due process grounds. The trial court ruled in the men's favor, but the state supreme court reversed its decision.[74]

While men's rights activists objected to the provisions of the UMDA intended to protect homemakers, some women objected to the idea of unilateral no-fault entirely and worried about the amount of judicial discretion allowed in the UMDA. Many feminists saw the almost uniformly male judiciary as inherently on the side of husbands. After all, judges had led the initial turn against alimony. One woman argued to NOW that it should not support the UMDA because "while judges have discretion to divide, given their male prejudices and the current definition of property . . . the judges may <u>consider</u> these provisions but the <u>decision will not reflect</u> that women should have half the economic assets."[75] Like the USDR, feminists understood judges to be stepping into the role husbands once filled. They rejected judges' patriarchal role along with other patriarchal structures, worrying that new divorce laws simply swapped one for another.

"The Rip Off It Was": Early Feminist Responses to No-Fault Divorce

At its founding in 1966, NOW established a Temporary Committee on the Family and appointed as its head Alice Rossi, a sociologist who simultaneously sat on the board of advisors overseeing the UMDA. Rossi set NOW's legal experts to carefully review divorce law not because she believed family law discriminated against women, but because she believed it discriminated against men. "If women are disadvantaged in the economic sphere, divorced men are disadvantaged in the family sphere, often carrying financial responsibility for a first family on top of that for a second family, despite the competence of his ex-wife to maintain her own household by employment," she said.[76] Rossi continued, "Women must shoulder some of the financial responsibility for their children if their marriages terminate in divorce, just as men should fulfill the social and emotional responsibilities for their children in intact families."[77] Similarly, an early NOW–New York meeting considered a motion "deploring alimony as a reinforcement of women's lower status."[78] In its earliest days, at the national and local level, NOW focused not on supporting homemakers but rather on moving women into the paid workface.

Despite these early statements advocating a formal equality approach to divorce, very shortly after its founding, NOW was flooded with appeals from divorced women asking for help winning alimony.[79] Women's decision to turn to NOW for help with their divorces in spite of the organization's initial position of sympathy with divorced men speaks to the critical place the organization played in the women's movement. NOW was the organization most women turned to when they needed to address what they understood to be a "women's issue" because in many parts of the country it was the only option. Even in places like New York, where there were many different feminist organizations, the women who turned to NOW for help with a divorce were generally not those women who were attuned to the variations in feminist ideology.[80] Instead, they were women who had not previously identified as feminists but found themselves facing a problem that they understood to be caused by their gender and its relationship to the law. In this situation, women went to NOW.

By reaching out to NOW, newly divorced women forced feminists to reconsider their stance toward alimony and transformed NOW into an organization focused not just on equality in the workforce but also in marriage. Throughout the 1970s, multiple NOW task forces drafted policy aimed at meeting the needs of divorced women and coordinated grassroots activism to demand that legislatures consider their bills. In addition, in 1971, NOW established a Legal Defense and Education Fund (NOW LDEF), tasked with spending at least some of its time working on the links between women's poverty, family law, and welfare policies.[81] Divorced women immediately asked NOW LDEF to challenge the constitutionality of the new no-fault divorce laws, and NOW became the main organization experimenting with these kinds of court cases.[82]

One particularly persistent woman, Ellen Sim Dewey of Nebraska, lobbied NOW for years to take her divorce case or the case of her friend Cleone Buchholz. Dewey, an associate professor of political science, and her husband of thirty-one years had two children.[83] Dewey claimed to have put her husband through a Ph.D. program at Harvard and also accused him of domestic abuse.[84] Despite what seems to have been an unhappy marriage, Dewey wanted to use her divorce as an opportunity to challenge the new Nebraska no-fault divorce law. She wrote to NOW that she and her attorney were considering sixteen different grounds on which to challenge the law's constitutionality including "irretrievable breakdown is unconstitutionally vague"; the law "assumes that women live in an economic system which at any point in their life allows them to take a job with equal opportunities and pay as men"; it "does not provide any recognition of the contribution women have made to the marriage, to their husband's career, and to his income and income potential"; and it "contributes to the breakdown of social morality."[85] Dewey identified as having professional expertise in the law and likely knew that most of the grounds she listed were not true constitutional violations. Her persistence in advocating a constitutional challenge to the no-fault law suggests how unjust Dewey believed new divorce laws to be.[86] By trying to push her claims into a constitutional argument, Dewey argued that marriage should endow women with basic rights—that, to be just, the law of the nation must recognize women's contributions to their marriages as having economic value.

Dewey met resistance not just from NOW LDEF, but also from her local NOW chapter where she encountered younger feminists who defended no-fault divorce laws. Dewey told NOW's midwest regional director that when she "pegged the no-fault law for the rip off it was. . . . I was ignored and hooted (behind my back as a menopausal old biddie whose husband was rejecting her)."[87] Despite this treatment, Dewey plugged on, arguing that feminism could offer as much to homemakers as it did to career women. After NOW refused to take her case, Dewey lobbied NOW LDEF to take another case, that of Cleone and Mark Buchholz. She wrote, "NOW needs this case, and needs to promote it hard if NOW is to rid itself of the public news-media inspired image that we are anti the family, anti the homemaker, and anti marriage."[88]

Cleone and Mark separated in 1972 and divorced in 1976 after nineteen years of marriage. At the time of the divorce, Mark was a judge in the Nebraska Workmen's Compensation Court and made $30,500 a year (roughly $127,500 in today's dollars). Cleone was a registered nurse, but had not worked in years.[89] The couple had two children, a twenty-year-old son and an eighteen-year-old daughter. In their original settlement Cleone was awarded custody of her daughter with $150 a month in child support, the house (as part of the property division in which both Mark and Cleone received about $27,000 worth of property), and $500 a month in alimony for two years and $400 a month for the next seven years. In addition, Mark was ordered to pay up to $2,000 for Cleone's retraining as a registered nurse, if she wished for the training and did it within three years of the divorce.[90] Dewey believed this was inadequate as Cleone was forty-five and "in frail health."[91]

Cleone and her lawyers decided to bring a Fourteenth Amendment challenge to Nebraska's no-fault divorce law. First, they argued that Cleone had a property right in her marriage. Unilateral, no-fault divorce therefore violated the Fourteenth Amendment's Due Process Clause, which they claimed should guarantee a right to a fair hearing.[92] To make this argument, Cleone and her lawyers sought to compare her position as a divorced woman under no-fault to a "tenured job holder who loses his position 'without fault.'"[93] Second, Cleone's lawyers claimed that the Nebraska law discriminated against women and thus violated the Equal Protection Clause because "women, after a divorce, are not as capable of supporting themselves as are men."[94] NOW's own attorneys considered this Fourteenth Amendment strategy viable and especially liked the Due Process Clause arguments.

NOW initially agreed to support Cleone's case and authorized Dewey to raise funds to support their work. NOW promised any of the money left after the *Buchholz* case would be used to start a fund to support other divorce litigation.[95] Dewey did raise much of the money, but NOW withdrew its support because of disagreement within the organization about whether or not it should attack the constitutionality of the new divorce laws.[96] Many feminists still believed alimony perpetuated discriminatory sex roles. Others argued that no-fault laws served as an important protection for women in bad marriages. Whether to prioritize these women's needs or the needs of homemakers left without a steady source of income after a divorce was a difficult question that highlighted generational and ideological divisions within the young organization.

Ultimately, the Nebraska Supreme Court denied Cleone's appeal. The court argued that women did not have a property right in marriage because marriage was not a contract like any other. The state had an interest in marriage and therefore could pass laws affecting the marriage contract, including dissolving it. The court also rejected the equal protection claim, arguing that the new divorce law clearly tried to address the economic situation of each party to a marriage.[97]

Losses like Cleone's affirmed feminists' suspicion of the judiciary. At NOW's national convention in 1973, the Marriage and Divorce Task Force refused to take a position on the Uniform Marriage and Divorce Act stating that it did not trust the parts of the UMDA that left a divorced spouse's economic fate up to a judge's discretion.[98] Feminists' distrust of the judiciary also led them away from prioritizing the challenging of no-fault divorce laws in court and toward a focus on further legislation to soften the effects of no-fault. In particular, they demanded the standardization of divorce settlements and the removal of discretion from judges.[99] In 1975, NOW–New York demanded legislators create alimony formulas and tables that took into account the "economic value of the homemaker's contribution[s]" as well as "the loss of earnings capacity during the period of full time homemaking and child care."[100] Such a formula would not only limit judicial discretion, but would also legislate a numeric formula that recognized marriage as an economic partnership and quantified homemakers' contributions to that partnership.

By 1976, NOW's take on divorce had changed dramatically. Reflecting back in 1976, Betty Friedan argued that early feminists "had fallen into a trap in the first few years of NOW." She explained, "When divorce laws began to be reformed in New York and other states, leading to the no-fault divorce law, we were so anxious to espouse full equality that we repudiated the very concept of alimony, now women who had been housewives, who hadn't worked in years or who made very little money, found themselves divorced, with no provision whatsoever for their maintenance or training for a job to earn real money, and often with the whole responsibility for the children to boot."[101] Friedan's statements marked the culmination of a very quick reversal. Forced by grassroots members to reconsider its position, NOW abandoned its formal equality agenda in favor of a more functionalist approach to divorce within a few years of its founding, long before it made a similar move on other issues.

Transitional Justice for the Women After the Divorce Revolution

In a 1975 newsletter to the NOW Marriage, Divorce, and Family Relations Task Force, Chair Elizabeth Coxe Spalding included a satirical open letter to marital court judges across the United States. "You boys want equality?" she wrote, "We're going to see that you get it. We want legislation in every state that mandates the state to discharge judges on the unilateral complaint of a homemaking wife." Spalding's letter parodied reports, which the NOW Task Force received from across the country, that judges were saying to divorcing women, "You girls want equality and I'm going to give it to you" before handing down decisions that left longtime homemakers without any support.[102] The letter highlighted NOW's increasing distrust of the judiciary and its members' sense that older women had married under one legal regime and were being divorced in another. A revolution not just in divorce laws but also in gender roles had led judges to argue that men need not be held economically responsible for their former wives, failing to recognize that years of expected economic dependence could not be erased overnight.

Two years after Spalding sent out her parody, in his ruling in *Brantner*, Judge Gardner defied Spalding's expectations and wrote of Flora, "Had she not been married those twenty odd years, she might now be well qualified as a typist, truck driver or tinsmith."[103] The list of jobs Judge Gardner imagined for Flora resulted directly from a decade of feminist insistence that women could be truck drivers or tinsmiths. But Gardner—like many feminists—had come to recognize that women who had spent twenty-five years raising children were unlikely to become either. A formal equality agenda simply would not do enough to help women like Flora; in some cases, it could actively hurt them. Judge Gardner explained, Flora had "spent her productive years as a housewife and mother and ha[d] missed the opportunity to compete in the job market and improve her job skills"; thus she had become, "when divorced, simply a 'displaced homemaker.'"[104] Judge Gardner overturned the automatic reductions and termination built into Flora's original alimony award.[105]

The *Brantner* case does not represent every divorce case in the late 1970s—among other things, divorce settlements were very rarely appealed.[106] In 1977, plenty of divorced women were still fighting to get their economic rights in divorce recognized. But Judge Gardner's decision is an important example of a hard-won success of the feminist divorce reform movement and shows the ground on which such successes were won. Flora's age played a critical role in Judge Gardner's decision. The problem Judge Gardner identified in Flora's initial settlement was that it ignored the fact that she had married and chosen to stay home and raise her family in an era when that was expected. As Gardner understood it, California's divorce laws had changed while Flora was married, leaving her trapped. This framing—that women caught in between changing eras needed special assistance—held broad appeal. While even feminist organizations did not always agree internally on what would constitute a feminist divorce law regime, almost everyone agreed that women who married in one legal regime and divorced in another were particularly vulnerable and deserving of sympathy.

While the *Brantner* case was not the start of a trend toward courts frequently reversing divorce settlements, the transitional justice argument that won the day in *Brantner* did signal the widespread acceptance of a feminist argument that proved to be key to feminist divorce reformers' legislative successes throughout the 1970s. On the one hand, it identified a particularly sympathetic group of women who could serve as the poster children for a broken divorce system. On the other hand, it allowed feminist activists to fight for women's right to support after marriage without arguing that all women needed the support of their husbands. Moreover, in individual divorce cases, the argument made a great deal of sense. When feminist divorce reformers brought the transitional justice argument to their legislative advocacy, however, it had much more insidious effects. By shaping what policies feminists advocated and the nature of feminists' legislative victories, the transitional justice narrative ultimately limited both the scope of feminist divorce reformers' legislative vision and their success in enacting it.

CHAPTER 2

From the Altar to the Grave

The Beginnings of the Feminist Divorce Reform Movement

On 19 January 1974, "despite a blizzard that shut down airports and made highways hazardous," over a thousand women and men, policymakers and activists, gathered in New York City for a Conference on Marriage and Divorce called by NOW–New York's Marriage and Divorce Task Force. In her keynote speech at the conference, Betty Friedan mused, "If there is any one thing that makes a feminist it is to grow up believing somehow that love and marriage will take care of the rest of your life. And then to wake up at forty or fifty or even at thirty and find it isn't so. And then to face the world—the reality of it."[1] The women in attendance understood the truth of this statement. Covering the conference, the *New York Times* wrote that each of the participants "seemed to have her own personal horror story to tell, and her own solution to 'obsolete' divorce laws."[2] These women had found their way to NOW because, in 1974, the feminist movement seemed to offer both an explanation for their experience and a means to make their proposed solutions a reality.

In the mid-1970s, women who sought out feminist organizations after divorce found an optimistic movement. In January of 1974, the Supreme Court had just handed down its decision in *Roe v. Wade*. Two years before, Congress had passed the ERA and, by the end of 1973, thirty states had ratified it.[3] The feminist movement was producing real wins. Perhaps because of feminists' success, despite being urged to try to overturn no-fault divorce laws by women like Dewey, leaders in the feminist divorce reform movement chose instead to focus their attention on imagining what a just social insurance and legal system that included no-fault divorce would look like. The women at the 1974 conference were for the most part not interested in turning back the clock. Rather, they wanted to win new laws that recognized women as earning economic rights and resources through marriage.

The feminist divorce reform movement flowered as divorced women found their way to NOW and other organizations. In the early 1970s, a divorcing woman had possible access to two economic protections: (1) alimony, if a judge awarded it, and (2) a Social Security benefit worth half of her ex-husband's benefit only at the point at which he started collecting and only if they had been married for twenty years. The women who flocked to the feminist movement after divorce had many ideas for legislation that would expand these limited protections while building on their basic structures. As they fleshed out these ideas, the work feminists had already done when considering challenging no-fault laws in court informed how feminist divorce reformers conceptualized marriage in a no-fault era. In particular, the due process argument that Cleone Buchholz's lawyers had pursued, the argument that women had a property right in their marriages, became central to feminist divorce reformers' efforts to construct a theory of marriage that explained why marriages, even after they ended, should guarantee women certain privileges.

Throughout the 1970s, feminist divorce reformers agreed on the basic idea that getting married, not staying married, should change women's status in the welfare state. But both the grounds on which feminist activists based divorced women's claims to resources and the kinds of resources they hoped to provide to women varied. This chapter looks at three women in particular—Betty Berry, Elizabeth Coxe Spalding, and Tish Sommers—who entered the feminist movement in the early 1970s and defined different feminist legislative approaches to the challenges of the no-fault era. Berry sought laws socializing the costs of divorce and recognizing marriage as an economic partnership; Spalding fought for laws that preserved married women's privileged economic status even after their marriages ended; and Sommers lobbied for programs that trained former homemakers for employment. As leaders in the feminist movement for divorce reform, their agendas represent three very different ideological strands that shaped their movement throughout the 1970s and 1980s. Despite their disagreements, over the course of a decade, these women's shared work turned divorced women into a recognized and privileged political group, entitled to special benefits, within the burgeoning category of single women.

"Another Financial Catastrophe That Can Befall a Family": Betty Berry's Proposal for Divorce Insurance

The woman most responsible for transforming NOW's position on divorce was Betty Blaisdell Berry. NOW-NYC Chapter President Ti-Grace Atkinson appointed Berry to serve as coordinator of the chapter's Task Force on Marriage, Divorce, and Family Relations in 1967.[4] From this position, Berry won fellow New Yorker Betty Friedan over to her vision for reformed marriage and divorce laws. When Alice Rossi dropped out of NOW's 1968 conference at the last minute, Friedan asked Berry to step in and run the discussion on marriage and divorce.[5] From there, Berry took over the national Task Force and shifted it away from focusing on absolute equality in divorce, as it had under Rossi, to working for the economic rights of divorced women.[6] Through this work, Berry proved to be one of NOW's most creative thinkers, notably willing to experiment with a range of proposals until she saw which had legislative legs. Berry's proposals rested on a key claim about marriage: She argued that homemaking was akin to a career and should earn women long-lasting economic protections similar to those earned through participation in paid workforce.

In rewriting NOW's positions, Berry transformed her own life. Like the women she sought to help, Berry was divorced. She had earned a B.A. from Smith and worked for a few years after college before leaving the paid workforce when she married.[7] After her divorce, Berry moved to New York City from the suburbs, a move she recommended for all divorced women. She explained, "In New York, you're so busy getting established again, coping with the job, making a whole new set of friends, that you hardly have a minute to think. By the time the emotional effects of the divorce catch up with you, you've restored your self-confidence and you can ask with some composure, 'Where do I go from here?'"[8]

Berry answered that question by throwing herself into changing the laws that had defined her own experience of divorce. Before her divorce Berry had no legal or policymaking experience. By 1973, she was drafting policy proposals for NOW, testifying in front of the United States Senate, consulting for the Presbyterian Church on marriage and divorce issues, and balancing all this with a job as executive director of the Industrial Designers Society of America.[9] A 1974 article in *Harper's Bazaar* described Berry as "chic, enthusiastic, and engaged in her work," "one of the seventies' bright and smiling breed of self-made, right-on divorcees who has taken over total responsibility for her own future."[10]

Berry arrived at the 1968 conference, where Friedan had asked her to take the lead on marriage and divorce, with a report outlining the legislative program her NOW-NYC committee hoped to enact. The report focused largely on the economic vulnerability of homemakers. It began by pointing out that 63 percent of married women worked in the home and that less than half of the 2,331,000 divorced women in the United States were employed. Nevertheless, alimony was becoming increasingly rare as legislators and courts had come to believe women could—and if not married, should—support themselves. To address this problem, NOW-NYC proposed a "program of education and legislation." They called for better collection of data on divorce, the creation of programs to reeducate and rehabilitate divorced women, and the reduction of the number of years a woman had to be married to draw a dependent Social Security benefit through her ex-husband. In addition, they planned programs to provide young people and legislators with a better understanding of the economic sacrifices women made through marriage. Finally, Berry's 1968 report called for a fundamental rethinking of alimony.[11]

After her own divorce, Berry received regular alimony payments. She told one reporter she viewed these payments "like a pension right for the years she contributed to the marriage." On the checks, she crossed out the word alimony and wrote "entitlement" before depositing.[12] Reflecting this personal practice, in Atlanta, Berry contended that NOW should advocate a legislative program that would provide women with actual entitlements in place of alimony. To make this claim, Berry argued that the law should recognize housework as an occupation. She wrote, "If housewife is an occupation, and if the woman has spent a number of years of service in it, she should automatically have some kind of compensation or economic rights or equity."[13]

Berry spent the next decade arguing that a critical piece of any attempt to reduce divorced women's economic vulnerability was recognizing their work in the home as a form of employment. For example, in 1971, when Berry was asked to comment on the Uniform Marriage and Divorce Act, she wrote that her feelings about the draft bill were "mixed." While she believed the UMDA's handling of marital property was "excellent and long overdue," she was "greatly disappointed that the proposed Act does not deal with the structure of marriage and with the necessary reform to make a housewife a bonafide occupation, and to lessen the dependency status and inferior economic status of the housewife or dependent spouse."[14]

Even as Berry argued that housewife should be viewed as an occupation, her boldest proposal rested on an understanding of marriage as somewhere between an employment contract and a status. She sought to socialize the risks of marriage—just as Americans had socialized the risks of wage labor and old age—and demanded for ex-wives the equivalent of unemployment insurance or Social Security. In 1968, Berry began drafting a "marriage insurance" proposal for NOW. The proposal called for a "comprehensive plan to be implemented that would reach from the altar to the grave whereby married women, or the dependent spouse, would be covered by health and medical insurance, divorce, and retirement insurance, and benefits."[15] Berry's proposals for health and retirement insurance advanced her claim that marriage and homemaking should be understood as a career. Her call for divorce insurance, on the other hand, sought to institutionalize her belief that the very act of getting married conferred on women a status that entitled them to a certain standard of living and that that status should not be lost just because an individual marriage ended.

Divorce insurance, as Berry conceived it, would insure both partners' standard of living at pre-divorce levels. Berry's plan was designed to fit within the public-private structure of the American social insurance system. As with most of the existing benefits in the U.S. social insurance system, Berry's divorce insurance would be offered through a combination of public and private providers. Through the Social Security system, at divorce dependent ex-wives would receive a benefit similar to that paid to widows. Berry explained, "The social benefits and insurance distributed by the government [would] be considered throughout as a minimum level, or a floor. This is a skeleton which would be filled out according to individual need and means, as indeed is already the case."[16] On top of this skeleton, Berry wanted families to purchase supplemental insurance—mirroring the private life insurance system—in units of $100 per month and to decide at purchase if the benefit would be paid to the dependent spouse or be split between the spouses.[17]

Berry was adamant that divorce insurance was a natural expansion of the current social insurance system. She frequently claimed that her plan was the logical next step for a Social Security system already intended to protect women from widowhood. She explained, "[Social Security was] conceived in an era when the traditional role of the woman was to be a wife and mother, the focus of this insurance was on the man and the wife obtained her benefits indirectly through him. (Private insurance plans paralleled this.) These benefits primarily related to her old age and subsequent widowhood. . . . Thus from the outset, widowhood was recognized as an insurable hazard of marriage."[18] Berry continued: "Another financial catastrophe that can befall the family is divorce. In this case the dissolution of the marriage is by judicial decree rather than death."[19] Berry argued the extension of Social Security to divorced women would make the creation of divorce insurance relatively simple.[20] When a couple divorced, the dependent wife and children would receive 75 percent of the benefits they would have received as surviving family members of a breadwinner.[21] To cover the addition of this new group of beneficiaries, husbands would begin to pay an additional Social Security tax for their wives.[22] How this tax would be calculated was left open, but Berry suggested that it be based on half of the husband's earnings, a suggestion which nodded toward older ideas about a "family wage."[23]

Berry's idea caught the attention of both public and private insurance officials. In 1970, she corresponded with U.S. Social Security Commissioner Robert Ball about the possibility of adding divorce coverage to Social Security. He wrote that he "could not question the logic of your argument that divorce is an economic hazard that may leave a wife or child without support of the family wage earner and therefore in the same economic position as if the husband and father had died."[24] That same year, Berry persuaded NOW-NYC to visit the New York State Department of Insurance as part of its activities during its 26 August 1970 Women's Strike for Equality, when an estimated thirty-five thousand to fifty thousand women gathered to protest in New York City and across the country.[25] On that visit, NOW members met with the New York superintendent of insurance and asked that he "direct insurance companies to develop marriage insurance policies." He agreed to further meetings and a feasibility study.[26] In 1972, NOW also convinced New York State Senator Donald Halperin to draft a bill establishing a commission to study the possibility of offering divorce insurance.[27]

Berry also managed to get at least one of the major insurance companies to consider her idea. Together with Friedan, she met with Charles A. Siegfried, the vice-chairman of the board and chairman of the executive committee of Metropolitan Life (MetLife), to discuss the possibility of creating divorce insurance.[28] Siegfried had MetLife's vice president for Insurance Relations draw up a report on the issue. The report considered a divorce insurance plan that provided divorced women, whose marriages had lasted at least five years, a three-year temporary annuity as long as they remained unmarried. In addition, under the proposed plan, if a divorced woman remained unmarried at age sixty, she would receive a benefit equivalent to the widow's benefit under Social Security.[29] The report took this idea seriously, but ultimately it raised more questions than it answered. To start, MetLife was not sure that divorce was a legally insurable interest, since such an interest had to be "beyond the control of the insured." Even if divorce cleared this bar, MetLife was not sure how divorce insurance could be structured to avoid deterring women from remarrying or finding employment. MetLife believed that to make the incentives work, divorce insurance would have to be compulsory. Yet the idea of compulsory insurance raised concerns about interactions with state alimony and child support laws.[30]

NOW's discussions with insurance companies and agencies led only to a deeper awareness of the challenges of establishing a divorce insurance program, but the organization remained interested in the idea. In 1973, NOW began to work with insurance companies to develop its own insurance offerings for its members. In these discussions, NOW representatives raised the issue of offering divorce insurance along with health and life insurance, but ultimately the organization was no more successful in designing a workable plan than MetLife had been.[31] Nevertheless, in her keynote speech at the 1974 NOW Marriage and Divorce Task Force, Friedan promoted the concept of divorce insurance as a replacement for alimony. She began by declaring alimony "a sexist concept, and doesn't belong in a women's movement for equality." But she admitted that because most women did not yet have earnings equal to men's, divorced women often had limited ability to find paid employment. Therefore, Friedan argued, "Maintenance, rehabilitation, severance pay—whatever you want to call it—is a necessity for many divorced women, as is child support. Maybe marriage and divorce insurance should actually be built into Social Security, like survivor's benefits at death."[32]

Friedan rejected alimony because it tied women permanently to their ex-husbands and was built on the assumption that women could not support themselves. She was, however, forced to admit that in 1974, many married women were still economically dependent. In response, Friedan turned to divorce insurance as a way of addressing at least the first concern and shifting whom women depended on after marriage. The feminist divorce insurance proposal would have created a new role for marriage within the American social insurance system. Legal historian Ariela Dubler argues that policymakers have historically used marriage to "privatize" women's financial dependency. Since the state takes responsibility for female poverty only when women are without husbands, judges and legislators have tried to push women into marital and marriage-like relationships in order to avoid this responsibility.[33] Divorce insurance proposals struck a novel middle ground between completely privatized female dependency through marriage and state support for dependent ex-wives.

Even as they offered a new interpretation of where to locate women's dependency, divorce insurance proposals affirmed an old idea about marriage. Unlike Berry's proposals for unemployment and health insurance for divorced women, which advanced a vision of marriage as analogous to other economic contracts for employment, the divorce insurance proposal affirmed the idea of marriage as a status. Arguably, by engaging this older understanding of marriage in her divorce insurance proposal, Berry contradicted and perhaps even began to undermine her other work to get marriage understood as a contract.

For Friedan and other feminists, a significant part of the appeal of divorce insurance proposals was their promise to grant divorced women the same privileged status married women had, by keeping divorced women from relying on existing and heavily stigmatized state support programs for low-income women and children. By socializing the cost of female dependency among all married people, Berry and Friedan believed they could save women the indignities of relying on the government or their ex-husbands. It is notable that Berry and Friedan sought to create new government programs to keep divorced women from depending on their ex-husbands instead of trying to strengthen AFDC or fold divorced women into the Social Security program's new Supplemental Security Income (SSI) program. Created in 1972, SSI unified and nationalized a number of state-run welfare programs for the disabled and elderly.[34] Feminist divorce reformers could easily have sought to use and improve either of these means-tested welfare programs. Instead they made keeping divorced women out of the means-tested welfare system one of their central goals.

Divorced women had many good reasons to want to avoid drawing on antipoverty programs; for example, such programs required them to spend down savings and sell off all property before receiving benefits.[35] These programs also supported women at a minimum level, not based on their wealth during marriage. Divorce insurance, on the other hand, would make it federal policy that formerly married women deserved to live at an income level to which they had become accustomed. The social stigma of welfare programs was also a chief concern. In 1971, Diana DuBroff, a member of NOW and a matrimonial lawyer, used Berry's work to spin off her own organization, NOISE (the National Organization to Insure Support Enforcement), which exclusively advocated for divorce insurance. Two years later NOISE had a mailing list of seven thousand women.[36] DuBroff explained to one newspaper that divorce insurance was necessary because while "the woman in the ghetto is accustomed to maintain her family on an inadequate budget . . . for the middle-income and the affluent family used to a certain standard of living, the sudden shortage of funds can be devastating."[37] DuBroff felt no embarrassment about flatly stating her belief that while AFDC might be good enough for women already outside the American middle class, divorced women, who had done their best to be in that middle class, deserved better.

Berry and DuBroff advocated a divorce insurance system that would define divorced women as a privileged and deserving class of women on the basis of a status conferred by their former marriages. At the same time, these proposals promised to make achieving this privileged status more difficult. The MetLife divorce insurance report made clear that in order for the economics and incentives of divorce insurance to work it would have to be mandatory; otherwise, adverse selection would lead only those in faltering marriages to invest in insurance. It could only be offered if the state required everyone to purchase insurance upon marriage in the same way that individuals were required to purchase car insurance when they bought a car. Thus, private divorce insurance rested on the idea that all married couples could be turned into a risk pool that took responsibility for all married people's standards of living. Berry's proposal for Social Security for divorced women rested on the same conceit since she proposed to fund it by taxing the wages of married men.[38] Whether private or public, for divorce insurance to succeed, it would have to make marriage more expensive.

Many feminists actively supported the idea of making marriage more difficult to enter. They said repeatedly that there should be more hurdles to pass through before marriage. In the same speech in which she called for divorce insurance, Friedan explicitly told her audience that they should consider "something making it more difficult to marry. Maybe there should be a large first premium for marriage and divorce insurance—a price of marriage, like you have to pay under no-fault automobile insurance to buy an automobile."[39] Friedan and Berry wanted people to recognize the risks of marriage and, by choosing to marry anyway, commit to supporting not only each other but also all married people's standard of living.

Elected officials did not share this goal. Indeed, the idea of taxing marriage likely made divorce insurance less politically popular than any of Berry's other ideas. During this period, policymakers and the public perceived the institution of marriage to be falling apart.[40] The idea of increasing the barriers to entering marriage while making it easier to divorce was politically infeasible at best. Thus, at NOW's 1974 Marriage and Divorce conference, Congresswoman Abzug spoke of a bill creating Social Security retirement pensions for homemakers, called for marriage to be recognized as an "economic partnership," and declared alimony a form of severance pay to which women had a "contractual right." But she steered clear of mentioning the divorce insurance proposal.[41]

Divorce insurance never became a reality through legislation or private action on the part of insurance of companies. Nevertheless, for the sheer scale of its ambition, Berry's proposal is worth considering. Divorce insurance was Berry's opportunity to imagine an entire entitlement program from the ground up. Yet, even at her most imaginative, Berry remained guided by the precedent of selective entitlements and the hybrid public-private social insurance system. Berry's divorce insurance proposal made a clear statement that the law should treat divorced women as a privileged class of single women who deserved special economic protections. This idea, along with Berry's belief that the existing social insurance system could accommodate it, shaped divorce reformers' activism for the next decade and a half.

"A Golden Opportunity to Bring Women to the Republican Party": Elizabeth Coxe Spalding and Support Enforcement

In 1973, Berry resigned from her official position as head of the Marriage and Divorce Task Force to found her own organization, the Marriage and Divorce Press.[42] She was replaced by another divorced homemaker and self-trained policy expert, Elizabeth Coxe Spalding. On paper Spalding and Berry seemed very different. Berry was childless, Spalding was the mother of six; Berry lived in New York City, Spalding stayed in the suburbs after her divorce.[43] Nevertheless, Berry and Spalding both agreed that the NOW Task Force on Marriage, Divorce, and Family Relations should fight for homemakers' rights. And they both embraced the idea that marriage should make women permanent members of a privileged class. While Berry looked to protect women by socializing the cost of their dependency and establishing homemaking as akin to paid employment, Spalding sought to hold husbands responsible for their wives in perpetuity.

Spalding first came to NOW seeking legal help with her own divorce. In 1970 she wrote, "I would like to meet with someone on your legal committee to discuss my particular case and how it might be of help to NOW. In brief, the case is a marital one, six minor children when it started 8 years ago; it has trust fund raiding; bigamy, custody; support—a little something for everyone in short. Four states are involved, eight law forces have come and gone." Spalding ended, "If we could settle on one such line of attack that could benefit your organization and the rights of women in the courts we might all benefit."[44]

Elizabeth Coxe and Charles Spalding married in 1945 in Pennsylvania and then moved to Connecticut, where they lived together and had six children.[45] In 1962, Charles moved to New York. In 1964, he received a divorce in Nevada. Then things got complicated. As one court put it in 1976, "Although living with Charles for reasons best known to them was not a model modus vivendi, Elizabeth did not wish to become unmarried—at least by a then-regarded renegade state whose procedural practices, re divorce, caused lifted eyebrows in more Victorian jurisdictions."[46] Elizabeth sued in New York and the court invalidated the Nevada divorce decree in 1968 because they did not accept that Charles was domiciled in state.[47] Nevertheless, in May of 1968, Charles married Amy McGinnis in California, which, unlike New York, recognized his Nevada divorce.[48] Charles lived with Amy in California until her early death in 1970. He quickly became engaged to a new woman, Bernice Grant, that same year. As part of this remarriage, and probably because he and Bernice hoped to return to New York, Charles seems to have tried to get a California divorce from Spalding to clear up the matter once and for all. Once again, Elizabeth sued, this time in Connecticut, for a judgment declaring this divorce null and void. This time she lost. The court also refused to grant her counsel fees because Spalding had significant assets at the time of judgment.[49]

Because of Spalding's ample funds and ability to hire her own expert legal counsel, NOW rejected her original request for legal support.[50] Spalding persisted, writing again in 1973, "Please do not tell me it is going to take a long time to litigate; and don't tell me it will be expensive; and don't tell me what I cannot do. All I want to hear is positive thinking, which I am certain you can come up with."[51] NOW LDEF expressed slightly more interest in her case in 1973 and raised the possibility of filing a writ of certiorari to the Supreme

Court to test the issues of domicile and jurisdiction that came up in her case.[52] This seems to be as far as the case ever got, but that year Spalding replaced Berry as coordinator of the National Task Force on Marriage, Divorce, and Family Relations. She reoriented its priorities to more closely match her own.

Spalding's priorities for the task force included the creation of a special NOW LDEF unit to help divorcing women; educating judges, lawyers, and women about the realities of divorce; and, at the top of her list, getting courts and legislatures to improve the enforcement of child support and alimony orders.[53] In her first proposed action program for the task force she argued, "The most oppressive problem of divorce is not the divorce, but the enforcement of the alimony and child support orders."[54] Unlike Berry and Friedan, Spalding had no trouble fitting alimony and child support into her feminist agenda. Instead of trying to create an alternate entitlement system to protect women and children in a divorce, she wanted to strengthen the existing system's enforcement mechanisms to keep ex-husbands responsible for their ex-wives and children.

Spalding linked her agenda to rising welfare rolls (something Berry also did on occasion). Spalding wrote, "All unsupported divorced and separated women know the states are forcing them on to AFDC because divorce and enforcement laws are going in opposite directions."[55] To illustrate this point, Spalding had NOW chapters conduct surveys of marital courts to show the ratios of divorces to support enforcement cases and to illustrate the relationship between rising number of divorces and the growth in welfare rolls.[56] In Connecticut this survey showed that in 1971–1972 there were seven enforcement cases already in the court system for every divorce granted and only one out of eight enforcement matters was successfully collected.[57]

Nationally, child support enforcement was similarly abysmal. At a point when the number of single mothers was rising quickly—in the early 1960s one in ten women headed families, by the mid-1970s one in nine did—less than half of the single mothers entitled to collect support payments regularly collected the full amount of their awards.[58] Spalding marshaled this data to argue that stronger economic provisions and enforcement mechanisms should be included in state divorce reform laws.[59] In addition, she pushed vigorously for a federal child support enforcement law. In support of these priorities, she urged NOW chapters to stage actions at court houses, including a Halloween-themed picket at court houses, where women held signs asking "Is It Trick or Treat on Support and Enforcement?" and another where women laid wreaths on the door of the Connecticut Superior Court to "mourn the loss of paternal responsibility by all fathers involved in divorce, separation and enforcement."[60] These actions showed a surprising commitment on the part of a NOW task force to upholding traditional patriarchal structures in the family and judiciary. Through these activities, Spalding and her task force argued that fathers had an obligation to support their families and judges had a responsibility to uphold that obligation.

Spalding herself does not seem to have seen a contradiction in advocating for the maintenance of patriarchal structure from within NOW. Historians can place her work within a long line of women's rights activists from the late nineteenth and early twentieth centuries called "maternalists" by many scholars. These women were committed to protecting women from the hazards of the market place, to using the power of the state to support motherhood, and to defending the value of care work in the home. While offering an inherently conservative defense of women's place as in the private sphere of the home, maternalists nonetheless understood themselves as women's rights activists.[61] In the early 1970s, the nature of the newly revived feminist movement was up for grabs. Women in the maternalist tradition like Spalding could make a home for themselves in it alongside women trying to tear down all vestiges of patriarchy.

Spalding also squared her fiscal conservatism with support for women's rights. For example, one of her priorities was shrinking growing AFDC rolls. In defense of this conservative stance, Spalding's 1975 Report to the National Task Force on Marriage and Divorce included a section titled "A Feminist View of the AFDC Mother," in which she argued that through AFDC, the state ripped off mothers by underpaying them for child care. Her calculations showed that a mother of two taking care of her own children instead of using institutional care saved the state $28,600 a year after deducting the cost of AFDC payments to that mother. And, Spalding pointed out, the mother got no employment benefits for the job she did.[62] Spalding's analysis here sounds similar to Berry's argument that homemakers should be considered important workers. Unlike Berry's, Spalding's proposals did not turn to social insurance to help protect homemakers. Instead, Spalding turned to fathers and ex-husbands to directly support homemakers. While Berry's divorce insurance program had aimed at providing divorced women with an alternative both to welfare and to direct reliance on their ex-husbands, Spalding's program saw these as the only two alternatives and sought to let women go back to relying on their exes.

Spalding's brand of conservative feminism allowed her to work closely with Republicans and Southern Democrats in Congress. Many of these alliances brought her into conflict with other feminists, but they also led to the passage of a new, NOW-endorsed, child support enforcement law in 1975. The law mandated that states establish "efficient programs" for the collection of child support. To aid in this, the federal government created a parent locator service to help find absent parents and allowed for garnishment of federal wages to directly pay child support and alimony. These programs were made available to all women, but custodial parents not receiving AFDC had to pay a small fee to use them. To enforce the mandate, the law required a yearly performance audit of every state's program; any state that failed the audit would lose 5 percent of its federal AFDC funds. Controversially, it also required mothers receiving AFDC payments to identify their children's fathers or risk losing support. Spalding's legislative agenda, unlike Berry's, was built not just on rhetorical fear of expanding AFDC but included provisions that would directly punish AFDC recipients with the loss of funds.

Spalding's work encountered pushback from within NOW and from other women's organizations, for example, the League of Women Voters and the Women's Equity Action League.[63] In 1975 Spalding's co-coordinator of the Marriage and Divorce Task Force, Norma Card, resigned, citing disagreement over the federal support enforcement bill. Card wrote to NOW president Karen DeCrow, "I feel the bill as originally passed imposes a serious limitation on women who are applying for welfare, and that NOW should not take a positive stand upon any issue which oppresses a large segment of women. Betty [Spalding] is not concerned about the women on welfare; she is concerned about middle-class women whose ex-husbands owe thousands of dollars in back child support." Card demanded, "Are we a middle-class organization, only out to help other middle-class women, willing to oppress our poorer sisters in making gains for ourselves?"[64]

Card's question resonated throughout NOW, which had debated versions of it for its entire short history. In 1976, in response to NOW's continued support for the child support enforcement legislation, the Task Force on Poverty called on NOW to pass a resolution clarifying its position on AFDC and child support. Pointing out that NOW had passed a resolution in 1971 demanding no woman be denied public assistance or services for refusing to identify a child's father, they asked for a new resolution that NOW "should never support any legislation or government program which protects the rights of one class of women at the expense of destroying or damaging the rights of another class of women."[65]

Spalding was terse in her response to Card's resignation, writing that the problem of mothers on AFDC should be dealt with by the Women and Poverty Task Force, not the Marriage and Divorce Task Force.[66] She nevertheless tried to address some of poor women's concerns, at least as she understood them. To Senator Sam Nunn, a Georgia Democrat who helped introduce the child support legislation, Spalding wrote about the concerns of women on AFDC. She believed their biggest fear was being "beaten up by the identified father" and asked for the bill to include protections for women who cooperated with enforcement authorities and named their children's fathers.[67] After the law passed, she argued that it addressed many of the Poverty Task Force's complaints, noting that it guaranteed hearings for AFDC recipients who did not want to name their children's fathers.[68] Here again, Spalding sounds remarkably like early twentieth-century reformers who believed they and the state knew better than poor women and sought to use the state to "protect" women from bad husbands rather than empower women to be independent.

The fight between Spalding and the Poverty Task Force highlighted deep divisions within NOW about class—augmented by racial divisions—as well as political party. The Poverty Task Force pointed out that "every child support bill proposed in Congress has been attached to welfare legislation" and supported by conservative Republican and Southern congressmen who were historically against AFDC.[69] This was by design. Spalding wanted her work to help the Republican Party. She sent letters to Republican members of Congress and women in the Ford administration arguing that if the Party took credit for the child support enforcement legislation they could bring feminists into the fold. Spalding wrote, "There is a vacuum in the women's movement as to political party. We are dissatisfied with both parties. . . . The Party could move into that vacuum and take the women's vote with the proper administration" of child support legislation.[70] To Patricia Lindh, special assistant to President Ford, she complained that the Republicans were "missing a golden opportunity to bring women to the Republican Party" by claiming the child support legislation as their own.[71]

Even as Spalding tried to carve out a place in the Republican Party, she notably refused to make common ground with another rising voice for women in the Party: Phyllis Schlafly and her anti-ERA and antifeminist movement. Schlafly's movement shared many of feminist divorce reformers' concerns about marriage and, like Spalding, wanted to defend patriarchal responsibility for the family. But Schlafly and her followers found other proposals of feminists—in particular the ERA—threatening instead of empowering. A defender of the ERA, Spalding rejected building common ground with these women. When Ellen Sim Dewey wrote to Spalding proposing that NOW meet with the chair of the Indianapolis anti-ERA committee with whom she saw "eye to eye on the no fault," Spalding wrote back, "Why waste time converting when you can use it to better advantage in aiding a believer!"[72]

Despite Spalding's best efforts, it was Schlafly and her vision that came to dominate the Republican Party in the following years. Yet, while Spalding failed to attract significant numbers of feminists to the Republican Party, her work did affect public policy. By accepting women's status as dependents of their ex-husbands, and by seeing AFDC as charity that could be taken away, Spalding promoted a maternalist version of feminism that defended women's right to be dependents and upheld men's patriarchal roles from within NOW. She paved the way for compromises between feminist divorce reformers and the government that supported divorced women's continued dependence on their ex-husbands but did nothing to broadly support child care and homemaking. These compromises were part of a longer process of rewriting marriage law to favor wealthy over low-income women and push poor, unmarried women with young children into the workforce.[73]

"A Real Hot Flash from the Post-Menopausal Zest Set": Tish Sommers and the Invention of Displaced Homemakers

Spalding found the idea of rehabilitative maintenance insulting. She argued, "If all labor contracts severed workers from their jobs after 5, 10, 20, and 30 years without pension or severance pay; and instead gave 'rehabilitative maintenance' to the worker so they could go out and get another job, how do you think the workforce would respond? There would be a nation-wide strike, right?"[74] Here again Spalding found herself in disagreement with another NOW Task Force—a group of women on the West Coast organizing to win employment rights and programs for older women. These women were led by Tish Sommers, an activist in both the women's movement and the new gerontology movement.

From 1973 to 1978, Tish Sommers served as the first coordinator of the NOW Task Force on Older Women. From this position, Sommers articulated an analysis of the relationship between sexism and ageism. In an early statement on the new Task Force she wrote: "Sexism is compounded as women grow older. Jobs are harder to come by; the dependency status increases; self-image deteriorates; health care goes from bad to worse; marriages flounder; and for a large majority of older women poverty is no longer on the doorstep—it moves in. . . . Unless we tackle our specific problems, the very upheavals which are bringing about gains for younger women will worsen conditions for those whose roles were defined in an earlier day, and will thereby alienate the young from the old."[75] Sommers engaged with the same problem as Berry and Spalding: the economic vulnerability of longtime homemakers. But her solution differed from those offered by the Marriage and Divorce Task Force because Sommers's analysis centered on age instead of marriage.

Like Berry's and Spalding's, Sommers's agenda was based on her own experience. When she came to NOW, Sommers was twice divorced. Her first marriage ended in the early 1940s, after only about three years, when she was still young and childless.[76] Trained as a dancer and with an interest in radical leftist politics, she was able to support herself and maintain her political activities after her first marriage. Through these activities she met her second husband, Joe Sommers. The two married in 1949. Two years later Tish and Joe moved to Birmingham as part of the American Communist Party's underground efforts in the South. Since their political work was clandestine, Sommers acted the part of a full-time homemaker involved in her community through volunteer activities. While in Birmingham, the couple adopted a son. In 1957, under investigation by the FBI, the family moved to Milwaukee and retreated from politics. Joe entered graduate school at the University of Wisconsin, and Sommers truly became a full-time homemaker. The couple eventually relocated to Seattle and then Palo Alto. In both places, Sommers volunteered with the local civil rights movement, but did not hold any full-time jobs. In the late 1960s, Sommers was also drawn into the burgeoning feminist movement, which led her and Joe to confront the state of their twenty-two-year marriage and then, in 1971, end it.[77]

This time, Sommers divorced at fifty-eight. She had been out of the formal workforce for almost twenty years; she had a history of breast cancer; and her ex-husband was ten years her junior, which meant she would not be eligible for any Social Security benefits through him until he reached the age of eligibility at sixty-five, more than fifteen years later.[78] Sommers was unlikely to get a well-paying job or quality health insurance and she would soon need retirement benefits. Luckily, Sommers also had a deep reserve of political experience on which to draw as well as independent wealth inherited from her mother.[79] She was already involved with the new feminist movement and she joined the Gray Panthers, an old-age activist group. In 1973, she helped found the Women's Action Training Center (WATC) in Oakland, which offered women training on how to identify issues and organize to fix them. It quickly became clear to Sommers that the issue she had identified was the intersection of ageism and sexism.[80] Out of the WATC, in 1974, she began the Jobs for Older Women hotline, which eventually became an organization, the Bay Area Jobs for Older Women Project.[81]

That same year, Sommers helped found NOW's new Task Force on Older Women. The task force was created by resolution at NOW's sixth annual conference. Sommers announced that its initial focus would be on Social Security, discrimination in employment, the physical and mental health needs of older women, and consideration of how to give credit to homemakers' work.[82] Organizing a task force on the basis of age immediately raised the question of what defined an older woman. Officially, the Task Force on Older Women defined women over thirty as "older."[83] While they never specified exactly how they hit upon this number, it is likely they chose thirty because it was the age at which women felt their remarriage chances after divorce or widowhood decreased significantly. NOW representatives cited numbers showing that while three-quarters of women thirty and under remarried after divorce, that number fell to only half of women aged thirty-one through thirty-nine and only one-quarter of women forty and over.[84] Women's age category was thus defined by their relationships. This was true of their relationships both with men and with children. For her task force, Sommers reached out not only to divorced and widowed women but also to women who had received AFDC payments until their children had aged them out of eligibility.[85] For this latter group of women, their children's redefinition as adults moved them into the category of "older" and resulted in the loss of support for their homemaking role. Establishing this alliance immediately put Sommers's task force at odds with Spalding's despite their many overlapping interests.[86]

Perhaps because of the fuzziness of the term "older," Sommers began to look for a better term to describe all the women her organizing brought together. This became especially pressing as she began to work with legal services lawyer Barbara Dudley to draft California legislation specifically to help these women. In 1975, she hit on the term "displaced homemakers."[87] Sommers liked the term because it captured a useful "analogy between displaced persons 'forcibly exiled' through social upheaval or war and a whole generation of women caught in the 1970s, 'forcibly exiled,' displaced from a role, an occupation, dependency status, and a livelihood."[88] Implicit in the term was a critique of an unmodified, feminist formal equality agenda. By locating herself within NOW while advocating for special protections for older women, Sommers argued that the feminists had an obligation to accommodate older women's special needs in their agenda.

Having coined the term "displaced homemakers," Sommers and Dudley drafted a bill to create funding for three model "Displaced Homemaker Centers." Each center was to offer job training, counseling, and placement services, as well as health services.[89] Introduced in California in 1975, the bill quickly inspired the introduction of similar legislation in other states as well as a national bill first introduced by California Congresswoman Yvonne Braithwaite Burke.[90] To aid the passage of these bills Sommers formed the Alliance for Displaced Homemakers and recruited a widowed woman, Laurie Shields, to be its executive director.[91]

A bill creating a pilot displaced homemaker center was signed into law in California in September 1975.[92] By 1976, Maryland and Florida had enacted their own displaced homemakers laws. That same year, Congress had amended the Vocational Education Act to allow states to use Vocational Education grants to help displaced homemakers and a federal displaced homemakers bill, modeled on the California bill, had also been proposed.[93] In 1978, Congresswoman Burke and Senator Birch Bayh decided to tie their displaced homemakers legislation to reauthorization of the more general Comprehensive Employment and Training Act (CETA).[94]

As an African American congresswoman, Burke was a notable sponsor of displaced homemakers legislation, complicating frequent criticism that the problems of divorce were the problems of middle-class white women.[95] For Burke, the displaced homemakers legislation was a piece of her broader commitment to full employment legislation. A priority of many on the Left in the 1970, including the Congressional Black Caucus, full employment legislation would have required Congress and the president to make the goal of full employment (usually defined as 3 percent unemployment) the focus of fiscal, monetary, and social policy.[96] Early legislative proposals also promised public sector jobs to anyone seeking work and unable to find employment in the private sector. As full employment legislation developed over the 1970s, feminists became increasingly skeptical that it would address the specific employment concerns of women. Eligibility criteria for the promised public sector jobs changed to prioritize men with families to support while leaving women with wage-earning husbands essentially ineligible for these jobs.[97] Burke was a supporter of full employment legislation despite its faults, but also advocated a host of programs designed to specifically improve women's employment opportunities. In addition to the displaced homemakers legislation, she supported legislation to increase part-time employment opportunities in the federal government.[98]

Burke's focus on employment legislation for women spoke directly to the women she represented. Black women were more likely to have to work to help support their families. In 1974, over half of adult black women were members of the civilian labor force, while only 44 percent of white women were. Nevertheless, the unemployment rate for black women—the number of women actively seeking work but unable to find it—was almost twice the unemployment rate for white women and the divorce and separation rates for black women also surpassed those for white women.[99] Although Burke was concerned with the poor enforcement of alimony and child support, she assumed that most displaced homemakers would have to work and concerned herself with helping them do so instead of improving enforcement of support orders.[100]

Sommers and Shields traveled the country and used their organizational contacts to rally support for Burke's bill. One characteristically humorous notice sent to NOW women asking them to immediately send letters to Congress was titled, "Attention: All Members of N.O.W.: A Real Hot Flash from the Post-Menopausal Zest Set."[101] The CETA bill, including the Burke-Bayh measures for displaced homemakers, passed in 1978. It authorized $5 million for the creation of pilot programs for displaced homemakers across the country.[102] After the passage of federal legislation, the Alliance for Displaced Homemakers was dissolved and replaced by a Displaced Homemakers Network. By the mid-1980s, one thousand centers belonged to the Displaced Homemakers Network.[103]

While Sommers and Shields's organizing drew in the support of women who were not engaged with the NOW Marriage and Divorce Committee, it also alienated feminists like Spalding who were committed to marriage-based policy and organizing. To their initial surprise, Sommers and Shields also drew Phyllis Schlafly's ire. In her memoir, Shields wrote that throughout the 1970s, "I sincerely believed that if ever there was an opportunity to share a platform, or even a cup of coffee, with Phyllis Schlafly herself, the two of us could find common ground."[104] Schlafly often sounded remarkably like feminist divorce reformers. In late 1979, for example, she argued against no-fault divorce and in favor of alimony, explaining: "In very few cases are women getting more than a year-and-a-half of alimony. That's all right if the wife is young and healthy and can go out and get a job and doesn't have any children. But that's something else again when it's a 60-year-old woman who went into marriage in another era, doesn't have any marketable skill, and whose husband is making a pretty good income. I just don't believe he should be able to just simply walk out and say 'goodbye, Toots.'"[105] Nevertheless, Schlafly organized a letter-writing campaign against the proposed federal displaced homemakers bill. She told readers of her *Eagle Forum Report*, "Such centers which are already in existence are nothing but indoctrination & training centers for women's lib. The feminists who run such centers use them to push ERA, abortion, federal child care, lesbian privilege, etc. Now they want to do this at the taxpayers' expense."[106]

Schlafly's opposition grew out of her origins as an anti-tax, anti-government activist in the 1950s.[107] She told her followers, "The Federal Government cannot create jobs except by taking the wages out of another citizen's pocket. Only the private enterprise system creates jobs."[108] Even when they agreed on an issue, antifeminists and feminists were divided by their approach to government. Fundamentally, Sommers and Shields believed the government had an important role to play in helping keep homemaking an option for women, while Schlafly did not.

Despite the objections of women from within and without the feminist movement, Sommers and Shields's coalition was broader and more effective than the smaller one of divorced women led by Berry and Spalding. Like Berry's and Spalding's advocacy, the idea of displaced homemakers suggested that divorced women were members of a privileged status group of single women, but the term "displaced homemakers" allowed divorced women to join with others to form an effective political coalition. The term also created a compelling narrative for offering dependent women services when the marital relationship ended while avoiding the complex issue of how to think about the value of women's work in the home. Instead of extending benefits to divorced women because of their former marriages or their work in the home, displaced homemakers legislation extended economic resources to women because, through no fault of their own, changing laws and cultural expectations had left them behind. This language allowed feminists to move away from an agenda exclusively emphasizing absolute equality to one that recognized that such an agenda could harm women who had grown up in an unequal world. They became advocates not just for equality but also transitional justice.

Berry, Spalding, Sommers, and the Broader Movement for Reform

Berry, Spalding, and Sommers offered three different answers to the problems of lost income after divorce. Their answers were shaped by their own experiences of losing breadwinner husbands through divorce and their wider political outlook. For all their differences, all three women became recognized feminist experts on the issue of divorce. They testified before Congress, gave lectures, and promoted an awareness of the economic problems rising divorce rates posed for women. Through these activities, these women helped create a new understanding of how divorced women should be treated by the law. All of their proposals argued against feminists adopting a strict formal equality agenda and provided early examples of the kinds of laws that would allow women to achieve functional equality. The common denominator uniting all three agendas was a shared claim that divorced women were a special class of single women who deserved the government's protection and support.

The influence of Berry's, Spalding's, and Sommers's ideas was on display in the responses to a 1977 national essay contest that called for submissions on "A Practical Program to Achieve Economic Justice for Homemakers." The contest was hosted by Babson College with support from public relations tycoon Edward Bernays and his wife Doris.[109] About nine hundred women entered the Babson-Bernays contest. The judges included the president of Radcliffe; the president of Wellesley; U.S. Representative Margaret Heckler; and former U.S. Senator Wendell Anderson. The winning proposal came from Dorothy Woodworth of Palo Alto, California. Her focus was on improving homemakers' access to economic resources by helping them define their work in the home as real work and passing legislation that recognized it as such. "For adults," Woodworth wrote, "the major suggestion is to give females the same bootstraps that are given veterans, and to adjust social security and other economic laws to women's segmented lives."[110] For children, Woodworth wanted education about the Social Security system to be included in the high school curriculum.[111] Runners-up in the contest also wrote about the problems of Social Security benefits for homemakers, as well as the problems of divorce in states without community property laws, the need for better and more affordable child care, and the division of labor in marriage.[112]

Before and after the contest, NOW and other organizations were inundated with similar proposals. The women who participated in the Babson-Bernays competition and sent their own proposals to feminist organizations played an important part in redefining marriage's place in the law. By embracing and debating many of the ideas about marriage that Berry, Spalding, Sommers, and NOW's lawyers spent so much time promoting, they helped move these ideas into the mainstream conversation. By the end of the 1970s, as a result of these women, the idea that the act of marriage gave women a status that entitled them to special rights and could not be lost through divorce was widespread.

As this idea moved into the popular consciousness, it quickly ran up against the growing antifeminist movement. Schlafly consistently linked all aspects of the feminist agenda to the ERA, ensuring that any hope of an alliance between feminist divorce reformers and antifeminists disappeared by late 1970s. In the place of the feminist divorce reform agenda she rejected, Schlafly lauded the privileges she believed homemakers already had under the law. She cited alimony and necessaries laws that required husbands to provide basic necessities for their wives as evidence for her point.[113] She argued the ERA threatened these protections. Schlafly and feminist divorce reformers were debating the very reality of divorced women's economic and legal situation. Thus, in 1977 Dewey, who had by then given up on allying with anti-ERA activists against no-fault divorce laws, argued that NOW needed to "show homemakers how the 'privileges' they have as wives and mothers are albatrosses and degrading to them as persons and as homemakers." She continued, "Those privileges can be taken away whenever their husbands, their legislators, and the judges want to take them away."[114] Feminist divorce reformers sought laws that guaranteed women economic security as a result of their own labor instead of as dependents, because they believed such guarantees would leave women far more secure than the dependent benefits Schlafly defended.

As a result of Schlafly's movement, between NOW's 1974 Marriage and Divorce conference and the election of 1980, the generative optimism feminists felt in the early 1970s faded, and the family became an increasingly polarizing subject of political debate. Differences in how liberals and conservatives defined the family and its appropriate role in public policy helped deepen the growing fault line between Democrats and Republicans and created new divisions within each party.[115] Historian Jefferson Cowie argues that these years marked a fundamental political realignment in the United States. The first half of the decade saw the entrenchment of the new identity politics of the 1960s throughout the country and the passage of many laws that fit into a liberal legislative agenda. As wages began to stagnate in 1973 and 1974, however, support for the New Deal state and the reforms of the Great Society began to crumble. Starting in the mid-1970s, right-wing groups successfully attracted legions of members from newly economically unstable members of the white working class.[116] Phyllis Schlafly's anti-ERA campaign—and its broader critique of the feminist agenda—appealed to many women in this demographic who found themselves forced to help supply a larger and larger share of the family income.[117] Although in the mid-1970s, members of Congress on both sides of the aisle as well as both Republican presidents Nixon and Ford lent their support to the ERA; in 1980 the GOP removed support for the ERA from its official platform.[118]

Even as the divide between the parties deepened, both liberal and conservative activists who took up the issue of the family shared a concern for homemakers' fate after divorce. Arguments about how the government should treat divorced women played a central role in the politicization of the family. As consensus built around the economic challenges divorced women faced, antifeminism intertwined with a conservative backlash against the welfare state to create a powerful new movement to counter feminist divorce reformers. It became increasingly difficult for feminist divorce reformers to win the expansive legislative proposals they had imagined. Instead, policymakers and activists settled for compromises. They gravitated toward proposals creating small selective entitlements for divorced women, which all feminist divorce reformers supported, instead of passing more controversial laws that created more equal marriages or recognized the value of women's work in the home.

PART II

A Galaxy of Laws

CHAPTER 3

Partners or Parasites?

Class, Race, and Credit Rights

Before the antifeminist backlash that seized the country at the end of the decade, in the early 1970s newly divorced women reached out to feminist congresswomen and organizations about an immediate problem they faced: the loss of credit. One NOW officer recalled that in 1970 and 1971, "hardly a week passed that I did not receive a plea for legal assistance from some woman somewhere in the United States who was denied credit because of her sex."[1] NOW heard from women like Betty Binder who, in 1973, wrote to her congressman about her experience following her divorce earlier that year. Binder explained that after she and her ex-husband, Michael Schutz, divorced, she went back to her given name and applied for credit. She wrote, "I was told, again and again, that Betty Binder had no financial standing in California, although Michael Schutz, earning the same income, had no difficulty in getting new credit cards." Binder found this especially galling "because Michael Schutz had been a full-time student for nearly two years, and Betty Schutz had earned the family income and paid the bills." Binder told her congressman that there were clearly "two systems of credit in America"—one for men and one for women. Outraged, she wrote, "If I have to pay the same taxes, the same prices, the same interest rates, why can't I be granted the same credit for expenditures?"[2]

The credit application process was one of the key moments when women discovered how marriage affected their economic status. While single women often had a hard time getting credit, lenders most systematically denied loans to married women.[3] Standard lending policies dictated that married women carry credit only in their husbands' names. Lenders typically canceled any credit lines a woman had held before marriage. This practice of erasing a woman's financial independence upon marriage and subsuming her economic identity under her husband's was a clear vestige of coverture, the common-law doctrine that turned a married couple into "one legal person" represented by the husband. Under coverture, once married, a woman lost her legal and economic identity. She could not contract or sue and was not responsible for herself in criminal or civil law—her husband became responsible for her actions. Similarly, any property she held before marriage became her husband's, along with the results of any future labor.[4]

Women might ignore their loss of economic identity while married, but divorce forced them to reckon with this harsh reality. Betty Berry explained, "The various annoyances, discrimination and problems that happen in marriage because of the coverture doctrine are merely harbingers of the calamities that can overcome the financially dependent wife and mother upon divorce."[5] For example, divorced women, like Betty Binder, found that even if they had paid the bills for years, they had no credit history, no credit, and little chance of getting any. Without credit, many women's standard of living fell quickly; they often could not purchase the goods they needed or shop at the stores they had frequented. As a result, in the early 1970s, many divorced women became leaders in the fight to end sex discrimination in credit.

While new laws and practices had slowly chipped away at the doctrine of coverture over the preceding century, the revived feminist activism of the 1970s directly attacked coverture's continuing hold on American marriage, law, and financial practices. A representative from the Center for Women's Policy Studies told a congressional committee in 1973, "Most women today want to be regarded as partners in marriages, not as parasites."[6] This partnership model of marriage guided the formulation of feminist divorce reformers' demands over the next decade. Many feminists thought that in order to be understood as partners, they had to force men, the state, and businesses to recognize the economic value of their housework, but they were divided over how to win this economic recognition. On the one hand, women's liberationists demanded actual wages for their housework.[7] On the other hand, liberal feminists who were more focused on working within the system to enact legislative change—a sector of the movement where most feminist divorce reformers fell—came to believe that the Equal Rights Amendment would require the federal government to recognize the value of women's unpaid household labor in its social welfare programs, even if it did not force the payment of wages for housework.[8]

Liberal feminists' campaign for equal credit rights fit into their broader attack on coverture. Their faith in the ERA's ability to undo coverture had limits. As written, the ERA applied only to state action. Because credit was a privately issued resource to which the government did not guarantee a right, private entities would still be free to discriminate on the basis of sex unless further laws were passed.[9] Equal credit legislation was meant to serve as one of these laws. Through such legislation feminists proposed not only to change the financial relationship between husbands and wives but also to pass the first of what they hoped would be many complementary pieces of legislation to the ERA. The chair of NOW's Task Force on Credit was quite explicit about this. She explained, "I don't believe the ERA will help us, even when it is ratified, because we would have to prove the existence of state action and perhaps a 'right to credit.'"[10]

Feminist divorce reformers also recognized that the campaign for equal credit fit into their larger campaign to reform women's position within the American social welfare regime. Most scholars who study the development of the American social welfare regime ignore credit, focusing instead on health insurance, unemployment insurance, and retirement pensions.[11] By leaving out credit, these scholars present an incomplete picture of the tools the government has used since the New Deal to try and guarantee a basic standard of living to Americans. By building and supporting the contemporary American mortgage market, beginning in the 1930s the federal government has made affordable and well-regulated credit available to middle-class Americans, helping raise their standard of living to include a home, a car, appliances, and a host of other consumer goods.[12] For better or worse, the government used credit regulation as it used health insurance regulation, to support Americans through private companies.[13] Divorced women understood this. When they listed the economic resources they had lost as a result of their divorces, credit always appeared on the list next to health insurance and retirement pensions.

As with most economic resources it regulated in the twentieth century, the federal government's regulation of credit did not provide equal access. The government regulation of credit access deliberately reinforced not only gender but also racial lines and divisions between recipients of different sorts of public benefits. As a result, as women began to lobby to improve their credit access they ran into questions about the extent of their demands and whom new credit legislation should seek to help. These questions arose during women's legislative work and when they sought to create new forms of credit access outside of the traditional banking system. As a result of divisions over these questions, NOW's work on credit in the 1970s culminated in a series of public fights among members of the organization's leadership about its stance toward African American and low-income women.

In the end, the greatest success of women's credit access campaigns—the passing of the Equal Credit Opportunity Act (ECOA) in 1974—offered an early and important victory to feminist divorce reformers while deepening much of the discrimination already embedded in credit regulations. The narrow law banned discrimination on the basis of sex and marital status and required lenders to create separate credit histories for husbands and wives. It also mandated that lenders consider alimony and child support payments as income when evaluating a credit record.[14] This allowed married and formerly married women who worked in the home to build credit records on the basis of their administration of their husbands' (or ex-husbands') salaries. The new law thus offered married women with access to financial resources recognition as their husbands' economic partners, a rare win in divorced women's work for the understanding of marriage as a contract not a status. At the same time, Congress refused to include credit reforms that would have helped low-income women establish their economic independence in the final bill. As a law that helped married and formerly married women more than never-married women and that did little for low-income women, the ECOA presaged what feminist divorce reformers would demand and win when they addressed divorced women's loss of health insurance and retirement pensions later in the 1970s.

"A Loud Roar": Uncovering Sex-Discriminatory Policies in America's Credit Economy

At the start of the 1970s, the model of the breadwinner-homemaker family guided the administration of credit to married women just as it did the administration of health care and retirement pensions. The policies of federal lenders encouraged this model and the gendered assumptions of local credit managers supported its continued use. Although the practice of distributing economic resources to married women through their husbands was standard, credit presents a particularly interesting case, because the homemaker-breadwinner model of family labor was not only promoted by its administration but also by the daily use of credit. Easy credit in combination with a booming economy allowed for the development of the consumer capitalist culture of the 1950s and 1960s in which the breadwinner-homemaker family structure flourished.[15] In the 1970s, however, as the economy weakened and women increasingly entered the workforce to help their families maintain their standards of living, credit did not become any less important. Instead, families relied even more on credit to make ends meet.[16] Divorced women quickly discovered the critical role that both their marriages and easy access to credit had played in maintaining their place in the American economy.

Consumer debt in the United States increased sixfold from 1950 to 1970.[17] While Americans had a long history of consumer borrowing, new suburban lifestyles rested on more extensive borrowing and new forms of loans, many facilitated by the federal government through New Deal agencies and programs like the Federal Housing Authority (FHA), the Veteran's Administration (VA), and the Federal National Mortgage Association (Fannie Mae). The mortgages backed by these agencies enabled families to move to detached houses in the suburbs; installment loans allowed them to buy the newly necessary cars and appliances; and revolving credit allowed them to make purchases at chain stores.[18] By 1975, consumer credit was used in approximately 48 percent of all retail purchases.[19]

Contemporaries felt rising debt levels as something new and notable. By the late 1960s government officials recognized credit as essential to full participation in the American economy. For example, in 1969, the Office of Economic Opportunity published a booklet, *Consumer Action for the Poor*, which announced, "The American economy in general depends largely upon credit. For the middle class, credit is often the avenue to a high standard of living; for the poor, it is often the only means of acquiring life's necessities."[20] In a 1974 address to the American Banking Association (ABA), Dee Dee Ahern, the ABA's director of the Women's Financial Education and Counseling Service said, "Never since the advent of money has a single factor so greatly affected our financial and economic world. Credit has changed the habits, lifestyles, and economic lives of every American."[21] The trend even received attention from popular women's magazines. In 1972, a *Glamour* magazine editorial declared, "Credit is, after all, a way of life in our society."[22]

In recognition of how essential consumer credit had become, Congress began to regulate it more aggressively. In 1968 it passed the Consumer Credit Protection Act, which among other things chartered a National Commission on Consumer Finance (NCCF) to evaluate fair and unfair lending practices.[23] The commission's hearings focused on various technical lending practices that had little to do with sex discrimination. It did, however devote some time to studying "special problems of availability"—under this category it included the availability of credit to the poor as well as racial, residential, and, eventually, sex discrimination in credit administration.[24]

The commission's decision to investigate sex discrimination came at the end of its life and resulted directly from pressure from women like Betty Binder.[25] NCCF chair, Ira Millstein, explained: "During the course of this Commission's existence, we have heard and read stories and received letters describing difficulties women have had when they applied for credit from banks, retailers, savings and loans associations or when they sought credit cards for specific or general use. When the letters and stories began to increase in length and frequency, we decided it was important for our overall study of the credit industry and consumer credit transactions to look into problems which seem to be peculiar to women seeking credit."[26] Privately, Millstein told his fellow commissioners that he wanted to hold the sex-discrimination hearings without having the NCCF staff actually spend much time on the issue. He hoped to simply gather a group of witnesses who would bring attention and publicity to the issue and leave it at that.[27] Yet Millstein also sensed that, even with limited staff time devoted to them, these hearings could have an impact. He said of the decision to hold them, "We [f]igure we will close our hearings with a lo[u]d roar."[28]

The NCCF hearings did inspire a roar. Witnesses described the near institutionalization of sex discrimination among mainstream lending institutions. Evidence showed that most banks and retailers refused to give married women credit in their own names. If women held credit before their marriage, banks required them to reapply in their husband's names when they married. One witness, Jorie Lueloff Friedman, told the committee that she had supported herself for nine years as a writer for the Associated Press and then as a newscaster for NBC News in Chicago, a job she continued to hold. For more than six years, she had held charge accounts at "most major Chicago stores." She continued, "I've always paid my bills on time and I never had a credit problem—until I got married." When she tried to change the name on her cards after her marriage, one store immediately closed her account, and all the others asked for her husband's name, bank, and employer. "There was no longer any interest in me, my job, my bank, or my ability to pay my own bills."[29] Lenders defended this practice to Friedman and other women by arguing that state laws required husbands to pay their wives' bills, but, as women pointed out in response, almost all states had eliminated such laws long ago.[30]

In addition to simply refusing to extend credit to married women as individuals, creditors often refused to count a married woman's income in full when a couple applied for a loan, unless she provided assurance—usually an affidavit on birth control practices—that she would not or could not get pregnant.[31] Creditors justified this policy, which was especially prevalent among mortgage lenders, with the false presumption that if a woman had a child she would automatically leave the workforce.[32] The NCCF hearings revealed that some government entities encouraged this practice. The FHA, Fannie Mae, and the VA all had different policies regarding counting wives' income when granting home loans to married couples. The FHA had changed its policies in the 1960s to count a wife's income in full. In contrast, the VA counted a wife's income only if the veteran's income was not enough to grant a loan and if "the nature of [a wife's] employment and family composition indicate that her income is likely to continue."[33] This clause suggested that if a VA loan agent believed a couple likely to have more children he or she should refuse to count a wife's income in full. Fannie Mae drafted rules in 1970 that counted only 50 percent of a wife's income in a home loan application. In response to protest from NOW and other women's groups, it eventually removed the 50 percent rule but put in its place language similar to the VA's.[34]

Women argued that these practices were based on stereotypes, not facts. Throughout the 1960s more and more women with young children entered, or chose to remain in, the workforce. By 1974, 40 percent of all women with children between three and five participated in the labor force.[35] Moreover, research showed that women of all marital statuses were better credit risks than men with the same marital status.[36]

In addition to discrimination on the basis of sex, lenders openly discriminated against divorced and separated people. After being asked to testify before the NCCF, the executive director of Parents Without Partners conducted a quick survey of the D.C. chapter of his organization. He told the commission that he was "appalled, really, overwhelmed, and somewhat stupefied by the extent of the discrimination practiced by the consumer credit industry."[37] The discrimination against divorced and separated people took a number of forms. Many credit scoring agencies interpreted divorce as a sign of unreliability and gave all separated and divorced people lower credit ratings. Furthermore, lenders argued that during a separation they had difficulty knowing who was responsible for debt. One bank representative explained, "Generally in divorce, you will find that a woman will blame a man, and the man will blame the woman. It's very hard to differentiate who has responsibility for indebtedness during the legal separation period that's required or that usually occurs."[38]

While lenders argued that discrimination against divorced people hit both men and women equally and therefore was not sex-discriminatory, feminists countered that such discrimination actually had far worse effects on women. Women had to apply for new credit when they divorced because creditors had erased any they held upon marriage and refused to allow them to carry credit in their own names during their marriages. While men could simply maintain their existing credit accounts after a divorce without notifying their creditors of the change in marital status, women had to start from scratch.[39]

Other lending practices discriminated even more directly against divorced women. Many lenders refused to count alimony and child support as income.[40] Most mainstream lenders also refused to count income from public assistance when deciding on a credit application.[41] Since women made up the majority of recipients of alimony, child support, and public assistance, these policies directly affected women's ability to get credit.[42] Interestingly, the NCCF understood only the discounting of alimony and child support as problems for the sex-discrimination hearings. Despite the fact that it considered the work of the largely female National Welfare Rights Organization during its hearings on low-income consumers, the NCCF separated the issues of sex discrimination in credit from the issues of low-income consumers' access to credit.[43] The commission's work implied that sex discrimination was a wealthy and middle-class women's issue—something that only arose once a woman had achieved a certain income and social status.

The NCCF separated sex and income discrimination in its analysis because it believed that some economic discrimination was justified in credit administration. After all, lenders took an economic risk when extending credit; they had to factor in the borrower's income when making the decision to do so.[44] Nevertheless, its acceptance of income discrimination led the NCCF to some bizarre conclusions. For example, it went so far as to declare itself unable to determine if racial discrimination occurred in lending decisions because income correlated so strongly to race.[45] By accepting income discrimination by lenders as necessary and inevitable, the NCCF ended many possible discussions about how to truly improve minorities' access to credit before they began. Similarly, the NCCF entirely separated the issues of income and sex discrimination. Since many middle-class women relied on their husbands' (or ex-husbands') incomes for their class status, separating the problems of income and sex discrimination paved the way for legislative solutions that worked to reward women for their marriages with access to credit.

The NCCF decided it did not have time to do anything about the problems exposed in the sex-discrimination hearings, but it celebrated their effect nonetheless. Chairman Millstein believed "the hearings worked out beautifully. . . . I think it was one of our most successful hearings in terms of getting publicity and in terms of apparently stirring up some people to worry about what they have been doing."[46] The commission's final report claimed, "The extensive publicity that accompanied the Commission's hearings has caused many credit grantors to reexamine their policies with respect to existence of sex discrimination."[47]

The NCCF hearings did play a critically important role in bringing national attention to the issue of sex discrimination in credit transactions; however, the commission's work did not occur in a vacuum. Women's organizations and civil rights groups had been highlighting the issue of sex discrimination in assessments of credit since the late 1960s. By 1972, NOW and WEAL had committees working on credit, and the Ford Foundation was funding a Center for Women's Policy Studies Project on Women and Credit.[48] Arguably, the NCCF hearings occurred as the result of all this work.

In response to women's activism, at the time of the NCCF hearing some lenders had already begun to voluntarily change their policies. As women moved into the workforce, many lenders saw a business opportunity to expand their customer base.[49] Increasing numbers of national lenders adopted policies mandating equal treatment of men and women. In 1973, for example, a National Businessmen's Council Report called for "absolute equality between men and women in credit granting."[50] Yet, even when national lenders or local laws mandated that lenders treat men and women equally in credit applications, many loan officers persisted in using old sex-discriminatory evaluations.[51] Moreover, while lenders might eagerly consider lending to single women with income, they remained considerably more hesitant about rethinking how marriage should affect women's access to credit.[52] It was clear to many women that voluntary action alone would not lead to truly gender-equal credit access.

"All Our Sisters with Incomes of Their Own": Women's Grassroots Credit Activism

Although the NCCF ignored the connection between income and sex discrimination, the first campaign for women's credit rights came not from an explicitly feminist organization but rather from an organization of low-income, single mothers. Between 1968 and 1969 the National Welfare Rights Organization (NWRO) waged a campaign to get large mainstream retailers to extend credit to its members. A few years later, NOW and other explicitly feminist organizations would kick off their work on credit in a similar fashion, sidestepping legislative activism and instead going straight to the banks. Unlike the NWRO, in pursuit of their goals, middle-class feminist organizations were able to draw heavily on their members' considerable resources as well as their class and racial statuses. The differences between welfare rights activists' and feminists' early corporate campaigns began the process of separating the issues of middle-class and low-income women's access to credit. The grassroots models for fair credit evaluations the organizations developed, which ultimately went on to influence national legislation, had class and racial biases built into them from the start.

AFDC rolls rapidly expanded in 1960s and 1970s and became associated not with the white widowed mothers for whom the program was originally intended, but with single mothers—black, in the popular imagination at least—who had never married.[53] Increased spending on women who generated far less sympathy than the original ADC recipients created political opposition to the program and spawned a host of reform efforts on the Left and Right.[54] This in turn led to welfare recipients themselves organizing to defend their rights and their dignity. The organization at the helm of this movement was the National Welfare Rights Organization.

Founded in 1966 by welfare rights groups from across the country, the NWRO quickly grew to have an official membership of approximately 25,000 welfare recipients in 150 communities. It launched a credit campaign in 1968 because its leadership realized that, although its members relied on credit to make many key purchases, women on welfare had severely restricted access to loans.[55] The chairman of the NWRO's Ways and Means Committee, Etta Horn, explained, "Unlike most consumers we cannot save for . . . purchases since our incomes are so inadequate. In addition, current welfare regulations discourage savings by confiscating any savings above a specified limit. When the possibility of savings are eliminated, large and emergency items must be purchased with credit."[56] Mainstream retailers and lenders, however, generally refused to lend to women receiving welfare. This left these women at the mercy of merchants whose entire business model rested on charging individuals with no other credit options exorbitant rates for low-quality goods.[57]

The NWRO defined itself first and foremost as a poor people's organization. Despite its largely female membership, the NWRO designed its campaigns and messaging around its members' status as poor people and mothers rather than as women.[58] The organization did not approach its credit campaign with a feminist analysis, much less with the analysis of the feminist divorce reform movement. Yet, in the late 1960s divorced and separated single mothers made up the largest block of welfare recipients, with never-married mothers coming in second.[59] While the NWRO did not conceptualize it as such, its 1968 credit campaign was one of the earliest instances of divorced women coming together to demand access to an economic resource as a right.

The NWRO came up with a plan to provide welfare recipients with credit by engaging department stores to organize a proto credit union. Credit unions are nonprofit financial cooperatives chartered around specific fields of membership. The members own the union and control its operation; membership in the union makes individuals eligible for credit.[60] The NWRO could not raise the capital to start its own credit union. Instead, it pressured large retailers to agree to extend $150 in credit to any affiliated NWRO member of at least three months, accepting a letter of reference from the NWRO as proof that an applicant was a good credit risk. This plan mimicked a traditional credit union in its use of organizational membership to determine credit eligibility, but relied on department stores for financing. For the NWRO this proposal had two key benefits. First, it created an incentive for women to join the organization.[61] Second, and more importantly, NWRO membership would stand in for the judgments based on race, gender, and income source that the organization believed led credit officers to deny their members credit. The organization wanted to minimize the subjective decisions that went into credit awards.

The NWRO decided to focus its national campaign on Sears, believing the chain's notorious intransigence in the face of grassroots pressure would allow them to build an exciting campaign that would draw in new members.[62] The organization began by demanding a meeting with Sears's management. When management refused, it kicked off a national boycott and series of protests.[63] NWRO members and supporters picketed Sears and staged "shop-ins." The latter involved entering stores en masse and causing chaos by ringing up large numbers of items, asking the clerks about the stores' credit policy, and then canceling the orders when the clerks gave an unsatisfactory answer.[64] In addition to these highly visible tactics, the NWRO sent teams of women to negotiate with local Sears's managers and convinced Sears's shareholders to give them proxy votes to attend a shareholders' meeting.[65]

The pressure the NWRO put on Sears resulted in no more than a meeting on the national level.[66] On a local level, however, the NWRO won agreements with Sears branches and other retailers in Winston-Salem, Cincinnati, and elsewhere.[67] Most of the individual Sears stores that reached agreements with the NWRO retained the right to conduct their own credit checks on individuals as they saw fit, undermining one of the NWRO's hopes for their campaign—creating an automatic right to credit for its members, freeing them from the subjective judgment of potential creditors. The NWRO unhappily agreed to this compromise, deciding improved access was more important to its members than waiting for a complete victory.

The organization also used Sears's intransigence to pressure other stores to offer credit to welfare recipients.[68] This strategy paid off. Ultimately, the NWRO's biggest victory was with Montgomery Ward, with which it won a national agreement establishing a pilot program of the NWRO's group credit plan for three thousand members in nine test areas across the country.[69] The program met most of the NWRO's demands, but, like the NWRO's agreements with local Sears branches, Montgomery Ward did retain the right to do a final credit check on individuals.[70] After the first year, the agreement disappears from the NWRO records, suggesting it was not renewed. In letters from late in the first year, Montgomery Ward executives express disappointment with the delinquency rate of 22 percent on the accounts.[71] High delinquency rates seem to have been a problem with some of the local agreements the NWRO won, as well.[72]

By its own measures, the NWRO's campaign was not particularly successful. It did, however, receive a great deal of news coverage. The *Christian Science Monitor*, the *Boston Globe*, the *New York Times*, and many local papers ran stories on the organization's protests.[73] The NWRO therefore created a precedent for the explicitly feminist campaigns for credit that followed in terms of both tactics and messaging. Two messages ran through the NWRO's credit rights campaign: that credit was a critical sign of respect in the contemporary economy and that, as mothers, welfare recipients deserved credit.

The NWRO argued that the extension of credit was equivalent to the extension of respect. The organization's executive director, George Wiley, wrote of the campaign, "We are not engaged in a discussion of credit buying, but rather we want welfare recipients and other poor people to have the right to make that decision for themselves."[74] He argued that having credit lines with mainstream retailers would allow poor people to decide how and where to spend their money and allow them to stop relying on exploitative merchants. One *Newsweek* article reporting on an NWRO protest explained that the NWRO's case rested "on the claim that welfare dollars are as good as any other kind."[75] The organization argued that how a woman received her income should not change how or where she could use it. Ultimately, middle-class feminists would make a very similar argument when they argued lenders should take into account alimony and child support payments when extending credit.

Of course, it was undeniable that women on welfare did not have large incomes. The national average monthly AFDC payment per recipient was $43.85 in June of 1969 (roughly $282 in today's dollars).[76] Sears plausibly argued that fair individual evaluations of applicants' ability to repay loans naturally ended up with few low-income individuals receiving credit.[77] The NWRO attempted to counter these concerns by framing its demands in terms of its members' status as mothers. For example, in 1969, Horn explained that the NWRO had encouraged its members "to apply for credit [at Sears] to buy Easter clothing for their children."[78] NWRO members also brought their children to accompany them at protests. In Chicago, twenty mothers and their children interrupted a Sears fashion show to show off "some 'welfare fashions' of 5–10 years vintage."[79] The NWRO's campaign suggested that its members' children made them more creditworthy. Children served as a sign that NWRO members could be, and deserved to be, trusted. In claiming credit for its members on the basis of their motherhood the NWRO drew on long-standing policy paradigms that awarded special financial assistance, such as AFDC, to mothers.[80] Just as motherhood made poor women eligible to receive welfare funds, the NWRO claimed it should also make them eligible for other critical economic resources.[81]

By the 1970s, the notion that mothers should receive financial support was under attack.[82] The NWRO's case for credit rested on a policy paradigm that had begun to shift as middle-class women entered the workforce. As more and more women defended their right to combine work and motherhood, policymakers questioned why taxpayers should support poor women who chose to stay home and care for their children.[83] Intentionally and unintentionally, middle-class feminist activists contributed to changing attitudes toward welfare. Their push for credit, which began in the years immediately following the NWRO's campaign, often mirrored welfare rights activists' work, but at times their message and tactics seemed to argue directly against the NWRO's claims. For example, as women fighting to get their existing economic resources recognized, middle-class feminist activists demanded that their potential to become mothers not affect how banks evaluated their credit worthiness. Fundamentally, feminist organizations hoped to use their members' power as consumers to win women credit, while the NWRO fought for its members' right to be consumers.

NOW's earliest campaigns for credit reveal the assumptions the organization made about its members' resources. Early on, the organization urged members to conduct surveys of local lenders' practices in regards to women and file complaints with retailers' associations and management where they found evidence of discrimination. Where complaints failed, NOW suggested women organize boycotts and pickets of offending stores. NOW also organized women to use their own credit applications as opportunities to change policy. One early suggestion from NOW's Credit Task Force was for women to apply for credit cards, loans, and mortgages at banks "where you or someone over whom you have influence has money deposited in a savings or checking account." If the bank refused to lend to a woman, NOW urged that she and her friends withdraw any money they had saved there and announce they were going to deposit it at a rival bank.[84] NOW expected its members to have savings accounts large enough to affect their banks if they withdrew their money—a far cry from the situation the members of the NWRO found themselves in.

Local chapters of both NOW and WEAL came up with their own projects that also relied on their members' resources. The D.C. and Maryland WEAL chapters proposed declaring November 1972 "Women's Credit Month" in the area. "During this month," they explained, "we would urge all our sisters with incomes of their own to apply for credit in their own names wherever they want or need it. We want to make it clear to credit managers that they should expect to deal with the individual women as applicants and that their staffs ought to get used to processing applications for us properly."[85] Through this kind of statement, feminists framed credit as proof of women's independent earning capacity rather than as a tool to help women become economically independent. Likewise, in Dallas, a WEAL chapter orchestrated an action where women earning between $8,000 and $10,000 (roughly $45,000 to $56,000 in today's dollars) applied to various local lenders for credit in their own names. The Dallas chapter then tracked the response and found that while 70 to 75 percent of lenders initially refused to extend credit to these women, 60 percent of those who refused at first eventually extended credit to the applicant when the woman pressed to talk to the store manager. Data in hand, the Dallas group convinced these institutions to agree to training sessions for credit personnel. During its negotiations, Dallas WEAL also convinced many lenders to change their policies and grant homemakers credit accounts in their own names based on their husbands' incomes and to allow divorced women to maintain the good credit ratings they had established during marriage.[86] Many of the WEAL "sisters with incomes of their own" did not have to have their own paycheck, just access to family money.

Even as they negotiated with lenders, feminist organizations also began to engage another strategy for improving women's access to credit that rested on their access to significant funds: creating their own credit unions and banks. This work was often led by the women's liberationists who objected to feminist strategies that relied on convincing male lenders to change their policies. Instead, they preferred finding ways for women to provide credit to other women. They hoped that all-female credit transactions would demonstrate what a fair transaction would look like—a strategy not unlike the NWRO's attempts to set up a model of their vision for a fair credit transaction. One group of such women explained they wanted to be able to borrow "where we are not discriminated against because of our marital status or the credit rating of our husband or father. We can be honest about why we want a loan; whether it be for a divorce, an abortion, a vacation, or a means to become a self-directing person."[87] They believed the best way to be judged as individuals and not as dependents was by borrowing from other women. And they argued that these all-female credit interactions could eventually "change attitudes by proving that women are good credit risks in retail loans and, when our assets increase sufficiently, in commercial loans."[88]

Women interested in this approach considered founding both women-run banks and feminist credit unions. The first women's bank began in New York in 1973. It took two years to get off the ground, slowed in part by a recession. In those two years, women in seven other cities—from San Diego to Greenwich, Connecticut, to Washington, D.C.—also began the work of founding women's banks. These banks had a twofold purpose. First, they hoped to create opportunities for women bankers to advance to executive positions, something women in banking felt they had been unable to do at most male-run banks. Second, the banks planned to place a special emphasis on counseling women about "how to establish credit and qualify for loans." A representative from the organization planning a women's bank in San

Francisco said it would make a specialty of counseling young, divorced, and widowed people—women and men.[89]

Across the country, feminists had even greater success organizing credit unions than banks.[90] Women's liberationists found the credit union model attractive because of the ways in which its self-help and collective action roots resembled many of their other successful endeavors—for example, women's health clinics. The first feminist credit union in the country grew out of Detroit's Feminist Women's Health Center. Inspired by the Health Center's need for financing to move into a more stable space, the women who founded the Detroit Feminist Credit Union quickly came to understand that the credit union model had the potential to allow women to support each other by extending loans to women for projects that male lenders remained reluctant to support.[91] As the founders explained in an open letter in 1973, "We need a credit union in order to support each other in our attempts to free ourselves to lead more independent, healthier lives. We formed consciousness-raising groups to support each other emotionally . . . we formed self-help clinics to help us understand and have control over our bodies. Forming a feminist credit union is a continuation of this process of mutual support."[92]

When the first feminist credit union formed, 83 percent of credit unions had employment-based membership fields.[93] As with most employment-based benefits, credit union membership was generally attached to jobs dominated by men. The founders of the Detroit feminist credit union pointed out, "Many of us either don't work outside the home, only work part time, or don't work in places or in occupations in which membership in a credit union is one of the benefits."[94] In place of employment or marital status, feminist credit unions used membership in a feminist organization as their field of membership. The Detroit union welcomed women who were members of the Women's Liberation Coalition of Michigan and local NOW chapters.[95]

Like the NWRO, the feminist organizations that made up each feminist credit union's base membership saw the unions as having the potential to increase their own membership.[96] NOW thus promoted the creation and joining of feminist credit unions, seeing them as having the dual benefit of creating an incentive for women to join NOW while enabling women to get credit and helping demonstrate women's credit worthiness. A year and a half after the Detroit credit union incorporated, eight feminist credit unions operated across the country, based in cities from Cambridge to Dallas to Los Angeles.[97] The eight joined together to create the Feminist Economic Network, which began with 5,200 members and $1.2 million in assets.[98]

The organizationally based access to credit that both feminist and welfare rights organizations created in the late 1960s and early 1970s did more than just demonstrate that women could be trusted with loans. They also demonstrated what a fair lending operation would look like. Unfortunately, both the NWRO's work and feminist's work recreated the biases and blind spots of the women in each organization, limiting the analysis of the problem addressed through the new models. Even as both sets of women demanded that lenders recognize the incomes they received—whether from employers, husbands, or the government—they failed to work together. Instead, each organization developed alternative means of credit access tailored to their specific constituencies and the kinds of income on which they drew. The flaws in these models were carried over into efforts to legislate the models of credit feminists and welfare rights activists had created on their own.

"Marginal Consumer Protections": Legislating Credit Rights

Even as feminist and welfare rights activists pursued self-help strategies and direct negotiation with lenders to improve their access to credit, both the NWRO and explicitly feminist organizations also pushed for legislative reform. By 1974, fourteen states had passed equal credit laws and numerous proposals for national legislation had come before the House and the Senate.[99] The debate surrounding these national proposals quickly took on racial and class dimensions that, at times, were even more explicit than those which underlay grassroots efforts. Liberal feminists realized early on that to provide truly equal access, equal credit legislation needed to move beyond formal equality to include proactive rules about what counted as income and how credit histories were established. Such rules required policymakers to make choices about which women should be protected in the proposed legislation. As they made these choices, policymakers and feminists repeatedly chose to explicitly protect married and formerly married upper- and middle class women's access to credit while doing little to help low-income women.

Legislative advocacy around credit access almost always came up against the question of whether or not credit should be considered a right. During its hearings, members of the NCCF grilled witnesses on whether or not there should be a protected right to credit, as did senators at a 1970 hearing of the Committee on Banking Currency regarding improving poor people's access to consumer credit. In the end, both welfare rights and feminist activists came to strikingly similar conclusions. Both groups agreed that there was no right to credit—a typical NOW position statement on read, "Neither men nor women have an absolute right to credit"—but that there was a right to a certain kind of credit interaction.[100] Wiley, of NWRO, argued, "In an economy where such a large segment of our economy is dependent upon credit . . . the consumer must be recognized as having a right with respect to the credit transactions, and the government must intervene to enforce the rights of consumers."[101] Ultimately the NCCF reached essentially the same conclusion: "Credit was a privilege, not a right. But the corollary to that was that access to the credit market was a right."[102]

For women credit activists concerned with divorced women's or single mothers' ability to get credit, creating equal access to the existing credit market could only be the beginning of a solution. Because of women's work patterns and average incomes, an equal credit evaluation would not result in equal credit for women. In order to accomplish that, the market also had to be regulated so that women earned individual credit histories through their unpaid work in the home and so that common forms of income women received counted toward a credit determination.

In the wake of the NCCF hearings, members of the Senate Committee on Banking, Housing, and Urban Affairs who had sat on the NCCF introduced four pieces of legislation addressing the many unfair lending practices uncovered by the commission. The two-year debate that followed made it clear that while the idea of banning direct instances of sex discrimination in credit evaluations was fairly uncontroversial, laws introducing proactive steps to correct for gendered labor patterns and protect low-income consumers were not.

As the Senate committee worked to combine the four bills, debate centered on how far new laws would go to regulate the industry. Some senators worked to limit the legislation's effects on lenders, while others sought to use the legislation to aid low-income consumers. The proposed bills included two pieces of legislation addressing abusive lending practices—for example, tight billing periods—one offered by Senator Proxmire (D-WI) and another offered by Senator Bill Brock (R-TN) along with Committee Chair Senator John Sparkman (D-AL).[103] Proxmire, who had a long-standing interest in aiding low-income consumers, supported legislation that did more for these consumers than Brock and Sparkman, who took a more sympathetic stance toward lenders.[104] For instance, Proxmire's bill included a ban on minimum service fees unless lenders applied such fees to all customers. Proxmire argued that, although lenders claimed that such minimum charges existed to cover the cost of bookkeeping, they rarely applied them to all accounts. Instead, lenders disproportionately applied these charges to low-income borrowers' accounts. Proxmire wrote in disgust, "It costs just as much to mail out a monthly statement to a rich customer living in the suburbs as to a welfare mother living in a ghetto."[105]

Along with these consumer protection bills, Senator Brock and Senator Harrison Williams (D-NJ) both introduced legislation addressing the issue of sex discrimination in credit. The Brock bill banned discrimination on the basis of sex and marital status in the establishment of credit and the purchase of a home.[106] Williams's legislation extended this prohibition to cover business and commercial loans as well as personal loans.[107]

When combining these four bills into one piece of legislation to report to the full Senate, the committee created a bill with weaker consumer protections than those suggested by Proxmire. The final bill did not include bans on minimum service fees and included the lowest suggested cap on class-action settlements. Proxmire found these choices infuriating. The consumer protections in the final ECOA targeted those unfair lending practices that affected the middle-class and wealthy but not the practices that disproportionately affected the poor. Or, as Proxmire put it, with the exception of the bans on sex and marital-status discrimination, the bill offered only "marginal consumer protection."[108]

In the House even more members of Congress came forward with bills to ban sex discrimination in credit. Abzug introduced three bills addressing sex discrimination in credit on the same day she testified at the NCCF hearings. The first Abzug bill banned discrimination on the basis of sex and marital status by all federally insured lending and saving institutions; the second outlawed such discrimination in all mortgage transactions, and the third amended the Truth in Lending Act to ban all discrimination in consumer credit transactions. In the next two years, Margaret Heckler (R-MA), Ed Koch (D-NY), and Matthew Rinaldo (R-NJ) all offered similar legislation addressing sex discrimination in credit.[109] The Heckler bill was the bill in the House most similar to the Brock bill, but both Rinaldo's and Koch's bills had the same limited class-action provisions as the Brock. In contrast, the Abzug bill provided for more generous settlements in class-action suits.[110]

Leonor K. Sullivan (D-MO), the chair of the Consumer Affairs Subcommittee of the House Banking, Currency, and Housing Committee, initially stalled on moving any of the proposed legislation forward. Sullivan had been the principal sponsor of the 1968 Consumer Credit Protection Act, which created the NCCF, but she disliked bills directed exclusively at sex discrimination—she was the only woman member of Congress to vote against the ERA.[111] Under "extreme pressure" from members of her subcommittee, she eventually introduced her own bill addressing not only sex discrimination but also discrimination on the basis of race, national origin, and religion.[112]

Unlike many pieces of economic equity legislation for women—after it cleared Sullivan's subcommittee—the ECOA passed relatively quickly.[113] But it did not sail through Congress without debate. Many lenders supported an equal credit act in principle, seeing women as an untapped market into which they could expand, but they nonetheless lobbied to make sure that the legislation that passed had few requirements beyond a ban on sex discrimination. In particular, lenders tried to keep a ban on discrimination on the basis of marital status out of the bill. Lenders defended their use of marital status in credit determinations by pointing to state laws that regulated how they could treat married couples. In community-property states, they argued, spouses' legal responsibilities for each other's debts made a ban on discrimination on the basis of marital status impossible. For example, one lawyer from Texas wrote that the proposed ban "would place the lending institutions of Texas in a very hazardous position."[114] Lenders in non-community-property states also worried about how a ban on discrimination on the basis of marital status might conflict with their laws. A banker in Mississippi wrote about a law that specifically allowed wives to prevent their husbands from mortgaging their house: "The mere fact that he is married affects his ability to pledge his homestead as security."[115]

Women fought hard to keep the marital-status provisions in the bill, aware that many of the instances of discrimination that women experienced resulted directly from their marital status, not their sex. In her testimony before the NCCF, Sonia Pressman Fuentes—a co-founder of NOW—told the commission about her own reaction to lenders' refusal to extend her credit in her own name after she married: "While I was not financially injured by initial refusal of these credit services to furnish a proper card to me, I was hurt psychologically. These services told me that my financial responsibility, in fact my very existence was a nullity—all because I had gotten married." Fuentes went on to say that she still carried the credit cards she received "made out in the name of 'Roberto Fuentes.' When I use them, they remind me of my non-existence in the eyes of the issuing concern."[116] By the time Fuentes gave her testimony, members of Congress and lenders had been inundated with letters making similar claims that the experience of being denied credit left women feeling nonexistent and invisible. For example, in 1974, one newly married woman wrote to a lender who had denied her credit in her own name and erased her old credit rating, "Does the fact that I am married mean I cease to exist as a person and sweep this credit rating down the drain?"[117]

The description of denial of credit as denial of existence is a striking statement about the moment when many married women discovered the vestiges of coverture. In response to a letter from a constituent about Gulf Oil's treatment of a woman's application for credit, Representative Bella Abzug (D-NY) sent a quote from Supreme Court Justice William Douglas about coverture, or as she wrote, the "old common-law fiction that 'the husband and wife are one.'" She told the woman that Justice Douglas had said of coverture, "In reality this rule has worked out that though the husband and wife are one, the one is the husband." Abzug continued, "Gulf Oil has obviously employed this premise in their treatment of your credit application."[118] Abzug explicitly saw coverture guiding lenders' behavior, but even women who could not name the legal doctrine guiding lenders understood that their economic personhood was being denied.

Women accompanied their complaints about invisibility with a more specific set of grievances. They argued that in denying women credit, lenders refused to recognize married women as responsible adults who managed money as part of the daily work of being wives and mothers. One woman wrote to a national credit manager, "Your local credit manager told me that 'occupation: housewife does not count' as a real occupation because there is no regular income. . . . You must be aware that most of your customers are housewives."[119] Another woman wrote to a J. C. Penney credit manager after receiving a credit card in her husband's name: "My job is mother, wife, cleaner, tailor, gardener, business manager, dietician, student, chauffer, nurse, laundress etc. for our family of four. My position is one of enormous responsibility calling for the use of a great scope of resources and talents. To keep current in all my fields requires much reading and experimentation. Turnover in my field is lower than in most professions. Why then was my credit issued to my employer?"[120] By demanding recognition for their work in the home, women began to articulate what equal credit legislation should do.

In essence, feminists argued that effective equal credit legislation not only had to ban discrimination on the basis of marital status but also go one step further and recognize women's work in the home by providing them with credit histories on the basis of their management of joint credit accounts.

Abzug took a particularly strong stand in defense of homemakers' fiscal responsibility. When a male constituent wrote to her defending lenders' refusal to give credit to women on the basis of their tendency toward spontaneous spending, Abzug retorted, "Since these women are managing households and since credit generally facilitates that management, it is only right that women have the same access as do men."[121] But the person who stated this policy most explicitly was Betty Howard, a representative from the Minnesota Department of Human Rights, who testified at the NCCF hearings. "There are many of us who believe that [a wife] should be given credit for the credit rating that she earned with her husband," she said. "This of course goes along with many feminists' point of view that housewives should be paid salaries which would take care of all of this."[122] Howard's statement got to the heart of the matter. While many feminists hoped to win wages for women's housework, they also knew this to be unlikely. They could, however, give housework economic recognition by awarding homemakers economic resources like credit, health care, and Social Security for their work.

The economic recognition of housework was of particular importance to divorced women since this was often the only way they could establish credit on their own after their marriages. Divorced women expressed outrage when they learned they did not have the same credit ratings as their ex-husband, arguing that such ratings were as much a result of their hard work as their husband's. One woman even enlisted her ex to write to Sears on her behalf. After Sears denied his ex-wife an account "on the grounds that, as a recently divorced woman who had not worked for pay for several years she was a poor credit risk," James Stegenga wrote to Sears's national executives: "In this particular case you may be interested in knowing that: (1) My ex-wife is a very responsible person who managed our financial affairs during our 11-year marriage very well; & (2) she will be receiving from me a guaranteed, reliable, court ordered income of nearly $600 for the next three years and $400 monthly for twelve years thereafter (in addition, of course, to whatever she will earn on her own as a talented and experienced professional)."[123] Stegenga addressed two of divorced women's most common complaints in his letter: lenders' erasure of the credit history they had with their husbands and lenders' refusal to count alimony and child support payments as income.

In addition to these sorts of letters and testimony, supportive policymakers pointed to both the FDIC's and the Congressional Research Services' (CRS) defense of the ban on marital discrimination in credit. The CRS in particular worried that without the marital-status provision there would be endless litigation over the difference between discrimination on the basis of sex and marital status.[124] As women knew from experience, it was often hard to distinguish between the two kinds of discrimination, especially since discrimination on the basis of marital status disproportionately affected women, who invariably had to reapply for new credit accounts when their marital status changed.

NOW not only worked hard to keep the marital status ban in the bill, but also lobbied against a bill that addressed any form of discrimination other than sex and marital status. Although African American women had pointed out for years that distinguishing between race and sex discrimination was almost impossible, NOW seems to have been unconcerned with this overlap even as they worried about a similar difficulty distinguishing marriage and sex discrimination.[125] NOW opposed Sullivan's comprehensive ban on credit discrimination and favored the bill offered by Brock, accepting its lack of robust consumer protections as the price of winning a broad ban on sex and marital-status discrimination.[126]

NOW's drive to have a sex- and marital-discrimination-only bill seems to have come from a desire to have a legislative victory it could claim as its own and a belief—possibly misguided—that adding a racial discrimination ban would slow down credit legislation. Sharyn Campbell, the chair of NOW's Credit Task Force and notably also an attorney for BankAmericard, told members of the Task Force she was disappointed with the Sullivan bill because it provided "equal credit opportunity without regard to race, color, creed, national origin, age, sex or marital status." She continued, "While these legislative goals are noble, [Sullivan] has failed to support the NOW position of a women's bill prohibiting credit discrimination because of sex or marital status."[127] In a letter that looked back on the fight, Campbell further explained that "in the eyes of some observers" Sullivan had insisted on including the other prohibitions "to minimize the role of NOW in connection with this legislation."[128]

NOW's official insistence on a sex-discrimination-only bill led to a rift within the organization. In the build-up to passing the ECOA, NOW's vice president for legislation, Ann Scott, had contended that the "primary need for remedial legislation relates to equal credit opportunity regardless of sex or marital status" and promised NOW support for any legislation addressing only these issues.[129] Scott's statement was supported by the NCCF's own report, which argued it could not prove there was racial discrimination in credit because race and income overlapped so strongly. Neither Scott nor the

NCCF noted that marriage was the only reason sex and income discrimination did not overlap as strongly After all, it was still through marriage that the vast majority of women acquired the incomes that made them middle-class.[130]

The members of NOW's Minority Women's Task Force reacted strongly to Scott's acceptance of the NCCF's analysis. A representative of that task force wrote, "I shudder at the 'remedial' being restricted to women."[131] Another woman wrote, "The claims that there is no discrimination on the basis of race in areas of consumer credit are blatantly ridiculous. I find it hard to believe that any report based on even a cursory study of the subject would set forth such a claim. But if it did, I would put that report in the same category as the infamous Moynihan report and such other documents generated by the white-male establishment for the purpose of perpetuation of the inequities of the sexist/racist power structure."[132] These protestations made no difference. NOW supported the Brock bill and this was the bill that eventually became law.

Conflict in the House meant that the Brock bill became law through a parliamentary maneuver. While both houses of Congress passed a Consumer Credit Protection Act in 1974, only the Senate bill included a ban on discrimination on the basis of sex and marital status. The Conference Committee accepted the Senate provisions, but did make a few adjustments to these provisions so that it would look more like the bill that the House Subcommittee on Consumer Affairs had finally reported in early October. The Committee did not broaden the kinds of discrimination covered by the bill, but instead increased flexibility in regulatory authority and limited class-action suits.[133] The Conference Committee's addition of the Senate's sex-discrimination provisions to the omnibus banking bill already voted on by the full House meant that the ECOA never had to be voted on by the full House of Representatives.[134]

As passed, the ECOA simply amended the Truth in Lending Act to ban discrimination on the basis of sex or marital status in the administration of consumer credit, including mortgage credit.[135] It included significant limits on the size of class-action settlements and exceptions allowing for discrimination where state laws affected husbands' and wives' liabilities for each other.[136] The ECOA left it to the Federal Reserve Board to determine the actual regulations enforcing the ban on discrimination on the basis of sex and marital status and gave the board two years to do so. Therefore, even as feminists claimed victory with the passage of the ECOA, they found themselves fighting to get regulations with real teeth enacted by the Fed.

During the rule-making period, NOW continued to struggle internally over how robust the regulations in the ECOA should be, so much so that in 1975 the organization issued two sets of contradictory comments within two months in response to the Fed's proposed regulations. The first set of comments, offered in testimony by Susan Onaitis, the new coordinator of the Women and Credit Task Force, was quite conciliatory to lenders. Onaitis expressed "dismay" at a retroactive requirement that lenders attach both partners' names to all joint accounts in order to create a credit history for married women. This requirement was particularly important to homemakers in case of divorce because this is what would give them a credit history on which to draw when they needed to establish their own line of credit. Onaitis, however, said, "We know of no legislation that operates retroactively and NOW does not believe that it is necessary for this legislation to do so."[137]

After coming under fire from other feminist groups for this position, which would clearly hurt homemakers and divorced women, NOW retracted Onaitis's statement and issued new testimony.[138] NOW president Karen DeCrow told Onaitis that her original testimony had "endangered the economic welfare of millions of women who do not have their own incomes, but who desperately need to develop credit histories." Furthermore, Onaitis's testimony "meant NOW went on record opposing provisions of the regulations which would aid the woman who is not employed outside the home. The press and other commentators justifiably concluded that NOW stood for equal credit opportunity only for persons who work outside the home. This is contrary to NOW's position."[139] Onaitis resigned three months later.[140]

NOW's revised testimony focused especially on the problems of the women DeCrow believed Onaitis had short-changed: "a woman who has been an authorized user on her husband's credit card (but has never had credit in her own name) [and then] gets divorced or widowed."[141] To help these women, NOW strongly endorsed the Fed's proposal to remove "divorced" from the category of marital statuses creditors could ask about. Its testimony pointed out, "No rights inure to the creditor under State law if the obligor is divorced rather than single."[142] NOW's new testimony also specifically endorsed policies in the Fed's draft that would not only eliminate discrimination against divorced women but also proactively improve their credit eligibility. It strongly supported the provision of the regulation that gave the authorized user of an earning spouse's account an individual credit history, celebrating this proposed regulation as an acknowledgement of the value of the work that women did in the home. Although they lauded much in the Fed's proposed regulations, NOW also had critiques. It used its testimony to contend that the Fed should require lenders to consider income from part-time employment because many more women had permanent part-time work than men. Discounting this income effectively discriminated against women.[143]

The final ECOA regulations required lenders to give spouses with joint accounts separate credit histories upon request—ending coverture's long hold on the credit industry and providing one of the first formal acknowledgments by the federal government of women as their husbands' economic partners.[144] The regulations transformed the equal rights language of the ECOA into law that proactively sought to help middle-class homemakers but did little to help low-income women who could still be refused credit on the basis of how much they made and how they made it. Moreover, the rules did not limit lending practices—like selective charges—that simply made the poor pay more for loans. The 1974 ECOA was designed to help two sets of women: well-employed women and women who married, even if those marriages did not last. In particular, feminist groups hoped that it would make for a smoother transition between these two categories. If a homemaker divorced and was able to keep her credit record, as she moved back into the workforce she would have the ability to continue to draw on the good credit history she had earned through marriage. The ECOA explicitly did not help low-income or never-married women. In fact, the bill that NOW celebrated was one that had been stripped of consumer protections, like those proposed by Senator Proxmire, aimed at helping low-income consumers.

The ECOA created neither an absolute right to credit nor a right to fairly administered credit, but only a right to fair consideration of one's creditworthiness. As feminist activists knew, this was a meaningless right without specific proactive provisions and rules telling lenders what kinds of income to count and how to keep their records. In the end, the rules feminist fought for and won targeted aid to middle-class homemakers and women who were employed. It gave women credit for working in the home only if their husbands could support them, suggesting that the choice to be a homemaker was only valid under these circumstances. It offered nothing to stop credit discrimination against women who worked in the home supported by AFDC payments.

In 1976, Congress amended the ECOA to ban discrimination on the basis of race, national origin, or the receipt of public assistance.[145] This time NOW supported these provisions.[146] Of course, neither the original law nor the amendments ended credit discrimination. Throughout the 1970s and into the 1980s feminist activists continued to worry that too many women did not know about their credit rights, that the Fed had not written strong enough regulations, and that the Act was not adequately enforced.[147] Nevertheless, a new right—to a fair and equal consideration of creditworthiness regardless of sex, marital status, or type of income—had been created, opening the door for educational efforts on the matter.

Pyrrhic Victory

The 1974 Equal Credit Opportunity Act passed just as the tide began to turn against the feminist movement. The year before, in 1973, the Supreme Court decided *Roe v. Wade* and eight new states ratified the ERA, bringing the total number to thirty. In 1974, however, only one new state ratified the amendment, and antifeminist organizations began to successfully organize against feminist legislation.[148] The ECOA was one of feminists' last straightforward national legislative triumphs. As a result, many different feminist groups claimed the ECOA as their victory. A 1975 report written for the Ford Foundation claimed that "virtually every major women's organization" took part in efforts to end credit discrimination.[149] When Representative Yvonne Brathwaite Burke (D-CA) was asked, "What good has the women's movement been?" she answered by pointing to the Act.[150] Yet, despite these rightful celebrations, in the process of winning the ECOA, the feminist divorce reform movement began to publicly show the divisions and compromises that would plague it going forward.

More than any other legislation passed in the early 1970s, the ECOA advanced feminist divorce reformers' claims that marriage was a partnership. But it did so through the regulation of privately administered resources. As feminist divorce reformers strove to change married and divorced women's place in the public and private social welfare regime, they consistently found it easier to win laws—the ECOA was the first—mandating that private institutions treat married women as equals and partners than laws instilling this understanding of married women into the public social insurance system. Since low-income couples had worse access to privately administered economic resources and relied more heavily on the public insurance system, this outcome meant that while the marriages of the wealthy and middle-class were increasingly treated as economic partnerships, the marriages of low-income people were not.

As the ECOA went into effect, it also quickly became apparent that ending private entities' ability to discriminate on the basis of sex did not make them institutions that actively supported equality or economic security. In the same decade that Congress began to regulate how lenders selected recipients of credit, legislators began to deregulate how lenders managed those loans. States began to lift their usury laws and the Supreme Court ruled that the interest rates on loans could be set according to the home state of the lender rather than the borrower. Banks moved their bases of operations to unregulated states and interest rates rose.[151] Higher interest rates allowed banks to lend to less and less reliable customers while still making a profit. Women gained access to the credit market as that market became a more dangerous place.[152]

Despite these drawbacks, the ECOA was a critical victory for divorced women. Feminist activists understood the ECOA campaign to be about ending coverture's vestiges and creating a new understanding of marriage. Coming early in feminist divorce reformers' lobbying efforts, the ECOA suggested that women could win legislative acknowledgment for the idea that marriage was a contracted partnership where women's work in the home had value.[153] The credit history married women won for their work in the home was the clearest recognition of the economic value of their work that married homemakers ever received, bringing married women into a direct relationship with their lenders unmediated by their husbands.

CHAPTER 4

The Privileges of Marriage

Divorced Women and Selective Entitlements to Health Care

In 1974, Betty Berry began a speech to the NOW Marriage and Divorce Task Force by commemorating the task force members who had passed away. She said, "NOW women have suffered terribly because of divorce laws. Many of you knew our sisters, Millie Chatzinoff and Pat McQuillan who did so much for this Task Force and died of cancer without health insurance—on and off of Medicaid, etc. Other NOW divorced women are ill without adequate health care." She finished, "NOW must pledge itself to see that its dying sisters at least die in comfort."[1] Berry's speech reminded her audience that, because of the ways that America's social insurance system used marital status to distribute benefits, divorce could quite literally become a life or death issue for women. Her speech also served as a call to action. Refusing to sugarcoat NOW's record, Berry admitted that NOW–New York had been "outstandingly unsuccessful in changing matrimonial legislation here." She continued, "We must organize ourselves and other women to march right up this hill in Albany and say this is what we need, we're the experts on our own lives."[2]

By 1974, with the death of her friends urging her on, Berry argued that in addition to lobbying for legislation directly addressing inequities in marriage and divorce law, divorced women needed to fight for legislation that would grant them access to critical resources such as health insurance. Women lost health insurance in a divorce not because of the way marriage law had developed but because of the way the health insurance system had. Most married women received insurance through their husbands' employers as their husbands' dependents. Thus, when their marriages ended, so did their coverage.

Reestablishing it was, at best, difficult and expensive because of the rules governing what insurers could and could not exclude from coverage.

Tish Sommers, the founder of the Alliance for Displaced Homemakers, began working on divorced women's issues after encountering these problems following her own divorce. When her marriage ended, she lost the health insurance coverage she had had through her husband's employer. Because she had a prior history of breast cancer, she was denied all but the most expensive coverage when she applied for insurance as an individual. Many of these expensive insurance options still excluded any cancer treatment from Sommers's coverage because it was a "preexisting condition." At fifty-seven, Sommers was too young for Medicare; she decided to take a "gamble" and go without coverage until she turned sixty-five and qualified. Six months before she became Medicare-eligible, her cancer returned.[3]

Sommers and Berry's work on divorced women's access to health care occurred as activists across the political spectrum sought solutions to the bourgeoning crisis of rising health care costs in the 1970s. These activists faced a fragmented health insurance system that included both public programs like Medicare and Medicaid alongside employer-based insurance programs and the individual market. The system's complexity made a single solution to rising costs difficult and provided endless fodder for debate. Adding to the complexity of the challenge, many of the decade's identity-based rights movements had begun to demand improved access to health care and to experiment with novel forms of health care provision by and for the communities they represented.[4] In the 1970s, feminist divorce reformers attempted to use each of these broader reform movements to improve divorced women's access to care. As a result, feminist divorce reformers' health care demands took many different forms. Yet, almost all of their health care campaigns ended up making the argument that divorced women deserved special health care options as a result of their former marriages. At first glance, divorced women's claim to health care on the basis of their marriages looks analogous to their claim to credit. But a closer look shows that while their demand for a credit history rested on the idea that marriage was a contracted partnership, their campaigns for health care quickly turned into a demand for recognition of marriage as a special status that could not be lost through divorce.

Feminist divorce reformers' ultimate focus on special health care options for formerly married women was not inevitable. As they reasoned through their loss of benefits, women like Sommers often demanded universal health insurance and argued for decoupling marriage from determining eligibility for benefits altogether. Yet, as their demands became specific legislation, feminist divorce reformers repeatedly found themselves pushing for expansions to the welfare state that specifically targeted divorced women. Like many activists before and after them, feminist divorce reformers found themselves trapped by the selective entitlement system to which Americans had grown accustomed. Because it is often easiest to win extensions of social welfare benefits for select groups of people who convince legislators that they have a special moral status, this has become one of the dominant messages around which activists organize. Feminist divorce reformers were no exception. Struggling to win health care access in the 1970s, they increasingly gravitated toward the message that divorced women had experienced a disaster that made them especially deserving of aid. As a result, in the end, their work did not decouple eligibility determinations from marital status but instead entrenched both the marriage-based insurance system and the idea that marriage was a status, not a contract.

Sex and the American Health Care System

Over the course of the twentieth century, the American insurance system developed to offer health insurance to most people through private insurance companies. Until 1965, with the notable exception of veterans, Americans had access only to privately run health insurance.[5] Then, Congress created Medicare and Medicaid to offer government-sponsored insurance to the elderly and the poor respectively. By the time feminist divorce reformers began organizing in the 1970s, this public-private system, shot through with discrimination against women on the basis of sex and marital status, was firmly established.

The push for state-run health insurance began in the early twentieth century. Prior to that, because medical care was relatively inexpensive and ineffective, insurance made little sense and most Americans did not have it.[6] Progressive reformers, inspired by sickness insurance programs in Western Europe, put forward proposals for compulsory, state-run health insurance in the 1910s. Theodore Roosevelt called for compulsory national "sickness insurance" in his 1912 run for the presidency. In 1916 the American Association for Labor Legislation (AALL) campaigned for a state health insurance program modeled on Germany's, which provided both sick pay and coverage of medical bills for workers.[7] Both campaigns failed. Roosevelt's campaign divided the Republican Party, paving the way for Wilson's election, and employers, private insurers, and the American Federation of Labor successfully opposed the AALL campaign.[8] Health care costs began to rise significantly in the 1920s, as the quality of medical care improved and medical training was standardized.[9] Increasing demand for medical insurance followed and insurance companies began to experiment with using employment-based groups to spread medical risks.[10]

The employment-based medical insurance system gained a firmer hold during the Great Depression and World War II. The Depression both increased worker demand for life insurance to protect their families and encouraged employers to look to insurance as a way to guard against labor unrest and organization. While initially focused on life insurance, insurers began to offer package deals with health benefits and pensions bundled with life insurance.[11] The system of employment-based health insurance coverage grew during and after World War II. During the war, caving to pressure from labor unions, the National War Labor Board ruled that employer contributions to health insurance premiums fell outside of wartime wage controls. With competition for workers fierce, employers turned to offering health insurance as a way to win employees and their loyalty.[12]

In the years following the war, employers used insurance offerings to contain the growth of labor unions.[13] Union leaders experimented with offering their own health insurance plans in an attempt to break employers' use of insurance to control their workforce, but they had limited success. Then, in 1947, the Taft-Hartley Act further constrained labor's ability to create such plans.[14] In 1954, under the Eisenhower Administration, employer contributions to employees' health insurance plans gained favored tax status, further entrenching the employment-based health care system.[15]

Historian Jennifer Klein argues this employer-based insurance system created a new version of welfare capitalism. The system tied workers to their employers not only by offering them insurance benefits but also by offering such benefits to their family members.[16] Private insurers did not give workers who quit the opportunity to convert their employer-based plans to individual ones.[17] The system also tied women to their husbands. Just as workers could only maintain their insurance by staying at their jobs, women only maintained their insurance by staying married.

Even as this private health insurance system developed, efforts to replace it with a national insurance system continued. FDR considered health insurance to be the unfinished piece of the New Deal. As president, Truman tried to complete the job and failed.[18] After these failures, Kennedy proposed a more gradual approach. In his first State of the Union address, he announced his intention to create a health insurance program for the elderly to accompany Social Security.[19] Kennedy did not succeed at winning such legislation, but in 1965 Johnson did when Congress created Medicare and Medicaid. Government-sponsored health insurance for the elderly and the poor respectively, Medicare and Medicaid provided insurance to two of the groups who had the most difficulty in the private market. The administration of these programs was modeled on existing social welfare programs—Medicare on Social Security and Medicaid on AFDC.

Together with the existing employment-based health insurance system, the creation of Medicare and Medicaid meant that most Americans now had health insurance coverage. Political scientist Jacob Hacker has argued that this level of coverage made it incredibly difficult to mobilize popular support for a universal health insurance program. Insured Americans were wary of any proposal that would change the coverage they knew and with which they were comfortable, especially since the system hid its growing costs in tax increases and slow wage growth.[20] The message sent by the extension of health insurance coverage through selective entitlements also worked against reform movements. Not only did most Americans have health insurance through the fragmented system of employment, marriage, and status-based access, but also those who did have insurance believed they had earned it. Access to quality health insurance came to signal merit and privilege, and those with access grew determined to defend that privilege.

Nevertheless, the American health care system did leave space for discontent. A full 10 percent of Americans remained uninsured in the early 1970s, excluded from both the public and private insurance systems.[21] Even insured Americans who were generally comfortable with this complex system of health care delivery remained vulnerable. Loss of a job meant loss of insurance. This could be catastrophic not only because of the high cost of health care without insurance but also because acquiring a new plan after a break in coverage allowed insurers to exclude preexisting conditions from the new coverage. So, for example, if someone with a history of cancer lost her health insurance, she might find herself permanently unable to get a health insurance plan covering cancer in any form. In addition, women were increasingly aware of the many ways that both the public and private pieces of the American health insurance system discriminated against them. This sex discrimination affected how eligibility for coverage was determined, what coverage cost, and what kinds of procedures medical insurance would cover.

Private insurance offerings shortchanged women both as a direct result of insurance policies and as the indirect result of sex discrimination in the workforce. Most working women were concentrated in low-income, nonunion jobs and thus were less likely than working men to have health insurance offered through their jobs. If women did receive health insurance through their employers, or if they purchased insurance on the open market, it generally cost more and covered less than the insurance plans offered to men.[22] Private health insurance plans routinely excluded all pregnancy-related costs on the grounds that pregnancy was a voluntary condition, but, to the annoyance of feminist activists, the same plans covered vasectomies and sports injuries, which women contended were at least equally voluntary.[23] Despite these exclusions, health insurance plans, even those with identical coverage, cost more for women. A 1975 survey of seven Illinois insurance companies showed that on average women paid 68 percent more than men for health insurance.[24] Insurance companies defended this unequal pricing; they argued that, even excluding pregnancy, women under fifty-five received more medical care than men, and that the insurance premiums of men and women fifty-five and over were roughly the same.[25]

Women's groups disagreed with insurance companies' claims that older women fared better in the health insurance market than younger women. In 1985, when the Older Women's League (OWL) drafted a paper describing the problems women faced in getting insurance, they told the story of Dr. and Mrs. B. who were getting divorced in their fifties. Dr. B. would, of course, have continued access to his group health insurance plan through Blue Cross. Mrs. B., however, had to pay a new plan worth only "about 75 percent of the group policy in terms of benefits"; however, "Dr. B.'s premiums were to be approximately $300 per year, and Mrs. B's were to be $3,800."[26] Furthermore, private insurance companies structured their health insurance policies around the idea that dependence was women's appropriate role in the family. Companies denied even those women who had insurance through their employers the ability to add their spouses or dependent children to their plans as men could, suggesting that even if a woman could contribute to the family income, she could never become the main source of her family's support.[27]

Medicare's structure reinforced this notion. Just as young and middle-aged married women relied on their employed husbands for health insurance through their employers, elderly women were expected to rely on their husbands for health insurance through the government. Medicare, which was modeled on Social Security, provided health care benefits on the basis of employment.[28] The program assumed most elderly women would receive benefits as their husbands' dependents.[29] Meanwhile, single women were less likely to receive Medicare as a result of their employment records because they were less likely to have worked consistently in a covered job.[30] Elderly Americans not covered by Medicare as a result of their work histories could buy into the program, but the premiums were often prohibitively expensive, especially for elderly women.[31] Only about 2 percent of the non-entitled elderly enrolled in Medicare; women made up a disproportionate share of those still uncovered.[32]

Medicare's counterpart, Medicaid, was designed to provide health care to the indigent and served a disproportionate number of women. In part this was because the federal government required any state participating in Medicaid to offer it to AFDC recipients.[33] Medicaid did offer a significant protection to divorced women—40 percent of unemployed divorced women relied on Medicaid, compared to only 4.5 percent of unemployed married women. However, as with many programs relied on by single women, Medicaid was significantly less robust than the program available to married women, Medicare.[34] Moreover, qualifying for Medicaid, like qualifying for AFDC, required women to go through means testing, spend down any savings, and sell any property they might have.[35] Unlike Medicare, which was administered by the federal government, Medicaid was state-administered and therefore more variable. States could decide to opt out of Medicaid entirely and set different benefit levels and eligibility requirements, including rules against single women having men in their homes.[36] The program thus excluded many women who could not afford health insurance on their own. By 1984, estimates suggested that between two and four million American women between the ages of forty-five and sixty-five had no health insurance.[37]

The sex-discriminatory insurance system was a perfect storm for divorcing women. When they divorced, women almost always lost their health insurance because they lost their connection to an employed husband. If they were not yet eligible for Medicare, or if they never would be, they had to find a job offering insurance, try to purchase insurance on the open market, or turn to Medicaid and its stringent means testing. Divorce settlements consistently ordered fathers to maintain their children's health insurance but often remained silent on what should happen to an ex-wife's insurance.[38] Even where settlements ordered husbands to maintain insurance for their ex-wives, women could not remain on their ex-husbands' group insurance and had to find new coverage on the individual market. By 1985, divorced women were twice as likely as married women to be without health coverage.[39]

Feminist health care activists and divorced women seeking better access to health insurance coverage had to navigate this complex public and private insurance system. The fragmented system offered many options for where to target reform efforts, but also made comprehensive reform especially challenging. Feminist divorce reformers had to decide whether to prioritize pushing for a national health care system, eliminating sex-discriminatory pricing and practices, or designing new laws to get health insurance to divorced women.

Many of these options existed in tension with each other. For example, the recently created Medicare and Medicaid programs offered a precedent for the gradual development of a government-sponsored health insurance system through the creation of selective entitlements. Feminist divorce reformers could advocate for an expansion of these existing government health insurance programs to divorced women. This kind of expansion required arguing that divorced women formed a particularly deserving class—like the elderly—and accepting the limits of the public-private insurance system. Choosing this path thus seemed to run against the message embedded in efforts to win a new national health care system. Despite this tension, throughout the 1970s, feminist divorce reformers attempted to advocate for a wide variety of reforms. But as their claims that divorced women deserved new selective entitlements proved most effective, the idea became more and more widespread. Divorced women across the political spectrum demanded privileged access to health care, laying the groundwork for legislative reforms that entrenched marriage and wealth as determinants of access to care and moved health insurance further from becoming a national right.

Feminists Challenge the Private Insurance Market

Whether their ex-husbands or divorced women themselves covered the cost, purchasing an individual insurance plan on the open market was a challenge. Health care costs rose rapidly alongside the divorce rate: Between 1950 and 1975 national health care expenditures increased more than ninefold; between 1969 and 1975, alone, the national health care bill doubled. In the 1975 fiscal year, health expenditures represented 8.3 percent of the gross national product, a total of $118.5 billion.[40] Because many divorced women ended up trying to purchase individual insurance on the open market, addressing the high and rising cost of insurance became a critical first step for improving divorced women's health care access.

Many of the largest feminist organizations made ending sex-discriminatory health insurance pricing a priority in the 1970s. The feminist campaign to end insurance discrimination had much in common with the campaign for equal credit. Like that campaign, the insurance discrimination campaign began as a way to extend the formal equality agenda embodied in the Equal Rights Amendment to private, institutional actors. Also, like the campaign to end credit discrimination, the insurance campaign began with efforts to expose the unfair treatment of women by the insurance industry. In 1973, Representative Martha Griffiths chaired seven days of hearings on economic discrimination against women, during which the committee heard testimony about insurance discrimination from an ACLU representative and from Pennsylvania's insurance commissioner, Herbert Denenberg.[41] Both testified that sex discrimination pervaded all kinds of insurance offerings—not only health insurance, but also life, unemployment, and automobile insurance—and that insurance companies consistently offered women insurance policies that covered less and cost more money than the policies offered to men.[42]

In his testimony, Denenberg suggested a "Women's Insurance Bill of Rights" that declared rights to "equal access to all types of insurance," to "premiums that fairly reflect risks and not prejudice," and to "disability insurance which fairly measures the economic value of childcare and homemaking," among others.[43] As equal credit advocates had, feminist health insurance advocates quickly realized that insurance equity would require not just banning discrimination but also accounting for women's different life and work patterns. They embraced a united formal and functional equality agenda.

In the four years after the Griffiths hearings, eight bills were introduced in Congress prohibiting sex discrimination in insurance, but none went beyond a formal equality agenda. (Only one bill, offered by Congresswoman Bella Abzug, a close associate of NOW, also addressed marital status.) None of these bills addressed rate discrimination; they proposed to ban only discrimination in coverage and availability of insurance offerings.[44] More importantly, after a vigorous insurance industry campaign against the antidiscrimination laws, none of these bills passed.

As their efforts to legislate change dragged on, NOW began to explore offering its own nondiscriminatory insurance plans to members. A number of different insurance companies made insurance program proposals to

NOW, but the most thorough proposal came from a new feminist venture company founded by Elizabeth Forsling Harris, the first publisher of *Ms.*, and Anne Wexler, who went on to work for the Carter administration.[45] Harris and Wexler established a joint-venture with a Connecticut insurance company and began to work with an insurance brokerage agency, Smith-Sternau, to develop a feminist insurance plan to offer first to NOW members and then the members of other women's organizations.[46] Harris and Wexler, as well as Smith-Sternau, saw sex-equal insurance as a business opportunity. Profit was not, however, the only consideration. Their efforts stemmed from the same instincts that led feminists to found credit unions and banks in response to credit discrimination. Wexler and Harris explained, "Affirmative action can be achieved through pressure on business institutions as well as through political efforts."[47] They believed their insurance offering would pressure other insurance companies to meet their standards. They told the NOW board, "We see this as an opportunity to use the power and prestige of NOW as leverage to crack the privately owned, state-regulated insurance industry which still offers policies to women for higher premium cost and lower benefits than are available to men."[48]

Wexler and Harris worked with Smith-Sternau to explore offering many kinds of nondiscriminatory insurance plans. The original list included disability, life, accidental death, major medical, hospital, maternity-fertility, retirement, auto, dental, legal, and divorce insurance.[49] Developing the insurance offerings, however, proved more difficult than anyone expected. A year after beginning the project, a frustrated agent from Smith-Sternau wrote: "We optimistically estimated obtaining meaningful results in approximately 6 months. This estimate was based on what we thought was a sufficiently cynical appraisal of the degree of cooperation to be expected from the insurance industry and on what we thought was a fair knowledge of the prevailing mythology about women and insurance coverage. It is clear that we underestimated the difficulties involved."[50] Even seasoned insurance professionals were impressed by the depth and degree of sex discrimination ingrained in the industry. Smith-Sternau did develop some recommended policies for NOW. Wexler and Harris were particularly proud of a proposed plan that offered homemakers an "opportunity to buy insurance to cover the cost of necessary services in the event of illness or disability."[51] They wrote, "We believe that this recognition of homemaking as an insurable occupation would have status effects well beyond the limits of the insurance industry."[52]

All of the Smith-Sternau proposals used membership instead of marriage to qualify women for health insurance. Membership in NOW would make women eligible for group insurance, just as the feminist credit unions used membership to make women eligible for credit. The NOW board liked this piece of these insurance plans not only because it provided an alternative to the marriage- and employment-based eligibility determinations endemic to the social insurance system, but also because it offered a way to increase membership and revenues for the organization.[53] Despite the promise of these plans, NOW's board of directors could not agree on which insurance plan to offer in 1974 and postponed the decision in hopes of receiving more proposals.[54] Not until 1984 did NOW begin to offer its own health and life insurance plans; the organization never managed to offer divorce insurance.[55]

Meanwhile, feminists continued to pursue a legislative solution to insurance discrimination. They drew enough attention to the issue that Jimmy Carter made ending insurance discrimination part of his 1976 campaign for the presidency. He used the issue in ads and the committee advising him on women's issues, his Committee on 51.3%, which Ruth Bader Ginsburg sat on, called for a Permanent Task Force on the Status of Women in the Insurance Industry to investigate sex-discriminatory rate setting and underwriting practices by the insurance industry.[56]

The specific recommendations of the Committee on 51.3% did not become a reality during Carter's presidency, but there was a good deal of activity around insurance discrimination throughout his time in office. In 1979, Congressman John Dingell introduced H.R. 100, the Nondiscrimination in Insurance Act, which proposed to ban sex discrimination in individually purchased insurance plans. Explicitly modeled on Title VII of the 1964 Civil Rights Act and the Equal Credit Opportunity Act, the bill prohibited discrimination by insurance companies on the basis of race, religion, national origin, and sex (but not marital status).[57]

Although, five years earlier, the ECOA had passed with relatively little opposition from credit companies, the Nondiscrimination in Insurance Act faced intense opposition. H.R. 100 was reintroduced and debated every year between 1979 and 1984. Each year, insurance companies argued that the bill would hurt women as well as men. In 1981, Aetna ran a large ad in major newspapers titled "Our Case for Sex Discrimination."[58] It claimed H.R. 100 would drive up the cost of auto insurance for women and life insurance for men because women were safer drivers and lived longer.[59] In 1983, the Health Insurance Association of America and American Council of Life Insurance ran an ad in the *New York Times* with the headline, "A Bill Is Moving Through Congress That Will Force Single Men to Buy Maternity Benefits for Themselves in Their Health Insurance." The ad encouraged anyone who found this absurd to contact their Senators and Representatives and ask them to oppose nondiscrimination insurance legislation.[60] Another ad against the bill ran in the *Washington Post* with the creatively sexist headline, "Sex and Insurance: Is Congress Being Seduced?"[61]

Feminists attributed their difficulties passing H.R. 100 to increasing antifeminist activism. By the late 1970s, antifeminists had become a well-organized force in American politics, preventing further progress on the ERA and other components of the feminist agenda. NOW argued that insurance discrimination legislation was not merely collateral damage in this larger fight about feminism, but integral to the building of a strong antifeminist movement. As early as 1974, NOW was selling copies of a report attempting to document the connections between the insurance industry and Phyllis Schlafly's STOP ERA.[62] The report, which also linked the insurance industry to the John Birch Society and Nixon's vice president Spiro Agnew, showed the many ways in which Schlafly relied on funding from the insurance industry. For example, Schlafly's 1970 congressional campaign received the second largest contribution to a House candidate in that year from the founder and head of the Combined Insurance Company of America.[63] NOW believed insurance companies so feared a law against sex-discriminatory policies that they were bankrolling antifeminist organizations and politicians.

Ronald Reagan's decisive win in 1980, with the strong support of antifeminists, strengthened the insurers' hand, as did the death of the ERA in 1982. The new administration refused to support the nondiscrimination in insurance bill.[64] Without the president's support, insurance company lobbying easily defeated H.R. 100 in 1981. Over the following years, amendments systematically weakened H.R. 100. In 1983, an amendment passed that changed the law to allow employers and insurance companies to come into compliance with the bill by lowering men's benefits instead of improving women's.[65] This amendment began to draw support away from the bill because almost no one was willing to advocate reforms that could harm the quality of benefits they already had.[66] In 1984, Representative Billy Tauzin, a Louisiana Democrat, offered an amendment to remove sex discrimination from the categories of discrimination prohibited by the bill. The amendment passed and feminist groups withdrew their support.[67]

Divorced Women Reimagine the Health Care System

Feminist organizations' failure to legislate an end to sex discrimination in the individual insurance market and their failure to create feminist group health insurance plans of their own, meant that divorced women outside of employer-based group plans remained stuck in an extremely expensive individual insurance market that explicitly discriminated against them. Feminist divorce reformers thus found themselves looking to more comprehensive health care reform efforts. In 1976, for example, Tish Sommers told the California state legislature, "Many of our laws still presume that wives will be cared for indefinitely by their husbands, and if anything should happen, life insurance or other assets would take care of the problem. But inflation, and especially the rising costs of medical care have made this very chancy."[68] Sommers endorsed a national health insurance plan and, at the same time, began to explore the radical alternatives offered by the Women's Health Movement.[69]

Feminist divorce reformers were not the only activists concerned with the rapidly rising costs of health insurance. Indeed, in the face of extreme medical inflation, national health care reform was recognized as a pressing issue across the political spectrum in the 1970s. In 1971, Nixon announced that national health reform was the top priority for his administration.[70] That same year, there were twenty-two different pieces of health care legislation in front of Congress.[71] These plans ranged from offering tax credits to families to help them cover the rising cost of insurance to complete overhauls of the American insurance system. For example, Senator Edward Kennedy (D-MA) and Congresswoman Martha Griffiths (D-MI) proposed a bill entitling every American to insurance coverage on the basis of residency.[72]

The idea of a comprehensive national health insurance system drew the support of many women's groups throughout the 1970s (including the National Welfare Rights Organization).[73] At marches, at conferences, and in testimony, women called again and again for national health care legislation. For example, at an International Women's Day March, a coalition of women actively involved in NOW, the YWCA, labor unions, and other women's and community organizations issued a list of demands that included a call for Congress to "pass a comprehensive national health care program for all."[74] Yet, even as they supported efforts to create a national health care program, feminist activists insisted that any new policy specifically address women's health care needs. Feminist divorce reformers worked especially hard to prevent any new health insurance program from replicating the flawed structure of Social Security. Recognizing that the model for national social insurance programs—from Social Security to Medicare—left divorced women out, feminist divorce reformers only supported national health insurance plans that explicitly enumerated protections for divorced women.

As early as 1968, Betty Berry began writing sponsors of national health insurance plans to critique their use of Social Security as a model. She pointed out to Governor Rockefeller that his employment-based health care reform proposal left out divorced women.[75] In 1970 she wrote to Senator Jacob Javits (D-NY), saying that although she liked his national health insurance program, she was troubled that it was modeled on Social Security. "You will recall that in 1968 NOW adopted the policy that spouses should be insured individually for Social Security benefits thus providing maximum portability from marriage to job etc. and eliminating the problems that arise because of marital status," she wrote. "We feel the same reasoning holds true here."[76] At the same time, Berry used the flaws in national health insurance proposals to push NOW to take action on her proposal for Social Security for homemakers. In her "Preliminary NOW Marriage Insurance Plan," she wrote, "It is also important to note that Medicare and proposed government health insurance plans are based on the existing social security structure. Unless individual coverage is instituted, future plans and extension of social security benefits will just perpetuate existing inequities."[77]

Other women's groups picked up Berry's drumbeat of criticism as the decade progressed. The Carter Campaign's Committee on 51.3% warned, "Certain planning may be necessary in order that present inequities are not carried forward into National Health Insurance."[78] Committee members hoped their recommended Permanent Task Force on the Status of Women in the Insurance Industry would take responsibility for working with drafters of national health insurance legislation to make sure the plans were not sex-discriminatory.[79] The bipartisan National Women's Political Caucus (NWPC) also pushed hard to keep marital status out of the eligibility requirements for national health insurance. In 1977 its legislative chair, Marilyn deMara Clancy, argued, "The principles of universal, mandatory coverage and quality controls must be the basis for a decent national health insurance plan. To elaborate—NWPC believes that NHI must offer coverage to everyone without regard to employment, age or marital status."[80]

WEAL, too, lobbied to keep marital status out of any national health care plan's determination of eligibility. A guidebook on sex discrimination in insurance published by the organization in 1977 declared happily that "a national health insurance (NHI) program is no longer a mere possibility in this country" but continued with a warning: "Since 1973, at least 17 NHI proposals have been introduced in Congress, and even the most liberal and comprehensive fails to address all of women's health insurance needs."[81] WEAL thought the proposals failed both in how they dealt with delivery of care—the kinds of care covered and the kinds of providers supported—and how they determined eligibility for insurance. On the issue of eligibility the guidebook explained, "Upon review of past and current NHI proposals, it is instructive to distinguish between two principal eligibility definitions. The first is linked to family membership and employment status, and the second requires merely residency in the United States." WEAL critiqued the first option as leaving women vulnerable to loss of insurance if their marital status changed. Linking eligibility to family status and employment, they argued, "would only serve to reinforce women's economic dependence on men."[82] The guidebook suggested women push for the second eligibility option since it "leaves no room for sex discrimination."[83]

Feminist divorce reformers' visions for how a national health insurance plan should address women's needs were influenced not only by women's experience with existing social insurance programs but also by the Women's Health Movement, a grassroots movement that emerged in the 1970s as women began to discuss their frustration with their medical options. As they did, they discovered a shared sense that their generally male doctors were disrespectful, condescending, and often knew alarmingly little about women's bodies.[84] In response, these women advocated a health care system where care was provided to women by women who were trained to be sensitive to women's unique health care needs. They taught themselves to perform many basic procedures and opened women's health clinics that offered these services. These clinics became the base of the Women's Health Movement; by 1974 over twelve hundred women's groups were providing direct health services in the United States.[85] Even though these clinics never reached more than a small slice of American women, the medicine practiced in them offered a direct challenge to the male-dominated health care system by suggesting that laypeople could perform many of doctors' duties and at lower cost.[86]

By the middle of the 1970s, women throughout the feminist movement, including feminist divorce reformers, looked to women's health clinics as sterling examples of direct activism. The centers offered women immediate services while modeling practices intended to have long-term effects on national policies.[87] The model was not only adapted to meet women's financial needs through the creation of feminist credit unions, but also inspired Tish Sommers's NOW Task Force on Older Women to propose a "health oriented well-woman center for women from menopause to Medicare."[88] Sommers, like the younger members of the Women's Health Movement, felt that doctors were condescending and older women had come to depend too much on them.[89] She argued, "Nurse practitioners and paraprofessionals could give us more time and attention at less cost. . . . The self-help principle in relation to our bodies is especially important to women as they grow older."[90] Sommers also believed non-married, often newly single, women in this age group neglected their health because they lacked health insurance and were reluctant to apply for Medicaid because of the "stigma of welfare" and fear of risking "what small assets they may have."[91] She thought a well-woman's health center tailored to these women's needs might encourage them to get the care they needed in a space that preserved their dignity.

Sommers's task force envisioned centers staffed by nurse practitioners, who would perform basic physicals and make referrals, and medical social workers, who would help patients sort through their options. In addition, the task force suggested such centers offer a regular rotation of special examinations tailored to older women—osteoporosis and glaucoma checks, for example—as well as immunizations. To complement these services, like women's health centers aimed at younger women, the center would hold discussion groups on health and aging. Finally, the task force proposed that the center conduct research on menopause and train older women to work as paraprofessionals in the center as a means of expanding their work opportunities.[92]

When Sommers and her partners began advocating for displaced homemakers legislation on the state and federal levels, their proposals included health clinics for older women. The initial legislation for a pilot Displaced Homemaker Center in California mandated running a well-woman health clinic out of the center. The clinic was to be "based on the principles of preventative care and self-help."[93] It would be "designed to serve the needs of older women, particularly displaced homemakers, who have no health insurance, or receive inadequate health care."[94] Services were to be offered on a sliding scale based on income and include routine, preventative examinations, referrals to doctors, and discussion and activity groups about older women's health.[95] This method of addressing divorced and older women's health care needs through government-supported women's health clinics also appeared in early versions of the national displaced homemakers bills.[96]

Despite the appeal of women's health centers, by the end of its first year the pilot Displaced Homemakers Center in Oakland decided that running a health clinic in addition to its job placement and training services was overly ambitious. It scaled down its health services to offer "in-kind support and referrals to health resources in the community."[97] Because federal displaced homemakers legislation ultimately passed as amendments to employment legislation, directing targeted federal funding for employment and training opportunities toward displaced homemakers, women's health centers also did not appear in federal displaced homemakers legislation.[98]

If winning legislative support for women's health centers for displaced homemakers proved a challenge, keeping marriage out of the benefit distribution structure of national health insurance legislation proved impossible. Although in 1977 WEAL believed national health insurance to be around the corner, throughout his time in office Carter hesitated to introduce comprehensive health care reform legislation. Indeed, frustration with Carter's refusal to act on the issue was part of the reason Ted Kennedy decided to challenge him in the 1980 Democratic primary.[99] Pushed by Kennedy, Carter finally introduced a plan in 1979 that was employment-based, requiring all employers to provide a minimum package of benefits including coverage for all members of an employee's family without alternative coverage.[100] Carter's plan thus proposed to deepen the insurance system's use of both marriage and employment to determine benefit eligibility. The plan did propose to create a safety net for the unemployed and uninsured through the creation of a government health care cooperative from which the uninsured could purchase insurance, something the administration specifically argued would help displaced homemakers.[101]

Feminist divorce reformers' efforts to reimagine the national health insurance system from the ground up—whether through a comprehensive, universal plan or through grassroots clinics—met with limited success. Yet key ideas embedded in these comprehensive reform efforts continued to influence policy for decades to come. In the 1970s feminist divorce reformers, skeptical of any new social insurance program modeled on those that already existed, attempted to direct the momentum behind health insurance reform toward the removal of all marriage-based eligibility determinations from the American social insurance system. But as hope for national health insurance reform, much less national health insurance reform that did not reify the breadwinner-homemaker family structure, began to fizzle, it was the more limited theory embedded in the work of feminist divorce reformers' use of the Women's Health Movement that began to shape their public campaigns. The proposal for federally funded women's health clinics for displaced homemakers rested on the belief that the government had a special responsibility toward divorced and widowed women. Feminist divorce reformers who focused on creating women's health clinics to serve divorced women suggested that these women's former marriages should make them eligible for special health care. While displaced homemakers' health clinics did not last long, this idea did.

Short-Term Solutions to Divorced Women's Health Care Crisis

Although feminist divorce reformers sought to adapt proposed systemic reforms to the American health insurance system to their own needs, they also had a range of suggestions for legislation that could work within the existing system to get divorced women health care. These proposals targeted two different problems divorced women faced after losing insurance: first, the high cost of individual health insurance plans and, second, the exposure to new medical underwriting exams that led women to lose coverage for preexisting conditions when switching plans. Proposed solutions to these problems included requiring women's ex-husbands to continue to pay for their care, expanding Medicare to cover divorced women, and new public policies allowing divorced women to convert their group insurance plans into individual ones. All of these proposals built on the idea that divorced women deserved special treatment by the government.

One of the NOW Marriage, Divorce, and Family Relations Task Force's earliest proposals to address divorced women's loss of insurance was for the government to issue health insurance directly to dependent spouses upon divorce. Despite their weaknesses, Medicare and Medicaid provided a model for incrementally expanding access to health care benefits that many liberal interest groups considered the most viable option for expanding the welfare state in the 1970s.[102] Thus, in 1972 and 1973, the NOW Task Force on Marriage and Divorce argued that divorced women should be the next group of deserving and frequently uninsured Americans to whom the government extended state-sponsored health insurance.[103] In this proposal, as in Betty Berry's proposal for divorce insurance, we again see the reluctance of middle-class, or formerly middle-class, NOW members to use existing antipoverty programs. Although Medicaid already existed to help poor Americans—especially single women—get health insurance, divorced women did not want to draw on this existing means-tested, stigmatized social welfare program any more than they had wanted to draw on AFDC. Instead, as they had when demanding funding for older women's health clinics, feminist divorce reformers insisted divorced women had earned a privileged place in the welfare state through their marriages. Divorced women, they argued, deserved to be treated like seniors or disabled people rather than like poor single women, which, of course, is exactly what many of them were.

If the government would not expand Medicare to divorced women, Berry argued it could at least pass a law to require divorced breadwinners to provide dependent ex-spouses with insurance "until such time as they are assumed by an employer or new husband."[104] In 1968, when Governor Nelson Rockefeller included a compulsory health insurance program in his presidential campaign platform, Berry wrote to him suggesting that his proposal include a provision to keep dependent spouses on their ex-spouses' health insurance policies.[105] There was judicial precedent for this suggestion. Divorce settlements occasionally ordered husbands to maintain health insurance coverage for their ex-wives; to do this, however, husbands generally had to purchase a new, individual insurance plan for their ex-wives who were no longer considered their dependents.[106] Berry was suggesting a law allowing ex-wives to remain on their ex-husbands' policies.

Allowing women to stay on their ex-husbands' group insurance policies would have created cheaper insurance options for women, but it also would have made divorced women's continued dependency on their ex-husbands official public policy. The majority of Berry's policy proposals sought to find ways to support women without maintaining their connection to their ex-husbands; that she chose to support such a plan reveals the desperation many divorced women felt when they tried to find health care.

The New York State legislature considered a provision to make ex-husbands responsible for their ex-wives' health insurance as a part of a comprehensive divorce reform bill in 1977. Berry expressed skepticism of this plan, however, because the bill did not actually mandate that divorced women be allowed to stay in their ex-husbands' employers' plans. She told the legislative committee, "We should all be aware of what is available to the individual policy holder."[107] She explained that the insurance options husbands could purchase for wives in the individual insurance market were inadequate and expensive. If such plans became part of an alimony award they would be difficult, often impossible, for both exes to afford. Not only would they be an enormous tax on ex-husbands' income, but also they would be fully taxable on the part of the receiving spouse.[108] The bill never made it out of committee.[109]

Berry's concerns with the New York bill were born out by men's experience. Ex-husbands faced with the responsibility of purchasing insurance for their wives quickly came to understand the need for insurance reform. One insurance professional related the story of a Maryland insurance agent who got divorced in 1973. At the time of his divorce, his company insurance plan covered his wife and children, but the wife was removed from the plan when the marriage ended. As part of the settlement, however, he had agreed to maintain her insurance. When he went to purchase individual coverage for her, the cost shot up to three times what it had been when she was covered on his family plan. "The company had tripled the premium for the identical coverage."[110] He ultimately testified in support of a Maryland bill that would have given women the right to maintain group coverage even if their marital status changed.[111] It was this kind of continuation legislation that ultimately seemed to offer the most short-term promise to divorced women.

Beginning in 1970, Berry and other feminist divorce reformers across the country fought for state legislation to allow women to stay in their group plans after their marital status changed. These "continuation" laws allowed members of groups who lost eligibility to stay in the group for a set period of time and for a cost. Continuation legislation was often accompanied by "conversion" legislation, which mandated that individuals be offered individual policies when they lost group eligibility.[112] The conversion pieces of these proposals would save women from the exclusion of preexisting conditions to which breaks in health care coverage exposed them and the continuation pieces would provide them with group insurance options not available to other single women on the open market. Yet they would have to pay for this privilege. Under conversion and continuation laws, the cost of coverage fell on divorced women instead of on their ex-husbands or the government.[113]

Because of their high cost, conversion and continuation bills were of limited value to most divorced women and were originally framed as emergency legislation. Berry explained to one New York state senator she was lobbying that the conversion bill was an "emergency bill which must be enacted so that old and ill women being turned out can continue on their health insurance protection."[114] Berry was aware of the legislation's shortcomings—mainly, how expensive such policies would be for women. She noted that her own premium under a plan would be $213, while the premium for her coverage when she was married had only been $120. "However," she wrote, "compared to the thousands of dollars that hospitals cost today the disparity in cost is not as important as having the option."[115]

NOW made conversion and continuation legislation one of its demands—along with better-known agenda items like the ERA—at its 26 August 1970 Women's Strike for Equality.[116] It then helped to draft the New York State legislation, enlisting the pro bono services of the New York law firm Cravath, Swain, and Moore and the New York State Department of Insurance to help them with this work.[117] A year later, the New York State legislature passed Berry's conversion and continuation bill.[118] This was an early victory for divorced women. Colorado and Illinois then followed suit, but it took over a decade for such laws to become widespread.[119]

The spread of conversion and continuation legislation was aided by rising unemployment. At the same time that divorced women began to lobby for continuation and conversion laws, concerns about unemployed workers' loss of health insurance led labor activists and others to lobby for similar legislation for the unemployed. Congress held a series of hearings about how to address unemployed workers' health insurance needs in the 1970s. Early hearings considered a range of strategies similar to those divorced women had considered, including extending Medicare coverage to the unemployed, qualifying the unemployed for state Medicaid programs, subsidizing health insurance costs of unemployed and their dependents through state reinsurance pools, and mandating that employers provide extended health insurance coverage after layoffs.[120] Divorced women and unemployed people thus both argued that their history made them particularly deserving of an extension of selective entitlements.

As Congress debated what to do, states began to act on this last option. As they already had with divorced women, many states turned to conversion and continuation legislation that required employers to allow former employees to maintain their group health insurance plans. In 1977, to aid these states, the National Association of Insurance Commissioners adopted a model bill on group coverage continuation and conversion. Notably, it only addressed those who lost insurance as a result of a change of employment status, not marital status.[121] In the following years, feminist divorce reformers across the country fought to be included in these state continuation and conversion laws.

Selective Entitlements and Marital Privilege

At the end of the 1970s, divorced women continued to struggle to find affordable health care coverage. Certainly, as more women moved into the workforce, divorced women who followed this path found it easier to get employment-based coverage, but many who had relied on their husbands' group insurance plans still found themselves exposed to breaks in coverage and high costs when their marriages ended. Moreover, the political optimism that had allowed feminist divorce reformers to consider an expansive range of options for improving their access to health care—from national health insurance plans to women's health clinics to Medicare for divorced women—was dissipating. Not only did feminists increasingly run into virulent antifeminist opposition, but also a conservative backlash against expanded social welfare programs emerged in the second half of the decade, driven in part by the same contracting economy that fueled continuation and conversion legislation.[122] Contained in many of feminist divorce reformers' initial health care reform proposals, however, was the core premise that would allow divorced women to finally expand their access to care in an age of welfare retrenchment: the claim that, as a result of their former marriages, divorced women formed a privileged class of single women that the government should help.

As the decade came to close, a particular group of divorced women picked up on this message: military wives. The National Military Wives Association (NMWA) claimed that in the late 1970s, 75 percent of the calls it received came from ex-military spouses losing benefits.[123] Rising divorce rates affected the military as they did the rest of society, but legislation ending any presumption of long-term alimony and new expectations that divorced women would support themselves were especially damaging to long-term military spouses because of the nature of military life. It was difficult for military wives to build long-term careers with benefits because of the frequent moves demanded of their spouse. The challenges of military divorce thus threw into stark relief the problems with the social insurance system based on marriage and employment to which feminist divorce reformers had long called attention.

One woman who experienced the outcomes of a military divorce was Annette K. Smail, who, in 1977, divorced after twenty-eight years of marriage to an

Air Force officer and seventeen years of moving from base to base. As a result of the divorce, she lost the very good military medical benefits she had received through her husband. Smail's story was typical, but, unlike many military wives, Smail had a long history of political activism. Before she married, she had worked as a community organizer with Saul Alinsky. Smail left this work during the years of moving for her husband's career, but when she lost her health insurance, she put this organizing experience to use. She convinced local media outlets to carry her story. In response, letters poured in from women in similar circumstances across the country. These women became the founding membership of Smail's new organization Medical Equality for Dependents (MED).[124] She then convinced the National Women's Political Caucus to create an Older Women's Committee and brought MED under its umbrella.[125]

Smail persuaded her congressman, John Burton, to write a bill to give women who had been married to a member of the military for twenty years continued access to military medical benefits.[126] The bill proposed to create a new and extremely selective entitlement: a right to health benefits for women with an extremely specific marital status. Feminist divorce reformers and their allies in Congress rallied around this limited legislation, believing it to present a potential opening wedge into the larger issue of divorced women's medical benefits.[127] If ex-military wives could win continued access to a federal health care program, perhaps a similar expansion of Medicare might be close behind.

The embrace of military wives as the advance guard in the campaign for federal social insurance legislation for divorced women and the decision to support legislation that determined eligibility for benefits through a status determination shows the narrowing of the feminist divorce reform movement's goals. Military wives were effective messengers for a campaign built on a disaster narrative and selective entitlements. They were the ultimate blameless divorcees—unable to build their own economic security during marriage and so left with nothing after years of sacrifice for husband and for country. But making military wives the standard-bearer for feminist divorce reformers' campaign for benefits meant that the movement was no longer making common cause with efforts to build an entirely new, broad-based social insurance system; nor was it advancing a vision of marriage as a form of economic contract. It had settled around trying to extend the status-based privileges of marriage to the formerly married.

CHAPTER 5

Marriage as Work, Marriage as Partnership

Divorced Women's Fight for Social Security

At NOW's 1974 Marriage and Divorce Conference—the same conference where Betty Friedan first called for divorce insurance—Congresswoman Bella Abzug proposed a thought experiment. She asked her audience to imagine what would happen if American housewives ever stopped performing the unpaid work they did every day. Painting a picture of such a strike, Abzug said, "If America's housewives ever placed an embargo on dispensing their free labor, the pilot lights on gas ranges would go out all over the land, the washing machines and vacuum cleaners would fall silent, husbands would not be driven to suburban trains, children not be fetched and carried, and this nation would discover a whole new definition of crisis." Abzug insisted that she was "not suggesting that housewives flex—or unflex—their muscles in that way"; rather, she wanted to prove a larger point. "It is time," she said, "that [housewives'] work be given dignity and their personal investment in marriage and the family be given legal recognition." To do this Abzug proposed not wages for housework, as many women had over the years, but retirement pensions. Specifically, she announced a bill to create Social Security accounts for homemakers, calculated on the basis of the value of their work in the home.[1]

Abzug explained that divorced homemakers, in particular, desperately needed a right to their own Social Security accounts. Women who had moved in and out of the paid workforce—spending some of their lives as homemakers—rarely had logged long enough or consistent enough work records to be eligible for retirement benefits that would ensure a secure old age. Instead, as with health insurance, most married women's access to retirement security rested on their husbands' employment-based benefits. As the divorce rate rose among older couples, women discovered how little retirement security they had when their only access to a pension came through a husband. By 1980, unmarried women made up roughly three-quarters of the elderly population living below the poverty line.[2] Abzug's language of embargo and crisis, which placed the problem of homemakers' retirement security on a par with the high drama of international oil politics in the 1970s, captures the alarm many feminists felt at the rising numbers of elderly women living in poverty.

Abzug's proposal to provide homemakers with their own retirement benefits required reconceptualizing either America's employment-based retirement pension system, the way the social insurance system understood marriage, or both. As feminist divorce reformers campaigned for retirement benefits for homemakers, they had to make difficult choices—balancing political and ideological considerations—about what public policy should say and do about women's work in the home and the nation's obligations to the elderly. In the early 1970s, many feminist divorce reformers embraced Abzug's idea that homemakers should be understood as workers and receive retirement benefits as such. This proposal required detaching retirement benefits from real wages and somehow calculating a value for women's work in the home. By the mid-1970s the magnitude of these challenges led feminist divorce reformers to settle on a simpler proposal: rewriting the Social Security Act to treat retirement benefits as community property to be divided evenly between husbands and wives.

Although simpler than creating a benefit for homemakers, redefining Social Security benefits as community property still required rewriting public policy so that it recognized marriage as an economic partnership, akin to other contracted relationships, rather than a breadwinner-dependent relationship. This was an idea that met significant resistance. Although, by 1980, just over half of married women with their husband present and children under eighteen were in the labor force, most of these women still depended on their husbands for the majority of their income.[3] And, of course, close to half of married women remained out of the workforce.[4] Women in these different economic positions recognized that they had competing interests in Social Security reform.

Even as they debated the best way to move ahead on comprehensive reform, women across the political spectrum pressured Congress to pass smaller amendments to Social Security law that would enhance divorced women's access to retirement pensions immediately. These proposals drew on a less controversial understanding of marriage: the idea that marriage was a privileged status that divorced people should be allowed to keep. Ultimately, it was these proposals that became law. Despite the common historical narrative that marriage became more contract-like over time, the history of divorced women's access to social welfare benefits, especially their access to retirement pensions, reveals an alternative to this timeline. Marriage-as-status has had its victories too, particularly in the legislature. Congress debated legislative proposals to treat marriage like a contracted economic partnership and other proposals to treat marriage like an employment contract, but these proposals failed. The smaller-scale reforms that did pass simply expanded who received retirement benefits on the basis of marital status. Legislation in the 1970s entrenched the public welfare regime's use of marital status instead of dismantling it.

The Wolf at the Door: The Social Security System Entering the 1970s

In 1975, Tish Sommers gave a speech titled "Social Security: A Feminist Critique." She told her audience, "Social Security as it now stands is highly discriminatory against women—not in an abstract 'equal under the law' sense, but in the far more real test of how well it keeps the wolf from the door. It serves us poorly in that." Sommers believed Social Security served women so badly because it was structured around the "archaic presumption" that men were breadwinners and women were homemaking dependents. She concluded, Social Security "reinforces the economic impact of sexism and punishes women for the roles society most approves."[5] Sommers accurately described the way the Social Security system had developed to treat women since the 1930s. Over the system's forty-year history, almost every time Congress amended the Social Security Act it made legislative choices designed to support the breadwinner-homemaker model of a family.

The 1935 Social Security Act provided old age insurance only for workers in covered employment, with no added benefits for their dependents. In exchange for the votes of Southern members of Congress, the architects of the initial Social Security program excluded the vast majority of African American workers from eligibility for old age insurance by excluding agricultural and domestic employers and employees from the new Social Security program.[6] These exclusions, as well as the decision to base benefits on length of service in the workforce, also kept most employed women from receiving old age insurance benefits in their own right.[7]

In addition to the old age insurance program for which it is best known, the Social Security Act created a federal-state partnership to support a state-run, means-tested, old age assistance program that provided benefits for the indigent elderly. At first, far more elderly people qualified for the assistance program than for the insurance program. This worried the architects of Social Security legislation, who were committed to creating a contributory insurance system based on employment and not a universal pension system. Their concerns grew as the lag between the beginning of Social Security taxes and the first benefits being paid out created a surplus of funds. In response to calls to use surplus funds to create more universal benefits, Social Security's architects decided instead to spend the surplus on expanding benefits for those already covered by Social Security.[8]

In 1939, Congress amended the Social Security Act to provide dependent benefits. Married men in covered employment would receive an extra 50 percent of their Social Security benefit to help them support their wives; wives who worked could choose between their husbands' benefits and their own. Widows and the children of deceased covered workers would also be eligible to collect a dependent benefit, but widows lost eligibility for benefits if they earned more than $15 a month.[9] Divorced women, a relatively small group in the 1930s, received no Social Security benefits through their ex-husbands.

After 1939, women could receive Social Security benefits either as employees in covered jobs or as their husbands' dependents, but not both. The majority of married women—even employed married women—chose the latter option because it almost always paid more.[10] Many women did not work in covered employment, and those that did found that low wages and breaks in employment to raise families kept benefits based on lifetime earnings low. Forgoing the Social Security benefit, however meager, that their work record had earned in order to draw the dependent benefit for which they were eligible regardless of work history angered many women. They believed they paid into the system without getting anything out.[11]

One of the first comprehensive governmental examinations of the Social Security system's treatment of women came from John F. Kennedy's Presidential Commission on the Status of Women (PCSW). Convened at the start of the Kennedy administration, the new commission took on the task of investigating sex discrimination in the Social Security and tax systems and quickly concluded that the social insurance system was failing older women.[12] It noted that in 1961 almost 17 percent of older women relied on public assistance (rather than Social Security's old age insurance program) to make ends meet while another 11.5 percent received no income from any public old age assistance or insurance program. Even women who could draw Social Security benefits on the basis of their own work or their husband's work received very low benefits. The average monthly retirement benefit for women was less than $65.00 (roughly $505 in today's dollars). The median annual income for all women sixty-five and over was $640 in 1960; for men it was $1,620.[13]

The startlingly large number of older women living in poverty in the 1960s was due in part to the increasing number of single older women. By 1960 there were 1.6 million more elderly women than elderly men, and the proportion of aged women to aged men was predicted to continue to grow.[14] Not only had couples begun to divorce later in life, but women had begun to outlive their husbands. By 1974, a quarter of all divorces filed in the United States were filed by couples that had been married for fifteen years or more.[15] The number of never-married women was also on the rise. Between 1960 and 1980, the percent of never-married women rose by three each decade.[16]

The PCSW's Committee on Social Insurance and Taxes expressed concern over these trends. It noted that Social Security made no provision for divorced wives of covered workers, even if these women had depended on their husbands' support throughout their entire working lives. A divorced woman without her own employment record was only eligible for support through Social Security's Old Age Insurance program if her ex-husband died while she had his minor child in her care. Even then she was eligible "only if she had not remarried and if she was receiving at least one-half of her support from her former husband after a court order or agreement at the time of his death."[17] Similarly, widowed women who had relied on their husbands' Social Security entirely for support were eligible for widows' benefits only if they had children or were sixty-two or over.[18] Such benefits cut off if a widow remarried.[19] Single women with children living below a certain poverty level could draw on AFDC and elderly women who also met means-testing requirements could draw on Old Age Assistance. In the early 1960s then, the Social Security system determined most women's eligibility for benefits on the basis of their connections to their husbands, their children, or both. The committee argued that this left women who lost these connections overly vulnerable.

Nevertheless, the PCSW's suggestions for reform did not promise the complete elimination of the system's reliance on relationally based benefits.

Its main recommendations for women were (1) to make divorced women, with or without children, eligible for a Social Security dependent benefit on the basis of their former husband's wage record if their marriage had lasted at least ten years and (2) for widows over sixty-two who lost widows' benefits upon remarriage and subsequently divorced to regain their original eligibility. The PCSW also suggested that employed married women be allowed to draw both dependent and employee benefits with the dependent benefit reduced in relation to the work benefit.[20] And it proposed that childless widows under sixty-two who were ineligible for all other Social Security benefits receive temporary benefits along with training to help them become self-supporting.[21] Each of these suggestions left in place the use of marriage to determine eligibility for benefits while expanding the categories of marital status through which women could become eligible for benefits.

In fact, the PCSW's proposals would have done more to remove the use of motherhood from benefit determinations than they did to remove the use of marriage. The commission justified this by arguing that many women waited for their children to leave home before they divorced; they did not believe women should be punished for postponing divorce for the sake of their children.[22] In the next ten years, legislators and activists lobbied for versions of each of the PCSW's proposals. The PCSW's initial decision to leave marriage in place as a determinant of eligibility but to remove motherhood shaped the decade's policy debates and outcomes.

Members of the commission did consider ways to give married women Social Security benefits of their own. They debated recommending Social Security credits for homemakers as individuals on the basis of the imputed value of their work in the home, but rejected the idea because of the practical difficulties it raised.[23] As longtime feminist and technical adviser to the PCSW Catherine East explained, the idea "was ahead of its times."[24]

Members of Congress quickly responded to the problems raised by the PCSW's 1963 report on Social Security. In particular, Representative Martha Griffiths (D-MI), the original champion of Title VII of the Civil Rights Act, lobbied for the proposed reforms.[25] Griffiths argued that married homemakers contributed to their husbands' Social Security accounts through their management of household budgets and thus had earned a right to their dependent benefit. She said, "In as much as married women who have never worked go without a great many things to pay the social security tax, I think there should come a moment when a wife has some rights all her own—let her have some protection against being divorced and receiving no help at a time of life when it is so very difficult to gain employment."[26] As a result of the work of Griffiths and others, in 1965 Congress amended the Social Security Act to give divorced women a limited Social Security benefit through their ex husbands.[27]

Despite the lip service Griffiths paid to the value of women's work in the home, the law she supported did not truly recognize women as having an earned right to Social Security benefits. To be eligible for the new benefits, a woman had to have been married for at least twenty years and be receiving substantial support—defined as half or more of her income or substantial contributions pursuant to a written agreement or court order—from her ex-husband. Even under these circumstances, an ex-wife could start drawing a dependent benefit on her ex-husband's Social Security account only once he started claiming his benefits. Her benefits cut off if she remarried, but the 1965 amendments did allow those benefits to be reinstated if the new marriage ended in divorce before twenty years of marriage.[28]

Even if a woman met all of these requirements, she could only draw a relatively small Social Security benefit. She and her ex-husband did not split his benefit evenly. Rather, a man received his full benefit and his ex-wife received half of whatever he received. This was the extra amount the husband would have received had the couple stayed married and he had drawn a dependent benefit. Although the combined benefit—150 percent of the benefit a husband had earned—might have supported two people living together, 50 percent of the husband's benefit was often not enough for the ex-wife to live on by herself. The value of the dependent benefit sent a powerful message about homemakers' contributions to their marriages. Rather than seeing marriage as an equal partnership, the 1965 Social Security amendments valued a woman's work in the home as worth exactly half of whatever her husband earned.

Under the 1965 amendments, women continued to receive Social Security benefits as a result of their status in relation to their ex-husbands. To be eligible for benefits they had to have been married for a certain length of time and to still depend on their ex-husbands for support. These requirements made clear that divorced women receiving Social Security benefits through their exes had not earned these benefits. Earned benefits do not cut off when a person's marital status changes, but remarrying ended divorced women's Social Security benefits immediately. Divorced women also could not draw benefits at their discretion, but had to wait until their ex-husband began to draw his own benefits. Since older divorced women often had a difficult time finding a job, this posed a problem for many women. In the end, the 1965 amendments simply expanded the variety of marital statuses through which women could be eligible for dependent benefits. Divorced-after-twenty-years-of-marriage was now a status position that merited dependent Social Security benefits. Divorced women's economic citizenship rights continued to flow to them through their ex-husbands.

The 1965 law drew immediate criticism. The early focus of most of this criticism was the twenty-year rule, not the continued use of dependency and status more generally. Feminist divorce reformers demanded to know what made a twenty-year marriage worth more than a marriage of nineteen and one half years.[29] They lobbied to lower the number of years of marriage at which a divorced woman became eligible for dependent benefits. Many pointed out that the PCSW had actually suggested a ten-year marriage as the eligibility cut-off.[30]

Supporters of the original twenty-year rule questioned the suggested reductions in the duration of marriage requirement.[31] For example, Griffiths initially resisted lowering the marriage requirement. She wrote, "The whole problem in reducing the Social Security duration-of-marriage requirement for divorced women, from 20 to 10 years, is the feeling among Ways and Means members that it would permit a number of women to draw on the earnings record of one man."[32] According to Griffiths the twenty-year requirement prevented too many women from claiming benefits through one man. Since men would be entitled to a full dependent benefit for their current wife and any woman they had been married to for at least ten years, multiple women could draw a full dependent benefit based on the same man's record.[33] This threatened to be quite costly for the government.

As policymakers debated how to address divorced women's retirement security over the next twenty years, this issue of men having multiple dependents came up repeatedly. It was not just the members of the House Ways and Means Committee who expressed this concern. In the lead-up to the passage of the 1965 amendments, one woman who had worked because her husband was disabled and ultimately earned a greater Social Security benefit than he did wrote to Griffiths, "A widow cannot have two pensions. But a man with serial wives can. Why is this?"[34] Congress could have solved the problem easily by awarding women Social Security benefits on the basis of the number of years they spent in any particular marriage—a policy for which many feminists lobbied. But at every turn, Congress decided that it would rather allow a man to claim a full dependent benefit for multiple wives. That policymakers chose this path, despite concerns about its costs, shows just how committed they were to bolstering men's breadwinner status through the Social Security system.

"What's a Wife Worth?": Reforming Social Security to Recognize the Value of Women's Work in the Home

In 1965, Chase Manhattan Bank grabbed public attention with a window display at its New York headquarters titled "What's a Wife Worth?" Working with economists and accountants, Chase had broken the work women did in the home down into a series of jobs: nursemaid, housekeeper, cook, dishwasher, laundress, food buyer, gardener, chauffeur, maintenance man, seamstress, dietician, and practical nurse. Researchers then approximated time spent in each role and declared that the average homemaker worked 99.6 hours a week performing tasks worth $159.34 on the market (roughly $1,203.00 in today's dollars).[35] The Chase study predicted a question that feminists became increasingly engaged with in the following years as they tried to find ways to reduce women's dependency on their husbands by compensating them for their work in the home. In the 1970s, numerous bills to give homemakers Social Security forced policymakers to consider how to calculate the value of women's unpaid labor. Feminist divorce reformers offered many possible approaches to this problem, but policymakers ultimately chose not to implement any of these options, preferring instead to affirm the breadwinner-dependent model of marriage.

At their inception, most feminist organizations expressed more concern with eliminating facial discrimination in the administration of Social Security than with addressing how discriminatory work patterns created gendered benefit structures. An early NOW position paper stated support for reforming Social Security laws "to assure equitable coverage for married and widowed women who have worked, as they do now for married women who did not work."[36] In other words, like the rest of its earliest agenda, NOW's early Social Security policy priorities focused on ending discrimination against employed women. The organization especially attacked employed married women's inability to draw dependent benefits for their husbands on their own work record. Only when Betty Berry took over the organization's Marriage and Divorce Task Force did NOW begin to focus its Social Security work on homemakers' economic rights.

The ACLU Women's Rights Project (WRP), led by future Supreme Court Justice Ruth Bader Ginsburg, provided the language and strategy for combining the interests of employment- and family-focused feminists' Social Security agendas. In a 1974 memo, the WRP explained, "Most of the sex discriminatory aspects of [the Social Security system] stem from a basic model which has pervaded it from its inception—the male worker and the female dependent housewife." Unfortunately, most of the overtly discriminatory provisions in the Social Security Act—the discrimination which the ACLU could challenge in court—was against men who could not draw dependent benefits on the basis of their employed wives' records.[37] This discrimination against men also affected women since it meant "the contributions of women as wage earners buy less protection for their families than do the same contributions by men."[38] The WRP spent most of the 1970s focused on eliminating sex discrimination in Social Security by winning dependent benefits for men in court.[39] Meanwhile, NOW and other feminist activist organizations lobbied Congress to change the policies that made the "the male worker and female dependent housewife" the family model at the center of Social Security.

By 1970, under the leadership of Betty Berry, NOW had made Social Security for homemakers a central plank in its platform. Berry's Social Security for homemakers proposal sought to give women who worked in the home the equivalent of Social Security retirement benefits not because of their marriages—as her divorce insurance proposal did—but because of the value of their work. In her first report to a national NOW conference in 1968, Berry argued that Social Security should "insure the housewife as an individual and not as her husband's dependent" because "if the woman were insured individually her coverage would go automatically with her from job to job as it does now, but in addition would also go with her into the occupation of housewife."[40]

NOW embraced the idea of Social Security for homemakers wholeheartedly during the 1970s in part because it believed the issue would bring new women into its ranks.[41] A 1974 NOW resolution explained that the organization would work for Social Security for homemakers in order "to broaden its appeal to include more women in traditional roles in the movement."[42] By 1974, the feminist movement had acquired a reputation for being anti-family. Liberal feminists were widely known for their work on employment discrimination, not family issues; women's liberationists had become an increasingly vocal presence in the movement; and, in the wake of the 1973 *Roe v. Wade* decision, feminists' work on reproductive freedom had become the flashpoint, which, along with the ERA, defined how most Americans understood the feminist agenda.[43] As NOW sought to overcome its anti-family image, Social Security for homemakers presented an issue around which they could organize a new constituency of women. The organization's Older Women's Task Force argued for supporting Social Security for homemakers specifically in order to ensure that older women who "invested years of (non-paid) labor in marriage, with the expectation of social and economic security in the future . . . [do] not become victims of unwelcomed 'liberation.'"[44] NOW's Social Security for homemakers campaign thus became a way for it to acknowledge that the feminist agenda affected women in a variety of ways and that some of these effects had to be addressed by further feminist action.

The broad appeal of Social Security for homemakers meant the idea quickly gained the support of many members of Congress. In 1971, Bella Abzug's staff put together a "complete package of social security bills . . . [to] make the system more equitable for women."[45] The bills included legislation to equalize the dependent benefits available to men and women, to reduce the length of the marriage requirement to five years for divorced women seeking to receive Social Security benefits through their ex-husbands, to eliminate the rule that forced women to choose between their dependent and employee benefits, and to guarantee Social Security benefits to "any person in a domestic relationship who remained in the home during the working years."[46] This long agenda addressed the concerns of men and women, employed women and homemakers, as well as married women and divorced women. It took on both overtly discriminatory policies in the law and policies that reproduced the problems of a gendered workforce.

Abzug's staff argued that all of these proposals aimed "to liberalize benefits under the same structure that exists today." The aide who drafted the proposals believed they were not "conceptually or practically radical in any way."[47] Nevertheless, many saw legislation to guarantee married women (or men) who worked in the home Social Security benefits despite their lack of formal employment as a radical departure from the employment-based social insurance system. Nixon's Secretary of Health Education and Welfare, Caspar Weinberger, explained, "Proposals to impute earnings for housewives raise a basic question as to the appropriateness in wage-related social insurance programs, such as Social Security, of a provision for basing benefits in whole, or in part, on services for which there is no remuneration paid."[48] Weinberger made clear that any addition of unpaid recipients required a dramatic rethinking of the system.[49]

Drafting legislation to offer homemakers Social Security required tackling many conceptual problems. First, there was the issue of definition. Almost all women performed homemaking tasks, but not all women were married. Did only married women constitute homemakers eligible for Social Security? Second, married women who held paid employment still performed many of the same tasks as women who worked exclusively within the home. Why should only women who held no other job be compensated for this work? Third, there was the problem of how to value women's work in the home. The Chase "What's a Wife Worth" study provided one possible answer—simply add up the value of many different tasks homemakers performed—but many other ideas surfaced as well.

All of these questions were tied to the largest challenge facing legislation giving homemakers Social Security: who would pay for the new benefits? Social Security's design meant that Americans generally understood the program to pay out in benefits what employees and employers paid in through taxes.[50] Unpaid homemakers could not make such contributions and had no employers to do so either. It was by answering the question of who should pay that policymakers and activists found their answers to the other conceptual problems.

Abzug's proposal provided a broad definition of homemaker. Anyone between the ages of eighteen and sixty-five who performed "householder services" and did not receive Social Security coverage from a full-time job or in any other manner would be deemed eligible. Furthermore, she specified, "A homemaker may be male, female, single, married, widowed or divorced (having been married any number of years)." The only requirement was that the household services performed had to support at least one person who was a wage earner.[51] Abzug's bill calculated homemakers' Social Security benefits on the basis of the value of the average national wage for "employment in the service occupations" and suggested the new benefits be paid out of the general tax fund in order to recognize the importance of homemakers' work to the national economy.[52]

Abzug's bill required that homemakers be tied to a wage earner, but not as a way of paying for benefits. Other proposals to give homemakers Social Security benefits also required homemakers to be tied to wage earners but used this connection to fund the benefits and, often, determine benefit size. For example, NOW's initial proposal drew on women's connection to their husbands to argue that husbands' employers should pay for homemakers' individual Social Security accounts. In an argument that embraced the older family wage ideal, NOW argued that this would acknowledge "the fact that the employer is receiving services of the household spouse as well as the employed person."[53]

In 1974, Congresswomen Barbara Jordan (D-TX), the first Southern black woman elected to Congress, joined with Martha Griffiths (D-MI) to offer a different approach to covering homemakers.[54] Their bill proposed to treat homemakers like self-employed workers: Under it, homemakers could earn Social Security credits, but they (or more likely, their husbands) would have to pay taxes to fund the credits themselves. Jordan and Griffiths's bill did not directly require homemakers to be supporting wage earners as Abzug's bill did. To qualify for the homemaker benefit a person simply had to be eighteen or over, conducting or supervising the affairs of a household, and not engaging in paid employment for more than 135 hours per month.[55] Nevertheless, by requiring homemakers to pay their own Social Security taxes to fund their eventual benefits, the Jordan-Griffiths bill essentially required homemakers be connected to a source of income. In determining her funding source, Abzug focused on the ways in which homemaking benefited the nation and therefore proposed that her plan be financed by existing funds. Jordan and Griffiths's bill instead focused on the benefits homemakers provided for the breadwinners their work supported and proposed these breadwinners pay.

Perhaps because their legislation did not require the federal government to foot the bill, Jordan and Griffiths's proposal attributed a higher value to women's work in the home than Abzug's did. Their bill offered three options for calculating the Social Security tax and benefit. From most expensive to least expensive, homemakers could choose a benefit plan based on the maximum amount payable by all self-employed workers, based on the median amount earned by all individuals who had worked four quarters in the most recent year, or based on the median amount earned by all women who worked four quarters in the most recent year.[56] By calculating the value of homemakers' work based on the market wage of workers in the service industries, Abzug's bill reproduced the market's consistent undervaluing of service work performed by women.[57] On the other hand, Jordan and Griffiths's plan allowed homemakers' work to be valued at the median amount earned by all individuals who worked four quarters in a given year. Their proposal, unlike Abzug's, might have helped to increase the market value of the kind of labor homemakers performed. This was especially important to women of color who were disproportionately represented in the service industries.[58]

Griffiths left office at the end of 1974, but Jordan again introduced their version of Social Security for homemakers legislation in 1975 and 1976—Representatives Yvonne Brathwaite Burke (D-CA) and Margaret Heckler (R-MA) joined her as cosponsors.[59] After Griffith's departure, two African American Democratic congresswomen and one white Republican congresswoman sponsored the bill. While parts of the feminist divorce reform agenda frequently led activists to clash with both women of color and poor women, African American congresswomen actively supported other priorities of feminist divorce reformers. African American women were still far more likely than white women to participate in the paid labor force in the 1970s, most frequently as severely underpaid care workers. Unsurprisingly, African American congresswomen showed particular interest in those pieces of the feminist divorce reform agenda that promised to boost women's wages and employment opportunities.

The potential cost of Social Security for homemakers legislation made these proposals immediately controversial. One angry husband wrote to Griffiths, "If you think for one minute I'll pay triple the amount of SS tax I'm now paying, you are crazy as hell. The minute a law of that sort comes into being is the same minute I apply for divorce."[60] Another woman who favored the idea behind the Jordan-Griffiths bill still expressed concerns. She wrote, "Your proposed bill is great if a young wife can persuade herself and her husband to take one of its options. For a young family, however, the 'option' is another grim decision. Homes with fulltime homemakers often already suffer serious economic penalties and adding an extra large tax will pose a grim decision."[61] While this woman generally favored the idea of Social Security for homemakers, others found the idea of taxing homemakers too high a price for their improved retirement security. In her dissertation, "The Problem of Marriage in the Era of Women's Liberation," Alison Lefkovitz argues that antifeminists believed that monetizing women's work in the home would open their care work up to competition from other workers and ultimately push all but the wealthiest women into the workforce.[62] These concerns led them to strongly oppose all proposals to change how homemakers received Social Security and fed into their opposition to the ERA, which they worried would require such changes to homemakers' relationship to Social Security.

The 1970s were not an easy moment to raise taxes. Local tax revolts, mostly over property taxes, presaged the beginning of a national politics focused on welfare retrenchment that was both anti-state and anti-tax.[63] The cost of Social Security for homemakers proposals made it difficult for elected officials to agree on a plan, even if the general idea of offering homemakers retirement security had broad support. Any expansion in benefits to homemakers required either a cut to some other part of the budget or raised taxes, but there was no agreement on who should pay those taxes. Progress toward passing legislation stalled over disagreement about how to best distribute the costs of new Social Security benefits.

It was a particularly hard moment for feminist divorce reformers to win expensive reforms because, increasingly, the politics of welfare retrenchment focused on single mothers receiving AFDC.[64] Although feminist divorce reformers had often tried to use the comparison between divorced women and never-married mothers to their advantage, the same similarities that made single mothers receiving AFDC attractive foils in some feminist divorce reform campaigns also threatened to allow divorced women to be understood as another undeserving group draining the public purse. Divorced feminist activists had to tread carefully, maintaining their differences from never-married single mothers by pointing to the ex-husbands who could be held liable for their dependency even while—at their most expansive—asking for the state to step into that role. This complicated political message never succeeded in moving major reform efforts.

Ideological commitments to Social Security System's extant structure also challenged proposals for Social Security for homemakers. Adding benefits for unpaid work to the Social Security system seemed to undermine the most basic premise of the employment-based insurance system. In addition, policymakers had a deep attachment to using the social insurance system to actively encourage marriage and the breadwinner-homemaker model of the family. Thus, while policymakers endlessly debated offering benefits to homemakers in order to attenuate women's dependency on their husbands, they quickly passed amendments that expanded women's access to benefits while further entrenching the Social Security system's use of the breadwinner-homemaker model. In 1972, for example, feminist divorce reformers convinced Congress to remove the requirement that divorced women prove their dependence on their ex-husband in order to receive a dependent Social Security benefit on his work record. Part of a larger set of Social Security amendments, this change passed the House by a vote of 344 to 32.[65]

Women's ability to pass such legislation rested on the fact that the change actually affirmed a model of marriage with which policymakers were comfortable: it suggested that all wives were dependent—no means testing required. Like the 1965 law allowing all wives of twenty years or more to claim dependent benefits through their ex-husbands, this 1972 change shows cost was not the only issue influencing policymakers' approach to the Social Security system. Adding non-dependent divorced women to the Social Security rolls necessarily increased the cost of the program. As they had when they opened up the Social Security system to pay dependent benefits to multiple wives of the same husband, Congress chose not the cheapest reform but the reform that best upheld the ideal of a family with a breadwinner husband and homemaker wife. While the new Social Security amendment was critical for many divorced women's immediate financial security, in the long term, the ideology affirmed in the new law only made it more difficult for feminist divorce reformers to win reforms advancing an understanding of marriage as a contracted partnership.

"A System That Will Minimize a Woman's Dependence": Earnings Sharing and the Partnership Model of Marriage

Throughout the early 1970s, as policymakers struggled to find a workable plan to provide Social Security credits to homemakers, there was a consistent murmur from the grass roots that there must be a simpler solution. "Why not split the payments' [*sic*] credits fifty-fifty and recognize in law that a homemaker has earned half of the payments?" wrote one woman, F. B. Mitchell, to Martha Griffiths.[66] "Then, come divorce, the first wife would have credits in her own name and the second wife, under her own Social Security number, could have the payments credited to her for the actual years she helped earn benefits." She finished, "I am sure that I must not fully understand Social Security regulations, for my simple solution must have occurred to you ladies."[67] The solution Mitchell proposed did indeed seem simple. Many elected officials, including Griffiths, had considered such proposals. But early on most feminist divorce reformers were set on using Social Security reform to win economic recognition for homemakers independent of their husbands' earnings.[68] By the middle of the 1970s, however, in the face of continuing opposition to Social Security for homemakers legislation and considering the rising number of women in the workforce, feminists began to cast around for new solutions. They moved away from debating the best way to value women's work in the home and began to try to reconceptualize marriage in ways that offered women who worked in and women who worked out of the home more economic protection. In the process, they found themselves reconsidering proposals like Mitchell's.

The Women's Equity Action League (WEAL) led the way in this shift.[69] WEAL was founded by a Cleveland-based lawyer, Elizabeth Boyer, in 1968. A founding member of NOW, Boyer believed that a group more focused on women's legal rights and economic issues—as opposed to abortion rights and the ERA—was necessary to attract a different set of women into the feminist movement. From the beginning, WEAL attracted the same women that NOW had tried to woo through its Social Security for homemakers campaign. In Washington, D.C., for example, WEAL gained an entire chapter when a group of older women who had begun meeting on their own decided to join its ranks.[70] This group had been convened by Arvonne Fraser, a longtime political operative who had worked for labor unions and on the congressional campaigns of her husband, Don Fraser (DFL-MN).[71] When Fraser began to reach out to feminist organizations, she decided the Washington chapter of NOW was too "politically naive" and that women's liberation groups were for young, unmarried women. She started her own feminist group of women who wanted to work within the political system. The new group dubbed itself "the nameless sisterhood" because the women in it refused to be identified by their husbands' names.[72] Their new moniker signified a group of women intent on establishing themselves outside of their husbands' shadows. The Nameless Sisterhood's agenda thus focused on giving economic recognition to homemakers.[73]

By becoming the Washington chapter of WEAL, the Nameless Sisterhood also became the organization's national lobbying arm. Fraser quickly became the organization's national president. In 1974, she proposed reforming the Social Security system so that it treated marriage as an "economic partnership."[74] Under Fraser's "earnings sharing" plan, any year that a couple filed a joint income tax return, each member of the couple would receive individual Social Security credits based on half of their combined earnings. This plan addressed the problems that both married employed women and married homemakers found in the Social Security system. It also reduced divorced homemakers' dependence on their ex-husbands. For example, without earnings sharing, if a divorced primary breadwinner chose to continue to earn wages above a certain limit after becoming Social Security eligible, his benefits were reduced and so were his ex-wife's. Earnings sharing disconnected the benefits of divorced spouses.[75]

WEAL and Fraser took up the fight for Social Security reform because of pressure from the grass roots. In 1975, Fraser testified that the national WEAL office received weekly letters from women "complaining about Social Security."[76] She divided these letters into two categories: those from women working outside the home who felt they made Social Security payments they never collected and those from divorced women "who are left without benefits."[77] Fraser argued that these two problems were rooted in the same inaccurate "assumptions about marital status that have come to have the force of law." She continued, "It is the role of the married woman as worker and as homemaker which raises the question of inequity in a social program which pressures the married woman to be the economic dependent of her husband."[78] Her proposal allowed women to decide what role they wanted to play in their marriage by reducing the financial reward given to breadwinner-homemaker couples.

Fraser argued her plan accurately reflected the nature of modern marriage. As an example of what such a marriage looked like, she told her own family's story. The bulk of her family's income came through her husband's salary. Fraser ran a small political consulting business, but also spent much of her time working directly for her husband's career. She explained, "Though I work in his office part-time I am prevented by nepotism rules from receiving a salary. We share a joint career. He earns most of the income. I manage the household, the campaigns, the children and what investments we have. I do our income taxes and pay all the bills. I am not unique."[79] Despite the many marriages that looked similar to hers, Fraser argued that, rather than treat marriage as a partnership, the Social Security system treated marriage as "an endurance test. . . . If one can last through a marriage with a covered worker for twenty years, it's possible to have a claim on benefits even after divorce."[80] Her plan, on the other hand, suggested that marriage was an "economic contract between two people."[81]

Arvonne Fraser's husband, Congressman Don Fraser (DFL-MN) first introduced earnings sharing legislation in the House of Representatives in 1976.[82] The legislation allowed couples to opt in to a partnership model of marriage by filing a joint tax return. Those who did would receive individual Social Security credits on the basis of whichever was higher: 50 percent of their combined earnings in covered employment or 75 percent of the higher earner's income in covered employment. This ensured that single-income couples would not lose benefits under the new plan.[83] In fact, single-earner couples would continue to receive larger benefits than dual-earner couples with the same total income.[84] Don justified his bill by pointing to the fact that in 1975, for the first year in history, over one million couples in the United States got a divorce. He wrote, "Marriages are no longer necessarily permanent. Be this good or bad, women suffer because the system has not recognized the frequency of divorce."[85] Don Fraser argued that his bill was premised on the ideas that "work in the home has economic value, that marriage is a partnership and that each partner contributes to the economic viability of the marriage unit."[86] All of this was true, but the details of the policy emphasized "economic partnership" more than the value of women's work in the home.[87]

Earnings sharing still explicitly rewarded marriage. Unlike most of the Social Security for homemakers bills, it only provided Social Security credits to *married* women who worked in the home. And it still allowed married people to claim credits on an extra 50 percent of a breadwinner's income. Moreover, instead of assigning a value to homemakers' work—or even a range of possible values to homemakers' work as the Jordan-Griffiths bill did—the Fraser earnings sharing bill rewarded homemakers on the basis of the couple's earnings. The marriage as an economic partnership model not only rewarded marriage but also suggested that some women's work in the home was worth more than others. Under the Fraser bill, the work a woman did in the home was deemed more valuable because she married a doctor instead of a factory worker.[88]

Because earnings sharing was not a perfect replacement for Social Security for homemakers legislation, some legislators, for example Burke and Abzug, supported both.[89] Effectively this meant they were trying to change how the law understood marriage, through earnings sharing, and how the law valued homemaking, through Social Security for homemakers. Importantly, they did not conflate these two goals. Likewise, the Frasers' plan included a nod to the complex relationship between the two ideas for improving women's status within the Social Security system. Their 1975 plan included a "constant attendant allowance" for anyone who was taking care of another person who was not their spouse but was "disabled or unable to care for himself/herself and who, without this constant attendant, would have to be institutionalized."[90] This last provision would have been especially important to poor women and women of color, who were most likely to end up in these caretaking roles, but it received less attention than the rest of the bill.

Despite its drawbacks, the Frasers' earnings sharing proposal was broadly popular among feminist divorce reformers. Just as NOW had tried to do with its Social Security for homemakers proposal, Arvonne Fraser tried to use earnings sharing to demonstrate the inclusivity of the women's movement. In 1975 testimony on earnings sharing she argued, "Many people believe that the women's movement is only of interest or importance to white, middle class, professional women. That's simply not true. Our subject today is an excellent illustration of one problem common to all women—all people in fact—and that problem is financial security in one's old age."[91] In recognition of both the substantive and political benefits earnings sharing offered, NOW's Older Women's Task Force endorsed the plan in 1975, soon after Arvonne proposed it.[92] The task force's chair, Tish Sommers, regularly promoted the Fraser proposal over the Social Security for homemakers bills on the table.[93]

Throughout the decade conservatives sought their own alternative solutions to address women's concerns with the Social Security system. For example, in 1975, the Social Security Advisory Council—a body that the 1935 Social Security Act required to meet every four years to review the program—released a report on the treatment of men and women. The report rejected earnings sharing as a solution to the problems caused by the system's reliance on the breadwinner-dependent model of marriage.[94] Instead, the chair of the committee, libertarian economist Rita Ricardo Campbell, called for eliminating dependent benefits entirely over the course of thirty years in order to encourage couples to save and women to work.[95] As an intermediate step, Campbell suggested requiring both men and women to prove their dependency in order to receive dependent benefits.[96] Proposals to level social benefits down instead of up soon became economic conservatives' favorite response to the unequal treatment of men and women.[97]

Although it never became law, the Frasers' earnings sharing plan succeeded in introducing a new policy paradigm into debates about how to help divorced women. Over the next decade, many policymakers and activists would wholeheartedly embrace the notion that marriage was an economic partnership. By introducing this concept, the Frasers helped move the debate about divorced women's retirement security from one focused on how to value women's work to one focused on how to understand marriage. Both sides of the issue received attention in the presidential campaigns of 1976. In that election, Jimmy Carter ran a campaign ad that spoke directly to divorced homemakers. "More women still work in the home than outside, but the rising divorce rate jeopardizes your economic security," it read. "I will act to help homemakers achieve equity in divorce and Social Security proceedings."[98]

The year that Carter took office, 1977, turned out to be the year that feminist divorce reformers finally began to see real action—not just debate—on the issue of divorced women's right to Social Security.

Social Security Reform in the Early Days of the Conservative Turn

Nineteen seventy-seven was a high point for feminists' efforts to reform Social Security. By the end of the year, divorced women and widows had more secure access to Social Security and courts had ruled that the system could not directly discriminate on the basis of sex. Nineteen seventy-seven was also a turning point year for feminism, marking the new prominence of the antifeminist movement. In 1977, feminists and antifeminists gathered in Houston for the federally funded National Women's Conference. While feminists from across the country met to outline a national agenda in which Social Security for homemakers featured prominently, Phyllis Schlafly gathered her followers for a large counter rally that stole headlines.[99] This antifeminist opposition began to offer a sustained and effective challenge not only to the ERA but also to the feminist critique of Social Security. By the time Congress began to truly consider removing dependency from the Social Security system, no comprehensive reform to the system could pass without an intense fight.

In 1977 the ACLU Women's Rights Project's litigation strategy around Social Security also bore fruit. Ginsburg's first success with Social Security came in 1975 when the Court ruled in *Weinberger v. Weisenfeld* that widowers with minor children in their care had to be eligible for the same Social Security benefits as widows in the same circumstances. In this case Ginsburg successfully argued that the law discriminated both against men by refusing to recognize them as caretakers and against women by giving them unequal benefits for their contributions to Social Security.[100]

Weisenfeld began the process of declaring women's contributions to Social Security equal to men's, but a bigger blow to the Social Security system's presumption of the breadwinner husband and homemaker wife came in 1977 with the Supreme Court decision in *Califano v. Goldfarb*. In that case, the Court declared unconstitutional the requirement that, in order to claim dependent benefits, which women received as-of-right, men prove that their wife earned three-quarters of their combined income.[101] *Goldfarb* did not eliminate dependency from the Social Security system, but it did force policymakers to consider whether all married people should be understood as dependent on each other solely by virtue of being married or if anyone claiming dependent benefits should have to prove their dependency.

Carter seized on the *Goldfarb* decision as a cost-saving opportunity for the Social Security system. Though he used the issue of divorced women's retirement security to try to win women's votes during the 1976 election, when Carter took office he focused more on Social Security's overall solvency.[102] Starting in 1975, the Social Security Administration had paid out more than it took in as a result of increasing rates of inflation and unemployment. Concern grew about a looming Social Security deficit.[103] Yet, without a response, the *Goldfarb* decision was predicted to simply add 520,000 new male beneficiaries to the Social Security program, further straining its finances. Instead, Carter advocated reducing the number of individuals receiving benefits as dependents altogether.[104]

Carter suggested that both men and women have to prove dependency in order to claim dependent and survivor benefits. In other words, instead of equalizing the system to be more generous to men, Carter proposed to make it less generous to women. To soften this blow, Carter suggested a looser definition of dependency than the Social Security system had imposed on men before *Goldfarb*. Under his proposed reforms, to be a dependent, a spouse merely had to earn less than his/her partner for the three years preceding the benefits claim.[105] As feminist divorce reformers argued for a new understanding of marriage that valued women's work in the home, Carter attempted to use women's increasing ability to support themselves through paid labor to financially shore up the Social Security system.[106]

When Congress began to consider Carter's Social Security proposals, most members were primarily concerned with Social Security's solvency, but years of lobbying by feminist divorce reformers meant that some vocal members of Congress responded with immediate skepticism to Carter's dependency proposal. In July hearings, Representative Don Fraser led the charge against Carter's proposed dependency test, arguing it was "totally unrealistic and, in fact, promises to offer some very bizarre results." He offered a number of examples of women who would lose benefits under the Carter plan such as the case of a woman who had served as a homemaker for the entirety of her marriage until her husband lost his job at sixty-one. If such a woman went to work until her husband turned sixty-five and became eligible for full Social Security benefits, she would be unable to draw dependent benefits on his record. By serving as the primary breadwinner for a mere the three years this woman would have lost her dependent status even though she could not plausibly have worked enough quarters to ensure a secure retirement for herself.

Fraser also pointed out that it was not at all clear how a divorced, longtime homemaker who received alimony for years and then took a part-time job to support herself would have her dependency on her ex-husband evaluated. Even though such a woman would not be eligible for any Social Security in her own right, she would likely not be eligible for a dependent benefit through her ex-husband either.[107] He concluded, "Dependence represents an artificial method of limiting participation in the social security system."[108] Fraser used his testimony to push for the elimination of dependency in the Social Security system altogether and rally support for his earnings sharing proposal. Other members of Congress and women's rights activists such as NOW's Eleanor Smeal and the Urban Institute's Nancy Gordon agreed with Fraser's analysis.[109]

As a result of this opposition, Carter's proposed Social Security amendments emerged from committee without the new dependency requirement. Instead the committee proposed a package of amendments that included a mandate that the Department of Health, Education, and Welfare (HEW) conduct a study about how to entirely eliminate the use of dependency to determine Social Security benefits. The final bill, passed in December of 1977, required HEW to produce this report with the Department of Justice Task Force on Sex Discrimination.[110]

While the called-for study might suggest that Congress was serious about eliminating dependency from the Social Security system, two other amendments passed in 1977 continued to use the Social Security system to encourage marriage. First, after 1977, widows and widowers over sixty who remarried could continue to draw survivors' benefits on their former spouses' Social Security records.[111] For years, members of Congress had received complaints from divorced older women about their inability to remarry without losing such benefits. Congressman Mark Hannaford (D-CA) testified that he heard stories from older couples who chose to "cohabitate and live as man and wife without the benefit of matrimony because of this loss of benefits. Needless to say most people of such age suffer psychologically because such an arrangement does violence to the mores of the time and places in which they were reared."[112] Concern for the "mores" of these older couples created broad support to allow them to keep their benefits even if they remarried.

More importantly to divorced women, another 1977 amendment lowered the duration of marriage requirement from twenty to ten years.[113] After 1977, anyone married for ten years or more could claim dependent benefits on the basis of their ex-husband's (or ex-wife's) full Social Security benefit. This legislation proved once again that, even at a moment when politicians were consumed with cutting the cost of the Social Security system, they remained wedded to using the system to promote the breadwinner-homemaker model of marriage whatever the cost. Both 1977 amendments encouraged marriage—specifically marriage arranged along breadwinner-homemaker lines—by improving its financial consequences.

In 1979, HEW finally published the report Congress had ordered two years earlier. *Social Security and the Changing Roles of Men and Women* examined two main proposals for eliminating dependency from eligibility determinations in the Social Security system: earnings sharing and a new proposal termed the "double decker system." The double decker system would have guaranteed all Americans a basic retirement benefit and, layered on top of that universal base pension, a second tier of benefits calculated based on earnings in covered employment.[114] This proposal would have ended the exclusive employment-basis of the Social Security system, but it did nothing to recognize the economic contributions women made to their marriages through their work in the home. As a result, the report also considered combining earnings sharing and double decker proposals. Under this model, married people's second tier, earnings-based benefits would be calculated using an earnings sharing model.[115] There were international precedents for both of these suggestions. By 1979, Canada and Sweden both had double decker systems; Canada's second tier also included a version of earnings sharing. Germany had an earnings sharing system in place for couples that divorced after 1979.[116]

Women's groups quickly weighed in on the two options the report presented. NOW, WEAL, the National Women's Political Caucus (NWPC), and the National Federation of Business and Professional Women's Clubs all endorsed earnings sharing over the double decker plan.[117] WEAL argued that, while the double decker system might make sense in an ideal world, "in today's world, no matter how high the minimum benefit, women will not be provided for sufficiently. Homemakers especially will have to cling tenaciously to their spouses and female workers who are happy in their pink-collar, underpaid jobs will have to drive trucks or look for other non-traditional work before this system as presented begins to be equitable."[118] Other women's groups echoed this sentiment. Feminist divorce reformers firmly believed any Social Security system that did not directly recognize women's contribution in the home would perpetuate the workplace's rampant sexism. They prioritized this recognition over the creation of more universal benefits.

Antifeminists also weighed in on the HEW report. Phyllis Schlafly's organization, the Eagle Forum, published a document, evoking Vietnam War draft card protests, titled "Don't Let the Libs and the Feds Tear Up the Homemaker's Social Security Card." It argued that the possibilities discussed in the HEW report would push women to enter the workforce by punishing homemakers with either diminished Social Security benefits or raised taxes.[119] In an issue of her *Phyllis Schlafly Report,* Schlafly told women that they could determine if they were being targeted by the "Women's Lib Movement and Federal Bureaucrats" by calculating whether their income over the course of their married life was less than one-quarter of their husband's. If so, she wrote, "YOU are the type of Traditional Family which Women's Lib is out to eliminate."[120] The Eagle Forum used its growing strength, which only a year later would help Ronald Reagan win the presidency, to encourage its members to attend regional symposia on Social Security that HEW held in 1979 and to oppose the proposed changes. They showed up in force.

As 1979 came to close, then, the promise of 1977 began to dim. Despite feminist divorce reformers' victories in court and the smaller reforms they won in the 1977 amendments, the momentum behind comprehensive reform that appeared in 1977 hearings on Social Security began to stall. The HEW report on eliminating dependency from the Social Security System helped encourage feminist consensus around earnings sharing but also drew the fire of powerful antifeminists. The battle between feminists and antifeminists that heated up in the final years of the 1970s would shape feminist divorce reformers' agenda and victories going forward. As they had in 1977, Congress would settle again and again on legislative reforms both sides supported—those that rewarded marriage through expanded access to marriage-based selective entitlements—but did not remove dependency from the social insurance system.

CHAPTER 6

"How You Lose Money by Being a Woman"

Divorce in an Age of Proliferating Retirement Savings Options

In what turned out to be the final months of his administration, Jimmy Carter at last made good on a 1976 campaign promise and took the stage at the White House Conference on Families (WHCF). Carter's goal at the conference was the same as it had been when he promised to hold the event four years earlier: to reclaim "the family" as an issue for Democrats, or at the very least, to counter Republican insistence that the GOP was the party of family values. In his speech to the conference, Carter tried to promote a language of family values that accepted and celebrated a diversity of family structures. He began by joking about the eclectic careers of his brother, sisters, and mother (a gas station owner, motorcyclist, holy roller preacher, and sixty-eight-year-old Peace Corps volunteer, respectively).[1] On a more serious note, he pointed out that a single mother had raised his wife, Rosalynn, after her father died when she was thirteen. He traced his commitment to helping single-parent families to watching families like Rosalynn's struggle, "emotionally and financially, to keep the family together." He concluded, "Every family is unique. If I ever doubt that, all I have to do is look at my own."[2] The presidential election five months later proved that Carter had done little to help Democrats win over Right Wing, "pro-family" activists. Instead, according to one Republican analyst, the conference had only ended up highlighting "a deep division over a fundamental question: what is the family?"[3]

Debates over the question of what forms the family should take and what role the government should have in promoting and protecting those forms raged throughout the late 1970s. They formed a critical backdrop to feminist divorce reformers' campaigns for better access to health benefits and Social Security. But the issue on the feminist divorce reformers' agenda that truly put the diversity of family economic arrangements on display was their work to improve access to men's job-specific retirement benefits. These campaigns highlighted not only the diversity of family forms—single-parent, married, divorced—but also the diversity of economic arrangements within families.

Private retirement benefits became an increasingly important component of American's retirement security over the course of the 1970s. This resulted in part from a general narrowing of support for government-backed benefits as well as a concerted effort by conservative elected officials to push more people into privatized social insurance programs. By 1970, 45 percent of all private sector workers received a pension plan through their employers.[4] As private retirement savings products began to play a larger role in Americans' lives, the government began to impose greater regulation on them. It also began to create new retirement savings devices through the tax code—for example, IRAs (individual retirement accounts) and 401(k) accounts—that transformed American's retirement security, leading increasing numbers of Americans to rely on these new, individual retirement products rather than employer-backed defined benefit pensions.

As these varied retirement savings products took on a greater role in Americans' lives, feminist divorce reformers found their attention pulled to this new multitude of employment-based retirement benefits and savings products. Often modeled on Social Security, the vast majority of retirement benefit programs took the breadwinner-homemaker model of the family as part of their basic structures. As a result, whether they had planned on retiring on their husband's employer-based pension or an IRA, divorced women were cut off from yet another form of economic security when their marriages ended. At the same time, each new retirement savings product or regulation offered feminist divorce reformers an opportunity to try and win federal regulations that recognized marriage as an economic partnership. Inserting an earnings sharing model into the regulations governing IRAs or military pensions, for example, might not have the same widespread effect as winning earnings sharing for Social Security, but it would make a strong statement and potentially open the door for further reform of public and private pensions.

Despite the hope that winning reforms to private retirement savings devices would lay the groundwork for more comprehensive change, in the short term, feminist divorce reformers' new focus on private and employer-sponsored benefits did not bode well for low-income women, particularly women of color. Both low-income women and their husbands were less likely to work in jobs that offered pensions. Similarly, low-income women and women of color were unlikely to have the finances to take advantage of new retirement savings devices. They relied more fully on Social Security for protection in old age. Feminist divorce reformers' shift toward focusing on private retirement benefits instead of Social Security thus focused their agenda more tightly than ever on preserving middle-class and wealthy women's class status.

Feminist divorce reformers ran their campaigns to change divorced women's rights to market- and employer-based retirement savings products while the debate over how the federal government should view the family moved to the national stage and as the antigovernment right wing solidified its grip on the Republican Party. Jimmy Carter's four-year struggle to host a White House Conference on Families was only one in a series of public battles to define the family in the late 1970s. As both Republican and Democratic elected officials tried to respond to increasing polarization around these issues, the feminist divorce reform agenda for private retirement benefits often seemed to offer the best possibility of compromise. Pursuing feminists' private pension agenda did not require the expansion of the federal welfare state and, arguably, was intended to protect breadwinner-homemaker families. Seeing its potential, elected officials flocked to the cause. At one point in 1979 there were close to one hundred bills addressing women's pensions access before Congress.[5] Nevertheless, success in reforming private employer-based pensions, federal employee pensions, and IRAs did not come quickly to feminist divorce reformers. Despite their efforts at compromise through narrowed demands, feminist divorce reformers ended the 1970s in the same position on private and public retirement benefits: with a clear agenda but little legislative movement.

"The American Family Is in Trouble": Claiming Family Values for the Left and Right

In the final months of his 1976 presidential campaign, Jimmy Carter began to frame his message around the American family. At a speech in Manchester, New Hampshire—his first after winning the Democratic nomination—he told his audience, "The American family is in trouble. I have campaigned all over America, and everywhere I go I find people deeply concerned about the loss of stability and the loss of values in our lives. The root of this problem is the steady erosion and weakening of our families."[6] Carter promised "to construct an administration that will reverse the trends we have seen toward the breakdown of the family in our country."[7] He received hundreds of enthusiastic responses to his speech. Capitalizing on this momentum, at a speech before the United States Catholic Conference in October, Carter promised that if elected he would hold a White House conference on the American family.[8]

Conceived as a benign campaign promise, the conference quickly became a political nightmare. Feminists and antifeminists competed to control it and hosted conferences of their own as they fought over questions as broad as how to define the family and as minute as the details of pension reform.[9] Carter found himself, not for the last time, attacked from both the Right and the Left for trying to stake out a middle ground. The history of the WHCF and competing conferences shows how issues still considered bipartisan in the mid-1970s were transformed into fodder for partisan political battles by the decade's end. The ultimate failure of the conference to move forward feminist divorce reformers' agenda shows the limits of the movement's political power at the end of the decade. While feminist divorce reformers retained agenda-setting power because of their ability to fit the issues behind their agenda into a range of politicians' concerns about the family, they did not have the political weight to pass their preferred reforms.

When Carter proposed a conference on families, he was thinking of congressional hearings held on the same topic in 1973 by his running mate, Minnesota Senator Walter Mondale (D-MN). These hearings on "American Families: Trends and Pressures" encouraged the government to evaluate exactly how its policies helped or hurt families while emphasizing and celebrating the diversity of the American family. Mondale himself began the hearings by warning, "To envision a single model family or a single way to raise children would do great damage to the pluralism and diversity that makes this country strong; would be beyond the legitimate concerns of government; and could produce at least as serious problems as ignoring altogether the impact of policies on families."[10] The dual emphasis on the importance of the family and recognition of the diversity of family forms was, by and large, accepted by all present at the hearings in 1973 and the hearings passed without much attention from the public.[11]

The new administration began planning its conference on families immediately upon Carter's entering office. By October of 1977, it had received congressional authorization for the conference, which it hoped to hold within two years.[12] A month later feminists and antifeminists clashed in Houston at the long-planned, federally sponsored, National Women's Conference. As feminists convened, Phyllis Schlafly and eleven thousand of her followers held a "pro-family" protest (some news reports estimated thirteen thousand and the protest leaders put the numbers between fifteen thousand and twenty thousand). The protesters attacked the ERA, abortion rights, child care, and gay rights, as well as the federal government funding that supported the women's conference, and they successfully shaped the press narrative about the conference into a story about feuding women.[13] The success of Schlafly's rally served as a warning to Carter: claiming family values as the Democrats' issue would be no easy task.

In Houston, feminists and antifeminists explicitly struggled over the appropriate role of government in protecting homemakers and the definition of the family in public policy. The conference released a comprehensive plan of action—voted on by the delegates in attendance—that called for government support for contentious legislative items such as abortion, the civil and parental rights of same-sex couples, and child care. In regards to family law, the plan of action demanded that the federal and state governments "base their laws relating to marital property, inheritance, and domestic relations on the principle that marriage is a partnership in which the contribution of each spouse is of equal importance and value."[14]

The opposition, meanwhile, released its own "minority report." This report began by announcing that, although it represented the minority of women at the conference, it spoke for "the majority of women, the homemakers and professional women of the United States."[15] It went on to accuse conference organizers of giving only token representation to the views of "family-oriented women."[16] The minority report listed these views as including the rejection of the ERA, national health insurance, and Social Security benefits for homemakers along with support for anti-abortion laws and the free enterprise system. Revealing the fundamentally different attitudes antifeminists and feminists held toward the government, the minority report announced, "We feel it is time for women to stop seeking federal solutions to personal problems."[17]

The press devoted most of its coverage of the Houston conference to the conflict between feminists and antifeminists.[18] Yet, hidden within the minority report—which, after a showdown, International Women's Year leaders included in the final printed report on the conference—were a number of points of legislative agreement between antifeminists and feminist divorce reformers.[19] The report called for lowering the length-of-marriage requirement for divorced women to draw dependent Social Security benefits on their ex-husbands, for IRAs for homemakers equal to those of their husbands, and for courts to recognize the importance of women's work in the home when dividing marital property in a divorce.[20] These were, naturally, the most conservative components of the feminist divorce reform agenda—the proposals that offered aid primarily to wealthy women or did not fundamentally challenge the law's understanding of marriage as a breadwinner-dependent relationship—but they did provide a clear compromise agenda focused mainly on the division of private property, and especially private retirement savings programs.

The "pro-family" framing of the antifeminists in Houston was exactly what the Carter administration hoped to combat through the White House Conference on Families. But before they even encountered antifeminists, the organizers of the White House Conference found themselves fighting each other. In early 1978, Carter's secretary of health, education, and welfare, Joseph Califano, named one of his special assistants, Patsy Fleming, as conference director.[21] Fleming, a former congressional aide, was a divorced, African American woman with three teenage sons.[22] Her appointment drew criticism from the Christian Right almost immediately.[23] In June, Fleming publicly quit as director alleging that Califano had caved to these critiques and ordered her to choose a white, married, Catholic, male co-director.[24] Just as Fleming's appointment angered many on the Right, Fleming's allegations incensed feminists and others on the Left. Feminists had never liked Califano, who actively opposed abortion.[25] They understood both his appointment and the Fleming debacle as representative of Carter's unwillingness to stand strongly behind their priorities.

Carter and Califano struggled to replace Fleming and postponed the conference, an early instance of the Carter administration's increasing appearance of haplessness. An article about the conference published in *Ms.* in September of 1978 explained that while the conference originally "sounded like a good thing: benign, well-meaning, apolitical," in the end it became "so political, so controversial, that no sensible President would consider going ahead with it until well after the next election."[26] Despite this analysis, Carter did eventually push ahead with the conference, making the political calculation that canceling the conference would look worse than holding it. Califano and Carter next offered the job of executive director to Sargent

Shriver, the former head of the War on Poverty agency, the Office of Economic Opportunity, who refused the appointment.[27]

As the White House Conference on Families floundered without leadership, NOW's Legal Defense and Education Fund decided to host its own National Assembly on the Future of the Family, scheduled for November 1979. NOW LDEF explicitly pitched the Assembly as outlining a new feminist agenda for the coming decade. In a *New York Times Sunday Magazine* piece published to coincide with the Assembly, Betty Friedan explained, "The great challenge we face in the 1980's is to frame a new agenda that makes it possible for women to be able to work and love in equality with men. . . . The second feminist agenda, the agenda of the 80's must call for the restructuring of the institutions of home and work."[28] This framing and the specifics of the National Assembly's agenda showed feminist divorce reformers' deep influence on NOW. The very first panel of the day was titled "With All My Worldly Goods—Marriage as an Economic Partnership."[29] The panel description explained, "Most couples enter marriage in total ignorance of marriage laws. Husband and wife agree privately to divide responsibilities for income, child rearing, recreation and basic services in the hope that their family can achieve a satisfying life." But, it warned, "existing laws all too often invalidate these private understandings, with the troublesome or tragic results that the partner who did not earn income outside the home is often denied ownership or control of the fruits of their collaboration. This panel will concentrate on the impact of these laws, both during the marriage and after it has ended."[30] Subsequent panels included "Helping the Homemaker—New Needs, New Problems," "The Single Parent Family," and "Divorce and the Family."[31]

By the time the NOW assembly met, the White House had found a new director for its own conference on families. In April of 1979, Carter appointed to the position Jim Guy Tucker, a former Democratic congressman from Arkansas, who had just lost a run for Senate. Tucker's appointment was an attempt by the administration to find someone whose biography represented a compromise between Fleming and the married white man who could have served as her co-director. Tucker was white and married. His wife, however, was on her second marriage and had two young children. The White House packaged Tucker as a perfect representative of the contemporary family. A *People Magazine* profile of him told the story of his appointment: "When the Carter administration asked Jim Guy Tucker to head its White House Conference on Families last Spring, Tucker answered, 'I don't have a dog or a station wagon. I am the wrong guy.'" But, the article continued, "He didn't realize that as a longtime bachelor who four years ago married a divorced woman with two children, his own life-style is as typical as any these days."[32] Tucker's wife, who was getting a law degree of her own, showed that Tucker was sympathetic to liberated women. Yet Tucker was tucked safely into a nuclear family in which he served as the main breadwinner. The Tuckers had even gotten a Labrador retriever since his appointment.[33]

Tucker came up with a plan for a decentralized series of conference meetings. The national committee urged states to hold their own conferences between September 1979 and March 1980. Each state conference would develop lists of the ten issues most important to the state's families and nominate delegates to attend one of three White House Conference on Families meetings—in Los Angeles, Minneapolis, or Baltimore.[34]

Almost immediately, Republicans on the national and state levels began to organize against the conference. In February, the governor of Alabama announced his state would not be holding a conference on families. He credited the decision to his wife who had convinced him the state should not participate in any conferences "which do not establish traditional Judeo-Christian values concerning the family."[35] Indiana soon followed suit. In response, supporters of the White House conference in both Alabama and Indiana convinced national conference organizers to allow sixty-six at-large delegates to attend.[36] These supporters did not, as the Alabama governor's statement might have suggested, represent radicals. The list of priorities Alabama's at-large delegates brought to the conference included "the ways traditional family structure can be encouraged" and "the rights of the spouse in case of divorce."[37] That the conference managed to divide not only the Right and Left but also Alabamians who shared a commitment to "the traditional family structure" shows how deeply politicized the family had become.

Right-wing senators also began to organize against funding for the Conference. Senator Gordon Humphrey (R-NH) circulated a petition protesting the conference. Pulling out all the stops, Humphrey told his constituents, "Your name on my petition is crucial to the survival of your family." "Believe it or not," he warned, "[Carter has] asked Bella Abzug, Mrs. Andrew Young, and Jean O'Leary to set future standards for American families."[38] The three figures Humphrey listed were clearly associated with a range of perceived threats to the "traditional family": a prominent New York feminist, an African American civil rights activist, and the co-head of the National Gay Task Force. Tucker responded forcefully to Humphrey's charges, not by defending Abzug, Young, or O'Leary, but by disavowing their participation in the Conference. Indeed, he pointed out that the Conference had refused the National Gay Task Force membership on the advisory committee and purposefully left gay families off the conference agenda.[39] Despite the rhetoric on the part of the Christian Right, the White House Conference on Families was a relatively conservative affair.

Early on, the conference's delegate selection process only enhanced its already conservative bent. The tight timeline tremendously advantaged organizations that could quickly mobilize to have a presence at the state conference.[40] By January 1980 it was clear that grassroots antifeminists had seized control of many state conferences. Phyllis Schlafly used her extensive network to drive her supporters to state conferences, and an active organizing effort by the Heritage Foundation also aided in the conservative takeover of many state meetings.[41] Thanks to these efforts, in November of 1979 "pro-family forces" won twenty-two of Virginia's twenty-five elected delegate positions.[42] In Oklahoma, they won all eight spots.[43] Part of their success came because, at first, feminist activists mostly ignored the state conferences. As one *Washington Post* article explained, "Guerrilla activists on the left were off fighting in other wars, leaving it to social work professionals to confront Phyllis Schlafly and her legions in the political trenches."[44]

Antifeminists' early success controlling the conferences left feminists embarrassed but unsure of how to respond. In response to predictions that the White House conference "will be the conservatives' answer to the Houston IWY Conference," NOW LDEF's president said, "Let's not have anything to do with them."[45] In contrast, at its December meeting, the NOW Societal Equality Committee decided to send action alerts urging NOW members to take an active interest in the conferences. In particular, they wanted to target the state delegate selection process in order "optimize our impact."[46]

In the end, antifeminists only won 250 of the 1,500 delegate positions. Feminists managed to retain influence over the official recommendations made by the conference.[47] These included many items on the feminist divorce reform agenda. One resolution read, "Marriage is also an economic partnership and financial resources earned by the spouses should be shared equally. Social Security and pension funds should be vested equally during marriage without reducing existing benefits. Assets accrued during marriage should be considered equally earned and owned so that at dissolution it can be divided fairly."[48] Yet, even as feminists controlled the conference resolutions, the press interpreted the WHCF as a conservative victory. The loud protests Schlafly organized to counter the conference she had failed to control dominated the press, making it more difficult for the conference resolutions to become legislative realities.[49]

In this increasingly polarized environment, policymakers and feminist activists turned toward legislation that could garner bipartisan support. Based on the minority report issued in Houston, private pension reform seemed to offer this room for compromise. Unlike Social Security reform, private pension reforms did not immediately intersect with debates about growing the social welfare state. Instead, these proposals focused on women's work and economic rights within marriage. These were by no means uncontroversial issues, but feminists nevertheless hoped they could find some legislative progress in spite of the deepening divide over women's "proper" role in marriage.

"Cheated of Their Fair Share": Women and Employer Pensions

In May of 1977, as feminists and antifeminists prepared to descend on Houston and Congress debated the Social Security amendments that would pass later in the year, the *Washington Post* reported on an issue riling the "the normally bland federal employee legislation front."[50] The typically staid House Subcommittee on Employment and Compensation had begun hearings on how federal employee pensions should be divided in divorce.[51] Feminist divorce reformers had identified federal employee pensions—the pension programs for civil servants, Foreign Service officers, military members, and others—as a potential wedge for their larger pension agenda. Feminists understood these pension programs as a middle ground between Social Security and employer-based, private pensions. On the one hand, the federal government acted like any other employer in offering these benefits. On the other, legislation regarding the division of federal benefits in divorce would amount to a federal policy statement about women's economic role in marriage. Feminists hoped that winning legislation that divided federal employee benefits along partnership lines at divorce would set a precedent for winning similar legislation not only for Social Security but also for private, employer-based pensions where they had struggled to make headway in the early part of the decade.

Married women relied on their husbands' employment-based retirement savings because of the myriad ways the retirement pension system discriminated against them. Early in the 1970s consumer advocate Ralph Nader published an article, aptly titled "How You Lose Money by Being a Woman," in *McCall's* that laid out the depth of this discrimination.[52] As with almost all employment-based benefits, women simply had worse access to employer-sponsored retirement pensions than men did. Pensions were a particular problem because women's work patterns did not fit the structure of the private retirement system any better than they did the public one. Private pensions rewarded lengthy service with the same employer. Women's frequent movements in and out of the workforce as the result of family obligations limited their opportunities to accrue pension benefits. As importantly, women tended to start working at a younger age than men, since they spent less time in school. Many employers, however, did not start counting years of service toward pension vesting until employees reached their late twenties, at which point most women had begun to have children and move out of the workforce, at least temporarily.[53] Moreover, even if a woman was lucky enough to have a job that offered pension benefits, private insurers offered women as a class smaller monthly retirement benefits on the basis of the fact that women tended to live longer.

While they rarely held retirement benefits in their own name, women often understood their husbands' pensions to result partially from their support work in the home. In the early 1970s, however, it was not clear what happened to such pensions in a divorce—courts in community-property states often divided them, while courts in common-law states tended to award them to the employee who had technically earned them.[54] Even in community-property states, women had to work to make sure that their lawyers fought for an equal division of pension benefits.[55]

As women struggled to establish a right to their husbands' employer-based pensions, the benefits themselves became increasingly critical to family economies and national retirement security. By the middle of the 1970s a panelist at an American Bar Association conference on divorce noted, "For many couples, employee benefits may be their most significant asset." He traced this state of affairs to the postwar growth in employee pension plans.[56] Congress also recognized the increasingly critical role employee pensions played in American's lives, stepping in to more tightly regulate this growing market. In 1974, the same year it passed the Equal Credit Opportunity Act, Congress passed the Employee Retirement Security Act (ERISA).

The debate over the ERISA legislation presented an opportunity to improve women's access to employer-based pensions. A NOW representative explained, "A long overdue private pension reform bill will be passed early in 1974 . . . . Unless women write and demand reforms in the bill now are kept in the bill, they will once more be cheated of their fair share."[57] She urged NOW women to write to Congress and advocate for, among other things, earlier vesting for pensions, an end to sex-discriminatory actuarial tables, pension portability, and automatic survivor benefits unless the survivor signed away those benefits.[58] Feminist policymakers took up the cause. Bella Abzug introduced legislation to make employees eligible for pension credits at twenty-five years of age or after three years of consecutive service, whichever came first, in order to allow women to build pension credits despite their shorter and earlier careers. In the Senate, a bill emerged proposing a uniform national vesting formula to make pensions portable across employers.[59]

ERISA faced many hurdles during the legislative process. The legislation got held up, first, by disagreement between insurance companies, large employers, and labor unions, as well as disputes over which executive branch department would oversee its implementation, and then by the Watergate impeachment hearings. During these debates, senators rejected amendments targeted at women, fearing that if they were added no bill would pass.[60] Women did not win earlier vesting, pension portability, or coverage in spite of breaks in service. ERISA did require that survivors' benefits be offered to employees, but it allowed the employee to waive those benefits without the consent of the dependent spouse.[61] The bill also did not address sex differentials in pension payments. The final bill thus did almost nothing to address women's problems with the private pension system.

Feminists registered their objections to the new law immediately. The NWPC issued a position paper that recognized the law as full of necessary improvements, but clearly demanded further legislation to advance women's pension rights through immediate eligibility for pension plans, immediate vesting for participating workers, pro rata benefits for part-time workers, and mandatory portability of pension credits.[62] Feminists also pointed out that ERISA had actually created new problems for divorcing women seeking a share of their husbands' pensions. The law contained a provision prohibiting the assignment of pensions to anyone other than the individual who earned them, a provision intended to protect pensions from being claimed in bankruptcy or as compensation for wrongdoing.[63] Some divorce court judges read this provision as prohibiting the division of pension benefits in a divorce.[64] Feminists campaigned for further reforms to employer-based pensions for the next decade, but met little success. By 1980, men were twice as likely as women to have pensions and, on average, those women who did receive pensions only received about half of what men received.[65]

It was in the context of this continued failure to win broad feminist reforms to employer-based pensions that newly elected Congresswoman Pat Schroeder joined both the Post Office and Civil Service Committee and the Armed Services Committee of the House. The first woman to sit on the Armed Services Committee, Schroeder fought for the posting because of her antiwar background. Once on the committee, she began to receive an enormous amount of mail from the ex-wives of military members asking her—as a feminist in a position of power—for help securing access to their ex-husbands' health and retirement benefits. This mail was matched by mail from the ex-wives of civil servants and post office employees who also looked to Schroeder for help. These letters made clear that federal employee pensions created problems for ex-wives similar to those faced by the ex-wives of men in the private sector. These problems were compounded by the fact that most government employees were not eligible for Social Security, so their ex-wives did not even have the minimum protections available to the wives of other employed workers. Moreover, many federal employees—especially military families—tended not to own property that could be divided. Instead their economic security rested on the very good benefits that came with a military or Foreign Service career, including retirement pay, pensions, commissary privileges, and health insurance.[66]

When Schroeder and her staff began to do research in response to this flood of mail, they identified sixty-seven federal pension programs with no provisions for divorced women.[67] In each of her committees, Schroeder began to push for legislation that applied an approach similar to the Frasers' earnings sharing proposal to different federal benefit programs.[68] Schroeder was frank about the fact that she took up the issue of federal employee benefits because she believed that, given her committee assignments, it was where she could "do the most" to help improve women's retirement security.[69] She understood these legislative campaigns as not only offering the possibility of immediate assistance to specific groups of women, but also as creating another opportunity to win federal recognition of marriage as an economic partnership.

The language of economic partnership suffused the testimony of those advocating for divorced women's access to their ex-husbands' federal retirement benefits. For example, NOW's Older Women's Committee sent Sarah Deane, the former wife of a Foreign Service officer, to testify on the division of Foreign Service benefits in divorce. In her testimony, Deane described her marriage as "twenty-five years of partnering" her husband's career. She explained, "My share of the partnership was in entertaining and representation, sharing in whatever work the ranking women at post felt American wives ought to be doing in that country." She added, "It was also in fulfilling women's traditional homemaking role, with the added measure of packing and moving house to establish secure home environments for the children's formative years in an alien, sometimes dangerous atmosphere."[70] Deane's inclusion of regular homemaking tasks along with the extra work expected by the Foreign Service advanced the argument that all marriages were economic partnerships, with all homemakers supplying vital support to their husbands. Foreign Service wives simply had an extra difficult job. Deane concluded by arguing, "Having fulfilled the role society expected of them in homemaking and family nurturing and performed loyally the function their government asked of them in support of their husband's careers, these women deserve a share of the rewards they helped earn."[71]

Despite the language of partnership marshaled by Deane and other supporters of the new bills to extend federal retirement benefits to divorced spouses, the legislation they lobbied for generally did not extend benefits on the basis of economic partnership. Instead, policymakers clung to the use of marital status determined by longevity of marriage that had entered into the Social Security system in 1965. Almost all of the bills to give divorced women access to federal retirement benefits adopted the Social Security system's requirement that a couple be married for at least twenty years before an ex-wife became eligible for any benefits.[72] Some of the proposed legislation—especially those bills championed by Schroeder—also included a nod to the partnership theory of marriage by requiring that after twenty years of marriage benefits be divided on a pro rata basis using a formula based on the number of years of marriage in relation to the number of years a husband had spent earning benefits on the job.[73] If passed, bills including this pro rata provision would have recognized marriages of a certain length as partnerships. This would have given some former wives of federal employees better access to their ex-husbands' benefits than divorced women received through Social Security, which continued to only provide divorced women with a dependent benefit worth half the benefit their husband received.

Even these limited bills ran "into a wall of opposition from groups ranging from the retirees themselves, second spouses, and civil liberties organizations who argue that states' rights would be trampled by the imposition of federal pension-setting rules."[74] In a 1980 hearing on the military pension proposal, one major general testified, "My wife probably deserves more of my retirement than I do. But I think the issue here is that the federal system would be violating what is left to the states."[75] Offering fewer plaudits to spouses, a vice president from the National Association for Uniformed Services testified, "The argument that the divorced spouse earned a share in the service member's retirement and survivor benefits is not a valid one. Under H.R. 2817, no measure of such a contribution is required, nor would such a measure be possible. The spouse could have been a hindrance to the member's career, as some spouses are, but it would make no difference."[76] He continued, arguing that Schroeder's proposal entirely ignored "the damage done to second wives and their children. It will create staggering problems for thousands of people who are innocent of any wrongdoing in marriage for the sake of a tiny handful of aged divorcees who may have been treated unfairly by their service member spouses."[77]

This opposition to military pension reform came from a specific place: those men and women directly affected by the proposed legislation. Otherwise, the feminist pension reform agenda received remarkably bipartisan support in the late 1970s. In part, this may have been because federal employees—especially those in the military and Foreign Service—seemed to embody the breadwinner-homemaker image of the family that conservatives were wedded to. To many, improving these women's access to benefits in case of divorce seemed to support the continued creation of this form of family instead of undermining it.

In 1980, President Carter signed into law a bill specifically addressing the access to federal pensions by ex-spouses of Foreign Service officers. The House bill had merely permitted courts to divide federal retirement pensions as the judge saw fit, but the Senate bill contained a presumption that such benefits should be divided on a pro rata basis through a formula that took into account years married in relation to years of service by the employee. The combined legislation that Carter signed compromised by implementing this pro rata provision for any couple getting divorced after 1981.[78] This formula was based on the notion that marriage was an economic partnership analogous to other contracted partnerships; it was the first legislation that forced the government itself to operate along this principle. The Foreign Service bill became the model for which other divorced women would fight in the years to come.

"Something a Woman Has Created for Herself": IRAs for Homemakers

In 1979, Senator Paul Laxalt (R-NV) introduced the Family Protection Act (FPA).[79] This omnibus legislation, described as a "Blueprint for a Moral

America," was a direct response to the White House Conference on Families; many of its provisions came straight out of the minority report issued at the Houston National Women's Conference. The first title of the act focused on education, for example, encouraging prayer in schools and offering special right-to-work laws for teachers. Under the broad heading of "welfare," the second title would have prohibited students enrolled in post-secondary education from receiving food stamps and offered small income tax credits or deductions to families taking care of seniors over sixty-five. A third title tried to increase parents' authority over their children's education. Under the title on domestic relations, the FPA contained provisions that removed the federal government from involvement in domestic abuse, affirmatively allowed corporal punishment of children by their parents, and required all federally funded abortion clinics to notify parents about minor patients.[80] Buried among these provisions to turn back the clock on feminist and other liberal reforms of the last few decades was a provision to allow married individuals to put equal amounts into tax-exempt retirement savings accounts—something feminist divorce reformers had advocated for years.[81]

Private, tax-exempt retirement savings accounts took off in the 1970s, especially after the passage of ERISA, which, in addition to regulating employer-based private pensions, created a new, tax-exempt retirement savings device: the IRA.[82] ERISA was intended to help foster the growth of the private-pension system as a critical supplement to Social Security.[83] The legislation signaled legislators' move away from efforts to expand Social Security benefits in favor of privatized insurance systems, along with a growing intention to create retirement savings mechanisms based on individual risks rather than the shared risk built into the models used in employer-based insurance plans. While this conservative shift raised some alarm bells for liberal feminists, feminist divorce reformers saw new financial instruments as another opportunity to win access to retirement accounts for homemakers. They quickly organized to push a partnership understanding of marriage into the regulations for the new IRAs.

IRAs were not the first retirement savings device that feminist divorce reformers had sought to tailor to divorced women's needs. In 1970, Congressman Bertram Podell (D-NY) introduced legislation proposing to create Keogh accounts for homemakers. (Created in 1962, over a decade before IRAs came into existence, Keogh accounts are pre-tax retirement savings accounts for self-employed people and small-business owners.[84]) Podell's plan designated wives as "'independent proprietors' in charge of a specific amount of money—that used for the feeding, the housing, and the clothing of her family."[85] Women could pay into a personal Keogh account with money they saved—up to $25 (roughly $163 today) per week, a total of $1,250 per year—through their "weekly management of the household."[86] By relying on homemakers' shopping savvy, this plan made married women responsible for their own retirement savings and clearly assigned value to homemakers' work.

Podell discussed his bill as an important complement to any Social Security for homemakers legislation. He argued, "Social Security, as attractive as it is, is still something that comes from the Government. This retirement plan is something a woman has created for herself over the years, perhaps the only tangible reward of decades of hard work in making a home and raising a family she will know in her old age."[87] Podell thus argued his plan did more to recognize the value of women's work in the home than Social Security for homemakers because women's own actions resulted in the savings. Nevertheless, the underlying ideology behind his plan was quite similar to the ideology informing the Social Security for homemakers proposals. Both the Podell plan and Social Security for homemakers bills sought to value women's work in the home independently of the value of their partners' salaries.

Like the proposals for Social Security for homemakers, Podell's plan languished in Congress.[88] When Nader published his article on retirement pensions, he argued the failure of the Podell plan lay at women's feet. He wrote, "A number of proposals pending before Congress have been ignored, shunted aside, or defeated because women have not fought hard enough for their rights in this crucial area of security benefits for women."[89]

The same could not be said about the new IRAs. Almost as soon as the new retirement program was created, women began to suggest ways it could help divorced women. Betty Berry, for example, argued that the new law should allow women to use alimony payments to establish IRAs.[90] A woman from California, Rachel Liss, wrote to the chairman of the House Ways and Means Committee, "Sometime ago Congress held a hearing regarding Social Security for homemakers. I realize that this would be a considerable burden for the Social Security Administration, therefore, I would like to propose an alternate retirement plan for homemakers."[91] Liss went on to propose IRAs for homemakers. Under Liss's plan, women could set aside up to 15 percent of $8,500 a year (based on the Chase Manhattan study of the value of a wife's work) in an IRA account.[92] Another woman, Sophie Ross, wrote to her senator, William Roth (R-DE), about a similar idea. Ross objected to feminists' campaigns for wages for housework because she worried about how such income would be taxed. She preferred her IRA proposal because it allowed women to put aside money for their retirement tax-free.[93]

Roth liked Ross's proposal and drafted legislation allowing breadwinning spouses to create and contribute to IRAs for their dependent spouse if the couple filed a joint tax return. Under the bill, each spouse could have a yearly contribution made to their account with the maximum contributed to each account based on the couple's joint gross income for the year.[94] Roth's proposal had much in common with the Frasers' earnings sharing proposal, which emerged in Congress around the same time. Like earnings sharing, Roth's proposal treated each partner as an equal contributor to the marriage and allowed each to receive the same retirement pension. Also like the Fraser proposal, Roth only allowed marriages to be treated like an economic partnership if couples filed a joint tax return. While Social Security for homemakers proposals and Podell's plan sought to compensate all homemakers similar amounts for doing similar work, IRAs, like earnings sharing proposals, based a woman's future retirement security on a couple's combined earnings.

In 1977 Congress passed IRA legislation inspired by feminist divorce reformers alongside Social Security reforms. This legislation was far more limited than Roth's initial proposal. An employed spouse with his own IRA whose spouse had no other source of income could now choose to contribute to an additional sum to his IRA on behalf of his spouse; however, the maximum IRA contribution only went up by $250, to $1,750 total.[95] In the event of a divorce, a homemaker would be entitled to half of the account; but women receiving alimony payments still could not use them to set up their own IRAs. By creating an equally divisible account, the new IRA provisions for homemakers reflected the understanding of marriage that feminist divorce reformers had settled on as their policy ideal: spouses as equal partners, earning equal retirement accounts. Yet, by pairing this option with a miniscule increase in allowed savings, Congress discouraged the use of the new benefit, since it would decrease the retirement benefits for men who otherwise would likely keep their entire $1,500 IRA in a divorce.[96]

The new IRA law, like reformed Social Security laws, undervalued women's work in the home. By setting the maximum contribution to an IRA on behalf of a homemaker spouse at one-sixth of the contribution permitted by a worker, the IRA legislation offered even less recognition to homemakers than Social Security's dependent benefit. Women rightly found this offensive, but were defeated by the limited expansion's promise to have a very minimal impact on the federal budget—neither decreasing tax revenues as much as equally sized contributions would have, nor increasing expenditures in the same way that earnings sharing proposals might have required of Social Security. While policymakers might pay lip service to the value of women's work in the home, there was never a broad willingness to recognize that value monetarily. The limits of the new IRA for homemaker provisions ensured that the issue would continue to be debated well into the 1980s.[97]

Women and Pensions at the End of the 1970s

In 1977, after signing major amendments to Social Security into law, Jimmy Carter established a President's Commission on Pension Policy. The commission was asked to consider the relationship between public and private and federal and local pension systems as well as the future financial stability of pension systems. Given the breadth of its assignment, the commission's hearings and reports over the next two years provide an excellent view into where debates about women's place in the retirement pension system stood at the end of the Carter administration.

The treatment of women by the pension system entered almost every commission conversation; Martha Griffiths, one of two women commissioners, made sure of it. To illustrate how unfairly the pension system treated divorced wives and argue for earnings sharing, Griffiths chose to make an example of Wilbur Mills, the longtime chair of the House Ways and Means Committee whose career had come to a dramatic end six years before, after a drunken run-in with the press while in the company of Argentine stripper Fanne Fox.[98] Griffiths explained to the commission, "When Wilbur Mills was going with Fanny [*sic*] Fox, if he had divorced Polly and married Fanny . . . he would had to have been married to Fanny a year or nine months . . . before she could have inherited that pension. But she would have gotten his pension. . . . And Polly, who had been married to him for 40 years would not have gotten a dime."[99] Why, Griffiths demanded, couldn't pensions be allocated to spouses on the basis of number of years of marriage instead of on the basis of whoever was last married to the wage-earner? With an earnings sharing system in place—not just for Social Security but for all employee pensions—Polly would have received the bulk of the pension and Fanne a couple months' worth, or, as Griffiths put it, "just what she deserved."[100]

Griffiths's pointed example proved effective. In November of 1980, the Commission issued an interim report endorsing earnings sharing along with policies treating private pensions as divisible property in a divorce, requiring a spousal signature before a worker could waive survivor benefits, and the pro-rating of pension benefits to years married for divorced women.[101] That same month Ronald Reagan was elected president.

Reagan's election revealed widespread support for welfare retrenchment at the same time that the Commission's support for feminist divorce reformers' pension agenda revealed broad support for certain expansions to the social insurance system. The new president had to navigate this tension carefully. He quickly found that feminist divorce reformers, whose agenda had already been edited to focus on private benefits, could help him find a path forward.

Reagan's election also signaled the rise of antifeminists as a powerful force in the Republican Party. Here the feminist divorce reform agenda was of less help. While feminist divorce reformers had narrowed their agenda to appeal to neoliberals disdainful of an expansive welfare state, they had not changed their position that marriage should be treated more as a contracted partnership than as a status. This was the line from which they found themselves retreating as they continued to push their agenda in the 1980s.

CHAPTER 7

An Expensive Endurance Test

Compromising Toward Success in the 1980s

Ronald Reagan beat Jimmy Carter by almost ten percentage points in the 1980 presidential election. Among women voters, however, Reagan won by only a single percentage point (46 percent of the vote, compared to Carter's 45 percent).[1] This new voting pattern generated tremendous concern within the Republican Party and a sense of possibility in the face of loss among Democrats.[2] As Republicans sought to close the newly dubbed "gender gap" and Democrats moved to capitalize on it, both parties put women forward as party leaders and worked to articulate policy agendas that appealed to women. Divorced homemakers' economic rights lay at the center of these agenda-setting efforts because divorced women helped create the gender gap. In the 1980s, even as many members of the white middle class changed party affiliation to become "Reagan Republicans," divorced women in this demographic continued to vote for Democrats. At a critical moment of change in the political parties' relationships with women, the feminist divorce reform agenda helped define areas of potential compromise and fundamental difference.

During the 1970s, through much debate, feminist divorce reformers settled on a message and a philosophy about how to understand contemporary marriage. They argued that no matter how a couple chose to divide the responsibilities of marriage, public policies should recognize that each spouse had a right to half of what they, together, earned. Feminist divorce reformers drafted bills and gave speeches that successfully convinced many people that every marriage was a partnership, but failed to rack up many legislative wins around this idea. By the end of the decade, feminist divorce reformers had begun to focus their demands on private insurance benefits rather than on the nation's large social insurance programs. In the 1980s, feminist divorce reformers agreed to even further compromise and walked back their insistence that legislation recognize marriage as a partnership—acknowledging not only the neoliberal turn but also the rising power of social conservatives. These compromises bore fruit.

While historians of Second Wave feminism often portray the election of Reagan as the end of feminists' hopes, a closer look at Reagan's early years in office shows an administration struggling to balance the demands of its antifeminist, "pro-family" supporters with the goal of winning back a share of the women's vote for the Republican Party.[3] At the same time, in response to the political power of social conservatives, feminists in Congress offered an increasingly unified opposition agenda. These new political conditions shifted the center of feminist divorce reform activism from the grass roots to political officials. As both parties fought for women's votes, women increasingly won leadership roles in the White House, Congress, and party infrastructure. These new leaders saw feminist divorce reformers' agenda as a place where they could still make legislative progress. Democratic presidential hopefuls Patricia Schroeder and Geraldine Ferraro along with Republican strategist Elizabeth Dole—herself a future presidential candidate as well as cabinet secretary and wife of Senate Majority Leader Bob Dole—all became central players in advocating for the feminist divorce agenda.

Feminist divorce reformers ended up as the winners of this moment when both political parties renegotiated their relationship with women. More of their retirement security and health care agenda became law in the early 1980s than at any other point. But this remarkable success resulted from feminist divorce reformers' repeated decision to compromise and shift their focus away from broad reforms that redefined marriage and restructured the social insurance system toward more targeted legislation that affirmed marriage as a status through which social insurance benefits should be distributed. While Congress proved willing to allow judges to recognize individual marriages as partnerships, it remained unwilling to declare all marriages partnerships in the eyes of the social insurance programs it controlled. Rather, legislators showed their ongoing commitment to distinguishing between marriages on the basis of their length. In the early 1980s, feminist divorce reformers wrote a new understanding of marriage into the law, but not the understanding for which they had originally fought. New laws increasingly determined women's rights to social insurance benefits like health insurance and pensions on the basis of the length of their marriages or their ability to pay.

The Election of 1980 and the Death of the ERA

In the early 1980s, feminists found themselves on uncertain ground. Extensive debate among different strands of the feminist movement about whom women should support in the 1980 presidential election—a three-way race between Carter, Reagan, and third-party challenger John Anderson—ended with the election of an administration with strong ties to the antifeminist backlash. Then, in 1982, after twelve years of fighting, the Equal Rights Amendment officially failed. Along with Reagan's election, the devastating defeat of the ERA forced feminists to define a new legislative agenda and political strategy.[4] The 1980 election foreshadowed the important role homemakers' rights would play in these efforts; all three candidates responded to the rise of social conservatism by putting forward women's rights platforms rooted in defending homemakers.

Feminists had not enthusiastically supported Carter in the lead-up to the 1980 election. Like many Americans, they expressed disappointment with Carter's ineffective leadership in the face of the Iran Hostage Crisis, the 1979 oil crisis, and continuing inflation.[5] Feminists saw Carter's failure to lead as directly affecting their own priorities. They argued that Carter had offered insufficient support for the ERA and abortion rights.[6] Only one state ratified the ERA during the Carter administration and two rescinded their ratifications.[7] In addition, feminists claimed Carter's reductions in government spending had particularly hurt programs that served women and that he had dragged his feet on many issues he had promised to support during his first campaign, including displaced homemakers legislation.[8] In 1980, NOW refused to endorse Carter.[9] During the primaries NOW lent its support to Ted Kennedy. In the general election, the organization threatened to support independent candidate, John Anderson.[10]

Carter somewhat half-heartedly fought for the women's vote by highlighting his accomplishments improving homemakers' economic security. Surrogates for the Carter campaign were urged to advertise the 1977 Social Security amendments as an "outstanding achievement of the Carter administration."[11] Carter's assistant on women's issues, Sarah Weddington, compiled a report on Carter's feminist record that highlighted the creation of displaced homemakers centers and the ways in which Carter's proposed health care plan would help divorced women.[12] Nevertheless, feminists, like much of America, remained skeptical.

NOW's threat to support Anderson resulted from a deliberate strategy on the part of his campaign to take advantage of feminists' dislike of both major party candidates. Anderson, a Republican congressman from Illinois, decided to run as a third-party candidate after losing the Republican primary. He presented himself as the moderate alternative to Reagan, explicitly opposing the Republican Party's embrace of the Christian Right's social agenda and appealing to Republican feminists.[13] He began by hiring a woman to be his national campaign director, a historic first. Anderson also hired feminist activist and civil servant Catherine East as his coordinator on women's issues.[14]

East was a revealing choice. A longtime but relatively conservative women's rights advocate, East had led the opposition to the inclusion of a lesbian rights resolution in the International Women's Year Plan of Action.[15] For Anderson's platform, East developed a "Justice for Women" plank that focused on homemakers' rights as the source of Anderson's concern for women's rights and support for the ERA. In a campaign speech explaining this plank, Anderson argued, "The ERA is sorely needed because federal law and most state laws are based on the English common law, under which married women were chattel under the control of their husbands. They were considered incompetent to control their children, their property, or their own lives." Anderson promised that his administration would "seek modification of federal laws to conform with the principle that the contribution of wife and husband are of equal value and dignity."[16] Anderson thus rested his support for the ERA on a commitment to substantive equality and valuing care work done in the home. He promised action on feminist divorce reformers' priorities, including Social Security reforms to secure "equity for homemakers and wives employed outside the home" and a homemaker retirement rights bill.[17]

Despite the promise she saw in Anderson's campaign, East was ultimately disappointed. She resigned from the campaign a month before the general election in protest over its treatment of women. She wrote, "It seems clear that the campaign is not going to make a significant effort to attract the votes of women sympathetic to the issues on which Mr. Anderson has a positive position."[18] She pointed angrily to a series of public events at which Anderson had failed to highlight his support for women's issues. She continued, "I naturally cling to the belief that if I had been allowed to participate in the briefing, I could have convinced him of the importance of covering the ERA and economic security for the homemaker, as well as abortion," she wrote in her resignation letter.[19] Historians have seen the ERA and abortion dominating the debate over so-called "women's issues" in the 1980 election, but in East's analysis, there was a triumvirate of issues on which the women's vote would be won or lost.

While some GOP feminists defected to the Anderson campaign in 1980, others pushed back against Reagan's antifeminist supporters, unwilling to abandon a party that seemed to be turning on them. As the Reagan campaign tried to keep GOP women with them, it, too, turned increasingly to homemakers' rights. Reagan's campaign literature claimed to recognize homemaking as "as important as any other profession" and vaguely promised to address inequitable treatment of older women by Social Security and private pension plans.[20] More concretely, Reagan promised to expand individual retirement accounts for homemakers, a popular idea that fit easily into Reagan's larger agenda of shifting from a retirement system that emphasized shared public responsibility to a system emphasizing private, individual responsibility.[21]

Reagan's vagueness during his campaign allowed him to keep the remaining feminist Republicans and the growing antifeminist wing of the GOP in the same tent. In an effort to expand Reagan's base, his campaign created a Women's Policy Advisory Board, tasked with reaching out to women voters. Anti-ERA women quickly attacked the board, which the campaign purposefully filled with pro-ERA Republicans. In response, the campaign added Elaine Donnelly, one of Phyllis Schlafly's protégés, to the board. When this failed to satisfy the GOP's anti-ERA contingent, the campaign created a separate Family Policy Advisory Board.[22]

The Women's Policy and Family Policy Advisory Boards clashed over many policy issues, including the question of how to address homemakers' retirement security. In late October 1980, Ann Fairbanks, a Women's Policy Advisory Board staff member, wrote a memo arguing, "The traditional roles of a wife as a lifelong homemaker and a husband as a lifelong sole breadwinner are becoming less common, no one new pattern is emerging. Instead there is a growing diversity in family roles and lifestyles." Fairbanks had statistics on her side: Women had entered the workforce in unprecedented numbers; between 1970 and 1980 the labor force participation of women aged twenty-five through thirty-four increased by 20.5 percent and labor force participation of women aged thirty-five through forty-four increased by 14.4 percent.[23] Fairbanks claimed that this was undermining the current Social Security system. She wrote, "The proof of the inadequacy of the present system is the fact that widowed, divorced, and never married women account for 72% of all aged people living in poverty."[24] Fairbanks encouraged Reagan to endorse earnings sharing as the best solution to this problem because it "would reduce the penalties now being imposed on the increasing numbers of married women who opt to work outside the home, but not establish compelling incentives for women to enter the labor force. The rights of women who choose to be full-time homemakers would be preserved."[25] Fairbanks framed earnings sharing as an ideal policy proposal for Reagan. It would allow him to remain neutral on the appropriate role for a wife while offering support to the increasing number of married women in the workforce.

The Family Policy Advisory Board lobbied against any such neutrality. On 20 November 1980, the board sent the newly elected Reagan a memo claiming credit for his "stunning" victory and reminding him of their priorities. The memo informed Reagan, "It would be a tremendous blow to public confidence if the Social Security system were to terminate the wife's benefits, either through earnings sharing or any other method, thereby depriving a huge class of women of their anticipated retirement." The memo concluded, "The FPAB believes that the government's moral obligation to the wife is the same as it was in 1939. The traditional family structure of a lifelong marriage is more important today than ever before."[26] As soon as Reagan was elected, a critical group of his supporters informed him in no uncertain terms that he should ignore the tremendous changes in family structure that had taken place since the original creation of the Social Security dependent benefit for homemakers.

The conflict between pro- and anti- feminist Republicans continued to rage throughout the early years of the Reagan administration. But antifeminists won a huge victory in 1982 when the deadline (already extended once) for the ERA ratification passed without enough states endorsing the amendment to make it law.[27] The ERA had served as the heart of the liberal feminists' legislative agenda for over a decade. Feminists had argued that it would transform women's lives in the family and the workplace—making them equal political, economic, and social citizens with men. Antifeminists had also rallied around the ERA arguing it would hurt women more than it helped them. Efforts to reintroduce the amendment in Congress in 1983 and 1984 and begin a new ratification process failed. Equal citizenship for women in the home and in the workplace remained feminists' goal after the ERA died, but the nature of the fight changed.

By the time the ERA ratification campaign came to an end, feminists had lost support from the White House. In Congress, however, feminists could still count on a bipartisan coalition of legislators. Indeed, in the face of antifeminist opposition in the White House, congressional feminists offered a more unified agenda than they had through much of the 1970s because of the bipartisan Congressional Caucus for Women's Issues (CCWI), founded in 1977.[28]

The centerpiece of the CCWI's agenda-setting effort was the Economic Equity Act, omnibus legislation addressing a broad range of sex inequalities that was introduced by the CCWI every year from 1981 to 1996. The Economic Equity Act's first sponsors had intended the EEA to serve as enabling legislation for the ERA. Because they believed the ERA would require a reexamination of facial and substantive discrimination throughout the federal code, the EEA sponsors proposed omnibus legislation that began this process with bills covering everything from tax credits for child care to ending sex discrimination in insurance. When the ERA failed, the EEA remained. Throughout the 1980s, the individual provisions of the EEA were introduced separately in every congressional session and as a complete package. Although the EEA as a whole never passed, many pieces of it became law while the package itself continued to express the closest thing to a unified feminist legislative agenda.[29] It became a vehicle for feminists to win, one by one, the substantive changes they had hoped the ERA would have effected all at once.[30] These changes included a long series of provisions addressing the division of benefits in divorce.[31] Each of these bills was an opportunity for feminists to chip away at how federal law understood the roles of men and women in marriage—turning marriage from a breadwinner-dependent relationship in the eyes of the law into a partnership.

"Fear of Losing Government Benefits": Social Security Debates Under Reagan

In the first years of the 1980s, feminist divorce reform activist groups, new and old, embraced the EEA and, in particular, its Social Security provisions as a strategy for moving their larger agenda. In 1983, the NOW Legal Defense and Education Fund launched its Family Law Project, which directly replaced the LDEF's former ERA Impact Project, with staff moving from the one project to the other.[32] The new project's stated goals included achieving "legal recognition of marriage as an economic partnership."[33] NOW LDEF believed that the most strategically important place to win this recognition was in the nation's most universal retirement pension program: Social Security.[34]

At the same time that feminist activist organizations shifted their attention toward Social Security, feminist advocates within the White House also made this shift. Until just before the 1982 midterms, Reagan did little to address the gender gap. Then, worried that the gap might affect the upcoming election, Reagan created the White House Coordinating Council on Women in August of 1982. The new council failed to prevent a repeat of the 1980 election. When Democrats picked up twenty-six seats in the House of Representatives in the 1982 midterms, political analysts attributed Republican losses to their continuing failure to win over women voters.[35] Although the midterms did not change which party controlled the House (Democrats) or the Senate (Republicans), Reagan was increasingly concerned about the gender gap's potential consequences for his own reelection. He swiftly appointed Elizabeth Dole, the former head of the Coordinating Council, to be the first female Secretary of Transportation and continued to search for ways to reach out to women.[36] Before she departed, Dole wrote the administration a strategic plan suggesting that if they wanted to win back women voters they would have to focus on improving women's access to Social Security and retirement pensions.

Dole's emphasis on pension reform as a cure for the gender gap stemmed from a careful statistical analysis. When pollsters broke down the gender gap, they discovered that Republicans' biggest problem was appealing to nonmarried women. When they further analyzed the president's job approval rating among different groups of single women, pollsters found that widowed women disapproved of Reagan by eight percentage points, married women by ten percentage points, never-married women by twelve points, and separated and divorced women by a full fourteen points.[37] Reagan's pollsters thus credited the gender gap to "the confluence of population changes in the past decade (the growth of the number of single female headed households), the political predispositions of this group (liberal, Democrat), their general economic conditions (poor, dependent on government), and the impact of President Reagan's policies (hardest on those who rely on government to supplement their base incomes)."[38] In other words, single women could be understood as voting their economic interests when they voted against Reagan. The report explained, "Fear of losing government benefits appears to be causing women to oppose the Administration. Controlling for receipt of government benefits, the gender gap does decrease."[39]

Reagan's pollsters did not offer this explanation to make the administration feel better. They were careful not to let the administration blame the gender gap on race. "While the group of non-married women is disproportionately made up of Blacks, it is still 70 percent white," a memo to senior staff explained. "It would be a serious mistake to explain the President's poor showing among women as a factor of race."[40] The pollsters warned that as long as the number of never-married and divorced women continued to rise, the gender gap would continue to widen. If Reagan wanted to close the gap, he had to find a way to address these women's needs.[41]

The pollsters broke the numbers down even further to uncover that the divorced women most likely to break with their ex-husbands and vote against Reagan were those "with some college education (but no degree)." They explained that these women had generally interrupted their educations for marriage and then had the marriage dissolve, leaving them with "no degree and no marriage certificate." These women were thus "extremely vulnerable, without the support of either an education or a spouse, to the vicissitudes of the economy. This creates pressures that men who are separated or divorced (such men are twice as likely as women to have a college degree) do not face and results in a different appraisal of President Reagan."[42] In other words, Reagan had the weakest support among the very women that Tish Sommers had identified as "displaced homemakers" almost a decade before.

Displaced homemakers' dislike of Reagan was not just a response to his general attack on the social insurance system. In Reagan's first years in office, he specifically tried to cut Social Security programs that served single women. For example, in 1981, Reagan proposed eliminating the minimum Social Security benefit program. This little-known program provided a monthly benefit to retired workers who had a history of work in occupations covered by Social Security but who had not earned a sufficient Social Security entitlement through that work history.[43] Women composed over 75 percent of the recipients of the minimum Social Security benefit.[44] The women who received this benefit generally had left the workforce when young to care for their families, only entered the workforce after their children left home, or only worked part time. Often, they were women who, as the result of divorce before ten years of marriage or because they were married to an uncovered worker, could not collect dependent benefits. Congress passed an amendment cutting the minimum benefit in 1981. In response to pressure from feminist activists, the Conference Committee for the 1981 Social Security reforms restored the benefit to those already eligible for it but denied it to newly eligible recipients.[45]

Reagan's other proposed changes to Social Security also alarmed feminist divorce reformers in the first years of the new administration. Feminist divorce reformers pointed out that "60 percent of all unmarried women over 65 relied on Social Security as their only source of income."[46] As a result, the administration's efforts to cut Social Security benefits altogether by raising the eligibility age or by freezing the cost-of-living adjustments built into the program promised to be especially devastating to unmarried older women. Proposals to lengthen the work requirement to establish eligibility not only failed to take into account women's work patterns but would explicitly force women, who moved in and out of the workforce more often than men, to bear the brunt of cuts to the program.[47]

Along with defending against Reagan's proposed cuts to Social Security, feminist divorce reformers continued to push for their own agenda. In the early 1980s, the average divorced woman's Social Security benefit was only $283 per month (approximately $811 in today's dollars), compared to $406 per month for men.[48] In the face of this inequity, feminist divorce reformers continued to try and advance earnings sharing legislation, pitching the plan as a bipartisan, moderate solution.[49] They pointed out that both Elizabeth Dole and her husband, Senator Bob Dole, had voiced support for earnings sharing, as did Republican members of the National Women's Political Caucus.[50] Feminist divorce reformers also argued that in exempting estates passed from husband to wife from inheritance taxes, Reagan's own 1981 Tax Recovery Act had actually endorsed the idea that marriage was a "legally and economically equal partnership."[51]

Even as moderate Republicans offered their support to earnings sharing, Phyllis Schlafly's Eagle Forum continued to strongly oppose the proposal. Eagle Forum representatives argued that feminists were wrong to describe the status quo as awarding spouses "dependent benefits." Since spouses did not have to prove dependency in order to receive such benefits, the Eagle Forum argued the benefits rewarded their legal status as married, not their dependency.[52] One woman, Judith Finn, testifying on behalf of the Eagle Forum, argued that Social Security as "presently constituted allows women the freedom to choose different roles. By perpetuating the option to choose homemaking as a primary role, it stands in the way of the revolutionary notion of equality which says that men and women are not equal until the traditional division of labor within the family is abolished."[53] Antifeminists saw the original design of Social Security as an important protection for homemakers who they assumed were in permanent relationships; feminists saw the system as leaving women overly vulnerable because they believed relationships were unpredictable at best. Caught between these two positions, the Reagan administration focused on other reforms.

In his 1983 State of the Union address, Reagan promised to take action to "remedy inequities in pensions" as part of a continued effort to "promote equity for women."[54] The Social Security amendments that he signed in April of that year, however, did little to promote equity. The amendments, which passed relatively quickly and with bipartisan support, mainly focused on securing the finances of the Social Security system.[55] They did include small reforms allowing divorced spouses who were eligible to draw dependent benefits on their ex-spouses' records to collect when they reached sixty-two, whether or not their spouses retired (provided they had already been divorced for two years). In addition, the new amendments allowed disabled divorced spouses under sixty who remarried to continue to draw dependent benefits on their ex-spouses' records.[56] These amendments—which Dole had proposed in her strategy memo—continued the pattern established in the 1970s of amending the Social Security system to better serve ex-spouses in ways that specifically rewarded and encouraged marriage and dependency. Instead of ending the use of dependency to determine eligibility, they expanded the kinds of dependent status through which women could become eligible to draw benefits on the basis of their former marriages.

The 1983 amendments also mandated that the Health and Human Services secretary develop plans to implement earnings sharing proposals and report back to Congress by July of 1984.[57] To watchdog HHS's work on the mandated earnings sharing report, Tish Sommers quickly helped launch a new Citizen's Council on Earnings Sharing.[58] The new council issued a statement of principles in September of 1983, which began by rejecting any cost-neutral earnings sharing proposal, arguing that unless overall spending increased, any increase in benefits to one group would result in a reduction in benefits for another group. An early statement issued by the group read, "We believe a 'zero net cost' plan is unacceptable because it would be economically harmful to many women in the name of equity for others."[59] The council's principles also demanded that any earnings sharing plan cover not only retirement benefits but also disability and survivor benefits, balance equity and adequacy provisions, treat marriage as an economic partnership, and recognize the value of dependent care.[60] In addition, the council asked that special attention be paid to how any proposal would affect minorities. Following all of these principles would have moved the Social Security system away from privileging outdated familial labor arrangements that had never been the norm for any families outside of the white middle class.

When HHS finally issued its earnings sharing "implementation" report—six months late, in January of 1985—the agency expressed skepticism about all earnings sharing proposals. Indeed, it referred to the treatment of women by the Social Security system as only a "perceived" problem.[61] Although specifically instructed to develop proposals to implement earnings sharing, HHS did not include recommendations for implementation in the report.[62] Women's groups immediately protested. Congresswoman Mary Rose Oakar (D-OH), a sponsor of earnings sharing legislation, announced, "I am disappointed that rather than providing Congress with the recommendations we requested, HHS appears to have used the report to promote its own biases against earnings sharing."[63] Arvonne Fraser, who had proposed one of the earliest earnings sharing plans, expressed her disappointment in the language of the day by framing the issue in terms of taxes: "A taxpayers' revolt is threatening as young women, divorced women, and low income women are realizing they are subsidizing the system that is now filled with inequities," she warned.[64] Fraser suggested that without Social Security reform the nation would soon see single women fighting Social Security taxes in place of the middle-class suburbanites revolting over property taxes. In defiance of the report, earnings sharing appeared as a provision of the Economic Equity Act for the first time in 1985.[65]

Reagan's resounding reelection in 1984 allowed the administration to move away from worrying about the women's vote, and feminist Republicans' voices became further marginalized.[66] Despite its new place in the EEA, earnings sharing actually received less attention after 1984. Nevertheless, the debate within the Republican Party over earnings sharing proposals during the first Reagan administration reveals an often-overlooked moment of flux within the party. Ultimately, controversial and costly changes to the Social Security system had little chance of becoming law during an administration that wanted to spend less, not more, on social insurance programs, but the earnings sharing debate shows how complicated it was for the Republican Party to renegotiate its stance toward women and the feminist agenda. The defeat of earnings sharing along with the minor adjustments to the Social Security system that did pass between 1980 and 1984 signaled that social conservatism had joined fiscal conservatism in determining the realm of the possible. Marital status would continue to determine eligibility and size of Social Security benefits.

"We Serve, We Deserve": Ex-Wives' Rights to Federal Benefits

Social Security was not the only federally administered social insurance benefit through which the battle to redefine marriage as a partnership was fought in the 1980s. Throughout the decade, the EEA also contained a series of bills designed to give ex-wives rights to the pensions and health benefits of federal employees and military members. Pressure from ex-wives of federal employees led Congress to debate legislation along these lines in the 1970s, but a 1981 Supreme Court ruling that only Congress could decide if military benefits were divisible in divorce pushed the issue near the top of congressional feminists' agenda. The debate over how to handle federal benefits in divorce and the resulting variation in laws reveal the complicated ways that employment and marriage worked together to shape women's political and economic identities through the social insurance system. The legislation feminist divorce reformers ultimately won rested on their ability to convince legislators that divorced women were especially deserving of selective entitlements and, once again, deepened the use of marital status and dependency to determine access to social insurance benefits. Only women who met very specific qualifications—determined by both marriage and the nature of their husbands' jobs—won the privilege of a marriage recognized as a partnership.

In 1981, the Supreme Court heard the case of Richard and Patricia McCarty. The Supreme Court's involvement in a divorce settlement was exceptionally rare. In this case, however, federally controlled military retirement benefits ran into California's community property laws. Richard and Patricia had filed for divorce in California in 1976 after a nineteen-year marriage begun while Richard was in his second year of medical school. After the wedding, Patricia worked in paid employment for a year and then left her job.[67] Just before graduating, Richard joined the military.[68] For the next eighteen and a half years, Patricia did what so many wives did in the 1960s: She remained out of the workforce, raised four children, and supported her husband's career. In addition, as a military officer's wife, she relocated her family seven times.[69] When they filed for divorce, Richard was two years away from retiring from the military, at which point he would be forty-two, licensed to practice medicine in California, and drawing military retirement pay. He would also be eligible for lifelong military medical benefits and commissary privileges. Patricia was studying psychology and needed five to six more years of schooling to begin to practice.[70] The California divorce court divided Richard's military retirement benefits, along with the rest of the McCartys's property, equally between Richard and Patricia, as was the practice in community-property states. Richard challenged the ruling, claiming that Congress intended military retirement benefits to belong solely to the enlisted member of a couple.

In a 6-3 decision, the Supreme Court ruled in Richard's favor. It announced that military benefits could not be divided in a divorce unless Congress explicitly stated otherwise.[71] In the majority opinion Justice Blackmun argued, among other things, that Congress had designed the retirement pay system to encourage enlisted members of the military to retire and thus maintain a "youthful and vigorous" military force. Unless Congress changed its mind, Blackmun wrote, states had no right to do anything that might impair the achievement of this goal.[72]

By the time Blackmun issued his opinion, the organization of ex-military wives that had begun with the creation of Smail's Medical Equality for Dependents in 1977 had blossomed. In 1979, a group of ex-military wives in Virginia founded Ex-Partners of Servicemembers for Equality (Ex-Pose), which quickly became a national force.[73] When the Supreme Court issued its ruling, Ex-Pose and other groups of organized ex-military wives sprang to action, pushing Congress to state clearly that military benefits could and should be divided at divorce.

Activist ex-military wives argued that their marriages were the ultimate economic partnerships and insisted that the new expectation that married women build their own careers did not comport with the demands of military life. The National Military Wives Association reported that military families moved, on average, every two and a half years. While this level of moving "may be socially and culturally enriching," it wrote, "it becomes virtually impossible for the wife to establish a career which includes all the benefits of seniority, medical insurance, vesting in a retirement plan, and building the foundation of her own financial security."[74] This argument served as a direct rebuke to the increasing number of divorce court judges who questioned divorcing women who had allowed their careers and job skills to lapse.

Other military wives found statistics to show "the extent to which the former military wife had relinquished her own opportunity for a career to that of her husband's."[75] One study found that military husbands and wives generally entered marriage with same level of education but during the marriage the husband consistently had opportunities to advance his education and career. "At the end of their careers, 47% of husbands had a college education, 100% had well established job skills, 100% had substantial pensions, and 100% had free medical care for life."[76] Wives, on the other hand, had an average of one extra semester of college education and less than five years of work experience. Only 15 percent were involved in a pension plan.[77]

Military wives' absence from the workforce was not for lack of effort. By the late 1960s, outside the military, one in three married women was employed.[78] By 1979, military wives' employment rate matched that of civilian wives, but more military than non-military wives wanted jobs. The number of women looking for work but unable to find jobs was twice that for civilian wives.[79] Finding a job after each move was difficult especially since employers hesitated to hire women likely to move again.[80]

At the same time that they struggled to find paying jobs, military wives faced demands from the military for significant volunteer work. Organizations representing military wives did not complain about these demands, but they did argue that the expectations showed that even the military understood marriage as a partnership. The National Military Wives Association (NMWA) shared the story of one woman who was critiqued on her husband's evaluation. The evaluator described the husband as "outstanding" but went on to say, "I must criticize his wife's anti-social behavior which led to the disintegration of a group of wives who had been making significant contributions to the company and military community."[81] As a result, her husband was not recommended for any future assignments that would involve her. Another paper by the NMWA noted, "The Military services are fully aware of the importance of the wife's role and award special recognition certificates at the time of the serviceman's retirement for the wife's service to the country."[82] Women regularly sent these certificates to their elected representatives when asking for help.[83] These women accepted the demands of military life, but as one woman put it when sharing her story with the NMWA, "If I am required not only to work in my chosen career but his also, then why am I not entitled to half or part of the retirement benefits?"[84] Ex-Pose adopted the slogan "We Serve, We Deserve."[85]

Military wives viewed themselves as necessary partners in their husbands' service to the country but, in addition to arguing for benefits on this basis, they returned again and again to the idea that all homemaking was a job. One letter seeking support for the cause from a Catholic congregation argued, "Not to recognize the military wife's great contribution to our country demeans her as an individual and also demeans her God-given role as wife and mother."[86] With this sort of more general argument about the value of women's work in the home, military wives and their supporters engaged both strands of feminist arguments for Social Security developed in the 1970s: marriage was work and marriage was a partnership. Military marriage provided an extreme example of both of these aspects of a marriage.

Military wives' struggle became a bipartisan cause. A year before the court issued its ruling in *McCarty*, three members of Congress introduced bills addressing military wives' rights to their husbands' pensions. Congresswoman Schroeder introduced a bill—H.R. 2817—that mirrored earnings sharing proposals and proposed a pro rata division of military retirement benefits at divorce. At the same time, two congressmen introduced weaker bills compelling the military to abide by court orders to divide pensions, but leaving it to up to judges to divide benefits as they saw fit in each particular case. These bills gave those opposing Schroeder's bill an alternative way to express support for ex-military spouses, while refusing to change how federal law understood marriage.[87] Schroeder's bill was, as she explained, "based on the premise that, among other things, marriage is an economic partnership and that a spouse makes a significant contribution to the military employee's ability to go through the ranks successfully, and consequently receive a pension."[88] The alternative bills simply tossed the issue back to the courts, allowing judges to make decisions about the nature of marriage on a case-by-case basis.[89]

While military wives marshaled their partnership arguments in favor of Schroeder's bill, enlisted and retired military officers testified against Schroeder's bill and in support of the weaker legislation. Representatives from the Department of Defense argued that Schroeder's bill brought the federal government into decisions that should be left to the states.[90] Federalism arguments took on special significance in the military context because both military members and their spouses felt that they lacked control over their mobility. Enlisted members went where the military told them and their wives followed. Why, both sides asked, should their property rights be determined by the state where their marriage happened to end?[91]

The debate between legislation creating a presumption of a pro rata division of benefits and legislation simply allowing state courts to divide federal pensions as they saw fit ended in a standstill in 1980. The *McCarty* decision provided the push needed to get a bill passed. The unpopularity of the decision led both Democrats and Republicans to take up military spouses' fight. In September 1982, Congress passed legislation reversing *McCarty* as an amendment to the Defense Reauthorization Act of 1983. The new law addressed pensions, health insurance, and commissary privileges. It returned the power to decide what to do with military retirement benefits in divorce to state judges. In addition, it allowed select military spouses to continue to receive health benefits and commissary privileges, but this new access was granted to women as selectively entitled dependents, not as partners who had earned a share of military benefits.[92]

Feminist policymakers had faced a fundamental challenge as they advocated for a legislative response to *McCarty.* While the arguments that they marshaled rested on the extreme partnerships displayed by military wives, the benefits they demanded access to were extreme examples of the selective entitlement system. Military wives' initial robust social insurance benefits came to them through multiple selective entitlements. Their husbands had access to retirement and health security not only as employed men but also as men deemed uniquely deserving of strong benefits because of the risk of their job. Similarly, military wives received benefits not just because of their status as married women but because of their status as women married to enlisted men. The legislation Schroeder offered not only proposed to extend these benefits to divorced women but to change the basis on which they were offered. It was the latter part that proved impossible to win.

The new law, the Uniformed Services Former Spouses' Protection Act (USFSPA), favored the enlisted member of a divorced military member couple in its specifics. It did not contain Schroeder's provision creating a presumption that benefits would be divided on a pro rata basis. As importantly, the new law barred judges in community-property states from imposing community property rules on couples living in the state solely because of military assignment.[93] One of the traditional rights of the male breadwinner is to determine where his family lives. Under common law, a husband determined his wife's domicile—the location she lived in and thus the laws she lived under.[94] In the military, women's traditional lack of control over their domicile was matched by their husbands'. Through the USFSPA, the military restored and upheld men's traditional rights and reaffirmed women's dependence. The law established the federal rule that military retirement benefits not be considered joint property unless a military member actively chose to live under community property laws. It allowed husbands to maintain control over domicile even when they could not control where they actually lived.

Furthermore, the law awarded benefits to women on the basis of their continued dependency on their ex-husbands rather than as an entitlement earned through their work in their homes for their husbands and the military. This emphasis on dependency was especially clear in the legislation's health care provisions, which allowed women to continue to receive military health benefits if they had been married to a member of the military who had served for twenty years, if the marriage had lasted at least twenty years, and if at least twenty years of the marriage had overlapped with at least twenty years of creditable military service.[95] Under the new law, access to military benefits cut off if a woman remarried before age sixty. When the dependency ended—or, more accurately, was shifted to a new man—so did the benefit.

Divorced military spouses' campaign for benefits had rested on their contributions to their husbands' careers. They had argued for rights to benefits as partners. Instead, they won access to benefits as idealized dependents. Policymakers responded not to military wives' stories of work but to their stories of sacrifice. By the 1980s, many policymakers held the former wives of civilians accountable for not maintaining their careers during marriage, but the same policymakers recognized military wives as sacrificing their careers for their family and country. Mary Carson, one of the founders of Ex-Pose with a history of cancer had actually worked as a teacher for ten years, but had never built up any seniority because she started at the bottom each time she moved.[96] Policymakers suggested that it reflected positively on Carson and her fellow military that they remained dependent on their ex-husbands after marriage. Therefore they could be offered the protections of an expansive social insurance system.

Tellingly, while divorced wives of other federal employees tried to marshal similar claims about both the sacrifices they made and the value of housework in their campaigns for access to federal benefits, they failed to win the comprehensive legislation military wives did. Like military wives, Foreign Service wives pointed to the number of moves that came with an average Foreign Service marriage and their resulting inability to establish their own careers. One woman reminded members of Congress that Foreign Service wives actually received grades from the Foreign Service, which affected their husbands' chances of promotion, until 1972.[97] It was in response to these arguments that, in 1980, Congress passed a law regarding the division of Foreign Service pensions. But, while Foreign Service wives won earlier and better access to retirement benefits than military wives, they never won rights to medical benefits.[98] Foreign Service wives fought hard for these benefits, arguing that the Federal Employee Health Benefit Plan was one of the most valuable pieces of property that most Foreign Service families held.[99] Even arguments that it was only fair to give them the same privileges as military wives failed.[100]

By 1984, all ex-wives of federal employees had won some access to retirement benefits, with the striking exception of ex-wives of members of Congress.[101] The wives of Foreign Service officers and CIA agents had won a presumed pro rata division of benefits after ten years of marriage. The legislation regarding military and civil service spouses, on the other hand, simply allowed judges to divide retirement benefits as they saw fit.[102] Only ex-military spouses also won a right to health insurance through their ex-husbands.

Divorced military spouses spent the next ten years trying to win a more definite right to retirement benefits—a right based on their individual contributions to their marriages and the military, not their dependency on their ex-husbands. They pushed to eliminate the remarriage rule, lower the number of years they had to be married to access benefits, and create a presumption that retirement benefits would be divided on a pro rata basis.[103] These efforts met with limited success. Military wives never won a presumption of pro rata division of benefits, although they did manage to lower the number of years they were required to be married in order to access benefits to fifteen.[104]

On the surface, Congress had to answer the same question when passing each new law addressing former wives' access to their ex-husbands' retirement benefits: Should wives be understood as their husbands' dependents or as their partners? Ultimately, Congress answered this question by looking not just at what was required of wives but also what was required of husbands. As it had with Social Security, Congress proved unwilling to say that the average wife was an equal partner with her husband. Instead, Congress left it to judges to decide how civil service pensions should be divided on a case-by-case basis. Congress did decide that some wives served as partners to their husbands; specifically, legislators understood the wives of Foreign Service officers and some CIA agents to play a critical role in their husbands' work.[105] Notably, to be eligible for benefits, CIA wives had to live abroad for at least five years. Like Foreign Service wives, then, they could have spent a good deal of time representing the country—or blending in—abroad.[106]

Military wives performed jobs much like those performed by the wives of Foreign Service officers and CIA agents; however, it seems that in the eyes of Congress no amount of work on the part of wives could amount to a true partnership with a member of the military. In one hearing on the issue in the 1990s, Congressman Robert Dornan argued against the pro rata division of benefits using particularly revealing language. He claimed, "There is no spousal contribution that can even remotely compare to the ultimate sacrifice of the military profession—that of laying one's life on the line for our great nation."[107] Dornan's statement suggests that Congress refused to accept that spouses were truly equal partners in situations where one member of the couple routinely risked his life for the country. Instead, Congress chose to see military marriages as extreme examples of marital dependency. The sacrifices military wives made did entitle them to benefits but not as their husbands' equals.

The increasing complexity and variety in how federal employee benefit programs dealt with ex-wives was the logical outgrowth of the already fragmented social insurance system based on selective entitlements. Path dependency encouraged the elaboration of the welfare state through new entitlements for specific groups of people that legislators decided deserved support. These expansions of the welfare state that based new access to benefits on membership in a status group deemed worthy necessarily limited future expansions by pushing policymakers to weigh the claims of different possible recipients of benefits against each other instead of trying to achieve equality.

"As Personal to Me as My Lungs": Private Pension Reform in the 1980s

Only a few months after the Supreme Court's 1981 decision in *McCarty*, the Missouri State Supreme Court was asked to decide how to divide a private, employment-based pension at the end of another nineteen-year marriage. Eustis and Arlene Kuchta's marriage ended in 1979. Prior to that, Arlene had spent twelve years as a full-time homemaker. At her marriage's end, she was working three jobs—at a local hospital, as an adjunct at a junior college, and as a religion teacher—and earning an annual salary of $12,110. As was often true for such typically female-dominated jobs, none of these positions came with retirement benefits. Eustis, meanwhile, was an employee of TWA where he had worked for the last twenty-two years. He was covered by two retirement plans worth $11,505 at the time of divorce. He could begin to draw pension benefits of $300 a month within two years if he so chose, but if he worked until 1990, he would be eligible for payments of $771 a month. When dividing the couple's property, the divorce court had taken into account the present value of Eustis's retirement plan but did not consider the possible worth of future monthly pension payments.[108] The Missouri Supreme Court upheld this decision. Analogizing the case to *McCarty*, the court argued that the "Congressional purpose in setting up the military retirement plans mirrors the purpose of private market retirement plans as they have evolved to meet present social needs."[109]

In the wake of *McCarty*, feminist divorce reformers feared that unless Congress amended ERISA to specifically give divorced women rights to their ex-husbands' pensions, the Supreme Court could end up issuing a ruling about private, employment-based pensions very similar to the one it had in *McCarty*.[110] *Kuchta* proved how pressing this concern was. Feminist divorce reformers launched a fight for laws mandating a division of private retirement benefits along partnership lines in a divorce.

Congresswoman and 1984 vice-presidential candidate Geraldine Ferraro (D-NY) made women's access to private pensions one of her signature issues. She served as the sponsor of the Economic Equity Act's retirement equity provisions, which included provisions attacking women's unequal access to retirement pensions in two ways: first, by attempting to improve female employees' access to pensions, and second, by attempting to secure married and divorced women's rights to a share of their husbands' (or former husbands') employment-based pensions. Ferraro's Retirement Equity Act was a truly bipartisan bill, sponsored in the Senate by Republicans Bob Dole and Mark Hatfield.[111] Nevertheless, the act did not pass without debate and resistance on the part of men who felt they had earned their pensions on their own.

One fireman, Robert Cepale, wrote of his pension, "It is not 'PROPERTY.' It is my exclusive benefit I earned from all the fires I crawled towards. Earlier I stated that my pension is as personal as the skin and hair on my body. A better way to paraphrase is to say the pension is as personal to me as my LUNGS!"[112] Ferraro argued in response to Cepale that his wife had supported his work by caring for his home, his children, and even for him when he was sick.[113] Cepale did not accept this. "I haven't the foggiest idea what my wife 'nursing me back to health,' to use your words, has to do with my pension," he wrote back. "What has her tending my home have to do with my pension? I bring home a salary that justifies these efforts. She married me never expecting a share of my pension except in the event of my death."[114] Cepale neglected to mention the other circumstance under which his wife had expected to share in his pension benefits—if their marriage lasted. Many shared Cepale's anger. As with military pensions, men who believed their jobs came with special risks and sacrifices often found women's claim to be their partners galling.

Counterbalancing letters from men like Cepale was the flood of letters that Ferraro and others received from women about their lack of retirement security. Working women wrote about the problems caused by stringent continuous service requirements to collect pensions, widows wrote about the sudden discovery that their husbands had signed away survivors' benefits without telling them, and divorced homemakers wrote to defend their right to the pensions of men like Cepale. One divorced homemaker described her work this way: "I raised four highly successful children. My oldest daughter is an obstetrician and gynecologist at Yale Medical. She is also a scientist with a PhD. My son is a professor at Harvard. My two younger children also have advanced degrees and distinguished careers. My husband too retired with honors heaped on him. I worked hard for and with this family."[115] Like so many others, this woman argued that her work had been good for her family and for the country. Raising so many productive members of her society entitled her to a share of her ex-husband's pension.

Republican policymakers also received letters from women and men. For those trying to win women's votes for the GOP, pension legislation seemed to create an opportunity for Republicans to close the gender gap after the 1982 election. One member of Elizabeth Dole's staff wrote that the proposed pension reform piece of the EEA "reads like motherhood and apple pie—the essence is protecting widows from old age poverty by insuring that their interests are maintained in their own and spouses' pensions." She continued, "Pension reform has widespread support among women's organizations, both liberal and conservative, and this is certainly an issue which could demonstrate both sensitivity and compassion on the part of the President."[116] Other members of the Reagan administration, however, voiced concern. In particular, Michael Uhlmann, one of Reagan's special assistants, argued against including a mention of pension rights for women in Reagan's 1983 State of the Union. He wrote, "I want to emphasize once again here what I have on many occasions in the past. The pension issue is enormously complicated—legally, morally, financially, and politically."[117]

When Reagan finally settled on a private pension reform agenda, it was modest. He was willing to support requiring spousal signature to sign away survivor benefits; clearly allowing divorce courts to assign pensions in divorce; lowering the participation age for pensions to twenty-one; preventing retirement plans from counting maternity leave as a disqualifying break in service; and requiring retirement plans covered by ERISA to pay survivor benefits if a participant died after ten years of participation, whether or not they had fully vested.[118] Congress passed this list of provisions in the Retirement Equity Act (REA) of 1984.

Although feminist organizations supported the REA they believed it far from perfect. Testifying on behalf of NOW LDEF, one woman argued that while the REA did not punish women for maternity leave, it did not recognize maternity leave as work either. Moreover, the REA did nothing for women who took extended breaks from paid employment to raise children.[119] Much like the USFSPA, the REA clarified that pension benefits could be divided by a judge in a divorce but did not create a presumption of a pro rata division. Therefore, although Ferraro described the REA as "built on the belief that marriage is a partnership and that the work of both spouses should be rewarded with the retirement benefits they have earned together," the law actually did relatively little to advance the partnership model of marriage.[120] The REA's provisions to help homemakers gave them rights as their husbands' survivors and dependents. It also created the possibility of court division of pensions along partnership lines, a possibility not available for Social Security benefits in a divorce, but it did not entitle women to an earned share of their husbands' pensions as feminists had hoped.

In addition to the REA, Ferraro sponsored a bill to allow homemakers to create individual IRA accounts for themselves, up to $2,000 a year for each spouse.[121] This legislation was also introduced as part of the EEA and as a stand-alone measure.[122] The idea of IRAs for homemakers drew bipartisan support, including a 1983 endorsement from the Heritage Foundation.[123] Despite the idea's broad popularity, the Reagan administration proved hesitant to endorse IRA legislation.[124] The Cabinet Council on Economic Affairs worried about the tax revenue loss that would result from allowing homemakers to invest in IRAs and recommended against supporting the Economic Equity Act's IRA provisions.[125] The council noted, "The Administration has already adopted policies in this area to improve program coverage and availability . . . [and] this proposal is expensive, increasing the deficit by $.5 billion each year."[126]

Ferraro's work on IRAs turned them into a campaign issue in 1984 when she ran for vice president. Both Democrats and Republicans sought to claim the issue as their own, leaving many voters confused.[127] Ferraro received letters from women demanding that she use her power as vice-presidential candidate to get Democrats to pass the IRA for homemakers bill.[128] One woman wrote, "I want my four daughters, myself, every woman to have the freedom of choice—whether to work in the home or outside. . . . There are already many incentives for her to work outside the home, both monetary and psychological."[129]

The Mondale-Ferraro ticket's loss and Reagan's sweeping reelection seem to have closed the window of possibility for Republican feminists to truly influence the administration. In place of the Coordinating Council on Women, Reagan created a new Working Group on the Family to oversee policy on a similar set of issues in his second term.[130] As the name suggests, this new group was far more conservative than Dole's Council had been. The Working Group on the Family continued to debate making IRAs friendlier toward homemakers. In the last year of the administration, it again recommended allowing dependent wives to create individual IRAs at the same level as employed people.[131] The administration, however, remained hamstrung by the cost of such a proposal, and IRAs for homemakers were not expanded on Reagan's watch.[132]

By the end of the Reagan administration, feminist activism had won women better access to their former husbands' employment-based pensions. In a divorce court, judges could award women a portion of a pension if they chose. Divorced women received greater access to such pensions than they had to Social Security, which judges could not divide in a divorce, but they did not win any entitlements. This minor success did nothing to advance feminist divorce reformers' claims about the partnership nature of marriage. Unless a woman married a member of the Foreign Service or CIA, federal law did not understand her marriage as a partnership.

The new pension laws also began the process of making marriage a much better deal for women married to wealthier men. Universally available benefits could not be divided in a divorce, but women lucky enough to be married to husbands with pensions and IRAs might win access to those benefits in a divorce. Doing so required a good lawyer to make the case before a judge—another privilege available to wealthier women. Instead of creating the privileged status for the once-married that early feminist divorce reformers had advocated, the limited victories eked out by feminist divorce reformers in the 1980s reinforced the privileged status of the wealthy.

"They Left When He Did": Buying Back Health Benefits for Divorced Women

The outcome of feminist divorce reformers' fight for health care access in the 1980s provides one of the clearest examples of how social insurance regulations amended for divorced women came to reinforce income inequalities within the social insurance system. With Ronald Reagan's election, activists on the left lost the confidence they had held onto throughout the 1970s that there would be an inevitable overhaul of the private health insurance system. Liberals fought simply to hang onto the gains for women and expansions to the welfare state they had won in previous decades. Although feminist divorce reformers did not altogether abandon alternative options for getting divorced women health care coverage, they recognized that many of the reforms they fought for in the 1970s simply were not short-term possibilities. Insurance companies were winning on insurance discrimination; national health insurance proposals were falling apart; and federal money for women's health clinics was drying up.[133] In response, feminist divorce reformers focused more and more of their time on reforms specifically addressing divorced women's needs through targeted legislation that would allow women continued access to their ex-husbands' group health insurance plans. This strategy won women new access to health insurance, but as with pensions, this new access was mediated by wealth and marriage.

In October of 1980, Tish Sommers, the founder of the Alliance for Displaced Homemakers (ADH), which dissolved after the passing of the 1977 national displaced homemakers legislation, launched a new organization, the Older Women's League (OWL).[134] Like the ADH, OWL explicitly set out to appeal to older women suffering economically after the loss of a husband either through death or divorce. It ran recruitment ads with captions such as "When my husband was here, we had his pension, his medical benefits and his profit sharing. Unfortunately, they left when he did." And "For men, they created retirement plans, medical benefits, profit sharing and gold watches. For women they created Mother's Day."[135] At its launch OWL chose health insurance continuation and conversion legislation for divorced

Figures 2 and 3. The Older Women's League had these ads designed to recruit members. They capture the scope of loss and anger that women felt after a divorce when they realized how few economic resources they had access to in their own right. Images from Folder 16-20, Tish Sommers Papers, Special Collections, San Diego State University.

women as "one of three key national issues on which the organization will focus."[136]

Continuation and conversion legislation sought to create a way for those who lost access to group insurance through divorce or loss of a job to remain in the group pool. While limited versions of this policy existed in some states in 1980, OWL's first national agenda explained that existing state conversion bills typically provided only "limited benefits and [were] very expensive." It continued, "OWL will prepare a model conversion bill for introduction into state legislatures to provide a vehicle for bringing the problem older women face into the limelight." The objectives to be incorporated into the model bill were:

1. All group health plans should offer conversion rights to persons leaving the group.
2. The severed dependent should remain a member of the group at group premium rates for at least one year.
3. The conversion policy should contain benefits equal to the group plan.
4. Premium costs should not exceed group premium rates.
5. Premium rates should not be segregated by sex.[137]

These objectives acknowledged many of the problems that women had identified with the insurance system, but they also reveal a significant narrowing of feminists' goals. In the 1970s, Sommers had tried to address divorced women's health crises by channeling government money toward women's self-help clinics. This proposal had both challenged the male-dominated, sex-discriminatory insurance system and demanded expanded government support for divorced women's health care. In the 1980s, on the other hand, Sommers's organization supported conversion and continuation legislation that suggested insurance companies were the best hope for getting divorced women continued access to care and said nothing about the government assuming a share of the cost.[138]

OWL began its work by trying to get its model conversion bill introduced at the state level. For example, Alice Kitchen, the executive director of Kansas City's United Way, spearheaded a project to win health insurance conversion and continuation legislation in Kansas and Missouri. With support from OWL and also WEAL, she managed to get both states to pass the legislation, despite their conservative legislative bodies, but to do so she had to offer many significant compromises.[139] In Kansas, the legislation gave divorced women only six months on their ex-husbands plans; in Missouri, Kitchen won women nine months.[140] Nevertheless, WEAL and Kitchen celebrated the passage of these bills as victories for women in states where such victories were few and far between. They sent women with personal stories on the road to talk about the law's effects and make sure other women knew they could take advantage of it.[141]

Feminist divorce reformers' investment in conversion and continuation legislation was complemented by a similar turn by labor. In the 1970s, labor had fought for Medicare or Medicaid for the unemployed. In the meantime, labor unions also started negotiating continuation provisions into their contracts. By 1983, all major UAW contracts included continuing health insurance coverage paid for by the employer for up to a year after layoff, depending on seniority. At Ford and GM, the most senior employees could qualify for a lifetime of paid health insurance coverage after a layoff.[142] The Steel Workers negotiated similar contracts.[143] In congressional hearings, labor representatives tried to turn these contractual wins into public policy that would benefit non-union workers. UAW President Douglas Fraser called on Congress to require private insurance to provide longer continuation periods for laid-off workers and to offer public financing for the cost of continuing health insurance for unemployed workers for at least a year after layoff.[144] In all of these proposals labor was more ambitious in its demands than divorced women, who had abandoned any hope of the government's paying for most divorced women's continuing health insurance.

The combined lobbying of labor and feminist divorce reformers led to real success at the state level. By 1983, thirty-seven states had adopted some form of continuation or conversion legislation for unemployed workers; twenty of these states also included provisions for divorced women in these bills.[145] Sommers had always believed that success at the state level would put pressure on Congress to act.[146] In 1985 she was proven correct when continuation legislation for divorced women was incorporated into the Economic Equity Act.[147]

Before 1989, only three provisions in the Economic Equity Act proposed to expand women's access to health care: a ban on sex-discrimination insurance; health insurance for ex-military wives; and continuation and conversion legislation.[148] Divorced women had successfully convinced feminist lawmakers to make them the primary recipients of new selective health entitlements. The entitlements within the EEA were far less robust than the ones feminists had lobbied for in the 1970s. Continuation and conversion legislation was by no means equivalent to Medicare. Moreover, the EEA proposal did not even offer the level of aid that labor unions had pushed for in their continuation and conversion legislation. Under the EEA, the person continuing the insurance was responsible for its cost, and the government offered no subsidies to help. In same way that the ECOA and REA only truly helped the well-off and middle-class formerly married women, continuation and conversion legislation offered improved insurance options to only an elite group of women who had married and could afford the cost of care.

Despite their drawbacks, as the campaign for conversion and continuation laws progressed, feminist divorce reformers moved from framing the bills as "emergency legislation" that would complement the rest of the feminist divorce reform agenda to making them the centerpiece of their health care agenda. This was partially the result of the narrowing prospects for comprehensive health care reform legislation. Even Ted Kennedy, the longtime champion of a single government health insurance plan, came to believe that the only way to create a guarantee of health insurance coverage in the United States was through an employer-based system.[149] Employer-based plans, however, were inherently risky for women who moved in and out of the workforce. Thus, the inclusion of conversion and continuation plans specifically addressing divorced women's needs increasingly became the litmus test by which feminist divorce reformers judged employment-based national health insurance proposals.[150] Instead of advocating for a national health insurance plan that covered women as individuals, in 1985 OWL endorsed Kennedy's new Health Initiative Program even though it used the marriage and employment-based distributive mechanisms of Social Security.[151] One of the main things OWL celebrated in the legislation was the inclusion of insurance conversion rights for women who lost their husbands.[152]

The Health Initiative Program did not become law, but more than ten years of hearings about how to address loss of group health insurance coverage finally resulted in the passage of a national continuation and conversion law through the Consolidated Omnibus and Reconciliation Act (COBRA) of 1985.[153] COBRA allowed divorced women to stay on their ex-husbands' health insurance plans for up to three years (twice as long as it allowed the unemployed to continue their coverage) if they paid both the employee and employer premiums. It also allowed employers to charge women 102 percent of the cost of their insurance plans.[154] Despite the extremely high cost of this plan, women's organizations celebrated the passage of COBRA. OWL told its members to "Hold that Divorce!" until after that law went into effect and described the new law as a "lifesaver."[155] WEAL and OWL both planned major educational efforts around the law.[156]

Women's organizations were not wrong to celebrate COBRA. The law represented substantial savings for middle- and upper-income divorced women who could afford the high cost of continuation and conversion. Divorced women understood that continued access to group insurance plans represented both cost savings and comprehensive coverage that could represent the difference between life and death to economically vulnerable divorced women. Yet, the celebration represented a narrowing of divorced women's vision for the welfare state. After a decade of championing alternate health care delivery systems or expansions of national health insurance as the best ways to protect divorced women's access to health insurance, feminist divorce reformers ended up celebrating a law that allowed them to pay exorbitant prices to purchase privately run, sex-discriminatory health insurance.

Whereas in the 1970s divorce reformers' health insurance proposals had held out the promise of helping all single women by decoupling eligibility for insurance and marriage, COBRA gave divorced women access to health insurance options that women who never married did not have. On the basis of their former marriages divorced women could purchase, at least for a time, more affordable health insurance, potentially keeping them from having to rely on Medicaid or go without. They could maintain their privileged position in the social insurance system, if they were able to pay for it.

An Expensive Endurance Test

Aided by the active support of the most powerful women in both political parties, between 1980 and 1985 feminist divorce reformers managed to eke out a series of wins. National legislation specifically addressed divorced women's retirement and health security by giving them access to their ex-husbands' employment-based retirement pensions and health insurance. Feminist divorce reformers' success at winning expanded access to employment-based benefits in the face of an administration that was both affirmatively trying to roll back social insurance provisions and in the grips of an antifeminist revolt is striking. These wins, however, came with a price. The new laws addressed only limited employment-based benefits and the access they offered women was contingent on their marital status and, in some cases, wealth.

The new legal regime reinforced the existing divisions between low-income and middle- and upper-income women.

These new policies did almost nothing to make the law recognize marriages as economic partnerships. The breadwinner-homemaker model of marriage remained firmly embedded in public policy. The Reagan administration was unwilling to reduce benefits for marriages arranged along breadwinner-homemaker lines, unwilling to sacrifice revenue in order to recognize all marriage as partnerships, and unwilling to raise taxes. It therefore only expanded access to benefits by allowing courts to redistribute husbands' benefits to their ex-wives or force ex-wives to pay for new benefits. This satisfied many wealthy divorced women, but did little to implement the philosophy of marital partnership that feminist divorce reformers had articulated in the 1970s. Instead, the new laws created new access to benefits by forcing ex-husbands to support their ex-wives or ex-wives to pay for that access. These laws rewarded marriage and drew lines between single women who had once been married and those who had not. They continued a long tradition of policies that privatized solutions to women's dependency by finding a man to support them.

The new laws did not simply affirm old understandings of marriage. Even as Congress largely rejected the idea of marriage as a partnership, it slowly created a new legal regime that treated marriage as an exercise in longevity. Each new law created new divisions by transforming marital status from a uniform category to a series of statuses. Women gained increasing rights to their husbands' or ex-husbands' support over the course of their marriages. After nine months of marriage, married women had access to Social Security through their husbands; after a year they had a right to private pension benefits through their husbands; and after ten years they had a vested right in dependent Social Security benefits through their ex-husband. This changing menu of benefits suggested that marriage was no longer a single status, but a status that changed and improved over the years.

Policymakers could have chosen any number of other signifiers to judge whether a marriage made women eligible for selective entitlements: for example, presence of children, years of full-time homemaking, or just the simple fact of having a marriage certificate. Among these options, feminist divorce reformers and their supporters in Congress gravitated toward years married as the measure of a marriage. A charitable reading of this decision argues that by focusing on length of marriage, feminist divorce reformers refused to let legislators define marriage substantively.[157] A less charitable reading argues that their focus on the length of marriage as opposed to the presence of children grew out of class bias. By refusing to claim benefits on the basis of their role as mothers, feminist divorce reformers drew yet another line between their own position and that of women on welfare, whose eligibility for benefits rested entirely on their children. Either way, by choosing duration as the way of measuring if people were sufficiently married, legislatures made a statement about what being married meant.[158] Perhaps predictably, in a world concerned with the increasing likelihood that marriages would not last, policymakers signaled that marriage was about the length of commitment above all. As Arvonne Fraser put it, they signaled that marriage was an "endurance test."

PART III

Stable Divorce Rates and Unstable Politics

CHAPTER 8

"Responsibility, Equity; Not Cruelty"

Changing Venues for Feminist Divorce Reformers

As he prepared for his 1982 State of the Union address, Ronald Reagan found himself lobbied from many directions to take a stand in the ongoing debates about the nature of the family. Senator Roger Jepsen (R-IA) pushed for the speech to clearly support the Family Protection Act. He wrote, "Over the past decade we have seen government policies expand under the guise of solving human problems in the areas of health, education, and social service. These programs have been put into place and allowed to run their course with little or no consideration being given to the impact upon the family."[1] Jepsen believed the Family Protection Act would return "the balance" toward the family by, for example, encouraging educational materials to present homemaking as a choice for women and denying federal funding to legal aid clinics that took divorce cases.[2] At the same time that Jepsen and his allies sought to strengthen and further the federal government's active support of breadwinner-homemaker families through the FPA, Republican feminists continued to push the administration to recognize a diversity of family forms through the Economic Equity Act. Reagan mentioned neither bill in his 1982 State of the Union. The face-off over these two pieces of omnibus legislation was not resolved by a greater show of strength from one side, but rather through a slow process of compromise around the least expensive measures in each. Throughout the Reagan administration, both feminists and antifeminists failed to convince the president to invest in costly legislation regarding the family.

As they ground out victories and adjusted to setbacks in Congress, feminist divorce reformers consciously began to reorient their work toward the judiciary. This constituted a significant shift from the 1970s when feminist divorce reformers in NOW resisted enacting their agenda through the courts, which they viewed as overly patriarchal. This is not to say important victories had not been won in the courts in the prior decade. Arguably, the judiciary is where the most progress on the feminist agenda had been made, as Ruth Bader Ginsburg's ACLU Women's Rights project won a critical series of cases in the Supreme Court. Nevertheless, feminist divorce reformers' focus had been largely trained on legislative change. While Ginsburg had won facial equality in Social Security and other federal laws, feminist divorce reformers had sought to supplement these victories by winning legislative reforms to these programs that promised homemakers substantive equality.[3] In the 1980s, however, as they lost faith in the executive and legislative branches of government, feminist divorce reformers saw more room for success in enacting their partnership vision of marriage through litigation than legislation.

This shift toward the judiciary as a means of winning substantive equality was not unique to feminist divorce reformers. Feminists seeking an expansive interpretation of Title VII made a similar shift in the 1980s when they began to pursue comparable worth litigation.[4] In both cases, feminists took advantage of the legislative gains they had made in the 1970s when they turned to the courts in the 1980s. Even as newly empowered antifeminists sought to turn back the clock on these earlier victories, courts continued to be informed by them. Feminists' legislative successes also pushed activists to the courts more directly. Federal legislation won in the 1970s and early 1980s had often struck a compromise between feminist divorce reformers and their opponents by empowering judges to administer benefits as they saw fit. To ensure these new laws worked for them, feminists had to put resources into ensuring that judges understood marriage as a partnership.

Along with the shift toward the judiciary, NOW's feminist divorce reformers also turned more of their attention to state legislation as the 1980s progressed. This, too, was a response to unfavorable political conditions at the federal level. In 1987, a newly reconstituted NOW committee on marriage began advocating for common law states across the country to adopt community property laws. If they could not win community property assumptions for specific federal programs, feminists decided they would turn to state-by-state efforts and hope that state action would eventually pressure the federal government to act.

Both the turn toward the judiciary and toward the states were of a piece with the narrowing of the feminist divorce reform agenda. The federal legislation feminist divorce reformers had demanded in the 1970s was costly. Their proposals to socialize the risks of female dependency rested on creating collective responsibility for the hidden costs of women's labor in the home. Like the legislation they advocated in the 1980s, the venues in which they advocated necessarily narrowed this demand. The courts could not expand the welfare state's budget; nor could state laws ever reach as broad a swath of people as feminist divorce reformers' most expansive federal legislation.

By the end of the decade, the combination of the new judicial precedents feminist divorce reformers had won worked in conjunction with their legislative successes at the state and national level to create a legal system that favored wealthy women and recognized some, but not all, marriages as economic partnerships. Women with the means could go to court with lawyers and win divorce settlements that treated them as equal partners to their husbands. These divorce settlements might award women shares of their husbands' private pensions and continuing support in the form of health insurance payments. On the other hand, women who could not afford an expensive lawyer or, just as likely, whose husbands did not have robust, divisible benefits did not have similar outcomes available. Low-income women continued to be treated as their ex-husbands' dependents by the federal statutory regime that governed their eligibility for economic resources. As such, they had limited access to their ex-husbands' property, including government entitlements and employer-based benefits.

When Jepsen appealed to Reagan to endorse the Family Protection Act in his State of the Union address, he reminded Reagan of their "shared concern that the elitist attitude of the federal government has been one of the key factors in the breakdown of the family unit."[5] Jepsen and Reagan were right to see an "elitist attitude" in the federal governments' regulation of marital property, but this was the result of compromises they, along with their antifeminist allies, had advocated in the name of family preservation. The reforms won in the late 1970s and 1980s pushed low-income women into the workforce by refusing to value their work in the home, while increasing the likelihood that upper-income marriages would be recognized as partnerships. On Reagan's watch, marriage not only became a much better bargain for rich women than poor but also, more deeply than ever, an institution that reproduced class inequality.

"Great Society Twaddle": The Limits of Legislative Compromise Under Reagan

The Family Protection Act and the Economic Equity Act were almost mirror images of each other—one outlining the agenda of antifeminists in the 1980s, the other outlining the agenda of feminists. Neither of the full bills ever received a floor vote, but many of their individual provisions did.[6] Historians have paid little attention to either bill, and even those historians who have considered one of these pieces of legislation have not put them together.[7] Taken together, they can be understood as helping to define the ongoing struggle between the Right and Left in Congress over the appropriate definition of the family in public policy in the 1980s. Even as they disagreed vehemently on policy, the two sides came up against the same challenge: costly reforms proved nonstarters for the Reagan administration.

The Economic Equity Act became the centerpiece of congressional feminists' agenda in the 1980s. As we have seen, the Social Security and employer-based pension provisions of the EEA played a particularly crucial role in feminists' efforts to use the omnibus bill to redefine marriage as an economic partnership. In addition to its many pension provisions, early versions of the EEA included legislation that would have banned sex discrimination in insurance, created tax credits to help working parents afford child care, improved the enforcement of child support and alimony, created job training programs for women, and more.[8] All of these different components aimed to eliminate from the federal code the idea that, as Ruth Bader Ginsburg put it, "the adult world is (and should be) divided into two classes—independent men, whose primary responsibility is to win bread for a family, and dependent women, whose primary responsibility is to care for children and household."[9] In place of this concept, the EEA attempted to assign real value to women's work in the home and to treat marriages as partnerships.

In contrast, the Family Protection Act read as a "tidy wish list for the New Right."[10] The sponsors of the FPA believed the legislation would protect "the role of women as it has been historically understood." Pushed to explain what this meant, its supporters wrote, "Traditionally, the role of the woman has been that of mother and homemaker just as the role of the man has been that of father and provider."[11] In order to protect the breadwinner-homemaker family, the FPA would have removed the government from any action conservatives believed directed people away from this family structure. For example, the FPA proposed to ban the government from providing any funds to organizations that condoned "gay or lesbian lifestyles." But the FPA did not simply seek to promote the breadwinner-homemaker family by limiting government intervention. It also included legislation to affirmatively promote a particular vision of the family, for example, expanded IRA deductions for homemakers.[12] A *Congressional Quarterly* article from 1981 predicted these affirmative proposals would ultimately cost billions.[13]

Even more than it defined the fight between feminists and antifeminists, the debate over the EEA and FPA defined Republican feminists' fight for their party. Although they self-identified as a "dying breed," in the early 1980s, Republican feminists refused to go down without a fight.[14] They pushed for Republican endorsements of at least portions of the EEA instead of the FPA. The National Women's Political Caucus had a Republican leader, Kathy Wilson, from 1981 to 1985. Wilson worked to use her position to pull the Reagan administration in a more feminist direction.[15] The NWPC explicitly denounced the FPA and endorsed the EEA in 1981, writing that the FPA represented "a major attack against those who believe in civil liberties, family planning, sex education, freedom of speech, and a high quality objective education for children of every background."[16] Wilson spent the next year arguing with the Reagan administration directly and berating them in speeches for not endorsing the EEA.[17] Republican members of the Congressional Caucus on Women's Issues also lobbied the Reagan administration to endorse the EEA and reject the FPA.[18] In 1982, Congresswoman Olympia Snowe (R-ME), who co-chaired the CCWI, wrote Elizabeth Dole and Reagan's chief of staff, Jim Baker, expressing hope that Reagan would endorse the EEA at the start of the next session of Congress.[19]

Even after Republican's failure to win women's vote in the 1982 midterm election, Reagan did not endorse the EEA in 1983. In fact, by the middle of that year, he had made it clear in repeated meetings with Republican feminists that he would not endorse either the EEA or the FPA in full because of concerns about the cost of many of their provisions.[20] While Reagan did offer support for select portions of each bill, he shied away from any provision in either bill that threatened to diminish government revenues.[21] Even where tax cuts to aid homemakers were a shared priority of the Left and Right, the Reagan administration's opposition prevented them from becoming law. The

FPA contained a few items on feminist divorce reformers' wish list, including legislation directing the military to garnish support payments automatically from military members' monthly pay and legislation to expand IRAs for homemakers. Both of these provisions had parallel provisions in the Economic Equity Act. While military wage garnishment became law in 1981, IRAs for homemakers were not expanded in the 1980s.[22] It was not a coincidence that the provision that cost the government next to nothing was the one that moved forward. In 1983, Reagan's Office of Policy Development argued against an expansion of IRA deductions because the Treasury Department estimated increasing the limit on contributions to spousal IRAs would cost $500 million a year in foregone revenue.[23]

Reagan also opposed creating a dependent care tax credit, granting tax-exempt status to day care centers, and expanding tax credits to employers who hired displaced homemakers.[24] Again, he cited cost. The Office of Management and Budget estimated the total revenue lost through all the provisions of the 1981 EEA would amount to $12 billion by 1986.[25] Of the proposed tax credit to encourage the hiring of displaced homemakers, Reagan's special assistant Michael Uhlmann wrote, "Sounds like Great Society twaddle to me. How 'bout a job tax credit for 'Displaced Political Appointees'? Reformed Alcoholics and Drug Addicts? Ex-Cons? Somewhere, somehow, we've got to get away from the idea that the federal treasury (front door or back door) is the only or best place to petition for the redress of life's grievances."[26]

The Reagan administration's active opposition to tax cuts—even tax cuts explicitly designed to encourage the homemaking role of women—is striking. Reagan is frequently accused of attempting to balance the budget on the backs of women by cutting social welfare programs that specifically helped women. Scholars also generally show Reagan to have favored tax cuts and worked to reduce government tax revenues.[27] When it came to tax cuts designed to protect women who chose homemaking roles, however, the administration repeatedly refused to yield to pressure from antifeminist Republicans, feminist Republicans, or feminist Democrats, all of whom agreed on a set of tax cuts designed to help divorced homemakers. The administration simply had no interest in proactively supporting divorced women.

In 1983, NWPC president Kathy Wilson called on Reagan to step down and endorsed Mondale. Wilson did not find this easy to do. She told one audience, "You know as a long-time Republican, I share the President's concern for excessive government spending and believe we must chart a fiscally responsible course. But I'm talking about responsibility, equity; not cruelty."[28]

Republican feminists' failure to get Reagan to even consider supporting tax cuts endorsed by legislation with bipartisan support convinced many women that Reagan simply did not care about their issues.

Without Reagan's support and with a Republican-controlled Senate that leaned toward deferring to the president's preferences, even if the Democratic House of Representatives had managed to pass some of the more costly bills contained within the EEA, they would not have become law.[29] With little incentive to stick their necks out in support of controversial bills that redefined marriage, Congress passed only those provisions of the EEA that continued to privatize women's dependency—provisions that improved divorced women's access to resources by tying them to their ex-husbands. These bills drew enough bipartisan support to pass in the Senate and gain Reagan's signature. In the face of Congress's and the Reagan administration's ongoing indifference, and often outright hostility, to feminist divorce reformers' demands for legislation that recognized marriages as partnerships, women's groups turned away from their legislative strategy and back to the judiciary.

No Longer "A Woman's Ticket to Poverty": Feminist Divorce Reformers Revisit Litigation

Women first encountered the no-fault divorce regime in court. It was often the experience of facing judges who refused to recognize the economic value of their work in the home that brought women into the feminist movement. In feminist divorce reformers' analysis, judges were part of the patriarchal family law structures that needed to be dismantled. Thus in the early years of the feminist divorce reform movement, activists often viewed strategies that relied on the judiciary with skepticism. Instead, they tried to win legislation that would force judges to recognize marriages as partnerships and homemaking as work. As this strategy ran into new challenges in the 1980s, feminist divorce reformers reconsidered their stance toward the courts. As they returned to this previously hostile territory, feminist divorce reformers found that the legislative and public relations victories they had won over the prior decade opened up possibilities in judicial venues.

By 1976, ten states had adopted divorce laws that either allowed or required judges to take into consideration the homemakers' economic contribution to the marriage.[30] These laws were an important protection for homemakers, but they were a far cry from the formulas feminist divorce reformers had hoped to have bind judges' decision making. Indeed, the new laws actually increased judicial discretion—practically requiring judges to issue judgments on the quality of individual homemakers' contributions to their families when dividing economic resources.

On a national level, feminist divorce reformers' efforts to win legislation mandating that judges use specific formulas when awarding alimony and dividing property ended in a place similar to where state legislation did. Most Economic Equity Act provisions that mandated the division of benefits according to a pro rata formula did not become law. Instead, in many of the enacted provisions of the EEA, Congress *allowed* judges to divide employment-based pensions but did not mandate that they do so.[31] Congress, like the states, remained extremely hesitant to interfere with judicial discretion in divorce.

While disappointing to feminist divorce reformers, the laws clarifying that judges could divide marital property in a divorce actually created new opportunities for activism, empowering feminists to push judges to approach marriage as an economic partnership and divide resources evenly in divorce. When NOW LDEF announced the creation of its Family Law Project in 1983 it promised the new project would "combine litigation strategies with public education and research" to achieve six goals: first and foremost, legal recognition of marriage as an economic partnership; second, broadening the definition of marital property to include "intangible assets" such as pensions and professional degrees; third, establishing the presumption that martial property would be divided equally in a divorce; fourth, legal recognition of the equal value of a homemaker's contributions to the martial partnership; fifth, legislative and judicial reforms of the rules around support awards; and finally, legislation and judicial reforms to ensure economic security for older women.[32]

The Family Law Project centralized work that NOW LDEF had long done in the field. In 1979 and 1981, NOW LDEF unsuccessfully defended a dependent spouse's right to a portion of her ex-husband's federally controlled pension in the *Hisquierdo* and *McCarty* cases. In 1981, it had also unsuccessfully argued in front of the Missouri Supreme Court that the potential pension earnings of Eustis Kuchta should be taken into account when dividing property in the divorce case *Kuchta v. Kuchta*. In 1982, NOW LDEF turned a corner and began to win significant cases. First, in *Lundberg v. Lundberg*, a 1982 Wisconsin court ruled that the earnings power that came with a professional degree could be treated by the court as marital property and divided at divorce.[33] In the early 1980s, NOW LDEF also successfully defended women against challenges to Congress's newly issued laws allowing the division of civil service and Foreign Service pensions in a divorce.[34] Pursuant to the new legislation, trial courts began to award homemakers a piece of their husbands' pensions. Divorcing husbands repeatedly challenged these decisions. In each case, feminist divorce reformers rushed to file amici briefs in support of the trial courts' decisions to award homemakers a piece of their husbands' pensions.[35] In each, the court of appeals ruled in favor of the ex-wife and the Supreme Court declined to hear the case.[36] Congress had spoken and at the very least said that judges could divide these federally controlled employment-based pensions as they saw fit.

It was on the heels of these successes that NOW LDEF created the Family Law Project, for the first time seeing real potential for progress on their family law agenda in the courts.[37] The organization received an anonymous donation of $10,000 to start the project and set a fundraising goal of raising roughly another $10,000 for its first year.[38] Its applications for foundation funding emphasized the link between divorce and rising poverty rates among women. One explained, "It is now well established that poverty is a women's issue. . . . Much of this poverty is due to the fact that divorced women who are becoming single heads of household in rapidly increasing numbers and taking on the financial responsibilities of family and children—typically have job skills which are marginal at best." The application went on to explain that the problem divorcing women faced in courts was twofold: First, studies showed that lawyers and judges grossly overestimated the number of divorced women who received alimony and child support; second, judges and lawyers often could not, or did not know if they could, divide marital property evenly between partners instead of on the basis of title.[39]

This analysis gave rise to a two-part strategy. First, NOW LDEF embarked on a public education project to teach judges, lawyers, and women themselves about the economic realities of divorce. It argued that this would "help to cement the changes in public awareness which must accompany reformulation of laws and legal principles if truly long-term change is to be effected." Second, NOW LDEF sought cases allowing it to "articulate a new and more equitable standard of marital property," to "reformulate the legal principles governing enforcement of child and spousal support awards," and to "challenge discriminatory pension vesting requirements."[40]

The public education component of the Family Law Project also built on long-standing practice by local chapters. In 1973, the Connecticut chapter of

NOW's Marriage and Divorce Task Force had created a program of court watchers who would attend divorce trials and watch for bias on the part of judges and encouraged other chapters do the same.[41] After the National Assembly on the Family, in 1979, NOW LDEF had launched a judicial education program that routinely held sessions on the economic consequences of divorce at statewide conferences of legal professionals.[42] Nevertheless, the creation of a formal project marked the new emphasis NOW LDEF planned to give this work. The organization's directors explained, "the decision to pull together our family law work into a project format will result in important gains for women denied economic equity as a result of our current system of law."[43]

In its first year the new Family Law Project won a number of critical victories. It helped develop the legal strategy in *LaRue v. LaRue*, in which the West Virginia Supreme Court ruled that a homemakers' twenty-nine years of work in the home had to be considered as a contribution to marital property in a divorce settlement. NOW LDEF's brief focused on the poverty many older divorced women fell into if courts ignored their unpaid labor in the home when dividing marital property. The case established marriage as economic partnership in West Virginia.[44] Despite strong opposition from Allstate Insurance, the NOW LDEF Project also won an Illinois case mandating that an employee pension plan pay directly to the non-employee spouse the percentage of the plan a divorce court determined she or he owned.[45] In 1985, NOW LDEF recommitted itself to this work, pledging that by the year 2000, "the legal resolution of divorce and/or widowhood [w]ould not be a woman's ticket to poverty."[46]

NOW's shift in focus to the courts had consequences. The new strategy abandoned all of the redistributive pieces of feminist divorce reform agenda. Courts would change how wealth was distributed between husbands and wives, but social insurance programs would not expand. Unlike Social Security for homemakers or Medicare for divorced women, the litigation strategy added no new resources to the pot. The most a woman could hope for was a judge to deem her worthy of a greater share of the spoils of her own marriage.

Despite these limits, the Family Law Project's had notably more success than other NOW LDEF efforts. For example, in 1982, NOW launched the NOW Insurance Project. The Insurance Project resembled the Family Law Project in many ways. Described as a "major campaign to outlaw all sex discrimination in insurance as part of a comprehensive action plan for economic empowerment of women," the project was a coordinated effort to educate women about insurance discrimination, bring legal challenges against discriminatory insurance companies, and stage actions pushing for legislation to ban insurance discrimination.[47] Inspiration for the project grew out of recognition that the insurance industry was one of "the silent interests who profit from sex discrimination" and one of the strongest sources of opposition to the ERA.[48]

When it launched the Insurance Project, NOW LDEF had reason to believe that it might find more success in the courts than it had in the legislature. In a 1978 Supreme Court case, *City of Los Angeles v. Manhart* (1978), the court ruled that insurance plans offered by employers who were covered by Title VII of the Civil Rights Act could not discriminate on the basis of sex.[49] The Insurance Project's cases aimed to extend this decision to insurance offered on the individual market—the insurance on which divorced homemakers relied. Yet, despite feminists' success winning equal access to employment-based pensions, NOW LDEF lost its first two cases about individual insurance plans. In both case, courts ruled that legislators had had plenty of opportunities to ban insurance discrimination on the basis of sex and had explicitly chosen not to do so.[50]

NOW LDEF's success with its Family Law Project and failure with its Insurance Project suggest that even as activists shopped their ideas from political institution to political institution searching for the best outcomes, the decisions of one policymaking body affected the decisions of others. It was not that Congress was antifeminist and courts feminist or vice versa. Rather, both institutions worked off each other, referring sticky problems back and forth. When NOW launched the Family Law Project, feminist divorce reformers had won enough victories in Congress to give them an effective platform from which to organize the judiciary. In contrast, Congress had continually refused to ban sex discrimination in insurance.

Nevertheless, the Family Law Project's success in winning rulings that treated marriage as an economic partnership changed the institutional target of antifeminists. Republican antifeminists began to rethink their decade-old strategy of arguing that the division of marital property should be left up to individual courts. Even as they continued to use courts to challenge other pieces of the feminist agenda they disliked—for example, abortion—antifeminists backed away from challenging family law in the courts. While in 1981, Reagan administration officials argued "courts should be free to take account of all the varying circumstances in a divorce situation," by 1986, Reagan's Family Working Group argued for legislative control of family law.[51] Expressing disappointment with recent Supreme Court decisions, the group argued, "The Court should enforce express provisions of the Constitution that have an impact on the family, and should otherwise leave the formulation of family policy to the legislature and especially to the states."[52] As courts increasingly accepted the idea that marriage was a partnership while the legislature and the president refused to, antifeminists turned against the courts just as feminist turned back to them.

The success of the Family Law Project, like many of NOW's legislative successes, had a limited reach. The judicial recognition of marriages as partnerships could, at best, serve women in divorcing couples who came to court with enough property to divide in a meaningful way and a husband earning enough to pay substantial alimony. Judges' hands were still tied from dividing the most basic federal benefit: Social Security. Even in cases where women had potential access to meaningful alimony and property division, the reliance on the courts meant women needed to live in the right state and have access to a good lawyer to take advantage of NOW LDEF's wins. NOW LDEF's victories were important, but they were won from a position of retreat and reflect the limits imposed by the country's increasingly conservative turn.

"The Attention Necessary for Progress": The NOW Task Force on the Rights of Women in Marriage's State Strategy

In 1987, NOW created a new task force on marriage. The new task force's name, The Task Force on the Rights of Women in Marriage, pinpointed the area where the feminist divorce reform agenda had failed over the previous fifteen years. While a decade and a half of activism had won divorced women many new rights—from access to their ex-husband's pensions to the ability to maintain membership in their ex's health insurance plans—within intact marriages, married women's status relative to their husbands had changed little. Even in the state that had led the way on early divorce reform, California, progress had ground to a halt. Ending her tenure as chair of the California Commission on the Status of Women, Dorothy Jonas expressed frustration to her fellow commissioners about the California legislature's continued refusal to enact legislation equalizing spouses' control over to marital property. She wrote that this inaction told women, "We're willing to concede your right to enter the business world as an equal, but we're not prepared to grant you the legal protections necessary to assume full equality as a financial partner in your own marriage."[53] Jonas left her post to helm the new NOW Task Force where she intended continue her California fight. She wanted to help activists across the country address the continuing inequities between husbands and wives in state laws.

When Jonas introduced herself to her Task Force in 1987 she argued that the key first step to finally winning equality between spouses was to "bring publicity to this long-neglected area of women's rights in order to capture the attention necessary for progress."[54] Jonas's analysis of the problem shows how quickly the sense of crisis around divorce and inequality in marriage had dissipated and fallen from memory. She wrote, "I am convinced that what appears to be apathy is, in reality, total ignorance that property laws continue to discriminate against women; that this discrimination is a contributing factor in the deterioration of the family unit; and that women and their dependent children suffer economic devastation as a result."[55] A decade and a half before, popular women's magazines had regularly brought articles about the inequities of marriage into women's homes and congressional hearings had focused legislative attention on the challenge. Now, Jonas felt the Task Force faced nothing but apathy and neglect.

Nevertheless, Jonas was not starting from the same place as the feminist divorce reformers who preceded her. Unlike Berry and Spalding, Jonas had a wealth of resources to draw on. Jonas's letter to her new members concluded, "It is time to consider an educational campaign to carry directly to the public the writings and insights of Kruaskoff, Weisberger, Weitzman, Cantwell, Wenig, Brunch, Laughrey, Volkmer, Younger, and others who for years have analyzed and offered real solutions to the problem of women's inequality in marriage."[56] Notably, many of these scholars—Krauskoff, Weisberger, and Weitzman, for example—sat on the new Task Force. Members of Jonas's Task Force also included the drafters of the Uniform Marriage and Divorce Act and Uniform Marital Property Act. This was not the committee of housewives-turned-activists that Berry and Spalding had presided over. It was a committee of people whose professional work over the prior two decades had centered on the issues of inequality within marriage.[57]

The scholars Jonas wanted to bring to the public's attention were some of the first to formally study the effects of no-fault divorce laws. But the solutions these experts suggested often looked strikingly similar to the ones citizen activists had produced in the 1970s. For example, in her work, Lenore

Weitzman called for laws creating a presumption that all marital property was equally owned by husbands and wives and for the redefinition of employment-based benefits and privileges—the new property—as jointly held marital property.[58] Also echoing the proposals of earlier activists, in 1982, Marygold Melli, a University of Wisconsin law professor, proposed creating a child support tax to address the difficulties of collecting child support. Melli's child support proposal was made in the same spirit that Berry's divorce insurance proposal had been made a decade before. It would have replaced "the present semi-private child support system with a new one consisting of a child support benefit payable on behalf of all children with legally liable absent parents."[59] Both of these proposals suggested skepticism toward other feminists' willingness to settle for laws that clarified judicial discretion over marital property. For scholars who had been studying the effects of no-fault divorce, distrust of the judiciary continued to be a guiding principle. Reconciling this instinct with the new political realities at the federal level led some activists back to state legislation.

In its first year, the Task Force on the Rights of Women in Marriage devoted itself to the Uniform Marital Property Act (UMPA). First drafted by the Uniform Law Commission in 1983, UMPA focused on creating more equality within marriages by encouraging states to adopt a "full community property system."[60] UMPA proposed that states redefine all property acquired during marriage (with a few exceptions, for example, gifts to an individual spouse) as jointly held. Under UMPA, each spouse would be presumed to have a 50 percent stake in all marital property and share decision-making authority over it.[61] The draft language also carefully made clear that private, employment-based insurance benefits were marital property.[62] UMPA thus embraced both the partnership concept of marriage and the broad definition of property that feminist divorce reformers had long advocated.

At one of its first meetings, the Task Force on Women in Marriage formed a committee to formally review UMPA and resolved to prioritize helping state legislatures adopt and strengthen the proposed act. The strengthening proposals that the committee settled on all sought to bring marriage under the laws that governed other economic interactions instead of treating the economics of marriage as separate and distinct from other partnerships. For example, the Task Force wanted states adopting the act to create a fiduciary duty between the spouses.[63] For another example, while UMPA had always proposed spouses be allowed to create their own personalized contracts for the ownership of marital property, the Task Force wanted to legally require full disclosure when these agreements were drawn up and increase courts' ability to enforce such contracts.

Significantly, UMPA and the Task Force's efforts to strengthen it were both targeted at privately held property. By focusing on UMPA and not on legislation aimed at bringing a partnership concept of marriage to more widely available and federally controlled benefits—as earnings sharing legislation proposed to do for Social Security—NOW's advocates of equality in marriage solidified the compromise they had begun to strike earlier in the decade. Like the Family Law Project, the Task Force on the Rights of Women in Marriage advocated policies that would equalize property in the marriages of the middle-class and wealthy while leaving the working class in marriages where one of their primary forms of property—mostly state entitlements—remained controlled by a patriarchal understanding of the family.

As the number of women the feminist divorce reform agenda served narrowed, the activist base the Task Force drew on—the letter writers who forced legislators to focus on the issue, the local groups of divorced mothers demanding the attention of the press—dried up. Without boots on the ground, although the new Task Force was stacked with experts, it did not succeed in bringing renewed attention to their cause and made little legislative progress. When the Task Force on the Rights of Women and Marriage was founded, only Wisconsin had formally adopted the principles in UMPA.[64] To this day, no other state has joined Wisconsin.

Feminist divorce reformers' turn back to the states was far less successful than their parallel turn to the judiciary. By the late 1980s, electoral politics was too deeply shaped by antifeminists and anti-welfare messaging for feminists' state legislative agenda to find much more success than their federal legislative agenda. Indeed, this increasingly dominant political narrative allowed Republican activists and elected officials who explicitly identified as antifeminists to claim and transform pieces of the old feminist divorce reform agenda. In 1987, Reagan's Working Group on the Family revived the discussion of child support enforcement legislation (finally embracing the Elizabeth Coxe Spalding's decade-old belief that child support enforcement was a strong issue for GOP). The administration's proposed child support enforcement policies emphasized paternal responsibility by requiring the establishment of paternity, something many feminists had long resisted.[65] While the policy agenda pursued by pro-family Republicans often sounded remarkably similar to the feminist divorce reform agenda, a different ideology—one that discouraged government from ensuring (by insuring) family economic security and idealized the breadwinner-homemaker family structure—lay underneath.

Navigating conservative activists' seizure and corruption of portions of their agenda presented a real challenge to feminist divorce reformers. Feminist activists often willingly lent support to Reagan administration policies they believed advanced their agenda despite the compromises required. WEAL, for example, gave its support to the administration's proposed new child support enforcement proposals.[66] As a result, while the Right peeled off conservative women looking for a defense of homemaking, other sectors of the feminist movement began to speak more clearly to liberal women trying to support themselves and their children. For the growing numbers of never-married mothers, provisions of the EEA like earnings sharing and the Retirement Equity Act, changes in how courts divided property at divorce, and UMPA offered little. They did not need policies rebalancing the economics of marriage. Instead they needed child care and other programs that would allow them to raise children while in the workforce. Yet feminist divorce reformers focused on UMPA and compromised with the Reagan administration on legislation like child support enforcement that increased government oversight of poor women. By the end of the 1980s, as NOW's Rights of Women in Marriage Task Force presided over the continuing growth of apathy on feminist divorce reform issues, NOW as a whole—along with other leading feminist organizations—turned its attention away from selective entitlements for divorced women to improved benefits for employed women.

"The Rules Have Changed"

Between 1969 and the mid-1980s, feminist divorce reformers won a series of laws that improved women's access to benefits through selective entitlements and strengthened judicial patriarchy. Growing political opposition to redefining marriage, however, prevented these laws from providing women with benefits as individuals by recognizing all marriages as partnerships between equals. Instead, at the federal and state level, new laws allowed judges to rule that some extraordinary marriages were partnerships just as Congress had done for certain marriages—military and Foreign Service—through the creation of new selective entitlements. Increasing numbers of judges did so. But divorcing women almost always remained dependent on some entity—their husbands, a benevolent judge, or the state—for their access to economic resources after marriage. Rather than establish women's independence in and out of their marriages, new laws simply shifted the relationships between the institutions (all dominated by men) on which divorced women could depend.

Thus, despite NOW LDEF's victories in court, individual women still suffered in divorce. NOW LDEF continued to receive more requests for help litigating women's divorces than it could take. These requests made clear the dangers of relying on individual judges to fairly administer each divorce. In 1986, NOW LDEF received a plea for help from a woman from Princeton, New Jersey, who wrote, "My marriage was a classic 1960's marriage. When we married there was an unwritten understanding that I would stay home and raise the children and in the event of divorce I would have permanent alimony and get the house. Now that we are actually divorcing the rules have changed."[67] Another woman, this one from St. Louis, wrote after her husband walked out on their nineteen-year marriage, "Our life was arranged as a partnership, one member responsible for the major income and the other to do all the unpaid labor to benefit the unit. In 1986 I find that this form of marriage is no longer recognized in the courts."[68] NOW LDEF told both of these women they did not have the resources to help them. We do not know how their cases worked out.

By leaving it up to judges, Congress gave yet another advantage to wealthy women in marriage who had the resources to mount legal challenges and, as importantly, had husbands with economic benefits courts could divide. Meanwhile, the more broadly available Social Security retirement benefit continued to be divided by statute on a breadwinner-dependent basis with dependent benefits going to divorced women only after ten years of marriage. Courts increasingly recognized wealthy women's marriages as partnerships, to those women's advantage, while low-income women continued to operate in a legal world that assumed husbands and wives were respectively breadwinners and homemaker dependents, not equals.

Yet by the close of the 1980s fewer women than ever relied entirely on marriage for their economic security. As women entered the workforce, feminist divorce reformers had to make a case for the continuing salience of their agenda to a feminist movement that represented ever fewer homemakers. Feminist divorce reformers' few wins in the second half of the 1980s—largely pushed by the Family Law Project—did not present a solid rationale for a continued feminist focus on their agenda. Each case had rested on the story of a displaced homemaker, and, looking around, feminists saw fewer and fewer women at risk of this displacement.

At its final meeting in 1987, NOW's national board heard a report from the new Task Force on the Rights of Women in Marriage and unanimously adopted a resolution supporting its focus on UMPA.[69] This was a vote of confidence for the new Task Force, but, to those paying close attention, the full meeting demonstrated how low on feminists' priority list fighting for the rights of married women had fallen. At the same meeting, the board heard a proposal that NOW produce new brochures on its priority issues. Of the nine issues on the list—including marital rights—the board decided to move ahead with only three: child care, family leave, and affirmative action.[70] NOW may have remained committed to advocating for more equality within marriages, but the organization now ranked helping women in their workplaces a significantly higher priority.

CHAPTER 9

"Saving the Next Generation"

The Changing Politics of Divorce

In June of 1985, the *New York Times* ran an editorial titled "Saving the Next Generation." It announced, "America is in trouble. In the last few years, children have become, before our very eyes, the poorest segment of our population, and every day brings new evidence that their plight is, if anything, growing worse."[1] According to the article, one in five children were now living in poverty, twice the number for poor people of all ages. The *Times* argued that this was partially due to the rise in "illegitimate births."[2] That year, the National Center for Health Statistics announced that 20 percent of children were born to unwed mothers.[3] And the number was rising. By 1994, the number had reached 32 percent.[4] Ten years earlier divorced women had been the "new poor" capturing headlines. By the mid-1980s children had replaced them. Yes, these children had—and were usually living with—equally poor mothers, but it was the children who had become the object of political sympathy. The public's assumptions had shifted and single mothers no longer seemed to be the victims of a divorce crisis but rather willing participants in the creation of a new crisis of out-of-wedlock births.

In part, this shift in political sympathy can be traced to the stabilizing divorce rate. In a 1987 speech titled "Where Do We Go from Here? Women and Public Policy," longtime feminist divorce reform activist and WEAL director Arvonne Fraser pointed out that divorce rates were holding steady at 50 percent.[5] The divorce rate had hit its peak in 1979 and then leveled out.[6] This did not mean the problems faced by divorced women had gone away, but it did mean they had become familiar—no longer a national crisis, simply many individual ones.

The language of "displaced homemakers" had always relied on the idea that divorced women were the victims of sudden social and legal changes. They had made life choices in one world and their husbands left them in another. As a result, activists argued, these women had a special claim on society's sympathy and resources. By the late 1980s, however, fewer and fewer divorcing women could actually say that they married at a time when divorce and its consequences were an unknown possibility. Moreover, divorcing women were less often full-time homemakers and more often underemployed primary caregivers / secondary earners. Women divorcing in these years had work experience; they had credit in their own names; they might even have access to a pension, health insurance, and Social Security credits through their jobs. By 1985, just about 50 percent of mothers with children under three and roughly 70 percent of mothers with children over six were in the labor force.[7] In 1990, the Displaced Homemakers Network pointed out, "Women are now 'expected' to work regardless of their marital status."[8] Judges and legislators asked why women who had long held jobs could not take care of themselves after a divorce.

Yet, even as women moved into the workforce, they continued to do the lion's share of care work in a marriage. Women were expected to take more time off work than their husbands when children were born. If they stayed in the workforce, they often had reduced hours or forewent career advancement so they could continue to meet the needs of their family. And, of course, they continued to face sex discrimination in the workplace and a significant wage gap. All this almost guaranteed that, even if they had held consistent employment throughout marriage, after a divorce most women would be significantly less financially secure than their ex-husbands.

Middle-class women's entrance into the workforce and their ensuing "double shift" at work and home meant that their lives came to look more like those of lower-income women and women of color who had always had to seek paid employment. As a result, the narrow laws feminist divorce reformers had compromised on in the 1970s and early 1980s offered significant aid to ever fewer women. It was the never-enacted legislative proposals to recognize the monetary value of domestic work and make employment law and work-based benefits friendlier to women's work patterns that would have made a bigger difference. Despite feminist divorce reformers' hard-won successes, the compromises they had made meant divorce continued to lead to economic hardship for women. And the basic reason why divorce fell more heavily on women also remained the same: an unequal division of the unpaid, caregiving labor in the family and the economic and legal system's continued support of that unequal division.

While the fundamental division of labor in the family remained the same, as women entered the workforce it had come to look quite different and less directly visible. In *The Sympathetic State: Disaster Relief and the Origins of the American Welfare State,* Michele Dauber argues that disaster narratives like the one successfully spun by divorced women in the 1970s have always been the key to the creation of social welfare programs in the United States. Relief recipients who successfully argue that they are deserving because of events outside of their control—whether fire, old age, or divorce—generally face less scrutiny than other relief recipients.[9] But, Dauber argues, "there is also the contradiction at the heart of the disaster-based welfare state between compensation and blamelessness, a contradiction that becomes more intense as time passes. Relief turns victims into recipients, making it progressively easier for relief opponents to argue that if recipients are still poor it is their own fault, and hence not the responsibility of government."[10] In the 1990s, feminist divorce reformers faced this contradiction head on. Their success in the 1980s, along with the stabilization of divorce rates and women's growing presence in the workforce meant that they needed a new explanation for why women continued to suffer economically in divorce and a new agenda to compel politicians to address the particular economic challenges women faced after divorce.

Fraser ended her "Where Do We Go from Here?" speech with a call for women to focus on the needs of children, both as objects of political sympathy and as the central challenge women faced in the workforce. "We must insist that responsibility for the next generation gets as much attention and as many resources as are needed," she told her audience. As Fraser delved into specifics she called for an expansion of preschools and public health insurance for children alongside the redefinition of work to include and value "taking care of households."[11] For the previous decade and a half, Fraser had advocated public policies that assigned economic value to women's work in the home by treating husbands and wives as full economic partners; her new agenda focused on creating stronger supports for women who worked outside the home. Her attention had shifted to external supports for women and their children because women, while still primary caretakers, were no longer primarily caretakers. Alone, shifting the balance of economic power within the family could not solve the care work problems created by the new norm of dual-income couples. The challenges of balancing care and work could only be solved with new entitlements for working women and their children.

Feminist divorce reformers and the economic crisis of divorce fell out of the national conversation in the late 1980s. But the activists who had driven the feminist divorce reform movement over the previous decade and a half remained. As these women joined their agenda with feminists who had long focused on helping mothers in the workforce instead of married women, they turned their attention to shoring up women's place in the work-based social insurance system instead of the marriage-based system.

After decades of fighting for selective entitlements for divorced women and focusing on securing the marriage-based insurance system, former feminist divorce reformers faced significant hurdles as they shifted focus. On the one hand, these reformers turned to strengthening women's place in the employment-based welfare state at a moment of retrenchment. On the other, the decisions they themselves had made over the course of their many campaigns continued to reverberate. Feminist divorce reformers' struggle with these issues in the context of the Reagan, Bush, and Clinton administrations demonstrates the staying power of the policy compromises they struck in the 1970s and early 1980s. The politics of selective entitlements haunted the feminist agenda through the end of the century.

"Love Is Not Enough": Winning Women Equal Access to Employment-Based Benefits

In the 1980s, reflecting back on the early years of NOW, Betty Friedan recalled a conversation she had with Betty Berry. "What's the real answer?" Friedan had asked Berry, feeling the magnitude of what divorced women were up against as NOW's 1974 conference on marriage and divorce came to a close. According to Friedan, Berry replied, "A woman should never give up her job. She shouldn't stop working. Love is not enough."[12] This private conversation was miles away from the official message of the conference or anything feminist divorce reformers associated with NOW would say over the next decade. This is not to say that no feminists were advancing this message in the 1970s; but the women advocating the feminist divorce reform agenda spent the 1970s focused on laws that would protect women by lessening the economic risks of marriage and homemaking, not by helping them join the workforce. By the closing years of the 1980s, however, the ideas expressed in this private conversation between Friedan and Berry had become central to the work of activists concerned with the economic risks of caretaking.

If women were going to stay in the workforce and access their benefits through employment instead of marriage, feminist divorce reformers understood they would have to join forces with their feminist colleagues who had long advocated for child care and paid family leave. Feminist divorce reformers' shift to join longtime feminist advocates of these feminist social insurance programs late 1980s and early 1990s showed a remarkable amount of optimism in the face of welfare retrenchment. It showed a belief that not only could the American social insurance system expand, but the system and feminists could move away from the political imperatives of gendered, selective entitlements and demand access to work-based social rights for all women and men.

Family leave legislation was first introduced in Congress in 1984 when Republicans still held the Senate and the White House. At the time, the act's supporters had little hope of doing anything but raising the issue through hearings. Introduced by Congresswoman Pat Schroeder, the first family leave legislation was a broad answer to the central question Schroeder had raised during her campaigns for ex-military wives: How could women have children without taking on a disproportionate economic risk?[13] Schroeder's Parental and Disability Leave Act of 1985 proposed that employees be guaranteed eighteen weeks of job-protected, unpaid leave after the birth, adoption, or serious illness of a child. After the eighteen weeks, the employee would have the right to return to the same job with the same pay and benefits.[14] The bill also would have created a commission to study ways of creating paid leave and required the commission to propose legislation creating paid leave within two years.[15]

The immediate impetus for Schroeder's legislation was a challenge to the Pregnancy Discrimination Act (PDA) of 1978 that was winding its way through the court system. The PDA clarified that the Title VII ban on sex discrimination in employment extended to discrimination on the basis of pregnancy and mandated that employers treat pregnancy like any other disability.[16] In 1982 Lillian Garland, an unmarried mother working as a receptionist at a bank in California, sued her employer for violating the state's maternity leave policy, which required four months of job-protected, unpaid leave after a woman gave birth. In response, the bank argued that the California law forced them to violate federal antidiscrimination law by requiring them to treat women differently than men.[17]

In fact, many feminists shared the bank's position and had raised concerns that California's leave law along with other states' sex-specific, maternity leave laws were too close to sex-discriminatory protective legislation.[18] Once the case made it to the Supreme Court, the ACLU filed an amicus brief agreeing with the bank's analysis and arguing that the California law could end up forcing women once again into "a separate sphere of home and family."[19] NOW LDEF filed a similarly messaged amicus brief arguing that the court should reconcile the two laws and California's maternity leave policy should be extended to cover all temporarily disabled workers.[20]

Other feminists, including Betty Friedan; the Southern California ACLU, which broke with the national organization; and labor unions such as the ILGWU and the California Teachers Federation supported the California leave law as it stood.[21] Activists with roots in the feminist divorce reform movement joined them. In particular, Equal Rights Advocates, a San Francisco-based feminist advocacy organization associated with Herma Hill Kay, longtime feminist divorce reform advocate and one of the original authors of the UMDA, supported the California law. Kay helped author a brief arguing that reproductive differences could legally be recognized as a meaningful difference when a woman was actually pregnant.[22] Kay had pioneered this "episodic argument"—the idea that women should not be treated as a separate class because of the possibility of pregnancy but pregnant women could be treated as a meaningfully different class of people subject to special rules without its constituting discrimination.[23] Kay's episodic argument in favor of maternity leave followed naturally from her earlier work to ensure that divorce courts recognized the value of women's work in the home. Kay's feminism—like that many of feminist divorce reformers—was not about demanding equal treatment but rather recognition and protection in light of difference.

As the Garland case made its way toward the Supreme Court, Schroeder and colleagues in the House began working to defend maternity leave policies by passing gender-neutral national leave legislation. In 1987, the Supreme Court decided in favor of Garland and upheld gender-specific maternity leave laws, but the legislation the case helped inspire continued to wind its way through the legislative process.[24] By then Democrats controlled both houses of Congress. Early in the year, House committees held hearings on the Family and Medical Leave Act. This version of the act offered job-protected leave for the birth of a child or the illness of a child or parent to both men and women. The FMLA's supporters argued it was "the product of a natural evolution from the more limited concept of pregnancy disability leave."[25] NOW president Eleanor Smeal proclaimed, "This bill goes beyond maternity leave and we salute it. It is fitting today's family needs. It deals with parental leave. And that is what we need today. A maternity leave bill alone would be old fashioned today."[26]

While the new family and medical leave legislation proposed a universal benefit available regardless of gender, it continued to limit its reach by only guaranteeing unpaid leave. Without paid leave, like the protections women had won for marriage-based social insurance benefits—the bill could only actually help the relatively wealthy who could afford to take a job-protected leave of absence. Mainstream feminist organizations like NOW had pushed for a stronger paid leave bill. NOW only endorsed Schroeder's limited legislation "with reservations."[27] In fact, as a result of the issue, NOW only joined the organizations testifying in favor of the FMLA at the last minute. During her testimony, when asked by a committee member what compromises feminist organizations were willing to make in order to pass the bill, Smeal replied, "Unpaid leave was already a compromise."[28]

Although it followed a familiar pattern, feminists' grudging agreement to compromise on legislation that could only help the elite did not lead to legislative victory as it had with feminist divorce reform legislation. Even unpaid leave presented a potential cost to employers, and business interests killed the bill.[29] Unlike the class-biased legislation that feminist divorce reformers had managed to win—like COBRA or a right to private pensions—unpaid leave did not keep the costs of women's maternal role the responsibility of the private family. However limited a right family leave legislation proposed to create, it proposed a new social right and that came with a cost that American society more broadly would have to bear. Congress proved unwilling to impose such a cost.

The FMLA may also have been a harder lift for feminists than earlier feminist divorce reform legislation because it represented a departure from the model of social benefits that boosted the family wage and the privatization of women's dependency. The employment-based social insurance benefits created earlier in the twentieth century almost all included a benefit for male workers' wives. Health insurance, Social Security, and in many cases unemployment insurance compensated men not just on the basis of their jobs but also on the basis of their marriage. The programs provided married, male employees with a dependent benefit on top of whatever benefit they were entitled to through their job alone. The drafters of the FMLA, however, did not consider creating a subsidy for an employee's spouse who was staying home and taking care of children.[30] The FMLA was not intended to use the employment-based benefit system to subsidize care work; it was intended to protect women in the workforce from the economic vulnerabilities created by their need to perform unpaid care work. In the same way that earnings sharing proposals and divorce insurance had sought to protect women from the vulnerabilities created by care work by shoring up their place in marriage-based insurance system, the FMLA proposed to address the same issue by shoring up women's place in the employment-based insurance system.

While feminists did not support the FMLA primarily as means of subsidizing care work, they did believe subsidized child care would also play a critical role in giving women access to the work-based social insurance system. In 1987, the same year that NOW's board voted to make child care a top priority, the Congressional Caucus on Women's Issues added a vastly expanded section on child and dependent care to the Economic Equity Act—the most unified expression of the feminist agenda in the 1980s.[31] In the first half of the 1980s the EEA had included provisions on child care tax credits. The 1987 legislation not only expanded these proposals but also offered new provisions—for example, funding to improve training for child care professionals and mortgage programs to help child care providers afford facility space—that shared the goal of expanding parents' child care options.[32] Meanwhile, child support enforcement provisions were noticeably absent from the omnibus bill for the second congressional session in a row. Child support enforcement would return in later iterations of the bill, but its brief abandonment in exchange for expanded child care options marks the Congressional Caucus on Women's Issues recognition that "America has become a society in which everyone is expected to work—including women with young children," as Schroeder explained.[33]

Despite the alignment between congressional women and NOW's priorities, feminists quickly began to disagree about the substance of a quality child care bill. In 1988, NOW passed a resolution laying out what it believed child care legislation—and any "quality public early child care and education system"—should contain: early child care as well as before- and after-school and summer programs "modeled after the current public school system"; democratic and local control of these programs; federal public funding in combination with state matching funds; and sliding scale fees "designed with a phasing-in mechanism to reach a goal of total public funding."[34] NOW's resolution emphasized universal accessibility in terms of both cost and scheduling. The organization's effort to include before- and after-school programs along with early childhood education demonstrated its determination to use the bill to not only subsidize care work but also facilitate and ease women's entrance into the workforce as equals.

NOW believed that the child care package it proposed would cost at least $40 billion.[35] When Congress began to debate actual legislation in 1988—the first major congressional child care bill since Nixon's 1971 veto of comprehensive child care—the bill it considered offered only $2.5 billion in federal dollars.[36] The ABC bill, as the bill was known, included funding to help states subsidize child care for low- and moderate-income families; set standards on health, safety, and child-caregiver ratios; and created training funds for child care professionals. While many women's groups, labor organizations, and child advocates supported the ABC bill, NOW found it underfunded and "woefully inadequate."[37] At a national board meeting early in 1988, NOW members debated whether or not to support the less-than-perfect child care bill or fight for a new one. Their primary concern revolved around the bill's emphasis on vouchers, which they believed would funnel money to "churches that oppose us at every turn."[38] In the end, the organization attempted to make the same move it had with the FMLA and accepted the weaker, compromise legislation while working to develop stronger legislation for the next Congress.

Feminists' tepid support for the ABC bill met fierce conservative resistance. Advocates of the ABC bill had to push back regularly against Phyllis Schlafly, the Heritage Foundation, the American Enterprise Institute, and other conservatives.[39] In 1987, a Heritage Foundation representative wrote of the proposed child care legislation, "ABC money would not go to the working poor who actually need help taking care of their children but to child-care professionals with their Master of Social Work degrees—the same upwardly mobile urban professionals who wouldn't think of having their own kids."[40] The organization sought to paint a picture of women in the workforce, even social service workers, as the opposite of mothers. In 1988 a columnist from the *San Francisco Chronicle* expressed a similar option, writing of the ABC bill, "Do we really want Mom to work? Should we accept the two-paycheck family as the only viable future?"[41] Embedded in this comment was an understanding that the economy had forced women into the workforce and alarm that crafting public policy around this state of affairs might make them permanent.

Despite virulent opposition from the antifeminist Right, many GOP congresswomen (and some men) did support the ABC bill. Nevertheless, no major strides were made toward creating a national child care system in the 1980s. In 1988 the Senate could not muster the sixty votes needed to overcome a filibuster for a child care bill that also included ten weeks of unpaid family leave.[42] In 1989 the Senate managed to pass the bill but the House did not.[43] In 1990, President Bush signed the first child care legislation since 1971 into law, but it was a minimal bill. The $4 billion legislation increased funding for existing services for poor families under Title IV of the Social Security Act and created a small Child Care and Development Grant to expand and improve child care options for the working poor.[44] Needless to say, this amounted to a tenth of what feminists had believed necessary.

Both the FMLA and child care bills grew out of a desire to protect women from the economic vulnerabilities created by their care responsibilities—feminist divorce reformers' longtime guiding principle—but by the late 1980s enough women had entered the workforce that protecting women from these vulnerabilities meant securing their place in the employment-based social insurance system instead of fighting to expand the marriage-based system. As former feminist divorce reformers turned their attention to the employment-based system, the legislative compromises they accepted looked remarkably similar to those that had defined their fight to secure the marriage-based system earlier in the decade. The limited unpaid leave legislation and expanded child care access for low-income women to which they agreed reproduced the same class differences that had defined and limited expansions to marriage-based insurance benefits. Women with a substantial income of their own or married to a spouse who could keep their family afloat during their unpaid maternity leave would most directly benefit from the FMLA (if it became law), while low-income women would gain expanded child care access.

Combined, these two pieces of legislation offered a similar message to the one that American social insurance policy had conveyed about women's role in the workplace since the 1930s: poor, single women should be in it; wealthy, married, middle-class women should be able to decide whether or not to stay home with their children. Yet the message had also shifted slightly. Women on both ends of the economic spectrum were now being told that the workforce was the only place to find permanent economic security. The new laws allowed wealthier women to take time out of the workforce but assumed a desire to reenter.

Unfortunately, as feminists turned their attention to improving women's access to work-based benefits, these benefits—the most robust available in the United States—were beginning to weaken. In 1980, 38 percent of all private sector workers had a defined-benefit pension through their job. By 2008 that number would drop to 20 percent.[45] Similarly, employers shifted more and more of the cost of health insurance on to their employees in the 1990s. Between 1988 and 1996, the share of premiums paid by employees for single coverage more than doubled.[46] At the same moment that feminists were fighting to equalize women's access to employer-based benefits, the availability and generosity of those benefits contracted across the board.

"The More Things Change": The Tight Grip of the Selective Entitlement System

In 1990, the National Displaced Homemakers Network issued a status report titled "The More Things Change. . . ." The report began by celebrating how far women had come over the decade and their entrance into the paid labor market. But as the title suggested, it quickly turned darker, declaring that, despite the progress made, "displaced homemakers and single parents are still facing the same situations and challenges they faced at the beginning of the decade."[47] The report ended with calls for policy reforms to address the economic challenges faced by both older and younger women—stronger alimony awards that took into account women's support for their husbands' careers and the FMLA.[48] The report's ecumenical approach was common to feminists' work in the late 1980s and early 1990s. Even as feminists turned their focus toward the goal of securing the employment-based insurance system for women, they could not or would not totally abandon their defense of the selective entitlements of the marriage-based insurance system. Throughout the late 1980s, feminists continued to advocate for married women to keep the special status they had in the welfare state. Arguably, this was not only about maintaining a status symbol but also a response to the decreasing quality of work-based benefits. If even a full-time job guaranteed no more than weak access to benefits, married women demanded continued access to more options. But advocacy for both visions of women's place in the social insurance system had a cost. When feminists propped up a social insurance system that rewarded marriage, they made it more difficult to fight for new universal social insurance programs and to defend social insurance programs aimed at single women.

In the late 1980s a renewed effort to reform the American health care system forced feminists to weigh their campaign to shift women toward employment-based benefits against their long history of advocating for selective entitlements for married women. In 1987, Senator Ted Kennedy released a new national health insurance plan, this time called the Minimum Essential Health Benefits for All Workers plan. In the 1970s, the name alone would have raised red flags for feminist divorce activists, who would have recognized immediately that a plan built around "workers," or paid employment, would discriminate against women who worked in the home. In 1987, however, feminists focused their concerns on how the plan would affect *employed married* women.

Kennedy's new proposal called for all employers to provide a minimum package of health care benefits, including dependent benefits, to any employee who worked over 17.5 hours a week. Employers would be required to pick up 80 percent of the premium for most employees and the entire premium for low-wage workers. Because the plan required employers to cover all employees, members of dual-income couples would each receive coverage through their own employer. In exchange, because these couples were not using dependent benefits, their premiums would be reduced.[49]

Women's organized response to the plan was generally positive. Feminist groups pointed out that women continued to constitute a disproportionate share of the nation's thirty-seven million uninsured and that 46 percent of working women had to provide for their own health insurance as well as their children's.[50] Their enthusiasm did not stop women's groups from offering further changes.[51] Many of their demands focused particularly on the difficulties faced by low-income women who headed families. For example, the Older Women's League pushed for sliding scale subsidies for families for low-income families' out-of-pocket expenses. The organization explained, "Combined with lower earnings and increased family responsibility, the spiraling cost of health care has an even more adverse effect on women. Ignoring the out-of-pocket costs associated with covered health services, women still incur considerable costs for necessary services not covered by most insurance plans, such as family planning and preventative tests for female-related diseases."[52] This critique neatly encompassed many of the problems women's groups found most objectionable about the bill. Not only did it not go far enough in aiding low-income women, but it also left unfixed gendered inequities in the kinds of care covered that were endemic to the insurance system and which a decade of lobbying had failed to unseat.

Within feminists' campaign to expand the availability of health insurance subsidies and coverage to all women there was also a push to address a provision of the Kennedy bill that feminists believed shortchanged married women. The Women's Health Insurance Task Force—a coalition of feminist organizations including WEAL and Planned Parenthood's Alan Guttmacher Institute—lobbied for a revision to the bill that reinstated the use of marital status. The coalition demanded that married people who had received superior coverage through their spouse's employer-sponsored health insurance plan be allowed to continue to receive that coverage.[53]

In response to strong lobbying from women's organizations, Kennedy amended his proposal to allow spouses to improve their coverage by purchasing supplementary coverage through their spouse's employer.[54] The change created "a separate and lower premium category for the working spouse whose coverage is secondary to the primary coverage the spouse receives through his or her own employment."[55] A new category of deserving and potentially specially treated participants in the social insurance system—the working wife—was born.

The difference between feminists' response to health insurance legislation and the FMLA and child care bills shows how difficult it is to remove privileges from the social welfare system once they are created. Since the U.S. had no federal child care or family leave policy, it was possible for feminists to support new policies that treated all women equally, if not all that well. In contrast, women accustomed to being able to improve their health insurance options through marriage proved unwilling to give up their privileged position in the social welfare system. Feminists fought to increase the range of benefits covered by the Minimum Health Bill and to make those benefits more universally accessible, but they also demanded that married women retain special access to health insurance through their husbands.

While no form of Kennedy's bill became law—indeed passing comprehensive health insurance reform remained the white whale of the Democratic Party until 2010—the revision process showed the tight grip selective entitlements held over not only activists but also lawmakers when it came to the politics of welfare expansion. Feminists' demands that Kennedy change his bill to make health insurance more accessible and comprehensive went ignored, but Kennedy's team was able to quickly address feminist demands to expand access to specific groups of individuals who seemed to lose out in the bill.[56] Policymakers struggled to fit increased funding to improve access for low-income individuals into their proposals, but they could accommodate a new category of "deserving" individuals or expand the selective entitlements already available to a group. Doing so fit into an existing, accepted political framework and thus entered legislation at a speed that feminists' more comprehensive proposals could not.

Feminists' advocacy to preserve married women's existing privileged position in the social welfare state made their support for more universal additions to the social insurance system, like the FMLA, more vulnerable to antifeminist critiques. Conservatives were quick to exploit women's rights activists' concerns about the inequalities in the FMLA and child care bills and to lay the blame for that inequality on feminists themselves. Schlafly repeatedly argued that "universal policies" advocated by feminists would actually only offer support to wealthy, working, married women. She claimed that the FMLA would discriminate against middle-class mothers who worked in the home, testifying, "Mandated parental leave is another discriminatory benefit that would force the traditional family which provides its own child care on a lower average income to subsidize the two-earner couples who have a higher average income."[57] Similarly, Schlafly wrote of child care legislation, "If Congress really wants to help families, it should raise the personal income tax exemption for children and make the child care tax credit available for all families, regardless of the lifestyle of their mothers."[58] Schlafly thus framed the creation of these new benefits not as a step toward creating wider access to employment-based benefits but as a new selective entitlement that would explicitly reward rich women who worked outside of the home.

This was not a new tactic on Schlafly's part. She had raised a similar class critique when attacking wages for housework and earnings sharing proposals. In a 1979 interview with *Family Circle*, for example, Schlafly argued that plans that attached a monetary value to homemaking would "deprive the poor man of the opportunity to have a wife." Although strongly anti-tax, Schlafly did not ground her argument in the cost such a policy might impose on men through taxes, but rather asked how a poor man would feel if his future wife's work was valued at more than his own.[59] She asked, "If you're going to say her value is $14,000 a year, what's that going to do to the husband who doesn't earn that much?"[60] As the contracting economy of the late 1970s created its own challenges to the breadwinner-homemaker family model, Schlafly argued that efforts to further destabilize the model posed too great a danger to men's self-worth.

At a moment when many middle-class men were seeing their wages stagnate and their benefits cut, Schlafly's arguments hit home and would continue to for the decade to come. Women's demand for improved access to work-based benefits encountered opposition rooted in both notions of masculinity and the fears about a declining economy. If men's wages would no longer allow them to support a family, all that remained to defend their breadwinner masculinity was the good benefits they alone could provide their family. For some, equalizing women's access to work-based benefits, especially when the value of men's work-based benefits was decreasing, simply offered too great an affront to a gendered wage system that was already beginning to crack. For others, the new benefits to which women might win access just seemed unlikely to ever equal what their husbands earned. Selective, marriage-based entitlements were difficult to let go of and relatively easy to expand.

"Merging the Feminist and Poor Women's Movement": The Fight for a Feminist Welfare State Under Clinton

On 5 February 1993, new president Bill Clinton's second nominee for attorney general, Kimba Woods, announced she would withdraw from consideration because she had hired and underpaid undocumented immigrants to care for her children. It was the second time in two weeks the new administration's pick for the post had to make such an announcement.[61] Zoe Baird and Kimba Woods would each have been the United States' first female attorney general, but then Congress asked how they had managed child care while they worked outside the home. Feminists watched horrified as two women in a row were felled by questions they believed no man would ever have had to answer, yet they remained hopeful about the new administration and the advocacy environment in which they now operated—after all, the same day that Woods withdrew Clinton signed his first piece of legislation: the FMLA.[62]

Working under a president who believed both that women belonged in the workforce and that social insurance benefits needed to be expanded, feminists saw an opportunity to escape the politics of selective entitlements and win more universal benefits for all women.[63] Thus, NOW chose to frame the Baird and Woods scandals as exposing the challenges women faced on both ends of the economy—the challenge middle-class women had finding affordable care and the exploitation of poor women as a result. In the months after the scandal, NOW's executive board passed a resolution calling for the acknowledgement of the underground economy and the fact that "the present immigration, welfare, tax, and social security laws and system stigmatize domestic workers and penalize workers who earn additional necessary income to support themselves and their families."[64] After years of bowing to political realities and compromising on benefits that only helped select groups, NOW hoped to use "nannygate" to begin reconnecting their brand of middle-class equal rights feminism with low-income women's activism and forge a cross-class agenda based on the shared challenges faced by working women across the labor market.[65]

The renewed interest in forging an alliance between middle-class feminists and welfare rights activists grew not only out of the more favorable political context in which feminists now believed they operated but also the continued demographic changes that challenged the feminist divorce reform agenda. As the divorce rate stabilized and ever greater numbers of women entered the workforce, it became imperative that feminists find common ground with never-married mothers in and out of the paid workforce. In an internal document from 1993 on "merging the feminist and poor women's movement," NOW framed women's poverty as the result of three interrelated factors: sex discrimination in the workforce, vulnerability to the loss of a male breadwinner, and "the welfare system."[66]

The FMLA victory came so quickly after Clinton's election that first real test for feminists' attempt at cross-class politics under the new administration was the new campaign to pass comprehensive health care reform legislation.[67] In advance of the 1992 election, with health care reform on the horizon, feminist organizations led by OWL had created a coalition organization to monitor any new legislation.[68] The Campaign for Women's Health was made up of eighty member organizations; it brought women together around the idea that they had a common interest in health care reform legislation. At the helm of CWH was the former leader of the Older Women's League, Joan Kuriansky. CWH committed itself to advocating for a model benefits package for women that would ensure that any health care plan that moved forward included provisions addressing women's health needs.[69] The organization also continued to emphasize the issues long raised by feminist divorce reformers. Kuriansky explained to a *Chicago Tribune* reporter, "Women are 'much more vulnerable' when it comes to health care because they historically have received benefits through spouses."[70] Soon the Congressional Caucus for Women's Issues was echoing the CWH's talking points in its own statements.[71]

NOW advocated a more radical agenda than the CWH. In 1993, the organization passed a resolution calling for a single-payer health plan. In 1994, the organization chose to support the single-payer bill before Congress (the McDermott/Wellstone bill). In a document that asked "What's at Stake for Women in Health Care Reform?" the organization explained, "Women are less likely to have their health insurance covered by their employer and more likely to obtain insurance through their spouse, leaving them more vulnerable to losing benefits if they are ever divorced, widowed, or if an employer eliminates coverage for dependents."[72] Like the CWH, the organization continued to emphasize the ways the marriage-based social insurance system left women vulnerable, but its endorsement of a single-payer health insurance program showed NOW's move to emphasize social rights that would help rich and poor women of any marital status.

Clinton's effort to pass universal health care legislation famously failed for many reasons, but NOW's departure from the politics of selective entitlements continued into its next major legislative battle with the administration: Clinton's attempts to make good on his campaign promise "to end welfare as we know it" and reform AFDC.[73] In anticipation of the legislative fight to come, NOW and the NWRO agreed to work together for a guaranteed adequate income program. Specifically, the organizations proposed a negative income tax, paid for by "cashing out" existing entitlement programs including not only the AFDC program, but also Social Security.[74] NOW's leadership was now driving a policy that sought to move past selective entitlements, even those entitlements that offered positions of privilege to certain NOW women.

NOW had endorsed universal income proposals and tried to work with welfare rights activists in the 1970s, but the 1990s breathed new life into this coalition-building effort. In early 1992, for example, NOW LDEF brought together a roundtable of women's rights and welfare rights activists. In doing so, the organization admitted, "While the welfare recipients' movement is de facto a women's movement, many mainstream women's rights organizations have been slow to recognize the explicit sexism and assault on women's economic and reproductive rights inherent in the current welfare 'reform' movement."[75] At the roundtable, participants agreed "that child support should not be a central focus for feminist and low income advocates," seeing the emphasis on child support enforcement as a diversion from the real issue.[76] Almost twenty years after NOW's Task Force on Marriage had warred with its Task Force on Poverty over including child support enforcement in welfare reform legislation, the organization chose to put down any lingering emphasis on child support enforcement in favor of a more comprehensive approach to welfare reform.

NOW continued to advocate for a guaranteed adequate income as the stakes became concrete in the battle over welfare reform legislation that began in 1994 when Republicans seized control of Congress.[77] In 1994, in response to legislative proposals issued both by the White House and Congress, NOW again called for a universal guaranteed income program that would provide "coverage for all people who are needy regardless of their characteristics or family situations, including childless individuals and displaced homemakers and excluding irrelevant 'eligibility criteria' such as 'deprivation of parent,' 'disability,' or 'age.'"[78] The organization condemned welfare reform proposals with mandated work requirements and time limits on receipt of benefits as sexist and racist and argued that work requirements devalued women's work in the home.[79]

As NOW articulated strong support for a more universal approach to the social insurance system, conservatives continued to try and divide women. In a 1994 "Welfare Busters" fact sheet, conservative members of Congress—led by Tom Delay and Jim Talent—rejected as a "liberal myth" the claim that "over half of the women on welfare go on AFDC as a result of divorce, separation or death of a spouse." Instead, they insisted, "More than half (53%) of mothers on AFDC have never been married."[80] The barely unstated implication: never-married women did not have the same claim on the public purse as the formerly married.

NOW and other feminists struggled to fight this argument because for years they had advocated policies using the same claim. Conservatives turned feminists' long-used argument that women needed a robust social insurance system because of the vulnerability created by marriage back on them. Throughout the 1970s many feminist divorce reformers had drawn a firm line between their own need for state support and the needs of poor women receiving AFDC payments. By arguing that divorced women deserved substantial state support as a reward (or compensation) for their former marriages, feminist divorce reformers had sometimes unwittingly and sometimes quite purposefully based their campaign on the stigmatization of welfare and never-married women who received it.

As feminists sought to move beyond their advocacy for selective entitlements and create universal benefits, their old messaging about which women had earned state support through good behavior and which had failed to do so continued to haunt them. In 1994, the president of Michigan NOW gave a speech defending welfare in which she noted: "Single parents with children are either ignored or vilified in our society. . . . Welfare is not free. Recipients need to pay for their welfare with proof that they deserve it. Proving you are among the 'deserving poor' is becoming harder and harder to do. And the myths about women on welfare are increasingly driving the passage of punitive legislation, intended to create and strengthen barriers to receiving assistance."[81] In the 1990s, NOW recognized the challenging position women in need of welfare were in, but they did not recognize the extent to which their own organization had contributed to the stigma these women faced.

Far from winning a universal guaranteed income bill, feminists and welfare reform advocates lost big in the 1990s. In 1996 Clinton signed the Personal Responsibility and Work Opportunity Act (PRWORA). It replaced AFDC with Temporary Assistance for Needy Families (TANF). The new TANF benefits required beneficiaries to enter the workforce after two years and imposed a lifetime limit of five years for receipt of benefits.[82] As all welfare reform legislation had done since Elizabeth Coxe Spalding's fight for better child support legislation in the 1970s, the PRWORA also included provisions strengthening child support programs.[83] While there was debate over the form these child support provisions should take, Democrats and Republicans supported the inclusion of such provisions.[84] Feminist divorce reformers' decades-old messaging had deeply shaped welfare reform legislation not only by helping forge the link to child support legislation but also by devaluing the work of raising children and helping create a political discourse that allowed unmarried women with children to be forced into the workforce. Through their campaigns in the 1970s and 1980s, feminist divorce reformers helped perpetuate a politics that allowed for massive cuts in benefits to poor single women in the 1990s even after feminists themselves had changed their message.

In the aftermath of the failed efforts to win universal benefits during the welfare and health care reform battles, feminists turned back to the politics of selective entitlements that had provided a winning, if flawed, formula for them for so many years. As they pushed back against the PRWORA and formulated new campaigns to create new social rights, feminists found new uniquely sympathetic and deserving categories of women on which to focus their efforts. Despite the early hope of the Clinton years, the playbook for a successful campaign to create new social insurance benefits remained remarkably unchanged.

Feminist campaigns to soften the effects of the PRWORA came to focus on two different victims who activists argued deserved special protections because of specific, sympathetic disaster narratives: abused wives and children. Early documents put out after the PRWORA told the stories of how welfare had allowed women to escape violent marriages. One 1997 pamphlet told "Robin's Story." Robin was the mother of a four-year-old, a social work student in Kentucky, and a recipient of Medicaid and food stamps. She was also recently divorced. Robin wrote, "In my opinion, the people that wrote welfare reform really don't understand what it's gonna do to people that are living on it. 'Cause the people around me in low-income housing are on welfare because it was a way to escape abusive marriages. Just like me—that's the way I got out of my marriage. They really don't think about that."[85] Robin was the ideal, deserving defender of the old system: a formerly-married mother, a student with professional ambitions, and the victim of domestic abuse.

Stories like Robin's gave feminists early legislative traction against the PRWORA. Even before the bill had become law, NOW LDEF won an amendment to mitigate its effects against abused women. The Family Violence Amendment gave states the option of waiving work requirements and time limits for domestic violence victims receiving welfare. NOW LDEF believed it was "the first federal law recognizing the role of domestic violence in creating and prolonging poverty."[86] After the law passed, they turned their attention to getting states to take up the option—winning from Clinton a presidential proclamation urging states to use the option and a directive requiring HHS and DOJ to help ensure that states implemented the exception.[87]

In addition to expressing their concerns about its effects on victims of domestic violence, critics of welfare reform also argued that the new work requirements for women made few provisions for child care.[88] In a 1997 grant proposal for funds to research the effects of the PRWORA, NOW LDEF wrote that it planned to "focus national and local attention on the issue of whether child care is available for women who want to work or are being required to work, and whether lack of child care is being considered (as required by Federal law) a legitimate reason for failure to comply with work requirements."[89] NOW's campaigns for improved child care access had always been as much about supporting women as their children. But in the 1990s, progressive activists found that children and their need for care were the better front on which the battle for expanded social rights could be fought.

This "kids first" strategy applied not only to the feminist response to welfare reform but also to renewed efforts to expand health insurance coverage.[90] In 1996, following the defeat of Clinton's health care reform proposal, Senator Ted Kennedy and the Clintons decided to return to the strategy of extending government health insurance gradually through selective entitlements to populations deemed especially deserving. They chose to focus on children. In 1997, thanks to an alliance between Kennedy and Republican Senator Orrin Hatch, Congress passed the State Children's Health Insurance Program (SCHIP), which essentially expanded Medicaid to children of the working poor.[91] Like Medicaid, the program is administered by the states, which receive federal matching funds to help them administer health insurance to children from families with incomes too high to receive Medicaid but too low to afford private insurance. The matching funds come in the form of block grants, leaving the states discretion in how they administer the programs. The politics of selective entitlements had returned, but women's—even mothers'—ability to make claims on the state had weakened over the years. Going forward, children would be the objects of sympathy through which welfare state expansions were won.

Historians too often end histories of the welfare state in 1996. Instead, we should see the passage of the PRWORA and SCHIP as part of the same story. Read together, these two laws, one contracting and one expanding the welfare state, are a fitting cap on three decades of advocacy from the Right and the Left. They demonstrate a remarkable shift in sympathy away from women and toward children. No longer considered vulnerable and deserving, women saw benefits cut throughout the 1990s. Efforts to establish a cross-class feminism that improved the workplace for women ended with women pushed into the workforce without the social programs needed to ease their care work responsibilities. Children and women suffered as a result of these policies, but only children inspired enough sympathy to win new legislative attention.

"Caught"

In 1993, NOW representatives considering a guaranteed national income program wrote, "Policy-makers, the media and conservative think-tanks spend much time popularizing the idea that conditions for women are much improved. The reality for nearly every female worker today is that she is caught in a low-paying job at the bottom of the career ladder."[92] Getting stuck at the bottom of the career ladder left women without a firm hold on employment-based insurance benefits. Yet, after decades of rising divorce rates, women also knew that their claim to marriage-based insurance benefits could fall apart—especially when judges believed that a woman's time in the workforce, however brief or disjointed, meant she could support herself. In the face of women's continued tenuous grip on both sides of the marriage- and employment-based insurance system, feminists began to prioritize a more universal benefits agenda.

Even as feminist organizations attempted to broaden the scope of their demands and rise above a politics of selective entitlements, feminist activists were stalked by their predecessors' rhetoric. The effects of their earlier work for selective entitlements that favored the well-off made the public suspicious of their intentions. Conservatives eagerly and successfully called attention to this weakness, exploiting not only feminist rhetoric but also concerns about a contracting economy and social insurance system that loosened everyone's grip on the employment-based insurance system. In the face of continuous opposition to their agenda and a growing, broad push to cut welfare benefits, feminists eventually fell back to the political strategy they had honed throughout the 1970s and 1980s. They found that the political system was still most responsive to demands to expand the social insurance system for very specific groups of deserving individuals who could be understood as caught in a crisis beyond their own making.

Selective entitlements continued to prove key to expanding the welfare state, but these limited victories—while providing real benefits to some women—built a social safety net full of holes. Meanwhile, shifts in political sympathy—some created by previous selective entitlements—could have devastating effects on specific groups of vulnerable individuals. Women's entrance into the workforce, however difficult and incomplete, limited the political sympathy they inspired and the new entitlements they could win. From Clinton's early attorney general candidates to those women's nannies, women remained vulnerable in a world that demanded they work, but made few accommodations for them to do so. Caught in a social insurance system built around marriage and work, but with a tenuous ability to spend a lifetime in either the home or the workplace, women continued to easily slip through the holes in the American social insurance system.

CONCLUSION

No-Fault Divorce in a Morality-Based Welfare System

Reflecting back on the lessons of her first year at the head of the NOW Marriage and Divorce Task Force, in 1974 Elizabeth Coxe Spalding wrote, "A 'reform divorce law' that demands equal responsibility of mother or wife in any aspect of divorce in a state that does not give her equal protection in enforcement, equal protection in housing, credit, job opportunities and half of the assets of marriage is not a divorce reform bill. It is, instead, a bill that imposes servitude to the ex-husband on top of what was servitude to her husband."[1] Spalding, like most feminist divorce reformers, recognized the myriad problems created by the clash between public policies that demanded divorced women act as their ex-husbands' economic equals and public policies that continued to assume all women were their husbands' dependents during marriage. Yet, over two decades of effort, feminist divorce reformers failed either to get all public policies to assume that men and women were equal partners during their marriages or to entirely eliminate the use of marriage to distribute resources. Instead, they won laws that expanded the dependent statuses through which women could receive benefits to include divorced women. These new social insurance policies effectively maintained the long-held assumption that once-married women would and should depend financially on their husbands even as divorce laws came to emphasize equality between separating husbands and wives. Marriage, and specifically breadwinner-dependent marriages, remained firmly at the center of the social welfare regime's eligibility determinations.

Even as states adopted no-fault divorce laws that removed moral judgments from the terms of divorce, national social insurance policies continued to make moral judgments. From its beginning, America's social insurance system has grown through the extension of entitlements to groups deemed morally deserving: widows, children, single mothers, disabled former workers, the elderly, even the very specific category of late-stage renal patients.[2] Not incidentally, those deemed morally deserving have generally been middle-class and white. By defining morally deserving behavior as the behavior of the largely white middle class and immoral behavior as the behavior of poor people of color, policymakers built social welfare programs that maintained and perpetuated class and race privilege. The elimination of moral judgments from divorce law through no-fault divorce thus inevitably clashed with American social welfare policies built around morality-based entitlements.

Feminist divorce reformers began to organize shortly after the last major expansion of state-sponsored benefits and just as the retrenchment of the late 1970s and 1980s began. Their strategies, successes, and failures show how the fully developed, public and private, postwar American social welfare regime shaped the possibilities for reform imagined by those it left out and how the new politics of welfare state contraction eventually curtailed those possibilities. Feminist divorce reformers set their agenda in response to constraints stemming both from the ways in which the American welfare state had developed long before they began to organize and from the increasingly conservative context—both economically and socially—in which they operated. The policy compromises they struck reinforced the precedent of using the politics of selective entitlements and moral judgment to win limited expansions to the welfare state.

When feminist divorce reformers demanded recognition by the social welfare regime that had previously excluded them, they challenged the belief that divorced women were morally undeserving. But in doing so they simply redefined divorce as socially acceptable behavior, expanding who was selected for entitlement, but only narrowly. Feminist divorce reformers won a place for themselves in the social insurance system by convincing policymakers that they were more deserving than women who never married. The enacted feminist divorce reform agenda solidified and exacerbated race and class biases and the marriage-based welfare state, ultimately helping lay the groundwork for the simultaneous expansions of class inequality, on the one hand, and the civil rights of same-sex couples, on the other.

Feminist Divorce Reform's Political Moment

NOW's Marriage and Divorce Task Force, the Alliance for Displaced Homemakers, and other feminist divorced women's organizations grew out of a unique political moment created by rising divorce rates, new divorce laws, new expectations that divorced women would enter the workforce, and the reality that many of these women could obtain only low-paying jobs. The rising number of divorced women included many women who had left the full-time, paid workforce upon marriage. They had raised children and supported their husbands' careers. When they divorced, these women found themselves in a world of changed laws and expectations that encouraged them to cut all economic ties with their ex-husbands and support themselves.

These women also divorced amidst a culture of rights-based social movements. The civil rights movement, the women's rights movement, and more radical organizing efforts on the Left provided many of the leaders of the feminist divorce reform movement—from Tish Sommers to Annette Smail—with prior experience fighting for economic rights. When already politically active women divorced and discovered their limited economic rights, they turned to the feminist movement for institutional support. So did many women with no political background when they encountered no-fault divorce laws that they believed mistreated women. Together these women built an active divorce reform movement within the larger feminist movement.

The broad swath of the population experiencing divorce and new divorce laws further aided the organizing efforts of feminist divorce reformers. Across classes, couples that married in the 1970s divorced at roughly the same rate. The divorce rate for both college-educated and non-college-educated couples married in the 1970s rose together until it peaked in 1979 with just about 50 percent of marriages ending in divorce.[3] Also across classes, a surprisingly large number of divorcing women shared the experience of having stayed out of the paid workforce to raise children for an extended period of time.[4] The common experience of divorce allowed for a powerful and initially relatively economically diverse feminist divorce reform movement.

Feminist divorce reform activists generally accepted no-fault divorce laws. Early debates within NOW, for example, about whether or not to support no-fault did not last long. Feminist organizations wholeheartedly supported the goal of removing moral judgments from marital dissolution proceedings. But, they argued, if women could not be at fault for their marriages ending, divorced women had every right to claim state support. In fact, they insisted divorced women were more deserving than many current recipients of state aid, like single mothers who had never married. Like the unemployed in an economic downturn, divorced women had tried to live up to society's expectations and now needed society's support.

Between 1974 and 1986, this line of argument produced a series of laws designed to specifically assist divorced women. Congress created programs that helped divorced women reenter the workforce. New laws guaranteed that a divorced spouse could maintain the good credit record he or she had while married and pay to stay on an ex's health insurance plan. Divorced dependent spouses also gained a right to a portion of their ex's Social Security and other federally administered retirement benefits, if they had been married a sufficient number of years. Other new laws encouraged judges in divorce proceedings to take into account the value of women's homemaking and to divide privately administered retirement benefits evenly. All of this legislation effectively made marriage a better bargain for women.

The compromises embedded in these new laws ultimately undermined the feminist divorce reform movement's staying power. More equal outcomes between spouses at the end of individual marriages masked significantly unequal outcomes between divorcing couples in different classes. The economic resources most likely to be divided evenly in divorce—private retirement accounts—were those held by wealthy people, while the economic resources for which the law mandated that a divorced dependent spouse automatically receive a smaller share than her breadwinner ex were those on which middle-class and low-income people depended—specifically, Social Security benefits. By the middle of the 1980s, divorce no longer served as a unifying experience for women of different classes and thus served less effectively as the basis of a grassroots movement.

Women's entry into the workforce posed yet another challenge to the continued vibrancy of the feminist divorce reform movement. Women entered the workforce for a variety of reasons. New jobs and opportunities opened up by feminist activism pulled women into the workforce even as deindustrialization and men's stagnating wages pushed other women into the workforce. The number of women in the workforce with children under three peaked in 1998 at 62 percent; the number of working women with children over six peaked just shy of 80 percent in 2000.[5] Although this was not why most women entered the workforce, by earning their own salaries and benefits women protected themselves from a complete loss of economic resources in a divorce.

The compromise feminist divorce reformers had struck in the 1970s and 1980s—a social insurance system that rewarded marriage, even after divorce, and assumed the breadwinner-homemaker division of labor—ignored a brewing problem. As middle-class women entered the workforce to keep their families afloat in a stagnating economy, as middle-class men lost jobs in the face of deindustrialization, and as middle-class marriage rates fell and divorce rates continued to rise, the people who relied most on the federal social insurance system were also the people whose marriages looked least like the breadwinner-homemaker model on which that system was based. The laws governing the economic resources on which middle-class Americans relied encouraged middle-income couples to embrace a family structure—a breadwinner-dependent relationship—that the economy made almost impossible.

Feminist Divorce Reformers' Legacy in the 1990s and 2000s

The 1990s solidified the patterns that had developed as a result of feminist divorce reformers' political compromises in the prior two decades. New laws increased judicial power to divide economic resources in divorce and encouraged the equal division of privately administered resources while maintaining the breadwinner-dependent structure of publicly administered ones. The laws and legal institutions with which wealthy couples interacted suggested a good marriage was a contracted partnership. In contrast, those with which middle-income couples interacted continued to view marriage as a status defined by a breadwinner-homemaker division of family labor. Low-income couples who could not establish either a breadwinner-homemaker relationship or a steady partnership were punished by the laws regulating the economic resources that most directly touched their family lives. Despite the limits of feminist divorce reformers' victories, new groups of individuals excluded from the social insurance system—particularly same-sex couples—turned to feminist divorce reformers' playbook to win access to benefits.

In the 1970s and 1980s, with feminist divorce reformers' encouragement, Congress repeatedly passed laws that used duration of marriage to determine post-divorce access to benefits. This sent a powerful message that marriage was a status determined by longevity of commitment above all else. The federal government's administrative bureaucracy carried this understanding of marriage forward into the 1990s. For example, by the end of the century, the Social Security Administration routinely counted anyone who had been married for less than ten years as "never-married."[6] This was the number of years of marriage Congress had settled on as entitling women to a dependent Social Security benefit even after divorce. Marriages that lasted under ten years no longer mattered to the SSA, and, therefore, the agency no longer counted these shorter marriages as marriages at all.

Along with longer marriages, the SSA encouraged breadwinner-homemaker marriages. It did so by offering any currently married couple who had been married for at least nine months and any divorced couple who had been married for at least ten years breadwinner-dependent benefits. As late as 1998, 63 percent of women receiving Social Security payments still chose to draw dependent benefits based on their husbands' earnings because this amounted to more than benefits based on their own earnings records.[7] Numerous legislative proposals designed to push the Social Security system to treat marriages as economic partnerships instead of breadwinner-dependent relationships failed.

While the SSA was erasing marriages that lasted under ten years and persisting in splitting retirement benefits unevenly between ex-spouses, the courts were experimenting with a new way of dividing employer-based pensions equally between spouses. Lawyers and judges began to refer to the "coverture fraction"—years married divided by years a spouse participated in an employer-based pension plan.[8] To calculate a dependent spouse's share of a pension, courts simply had to multiply the value of the pension by the coverture fraction and divide the result in two.[9] Courts applying the coverture fraction gave women exactly half of all retirement benefits earned during the years they were married to a man. Throughout the late 1980s and early 1990s, as part of their strategy of using the courts to enact a feminist divorce reform agenda, women's groups filed amicus briefs advocating the use of the coverture fraction.[10] By 1990, six states had adopted its use as the default rule; by the early 2000s, twenty-nine states had. Almost all did so through judicial rulings.[11] These courts were essentially applying to private pensions the principle that all property earned during a year of marriage was joint property. They did this even as Congress refused to apply this principle to Social Security entitlements through the adoption of an earnings sharing law.

The use of the term "coverture fraction" by feminists and courts in the 1990s challenges the idea that by this time coverture had been thoroughly dismantled.[12] As late as the 1990s, feminist activists were fully aware that in most states the idea that a couple's property would be entirely in the husband's hands was alive and well even if it wasn't a matter of formal law. Rather than continuing to fight the vestiges of the coverture principle, many activists turned to creating tools—like the coverture fraction—that helped move women out from under coverture's remaining constraints only if their marriages ended. The coverture fraction was a tool that created a contractual relationship out of a status when a marriage ended, but only for women with access to a specific set of economic resources.

Feminist divorce reformers' work ultimately entrenched not only dated understandings of marriage in the law but also the use of selective entitlements for married people to expand the welfare state, paving the way for the agenda of the burgeoning same-sex marriage movement. In the 1990s and 2000s, same-sex marriage advocates followed in the path of feminist divorce reformers and tied their demands for marriage rights to the benefits that came with marriage—dependent benefits from Social Security and health insurance, for example. Instead of aligning with those who had been excluded from the marriage-based benefits of the welfare state, they sought to fit themselves into the same morally deserving status categories that divorced women had used in the 1970s and 1980s.[13]

By fighting for access to marriage-based entitlements as feminist divorce reformers had restructured them in the 1970s and 1980s, same-sex marriage advocates won access to a system that was particularly unfair to them. After all, same-sex couples won access to a system that awarded benefits on the basis of years of formal marriage. A member of a same-sex couple that has been in a formal partnership since 1985 but was only recognized by the state as married in 2010 would have to wait until 2020 to have any rights to Social Security through his or her partner after divorce.[14] Moreover, same-sex couples are even less likely than opposite-sex couples to fall into breadwinner-homemaker marriages. Like most couples today, same-sex couples are ill-served by dependent benefits that do not accurately reflect the primary-secondary breadwinner structure of most marriages. Same-sex couples, and indeed most Americans, would be far better off if the law reflected feminist divorce reformers' initial proposals to treat members of married couples as independent economic citizens engaged in an economic partnership.

Marriage, Morality, and Selective Entitlements Today

In 2005, the *New York Times* ran a sensationalist article about women at elite universities who wanted to be stay-at-home mothers.[15] In response, a former champion of this choice—Terry Martin Hekker—took up her pen. Thirty years earlier Hekker had written an op-ed for the *Times* defending her choice to be a "housewife" and castigating a society she felt was telling her at every turn that she was a failure for staying home and raising five children instead of entering the workforce. The op-ed made her famous and a poster child for antifeminism. But in the 1990s, on her fortieth wedding anniversary, Hekker's husband suddenly divorced her.[16] Now, she presented her life as a "cautionary tale" for women considering opting out of the workforce. She wrote of her experience, "'Divorced' doesn't begin to describe the pain of this process. 'Canceled' is more like it. It began with my credit cards, then my health insurance and checkbook, until, finally, like a used postage stamp, I felt canceled too."[17] Even after all the work feminist divorce reformers had done over the preceding decades, Hekker found herself in a familiar role: divorced woman forced to reckon with the gendered economic and social insurance system.

The feminist divorce reform movement was, fundamentally, about the nature of women's economic citizenship. A half century earlier, women's victory in their suffrage campaign transformed the nature of women's political citizenship. Prior to the granting of women's suffrage, their relationship to the state had been mediated by their husbands. After suffrage, women entered into a direct political relationship with the state. Through divorce, however, once-married women discovered that their economic relationship to the state was still mediated through their husbands. They organized to demand a direct economic relationship to the state to match their increasingly direct relationship to the market. In the end, what is most striking about the history of divorced women's attempts to reform the social welfare system is how little changed.

Feminist divorce reformers articulated a vision of marriage as a partnership and a site of work for women, rather than as proof of women's morality. Decades of organizing failed to achieve this goal. Instead, divorce reformers won selective entitlements for divorced women who met certain length-of-marriage requirements. New laws recognized divorced women as having a unique place in the social insurance system, distinct from both married and never-married women.[18] The act of having been married entitled women to some, but not all, of the benefits of marriage. This outcome reveals the tremendous path dependency of the selective entitlement system. Once the precedent had been set that proof of moral deservingness was the best way for a group to win new state-sponsored welfare benefits, that proof became the grounds on which most campaigns for welfare state expansions were fought.

This outcome also reflects the political and economic conditions under which divorced women worked. The selective entitlement system has always served those who claim to protect the public purse. By giving benefits only to those people deemed most deserving, the government purports to save money. In the 1970s and 1980s, as divorced women lobbied Congress to force both the public and private pieces of America's hybrid pension system to include them, they faced a Congress less and less willing to raise taxes or increase government spending. Thus, when Congress passed laws expanding divorced women's access to government-funded pensions, these laws came with lengthy marriage requirements—ten years served as the minimum. Congress also passed laws requiring the private pension and health insurance systems to include some divorced women, but these laws invariably came with shorter length-of-marriage requirements—often only one year. A lesson was learned here as well: The easiest way to expand access to the social insurance system was through government regulation of private benefits.

Both of these strategies were mobilized in the largest expansion of the American welfare state since Medicare and Medicaid: the passing of the Affordable Care Act in 2010. The law includes expansions of selective entitlements—for the poor—and a tremendous amount of regulation of access to the private market. For example, one provision of the law mandates that children be allowed to stay on their parents' private health care plans until they turn twenty-six. This is not dissimilar from the way in which health insurance access was expanded for divorced women through mandates that a woman be allowed to stay on her ex-husband's plan, for a price. The Affordable Care Act also still uses families—marriage and parenthood—to distribute health care benefits.

The continued use of marriage to determine eligibility did not inspire protests from feminist groups in 2010, but it should have.[19] In the late 1990s, the Social Security Administration predicted that by 2020 almost 6 percent of women would never marry.[20] This prediction—which would have amounted to a mere 2 percent increase in never-married women from 1991—alarmed the SSA because it meant that even fewer women would fit into the breadwinner-homemaker family model on which it relied. It was an underestimate. By 2009, just over 10 percent of women aged fifty through fifty-four had either never been married or had been married for less than ten years.[21] The drop in the marriage rate has been even starker for women without a college degree. In 2015, 65 percent of adults with a four-year college degree were married, but only 50 percent of adults with no education beyond high school had married.[22] The marriage-based social insurance system's structure is more out of synch with the structure of American's lives than ever.

Almost a half century ago, states realized that the law of divorce no longer accurately represented most couples' experience. The requirement that one spouse be morally at fault in order for the other spouse to end their marriage did not represent how marriages actually dissolved. The use of fault to distribute economic resources between spouses seemed equally unfair. Recognizing this truth, couples either developed elaborate systems to work around the law and end their marriages in ways that seemed fair to them or ended up in endless legal battles. When lawyers, judges, legislators, and everyday people recognized this system was broken, they forced a revolution in divorce law. The changes that followed did not come without pain and economic suffering. It required twenty more years of legal tinkering to make the economic outcomes of divorce closer to fair, and, as we have seen, still more legal adjustments are necessary.

If moral judgments should have no role in how economic resources are distributed between individuals at the end of marriage, they should have no role in how economic resources are distributed across society. Just as judges cannot determine who was at fault at the end of a marriage, legislators should not apply measures of morality to whole swaths of the population. Even if Congress continues to want to incentivize breadwinner-dependent marriages, the outcomes of the many laws it has passed with this goal in the last fifty years suggest how difficult that project is. Social Security's reward for dependent spouses may encourage some to marry while discouraging others whose economic status makes it impossible for them to take advantage of this reward. Yet, by persisting in using marriage to measure who deserves economic resources, Congress avoids passing laws that could give economic resources to people who need them. It also promotes a divisive politics that encourages competition for resources on the basis of claims of comparative moral deservingness, instead of creating a unifying social safety net.

In 1993, Catharine MacKinnon argued that in the legal regime feminist divorce reformers created, "not even divorce disturbs the power relations of marriage."[23] This is true of both the power relations between spouses and ex-spouses and of the power relations between whole classes of people who marry and who do not. It does not have to be this way. Recovering feminist divorce reformers' partnership agenda would change the power relations of marriage during and after marriage. If successful, the partnership agenda would force the law to recognize the true nature of most marriages and the value of care work in the home. It is also an agenda that could reach women across classes—uniting low-income women who hesitate to get married and high-income women who struggle to make their marriages and careers work together. Most importantly, however, the partnership agenda could push the government to evaluate and interact with spouses as individuals, making them equal economic citizens. Only when the state approaches everyone as an individual equally deserving of economic rights and resources can we build a truly comprehensive social safety net.

NOTES

Introduction

1. Geraldine Ferraro, "Keynote by Rep. Geraldine A. Ferraro, Corning Women and Money Conference," 5 November 1983, pp. 2–3, Box 129: Folder: Ferraro, Speeches, Corning, N.Y., Seminar on Women and Money, Geraldine Ferraro Papers, Marymount Manhattan College, New York (hereafter cited as Geraldine Ferraro Papers).

2. Sandra L. Hofferth and Kristin Moore, "Women's Employment and Marriage," in *The Subtle Revolution: Women at Work*, ed. Ralph E. Smith (Washington, D.C.: Urban Institute, 1979), 99, 103.

3. Daniel T. Rodgers, *Age of Fracture* (Cambridge, Mass.: Belknap, 2011), 146.

4. Betsey Stevenson and Justin Wolfers, "Marriage and Divorce: Changes and Their Driving Forces," *Journal of Economic Perspectives* 21, no. 2 (April 1, 2007): 29–30.

5. Alice Lake, "Divorcees: The New Poor," *McCall's*, September 1976, 18, Folder 1.2, Betty Berry Papers (MC 506), Schlesinger Library, Cambridge, Mass. (hereafter cited as Berry Papers).

6. Ibid., 2.

7. Ibid., 4.

8. For a more extensive discussion of this legal history see Janet Halley, "What Is Family Law?: A Genealogy," Parts I and II, *Yale Journal of Law and the Humanities* 23 (2011); Amy Dru Stanley, *From Bondage to Contract: Wage Labor, Marriage, and the Market in the Age of Slave Emancipation* (New York: Cambridge University Press, 1986); and Nancy Cott, *Public Vows: A History of Marriage and Nation* (Cambridge, Mass.: Harvard University Press, 2000).

9. Daniel Horowitz, *Betty Friedan and the Making of "The Feminine Mystique": The American Left, the Cold War, and Modern Feminism* (Amherst: University of Massachusetts Press, 1998), 226; Stephanie Coontz, *A Strange Stirring: "The Feminine Mystique" and American Women at the Dawn of the 1960s* (New York: Basic Books, 2010); Joanne Meyerowitz, "Beyond the Feminine Mystique: A Reassessment of Postwar Mass Culture, 1946–1958," *Journal of American History* 79, no. 4 (March 1, 1993): 1456–1458.

10. Alice Kessler-Harris, *In Pursuit of Equity: Women, Men, and the Quest for Economic Citizenship in 20th-Century America* (New York: Oxford University Press, 2001), 241–242, 258; Horowitz, *Betty Friedan and the Making of "The Feminine Mystique,"* 226; Cynthia Ellen Harrison, *On Account of Sex: The Politics of Women's Issues, 1945–1968* (Berkeley: University of California Press, 1988), 178–182, 191–203.

11. Sara M. Evans, *Personal Politics: The Roots of Women's Liberation in the Civil Rights Movement and the New Left* (New York: Vintage, 1980).

12. Bruce J. Schulman, *The Seventies: The Great Shift in American Culture, Society, and Politics* (New York: Free Press, 2001); Jefferson Cowie, *Stayin' Alive: The 1970s and the Last Days*

of the Working Class (New York: New Press: 2010); Judith Stein, *Pivotal Decade: How the United States Traded Factories for Finance in the Seventies* (New Haven, Conn.: Yale University Press, 2010); Daniel T. Rodgers, *Age of Fracture* (Cambridge, Mass.: Belknap, 2011).

13. Thomas Borstelman, *The 1970s: A New Global History from Civil Rights to Economic Inequality* (Princeton, N.J.: Princeton University Press, 2012), 77; Marjorie Spruill, *Divided We Stand: The Battle over Women's Rights and Family Values That Polarized American Politics* (New York: Bloomsbury, 2017), 162–163.

14. J. Brooks Flippen, *Jimmy Carter, the Politics of Family, and the Rise of the Religious Right* (Athens: University of Georgia Press, 2011), 262.

15. Betty Berry, "Marriage, Divorce and Family Relations Task Force Report of the National Organization for Women," February 1973, p. 3, Folder 3.10, Elizabeth Coxe Spalding Papers (MC 482), Schlesinger Library (hereafter cited as Spalding Papers).

16. Nancy M. Gordon, "Statement of Nancy M. Gordon Before the Hearings of the President's Commission on Pension Policy on 'Retirement Income and Coverage of Women and Minorities,'" 30 November 1979, p. 3, Box 24: Folder: Older Women, Collection: Records of the Office of the Assistant to the President for Women's Affairs, Sarah Weddington, Jimmy Carter Presidential Library, Atlanta, Ga.

17. Elaine Tyler May, *Homeward Bound: American Families in the Cold War Era* (New York: Basic Books, 2008), 212–213.

18. Herbert Jacob, *Silent Revolution: The Transformation of Divorce Law in the United States* (Chicago: University of Chicago Press, 1988), 42; Denese Ashbaugh Vlosky and Pamela A. Monroe, "The Effective Dates of No-Fault Divorce Laws in the 50 States," *Family Relations* 51, no. 4 (October 1, 2002): 317–324.

19. May, *Homeward Bound*, 212–213; Lenore Weitzman, *The Divorce Revolution: The Unexpected Social and Economic Consequences for Women and Children in America* (New York: Free Press, 1985), xviii; Justin Wolfers, "Did Unilateral Divorce Laws Raise Divorce Rates? A Reconciliation and New Results," *American Economic Review* 96, no. 5 (December 2006): 1806.

20. Rose M. Kreider and Renee Ellis, "Current Population Reports; Number, Timing, and Duration of Marriages and Divorces: 2009" (United States Census Bureau, May 2011: http://www.census.gov/prod/2011pubs/p70-125.pdf), 7.

21. Stevenson and Wolfers, "Marriage and Divorce," 30.

22. Barbara Dafoe Whitehead, *The Divorce Culture* (New York: Alfred A. Knopf: Distributed by Random House, 1997), 95.

23. "Script: National Judicial Education Program Presentation, 'The Economic Consequences of Divorce: Child Support and the Feminization of Poverty,' Panel at N.J. Statewide Conference on Child Support Enforcement," 9 May 1982, Folder 309.5, Records of the NOW Legal Defense and Education Fund (LDEF) (MC 623), Schlesinger Library (hereafter cited as NOW LDEF Records).

24. Yvonne Brathwaite Burke, "Women: Their Struggle Against Powerlessness [For Publication in Adelphi University Anthology]," 1 April 1977, p. 10, Folder 148.24, Yvonne Brathwaite Burke Papers, Special Collections, University of Southern California, Los Angeles, Calif. (hereafter cited as Burke Papers).

25. Lake, "Divorcees: The New Poor."

26. John B. Anderson, "Speech: Justice for American Women," no date [c. 1979–1980], Folder 26.12, Catherine East Papers, 1916–1996 (MC 477), Schlesinger Library (hereafter cited as Catherine East Papers); NOW, "ERA Countdown Campaign Facts Sheets: ERA and Home-

makers: Partnership in Marriage," 1981, Box 3: Folder F003: Equal Rights Amendment [1/3], Elizabeth Dole Files: Series I: Subject Files, Ronald Reagan Presidential Library, Simi Valley, Calif.

27. Catharine A. MacKinnon, *Women's Lives, Men's Laws* (Cambridge, Mass.: Belknap, 2005), 38; Martha Fineman, *The Illusion of Equality: The Rhetoric and Reality of Divorce Reform* (Chicago: University of Chicago Press, 1991), 112.

28. Task Force to Investigate Unfair Discrimination Against Women by the Insurance Industry, "Preliminary Report and Recommendations on Discriminatory Practices in the Insurance Industry," 10 September 1976, p. 6, Folder: Health and Disability Insurance Discrimination, Jimmy Carter Presidential Library.

29. Susan Faludi, *Backlash: The Undeclared War Against American Women* (New York: Three Rivers Press, 2006), 42.

30. Ibid., 734–737.

31. Kristin A. Collins, "Administering Marriage: Marriage-Based Entitlements, Bureaucracy, and the Legal Construction of the Family," *Vanderbilt Law Review* 62, no. 4 (May 2009); Kristin A. Collins, "'Petitions Without Number': Widows' Petitions and the Early Nineteenth-Century Origins of Public Marriage-Based Entitlements," *Law and History Review* 31, no. 01 (February 11, 2013); Theda Skocpol, *Protecting Soldiers and Mothers: The Political Origins of Social Policy* (Cambridge, Mass.: Belknap, 1992); Linda Gordon, *Pitied but Not Entitled: Single Mothers and the History of Welfare, 1890–1935* (Cambridge, Mass.: Harvard University Press, 1995); Gwendolyn Mink, *The Wages of Motherhood: Inequality in the Welfare State, 1917–1942* (Ithaca, N.Y.: Cornell University Press, 1995).

32. Alice Kessler-Harris's *In Pursuit of Equity* offers a full history of the debates behind these policy decisions that supported the breadwinner-homemaker family during the New Deal.

33. Kessler-Harris, *In Pursuit of Equity*, 140–141.

34. Ibid., 143–147.

35. Ibid.

36. Jill S. Quadagno, *The Transformation of Old Age Security: Class and Politics in the American Welfare State* (Chicago: University of Chicago Press, 1988); Michael B. Katz, *In the Shadow of the Poorhouse: A Social History of Welfare in America* (New York: Basic Books, 1996); Jennifer Klein, *For All These Rights: Business, Labor, and the Shaping of the American Welfare State* (Princeton, N.J.: Princeton University Press, 2003); Jacob Hacker, *The Divided Welfare State: The Battle over Public and Private Social Benefits in the United States* (New York: Cambridge University Press, 2002), 239.

37. Hacker, *Divided Welfare State*, 239.

38. Weitzman, *Divorce Revolution*, 323; Betty Berry, "Testimony by Betty Berry, Past National Coordinator, Marriage and Divorce Task Force, National Organization for Women, Marriage and Divorce Consultant to the United Presbyterian Church in the U.S.A. Before Assembly Judiciary Committee, New York Senate," 12 September 1974, Folder 4.15, Berry Papers.

39. Ferraro, "Keynote by Rep. Geraldine A. Ferraro, Corning Women and Money Conference," 5 November 1983.

40. With 113 official members, the Task Force on Marriage and Divorce had fewer members than the media, education, and rape task forces, but almost twice as many as the Women and Health Task Force and more than three times as many as the Minority Women and Women's Rights Task Force and the Sexuality and Lesbianism Task Force ("National Organization for Women, National Task Forces and Committees," 25 July 1975, Folder 42.3, National

Organization for Women (NOW) Records, 1959–2000, Schlesinger Library (hereafter cited as NOW Records).

41. Arlene Kaplan Daniels, "W.E.A.L.: The Growth of a Feminist Organization" (Northwestern University, March 1977), 14, Box 10: Location 146.E.9.7B, Folder: WEAL: Historical Background, 1975–1980, Arvonne Fraser Papers, Minnesota Historical Society, Saint Paul, Minn. (hereafter cited as Arvonne Fraser Papers).

42. A few historians have looked at this group of women previously: Flora Davis's survey, *Moving the Mountain: The Women's Movement in America Since 1960* (New York: Simon & Schuster, 1991) argues that rising divorce rates help to account for the timing of the second wave of feminism and looks closely at how divorce became a national issue in the 1980s as a result of pressure from women's groups. But Davis gives relatively little attention to the broader agenda of feminist divorce reformers, focusing on their work on divorce laws but not economic rights. Alison Lefkovitz's 2010 dissertation, "The Problem of Marriage in the Era of Women's Liberation," University of Chicago, argues that legal coverture came undone in the 1960s, 1970s, and 1980s by examining a range of challenges to traditional marriage, including no-fault divorce, marital rape laws, and demands for same-sex marriage. Lefkovitz looks closely at how demands for recognition of women's labor in the home came to a head in the debates over the ERA and Social Security for homemakers. Lisa Levenstein's article "'Don't Agonize, Organize!': The Displaced Homemakers Campaign and the Contested Goals of Postwar Feminism," *Journal of American History* 100, no. 4 (March 2014): 1114, takes a deeper dive into the history of feminists supportive of the homemaking role.

43. See, for example, Borstelman, *The 1970s*; Marisa Chappell, *The War on Welfare: Family, Poverty, and Politics in Modern America* (Philadelphia: University of Pennsylvania Press, 2010); Susan Faludi, *Backlash: The Undeclared War Against American Women* (New York: Random House, 1991); Nancy Fraser, *Fortunes of Feminism: From State-Managed Capitalism to Neoliberal Crisis* (New York: Verso, 2013); Daniel Rodgers, *Age of Fracture* (Cambridge, Mass.: Belknap, 2011); Spruill, *Divided We Stand.*

44. For the cohort that married between 1940 and 1960, the marriage rate rose and divorce rate fell across demographics. For the cohort that married in the 1970s, while black Americans were significantly less likely than white Americans to get married, the divorce rate for married white and married black Americans was very similar. In 1974, the Census Bureau reported that 4.3 percent of white women and 5.7 percent of black women were divorced. For the cohort born between 1950 and 1955, 42.9 percent of black marriages and 41.5 percent of white marriages ended in divorce by 2001 (May, *Homeward Bound*, 1–3; Stevenson and Wolfers, "Marriage and Divorce," 34–35; Jessie Bernard, *The Jessie Bernard Reader* (Boulder, Colo.: Paradigm, 2008), 174, 189).

45. Twila L. Perry, "Alimony: Race, Privilege, and Dependency in the Search for Theory," *Georgetown Law Journal* 82 (1994): 2493.

46. For examples of recent scholarship citing the formal equality agenda of the 1970s, see Patricia A. Seith, "Congressional Power to Effect Sex Equality," *Harvard Journal of Law and Gender* 36, no. 1 (Winter 2013): 7; Serena Mayeri, *Reasoning from Race: Feminism, Law, and the Civil Rights Revolution* (Cambridge, Mass.: Harvard University Press, 2011), 6.

47. Rhonda Y. Williams, *The Politics of Public Housing: Black Women's Struggles Against Urban Inequality* (New York: Oxford University Press, 2004), 16, 85.

48. Robert Self, *All in the Family: The Realignment of American Democracy Since the 1960s* (New York: Hill and Wang, 2012), 4.

49. Collins, "Petitions Without Number," 11.

50. T. H. Marshall, *Citizenship and Social Class* (London: Pluto, 1992); Kessler-Harris, *In Pursuit of Equity.*

51. Kessler-Harris, *In Pursuit of Equity*, 5.

52. Social and cultural historians have generally approached the history of marriage in the 1970s through a cultural lens. For excellent examples of cultural histories of divorce the 1970s, and indeed throughout the whole twentieth century, see Herbie J. DiFonzo, *Beneath the Fault Line: The Popular and Legal Culture of Divorce in Twentieth-Century America* (Charlottesville: University Press of Virginia, 1997), and Stephanie Coontz, *Marriage, A History: How Love Conquered Marriage* (New York: Penguin, 2006). Legal historians, on the other hand, have generally focused on the case record and, when looking at legislation, focused specifically on the development of no-fault laws. For examples of these two approaches, see Anne Alstott, "Private Tragedies—Family Law as Social Insurance," *Harvard Law and Policy Review* 4 (2010), and Herma Hill Kay, "Equality and Difference: A Perspective on No-Fault Divorce and Its Aftermath," *University of Cincinnati Law Review* 56 (1997–1998). The few books that have really engaged marriage as a political institution through history—for instance, Nancy Cott's *Public Vows* and Priscilla Yamin's *American Marriage* (Philadelphia: University of Pennsylvania Press, 2012)—miss this moment almost entirely, skipping straight from interracial marriages to the marriage equality movement.

53. My inclusion of credit is relatively unique among scholars of the American social welfare regime. Here, I follow divorced women's lead. They correctly understood that credit shared many characteristics with resources more commonly considered to be part of the social welfare regime. As a privately offered resource regulated by the government in order to ensure widespread access, credit epitomized the public-private nature of the social welfare regime. In these years, credit was also administered to women in the same way as health insurance and pensions: through their husbands. Such mediated access prevailed even though a diverse range of institutional sources actually provided these resources to men—pensions through the government and the workplace, health care largely through the workplace, and credit through consumer businesses. The shared aims and characteristics of credit, health insurance, and pensions knit them together into a coherent regime.

54. Hacker, *Divided Welfare State*, 44.

55. "Open Your Parachute Mom," no date, Box 124: Folder: Former Spouses Press, Patricia Schroeder Papers, Archives, University of Colorado Boulder Libraries (hereafter cited as Patricia Schroeder Papers).

Chapter 1

1. Doyle v. Doyle, 158 N.Y.S. 2d 909, 911 (Supreme Court, New York County, N.Y., 1957).

2. Herbert Jacob, *Silent Revolution: The Transformation of Divorce Law in the United States* (Chicago: University of Chicago Press, 1988).

3. *Doyle v. Doyle.*

4. In Re Marriage of Brantner, 67 Cal. App. 3d 416, 418 (Court of Appeals, 4th Dist., Div. 2, Cal., 1977).

5. Ibid., 418. The $1 a month award allowed the court to retain jurisdiction over the case for an extra four years; such awards were not uncommon (Weitzman, *Divorce Revolution*, 167–168).

6. Ibid., 419.

7. Ibid.

8. Ralph E. Smith, The Movement of Women into the Labor Force," in *Subtle Revolution*, 3–7; U.S. Department of Labor, "Labor Force Participation of Women by Age," https://www.dol.gov/wb/stats/NEWSTATS/facts/lf_prate_women_age_48_2016_txt.htm.

9. *Doyle v. Doyle.*

10. Ibid., 911.

11. Stephanie Coontz, *Marriage*, 235, 252.

12. Elizabeth Ogg, "Confidential Draft: Divorce," 20 August 1975, p. 7, Box 38: Folder 6, Uniform Law Commission (ULC) Main Office Papers, Tarlton Law Library, Rare Books and Special Collections, University of Texas, Austin (hereafter cited as ULC Main Office Papers).

13. "Proceedings of the Committee of the Whole: Uniform Marriage and Divorce Act," in *Proceedings: National Conference of Commissioners on Uniform State Laws in Its 79th Year, in Clayton, Missouri, August 1–6, 1970* (New York: Martin C. Johnson Reporting Service, Inc.): 6.

14. Robert Mnookin and Lewis Kornhauser, "Bargaining in the Shadow of the Law: The Case of Divorce," *Yale Law Journal* 88, no. 5 (Dispute Resolution) (April 1979), 950–997.

15. Lawrence M. Friedman, "A Dead Language: Divorce Law and Practice Before No-Fault," *Virginia Law Review* 86, no. 7 (October 1, 2000): 1512.

16. Ogg, "Confidential Draft: Divorce," 8.

17. Anna R. Igra, *Wives Without Husbands: Marriage, Desertion, and Welfare in New York, 1900–1935* (Chapel Hill: University of North Carolina Press, 2007), 43.

18. Elaine Tyler May, *Great Expectations: Marriage and Divorce in Post-Victorian America* (Chicago: University of Chicago Press, 1980), 151.

19. Davis, *Moving the Mountain*, 288; Faludi, *Backlash*, 39.

20. "Script: National Judicial Education Program Presentation, 'The Economic Consequences of Divorce: Child Support and the Feminization of Poverty.'"

21. Jacob, *Silent Revolution.*

22. Deborah Dinner, "The Divorce Bargain: The Father's Rights Movement and the Dual System of Family Law [Draft provided to author]," September 2014, 12.

23. George Partis, "Divorce Chats: How You Can Help!" 1 December 1968, Folder 12.15, Berry Papers.

24. Dinner, "Divorce Bargain"; Michael Grossberg, "Who Gets the Child? Custody, Guardianship, and the Rise of a Judicial Patriarchy in Nineteenth-Century America," *Feminist Studies* 9, no. 2 (Summer 1983): 235–260.

25. No author, "Memo: From: United States Divorce Reform, Inc.; To: Our Friends and Members; Subject: Family Preservation Month June 1970," June 1970, Folder 12.15, Berry Papers.

26. Dinner, "Divorce Bargain."

27. George Doppler, "Men's Liberation," *Playboy*, December 1970, Folder 12.15, Berry Papers.

28. George Doppler, "America Needs Total Divorce Reform—Now!" no date [c. 1970], Folder 12.15, Berry Papers.

29. Norman Lobsenz, "Can Divorce Be Fair?," *Redbook Magazine*, January 1959, p. 25, Folder 163.2069: Divorce, 1964–1972, Betty Friedan Papers (MC 575), Schlesinger Library (hereafter cited as Friedan Papers).

30. Ibid.

31. Ann Hirsch, "Letter to Griffiths from Ann Hirsch" (Southfield, Mich., no date [from Griffiths response 1970]), Box 39: Folder: 91st Women–Discrimination, University of Michi-

gan, Martha Griffiths Papers, University of Michigan, Ann Arbor (hereafter cited as Martha Griffiths Papers).

32. Ibid.

33. Alice Kessler-Harris, *A Woman's Wage: Historical Meanings and Social Consequences* (Lexington: University Press of Kentucky, 2014).

34. Lobsenz, "Can Divorce Be Fair?"

35. Alice Rossi, "NOW: Task Force on the Family" no date [penciled in 1967], Folder 47.42, NOW Records.

36. Jacob, *Silent Revolution*.

37. Phillip L. Hammer, "Divorce Reform in California: The Governor's Commission on the Family and Beyond," *Santa Clara Law Review* 9, no. 1 (January 1969), 32–74.

38. Jacob, *Silent Revolution*, 63; William J. Pierce, "Letter to William Pincus, Ford Foundation, from William J. Pierce, Chairman, Executive Committee, NCCUSL," 28 September 1966, Ford Foundation Grant # 06700066, Reel 1810, Rockefeller Archive Center, Sleepy Hollow, N.Y.; Herma Hill Kay, "Equality and Difference: A Perspective on No-Fault Divorce and Its Aftermath," *University of Cincinnati Law Review* 56 (1987): 44; Nina Totenberg, "Easy Divorces: No More Fights and Maybe No More Alimony," *National Observer*, 15 February 1971, Loose Folders: Folder: No Label, ULC Main Office Papers.

39. Pierce, "Letter to William Pincus"; Paul Ylvisaker, "Memo: To: Mr. McGeorge Bundy; Via: Mr. Joseph M. McDaniel Jr.; Subject: Board of Trustees—Public Affairs. Grant of $60,000 to the National Conference of Commissioners on Uniform State Laws to Assist in the Research and Deliberation Required to Promulgate a Comprehensive Uniform Family Law," 31 October 1966, Ford Foundation Grant # 06700066, Reel 1810, Rockefeller Archive Center.

40. William J. Pierce, "Letter to Miss Arlene Deder, National Affairs Division, Ford Foundation, from William J. Pierce, Executive Director, NCCUSL, Re: Grant No. 67-66," 12 January 1970, Ford Foundation, Grant #06700066, Reel 1810, Rockefeller Archive Center; Jacob, *Silent Revolution*, 51.

41. Harold E. Read, Jr., "American Bar Association: Report to the House of Delegates: National Conference of Commissioners on Uniform State Laws, Recommendation," 4 January 1974, p. 1, Box 38: Folder 6, ULC Main Office Papers.

42. Ibid.

43. National Conference of Commissioners of Uniform State Laws, Uniform Marriage and Divorce Act (St. Louis, Mo. [Annual Conference]: National Conference of Commissioners of Uniform State Laws, 2 August 1973), 7.

44. National Conference of Commissioners of Uniform State Laws, Uniform Marriage and Divorce Act, 21.

45. Ibid., 6.

46. Ibid., 25, 28–29; Harry D. Krause, *Family Law in a Nutshell* (St. Paul, Minn.: West Publishing Co., 1977), 274.

47. Michael Wheeler, *No-Fault Divorce* (Boston: Beacon Press, 1974), 32; Thomas B. Marvell, "Divorce Rates and the Fault Requirement," *Law and Society Review* 23, no. 4 (January 1, 1989): 552–553; National Conference of Commissioners of Uniform State Laws, Uniform Marriage and Divorce Act, 35–36.

48. Jacob, *Silent Revolution*, 113, 119–120.

49. National Conference of Commissioners of Uniform State Laws, Uniform Marriage and Divorce Act, 33–35.

50. Krause, *Family Law in a Nutshell*, 366.

51. National Conference of Commissioners of Uniform State Laws, Uniform Marriage and Divorce Act, 35.

52. Imposing means testing on alimony made the experience of receiving alimony notably more like the process of receiving AFDC, the means-tested welfare program for poor women. This means testing, which was often quite humiliating, was one of things that women on welfare objected to most. Lenore Weitzman and Ruth B. Dixon, "Alimony: A Quest for Justice in Changing Times, Paper Read at the Meetings of the American Sociological Association, August 1976" (New York City, August 1976), p. 9, Box 39: Folder 2, ULC Main Office Papers.

53. Totenberg, "Easy Divorces."

54. Jacob, *Silent Revolution*, 75–76.

55. Read, "American Bar Association: Report to the House of Delegates: National Conference of Commissioners on Uniform State Laws, Recommendation," 4–5. The ABA Family Law Section wanted "irretrievable breakdown" to be defined solely on the basis of a 180-day separation; the ULC refused to make the definition this narrow.

56. Ibid., 2.

57. John M. McCabe, "Letter to Professor Merril from John M. McCabe," 13 July 1978, Box 38: Folder 6, ULC Main Office Papers. The states were Arkansas, Colorado, Georgia, Kentucky, Montana, New Jersey, and Washington.

58. Ibid.

59. Jacob, *Silent Revolution*, 80.

60. John M. McCabe, "Memo to: Scope and Program Committee; From: John M. McCabe; Subject: Survey of Progress on the Uniform Marriage and Divorce Act; Date: July 23, 1988," 23 July 1988, p. 31, Box 22: Folder 7, ULC Main Office Papers.

61. Ibid., 1.

62. Wheeler, *No-Fault Divorce*, 31–32.

63. Denese Ashbaugh Vlosky and Pamela A. Monroe, "The Effective Dates of No-Fault Divorce Laws in the 50 States," *Family Relations* 51, no. 4 (October 1, 2002): 322.

64. A few states (Nevada and New Hampshire, for example) began to allow this practice as early as the 1930s. Before the 1970s, this was the closest any state got to allowing no-fault divorce, although some states offered many more grounds for divorce than others (ibid., 322–323).

65. Wheeler, *No-Fault Divorce*, 33–35.

66. National Conference of Commissioners of Uniform State Laws, Uniform Marriage and Divorce Act, 34.

67. Citizen's Advisory Council on the Status of Women, "Recognition of Economic Contribution of Homemakers and Protection of Children in Divorce Law and Practice," January 1974, p. 2, Box 611, Subject File: Women: Divorce, Rare Book and Manuscript Library, Bella Abzug Papers, 1970–1976, Columbia University in the City of New York (hereafter cited as Abzug Papers).

68. Martha Griffiths, "Draft: National Commission on the Observance of International Women's Year, 1975, Committee on the Homemaker; Memo: To: Jill Ruckelshaus, Presiding Officer; From: Martha Griffiths, Chair; Subject: Recommendation on Revision of Divorce Laws," 12 January 1976, p. 1, Folder 19.2, Catherine East Papers.

69. Elizabeth Coxe Spalding, "Dear Legislator Letter from Elizabeth C. Spalding" (Greenwich, Conn., 18 March 1973), Folder 47.42, NOW Records.

70. Vlosky and Monroe, "The Effective Dates of No-Fault Divorce Laws," 320.

71. "Women's Lobby of Virginia Press Release: Urging Governor's Veto of HB 1470," no date [c. 1974/1975], Folder 24.33, Catherine East Papers.

72. Clipping: Pat Franklin, "Opinions Differ on Divorce Law," *Ledger Star*, 31 March 1975, Folder 24.33, Catherine East Papers.

73. George Doppler, "Letter to John McCabe from George F. Doppler," 29 August 1977, Box 38: Folder 6, ULC Main Office Papers.

74. Ed Randegger, "National Conference of Commissioners on Uniform State Laws Memo: To: Newspeople; From: Ed Randegger," 6 July 1978, Box 38: Folder 6, ULC Main Office Papers; Kujawinski v. Kujawinski, 71 Ill. 2d 563 (Supreme Court of Illinois, 1978).

75. Ellen Sim Dewey, "Letter to Cindy Morse from Ellen Sim Dewey," 6 June 1977, Folder 46.38, NOW Records.

76. Maurice Merrill, "Uniform Marriage and Divorce Act, Commissioners' Prefatory Note," 29 November 1970, pp. 1–2, Loose Folders: Folder: No Label, ULC Main Office Papers; Alice S. Rossi, "NOW Temporary Committee on Family," 1967, pp. 1–3, Folder 47.44, NOW Records.

77. Rossi, "NOW Temporary Committee on Family," p. 3.

78. "Clipping: Domestic Relations: The Price of Guilt v. Need," *Time Magazine*, 8 March 1968, Folder 6.1, Berry Papers.

79. Betty Berry, "Civil Disabilities in Marriage and Divorce," no date, pp. 1–3, Folder 1.3, Berry Papers.

80. Stephanie Gilmore, *Groundswell: Grassroots Feminist Activism in Postwar America* (New York: Routledge, 2013), 3.

81. "Family Law Proposal," no date, p. 1, Folder 125.3: Family Law Project, 1982–1984, NOW LDEF Records.

82. Ruth B. Cowan, "Women's Rights Through Litigation: An Examination of the American Civil Liberties Union Women's Rights Project, 1971–1976," *Columbia Human Rights Law Review* 8 (1976–1977): 373. The ACLU Women's Rights Project also took a few divorce-related cases, but its focus was on eliminating explicitly different treatment of men and women in divorce law. NOW LDEF, on the other hand, was more concerned with finding ways to challenge divorce's economic impact on women.

83. Ellen Sim Dewey, "Letter to Laura Rasmussen, Attorney, from Ellen Sim Dewey," 7 January 1975, Folder 5.1, Spalding Papers; Ellen Sim Dewey, "Letter to the Editor by Ellen Sim Dewey," 21 March 1975, Folder 38.39, NOW Records.

84. Ellen Sim Dewey, "Letter to Mary Anne Sedey, Midwest Regional Director, NOW, from Ellen Sim Dewey," 21 March 1975, Folder 38.39, NOW Records.

85. Ellen Sim Dewey, "Letter to Betty Berry from Ellen Sim Dewey," 15 September 1972, Folder 368.7, NOW LDEF Records.

86. Hendrik Hartog argues, "Americans have been especially inclined to phrase their demands and 'needs' in arguments about constitutional rights, to expect remedies for their wrongs to be provided through processes provided by formal legal institutions, and to view their activities as touching on issues of constitutional interpretation." Dewey was working within this tradition, which Hartog argues often particularly captures the imagination of people, like Dewey, who "recognized themselves as still dependent and vulnerable, even as they aspired to autonomy." Hartog shows there is a long tradition of activists attempting to create a constitutional obligation for public authorities to help individuals achieve autonomy. Hendrik Hartog, "The Constitution of Aspiration and 'The Rights That Belong to Us All,'" *Journal of American History* 74, no. 3 (December 1, 1987): 1013–1034, quotes pp. 1030 and 1019.

87. Dewey, "Letter to Mary Anne Sedey."

88. Dewey, "Letter to Laura Rasmussen," 2.

89. Ellen Sim Dewey, "Letter to Betty Boyer, Attny, from Ellen Sim Dewey," 7 December 1975, Folder 5.1, Spalding Papers; Buchholz v. Buchholz, 248 N.W. 2d 21, 23 (Supreme Court, Nebraska, 1976).

90. *Buchholz* (1976), 24.

91. Dewey, "Letter to Betty Boyer."

92. Ibid.

93. *Buchholz* (1976), 22. This was an argument that a few other women across the country also tried (Krause, *Family Law in a Nutshell*, 31–32). For example, a California woman had already used this argument and lost in 1972 (In re Marriage of Walton, 28 Cal. App. 3d 108 (Court of Appeals, 4th Dist., Div. 2, 1972).

94. *Buchholz* (1976), 22.

95. Ellen Sim Dewey, "Memo: To: Cindy, Lynn, Sandy, Karen, Mary, Bea, Jackie; From: ESD; Re: Conference and MFRD Report," 30 October 1975, Folder 5.1, Spalding Papers; Dewey, "Letter to Laura Rasmussen."

96. Dewey, "Letter to Cindy Morse," 4.

97. *Buchholz* (1976), 23–24.

98. No author, "National Convention Resolutions Marriage, Family Relations, Divorce," February 1973, Folder 3.20, Spalding Papers.

99. Betty Berry, "Letter to Wilma Scott Heide from Betty Berry," 22 February 1972, Folder 8.3, Wilma Scott Heide Papers, Schlesinger Library, Cambridge, Mass.

100. NOW–New York State, Task Force—Marriage, Divorce, and Family Relations, "Proposed Resolution for Discussion for Presentation at Next National Conference," c. 1975, Box 17: Folder: Marriage and Divorce Committee, 1974–1975 (Folder 9), NOW-NYC Papers (TAM 106), Tamiment Library, New York University, New York City (hereafter cited as NOW-NYC Papers).

101. Betty Friedan, *It Changed My Life: Writings on the Women's Movement* (Cambridge, Mass.: Harvard University Press, [1976] 1998), 175.

102. Elizabeth Coxe Spalding, "For Newsletter, Fall of 1975," 1975, Folder 5, Spalding Papers.

103. *Brantner* (1977), 419.

104. Ibid.

105. Ibid.

106. DiFonzo, *Beneath the Fault Line*, 52–53.

Chapter 2

1. Betty Friedan, "Speech at NOW Marriage and Divorce Conference," 20 January 1974, Folder 89.1020, Friedan Papers.

2. Judy Klemsrud, "'Obsolete' Divorce Laws Assailed at N.O.W. Conference Here," *New York Times*, 21 January 1974, 32.

3. Sarah A. Soule and Susan Olzak, "When Do Movements Matter? The Politics of Contingency and the Equal Rights Amendment," *American Sociological Review* 69, no. 4 (1 August 2004), 472–476.

4. Nancy Ann Rella, "'Lib' Leaders Speak Out: Move Over Men, Women Demand," *Reporter Dispatch*, 14 October 1970, Folder 1.2, Berry Papers; Betty Berry, "Letter to Jacqui Ceballos from Betty Berry," 19 June 1971, Folder 1.1, Berry Papers.

5. Betty Friedan, "Letter to Betty Berry from Betty Friedan," 3 December 1968, Folder 1.1, Berry Papers.

6. Betty Berry, "For Discussion Purposes Only. Report of NOW-NY Marriage and Divorce Committee," September 1970, p. 1, Box 17: Folder 3: Marriage and Divorce Committee, 1970, NOW-NYC Papers.

7. Friedan, *It Changed My Life*, 5, 404; Betty Berry, "Betty Blaisdell Berry, President, The Marriage and Divorce Press, Inc. Resume," 1 November 1976, Folder 1.5, Berry Papers.

8. Natalie Gittelson, "Divorce, Suburban Style," *Harper's Bazaar*, June 1974, Folder 1.2, Berry Papers.

9. Beverly Grunwald, "Getting Around: Partners in Divorce," *Women's Wear Daily*, 1 April 1976, Folder 1.2, Berry Papers; Betty Berry, "Testimony of Betty Blaisdell Berry, Adviser to the National Task Force on Marriage, Divorce, and Family Relations of the National Organization for Women Before the Senate Finance Committee of the U.S. Government, Washington, DC, September 25, 1973," 25 September 1973, Box 611, Subject File: Women: Divorce, Abzug Papers; Berry, "Betty Blaisdell Berry, President, The Marriage and Divorce Press, Inc. Resume."

10. Gittelson, "Divorce Suburban Style."

11. Betty Berry, "Report to 1968 National NOW Conference, Atlanta, GA. December 7, 1968, by NOW New York Subcommittee on Divorce, Alimony, and Child Support. Prepared by Betty Berry Chairman," 7 December 1968, Box 17: Folder 2: Marriage and Family Committee, 1968–1969, NOW-NYC Papers.

12. Grunwald, "Getting Around: Partners in Divorce."

13. Berry, "Report to 1968 National NOW Conference, Atlanta, GA," 4.

14. Betty Berry, "Suggested Guidelines in Studying and Comments on the Uniform Marriage and Divorce Act," 11 April 1971, pp. 1–2, Folder 3.12, Spalding Papers.

15. Betty Berry, "Preliminary NOW Marriage Insurance Plan," no date, p. 1, Folder 2.13, Berry Papers. Berry's proposal for "altar to grave insurance" reformulated Sir William Beveridge's 1942 "cradle to grave" insurance proposal; however, her suggestions actually echoed some of Beveridge's original plans for married women's relationship to the social insurance system. In *Social Insurance and Allied Services*, Beveridge's report outlining his proposed comprehensive social insurance system, he wrote, "On marriage every woman begins a new life in relation to social insurance." Beveridge wanted the social insurance system to recognize this by stripping women of the entitlements to unemployment and disability insurance they might have earned by working upon marriage and in exchange giving them a marriage grant. After marriage, if a wife entered the workforce she could earn new unemployment and disability insurance credits, but they would not build on those credits she had earned before marriage. If a married woman lost a male-breadwinner through divorce, and if she was not at fault, Beveridge also proposed that the insurance system address her loss in the same way that it addressed a widow's, with a social insurance benefit. Notably, Beveridge was unable to let go of fault in his insurance system, whereas Berry accepted no-fault as a basic premise of her proposal (Great Britain, *Social Insurance and Allied Services* [Great Britain, Parliament, Papers by Command] Cmd. 6404 [London: H. M. Stationery Office, 1942], 50, 134).

16. Betty Berry, "Draft Proposal for a Marriage Insurance Plan," 5 November 1970, Box 17: Folder: Marriage and Divorce Committee, 1970, NOW-NYC Papers.

17. Berry, "Preliminary NOW Marriage Insurance Plan," 5.

18. Ibid., 1.

19. Ibid., 5.

20. Ibid., 5–6.

21. Even Berry did not ask for the whole widows' benefit for divorced women, signaling that she did not think divorced women and widows were in the exact same situation. She did not explain why she set her suggested the benefit for divorced women at 75 percent of a widow's benefit.

22. Berry, "Preliminary NOW Marriage Insurance Plan," 6.

23. "The National Organization for Women Would Like to Propose . . . Expanding Social Security to Include Benefits for Qualified Family Members in Case of Divorce [Draft Only Not Official Policy]," no date, Folder 2.13, Berry Papers.

24. Robert M. Ball, "Letter to Betty Berry from Robert M. Ball, Commissioner of Social Security, Department of Health, Education, and Welfare, Social Security Administration, Baltimore, Maryland," 2 December 1970, Folder 2.13, Berry Papers.

25. Betty Berry, "Press Release: NOW-NY Marriage and the Family Committee Delegation, August 26th, 'Women's Strike for Equality Day,' Background Sheet," 26 August 1970, Folder 2.13, Berry Papers; Davis, *Moving the Mountain*, 116; Alice Echols, *Daring to Be Bad: Racial Feminism in America 1967–1975* (Minneapolis, Minn.: University of Minnesota Press, 1989), 198.

26. Berry, "For Discussion Purposes Only: Report of NOW-NY Marriage and Divorce Committee," 4–5.

27. Enid Nemy, "Divorce Insurance Gains Varied Support in State," *New York Times*, 15 January 1973, 1.

28. Betty Berry, "Letter to Charles A. Siegfried from Betty Berry," 17 February 1971, Folder 2.13, Berry Papers.

29. K. Arne Eide, Assistant Vice President Insurance Relations, "Memo for Mr. C. A. Siegfried, Vice Chairman of the Board and Chairman of the Executive Committee of Metropolitan Life, Prepared for National Organization of Women, Betty Berry, Re: Divorce Insurance Plan," 9 March 1971, Folder 2.13, Berry Papers.

30. Ibid., 4.

31. Jack T. Hunn, "Smith-Sternau Organization, Inc. Memo: To: Ms. Elizabeth Forsling Harris and Ms. Anne Wexler; Re: Non-Discriminatory Insurance Product Development for Groups of Women," 2 April 1973, Folder 34.7, NOW Records.

32. Friedan, *It Changed My Life*, 416.

33. Ariela R. Dubler, "Wifely Behavior: A Legal History of Acting Married," *Columbia Law Review* 100, no. 4 (May 1, 2000): 969.

34. Edward D. Berkowitz, *The Other Welfare: Supplemental Security Income and U.S. Policy* (Ithaca: Cornell University Press, 2013), 1, 42.

35. Cynthia Gorney, "The Discarding of Mrs. Hill," *Ladies' Home Journal*, February 1976, 60.

36. Nemy, "Divorce Insurance Gains Varied Support in State"; Betty Berry, "Letter to Dr. Edwin K. Graham (Assistant Director, Education Services, Institute of Life Insurance) from Betty Berry," 30 January 1974, Folder 2.13, Berry Papers; Molly Sinclair, "NOISE About Divorce: Insure Your Marriage," *Miami Herald*, 4 December 1972, Box 17, Folder 6: Marriage and Divorce Committee—Equal Rights Divorce Reform Bill, 1972, NOW-NYC Papers.

37. Sinclair, "NOISE About Divorce."

38. Betty Berry, "Proposal for a Marriage Insurance Plan," second printing, 1973, p. 6, Folder 3.21, Spalding Papers.

39. Friedan, *It Changed My Life*, 416.

40. Self, *All in the Family,* 328–329.

41. Bella Abzug, "Speech by Congresswoman Bella Abzug to NOW Marriage and Divorce Conference, Hotel Commodore, New York, January 19, 1974," Box 759 A: Folder: NOW Marriage and Divorce Conference Speech, Abzug Papers, 2, 6–7.

42. Berry, "Betty Blaisdell Berry, President, The Marriage and Divorce Press, Inc. Resume."

43. "The Interlocking Relationships Between the Marital Courts and Welfare," *Alert: Women's Legislative Review,* January 1973, Folder 1.1, Spalding Papers; Elizabeth Spalding, "Letter from Elizabeth Spalding to NOW," 4 September 1970, Folder 2.17, Berry Papers.

44. Spalding, "Letter from Elizabeth Spalding to NOW."

45. Estate of Amy McGinnis Spalding v. Commissioner of Internal Revenue, 537 F. 2d 666 (U.S. Court of Appeals, 2nd Circ., 1976); Spalding v. Spalding, 171 Conn. 220 (Supreme Court of Conn., 1976).

46. *Estate of Amy McGinnis* (1976), 667.

47. *Spalding* (1976).

48. *Estate of Amy McGinnis* (1976).

49. *Spalding* (1976).

50. Faith A. Seidenberg, "Letter to Betty Berry from Faith A. Seidenberg, Vice-President for Legal Affairs, NOW," 7 October 1970, Folder 1.20, Berry Papers.

51. Elizabeth Coxe Spalding, "Letter to Sylvia [Roberts] from Elizabeth Coxe Spalding and Attachments [Litigation Currently Pending Between Elizabeth C. Spalding and Charles F. Spalding and Chronological Legal History of Elizabeth C. Spalding and Charles F. Spalding]," 6 February 1973, Folder 617.8, NOW LDEF Records.

52. Sylvia Roberts, "Letter to Elizabeth Coxe Spalding from Sylvia Roberts," 14 March 1973, Folder 617.8, NOW LDEF Records.

53. Betty Spalding, "Proposed Action Program for the Task Force," *National Organization for Women: National Task Force—Marriage, Divorce and Family Relations Newsletter,* August 1973, Folder 1.4, Spalding Papers; Betty Spalding, "Memo: To: Karen Decrow; From: Betty Spalding; Re: Reorganization of Substantive Feminist Issues within NOW," 19 November 1975, Folder 5.9, Spalding Papers.

54. Spalding, "Proposed Action Program for the Task Force," 1.

55. Ibid.

56. Ibid.; "The Interlocking Relationships Between the Marital Courts and Welfare."

57. Spalding, "Proposed Action Program for the Task Force," 1.

58. Congressional Caucus for Women, "Congressional Caucus for Women Fact Sheets," 7 February 1984, Box 76: Folder: Economic Equity Act Fact Sheet, Geraldine Ferraro Papers; Self, *All in the Family,* 110.

59. Elizabeth C. Spalding, Coordinator National Task Force on Marriage and Divorce, NOW, "The Galaxy of Attitudes Towards Women, As Reflected by Certain Laws" (NOW State Conference, Connecticut: Manchester Community College, 24 August 1974), p. 1, Folder 169.43, NOW Records.

60. Elizabeth Coxe Spalding, "Handwritten Note [Wreath Action]," no date [c. 1975], Folder 5.7, Spalding Papers; Mary Anne Sedey, "Memo: To: State Coordinators; From: Mary Anne Sedey, Midwest Regional Director; Subject: Marriage, Divorce and Family Taskforce Bulletin," 12 October 1974, Folder: 4.19, Spalding Papers.

61. For a classic discussion of "maternalist" women's rights activists and their effect on the social welfare regime, see Theda Skocpol, *Protecting Soldiers and Mothers: The Political*

Origins of Social Policy (Cambridge, Mass.: Belknap, 1992). For detailed discussions of the difficulty of squaring women's equality and maternalist agendas, see Ariela Dubler, "In the Shadow of Marriage: Single Women and the Legal Construction of the Family and the State," *Yale Law Journal* 112, no. 7 (1 May 2003): 1641, and Chappell, *War on Welfare*, 41.

62. Elizabeth Coxe Spalding, "First Report to the National Task Force on Marriage and Divorce, National Organization for Women," February 1975, p. 13, Folder 1.4, Spalding Papers.

63. Marisa Chappell, "Rethinking Women's Politics in the 1970s: The League of Women Voters and the National Organization for Women Confront Poverty," *Journal of Women's History* 13, no. 4 (Winter 2002): 166; Arvonne Fraser, "Letter to Doris Seward from Arvonne Fraser," 17 July 1975, Box 10: Location 146.E.9.7B: Folder: WEAL: Historical Background, 1975–1980, Arvonne Fraser Papers.

64. Norma Card, "Letter to Karen DeCrow," 7 August 1975, Folder 2.10, Spalding Papers.

65. NOW Task Force on Women and Poverty, "Save Our Sisters: Support the Task Force on Women and Poverty Resolution on Child Support," no date, p. 2, Folder 3.1, Spalding Papers.

66. Elizabeth Coxe Spalding, "Letter to Norma Card," 27 August 1975, Folder 2.10, Spalding Papers.

67. Elizabeth Coxe Spalding, "Letter to Senator Nunn," 14 August 1973, p. 3, Folder 3.9, Spalding Papers.

68. Elizabeth Coxe Spalding, "Memo: To: Eleanor Smeal, Chair of the NOW Board; Re: Proposed Resolutions of the Women and Poverty TF for Consideration by the Nat'l Board at the Phoenix, Ariz Meeting, Jan 24 1976," 18 January 1976, Folder 3.1, Spalding Papers.

69. NOW Task Force on Women and Poverty, "Save Our Sisters."

70. Elizabeth Coxe Spalding, "Letter to Mrs. Gwen Anderson," no date [c. 1971–1972], Folder 2.1, Spalding Papers.

71. Elizabeth Coxe Spalding, "Letter to Patricia Lindh," 10 July 1975, Folder 3.2, Spalding Papers.

72. Ellen Sim Dewey, "Memo to: To: Betty Berry, Betty Dwyer and Elizabeth Spalding; From: Ellen Sim Dewey; Re: Marriage and Divorce Taskforce," 15 June 1973, Folder 2.4, Spalding Papers; Betty Spalding, "Letter to Ellen Sim Dewey from Betty Spalding," 14 July 1973, Spalding Papers.

73. Kessler-Harris, *In Pursuit of Equity*, 135; Skocpol, *Protecting Soldiers and Mothers*, 465.

74. Elizabeth Coxe Spalding, "Reasons for Awarding Alimony in Divorce," no date, p. 2, Folder 5.5, Spalding Papers.

75. Tish Sommers, "Brief Statement on Task Force on Older Women," no date, Folder 210:39, NOW Records.

76. Patricia Huckle, *Tish Sommers, Activist, and the Founding of the Older Women's League* (Knoxville: University of Tennessee Press, 1991), 80–85.

77. Ibid., 121–138, 167–168.

78. Ibid., 169.

79. Ibid., 142.

80. Ibid., 185–186.

81. Ibid., 15, 189.

82. Tish Sommers, "NOW Task Force on Older Women [Handwritten Note Says This Is 'from Programs for NOW']," November 1973, Folder: 48.22, NOW Records.

83. Ruth Rosen, *The World Split Open: How the Modern Women's Movement Changed America* (New York: Viking, 2000), 272.

84. "Script: National Judicial Education Program Presentation, 'The Economic Consequences of Divorce: Child Support and the Feminization of Poverty,' Panel at NJ Statewide Conference on Child Support Enforcement," 9 May 1982, p. 30, Folder 309.5, NOW LDEF Records.

85. Tish Sommers, "Task Force [on Older Women] Statement for Letter to Congress (and Attached Displaced Homemakers Act)," 28 February 1975, Folder: 89.41, NOW Records.

86. Lisa Levenstein argues in her article on the Displaced Homemakers Campaign that Sommers and Shields opposed the inclusion of women on welfare in their definition of displaced homemakers. My own research contradicts this, but does suggest, along with Levenstein's work, that both women opposed means testing to determine if women deserved benefits as displaced homemakers (Levenstein, "'Don't Agonize, Organize!'," 1132).

87. Huckle, *Tish Sommers, Activist*, 190–191; Laurie Shields, "'All Rising to a Great Place Is by a Winding Stair': The Latest, and Possibly the Last UPDATE on National Displaced Homemakers Legislation," June 1978, Folder 7.14, Berry Papers.

88. Laurie Shields, *Displaced Homemakers: Organizing for a New Life* (New York: McGraw-Hill, 1981), ix.

89. "Displaced Homemakers Bill—California," no date, Folder 48.26, NOW Records.

90. "Legislative Background: Displaced Homemakers," *Civil Rights Digest*, December 1977, Folder: 89.41, NOW Records; Levenstein, "'Don't Agonize, Organize!'," 1123.

91. Shields, "All Rising to a Great Place Is by a Winding Stair."

92. Shields, *Displaced Homemakers*, 61.

93. *Displaced Homemakers: Programs and Policy: An Interim Report* (Washington, D.C.: Congress of the United States, Office of Technology Assessment, 1985), 15.

94. Shields, "All Rising to a Great Place Is by a Winding Stair."

95. Shields, *Displaced Homemakers*, 119.

96. Marisa Chappell, "Demanding a New Family Wage: Feminist Consensus in the 1970s Full Employment Campaign," in *Feminist Coalitions: Historical Perspectives on Second-Wave Feminism in the United States*, ed. Stephanie Gilmore (Urbana: University of Illinois Press, 2008), 256.

97. Ibid., 265.

98. Yvonne Brathwaite Burke, "Statement by the Honorable Yvonne Brathwaite Burke (D-Calif.) for Insertion into the Congressional Record, Subject: Part-Time Career Opportunity Act," 11 January 1977, Folder 135.13, Burke Papers.

99. Alicia Christian, "The Socio-Economic Status of Black Women in the United States (1970–1974): A Congressional Black Caucus Fact Sheet," June 1975, p. 5, Folder 148.13, Burke Papers; Bernard, *Jessie Bernard Reader*, 189.

100. Yvonne Brathwaite Burke, "Testimony of the Honorable Yvonne Brathwaite Burke Before the Subcommittee on Employment Opportunities: H.R. 28, The Displaced Homemakers Act," 14 July 1977, p. 2, Folder 135.18, Burke Papers.

101. Tish Sommers and Laurie Shields, "Attention: All Members of N.O.W.: A Real Hot Flash from the Post-Menopausal Zest Set," 14 July 1977, Folder 48.22, NOW Records.

102. Sandra Burton and Cynthia Marano, "Dear Network Member Letter from Cynthia Marano and Sandra Burton," 14 October 1980, Carton 95: Folder 2539, Boston YWCA, Records, 1858–1988 (89-M3), Schlesinger Library.

103. Huckle, *Tish Sommers, Activist*, 15, 191.

104. Shields, *Displaced Homemakers*, 130.

105. Quoted in Diane Weathers, "Is Liberation Really Good for Women?" *Family Circle,* 18 September 1979, 66.

106. Phyllis Schlafly, "Displaced Homemaker's Bill," Eagle Forum Report, August 1977, Folder 7-11, Tish Sommers Papers, Special Collections, San Diego State University (hereafter cited as Tish Sommers Papers).

107. Donald T. Critchlow, *Phyllis Schlafly and Grassroots Conservatism: A Woman's Crusade*, Politics and Society in Twentieth-Century America (Princeton, N.J.: Princeton University Press, 2005).

108. Schlafly, "Displaced Homemaker's Bill."

109. No author, "National Essay Contest: Housewives Decry Lot," *Patriot Ledger*, 15 February 1979, Box 1: Folder 1: Contest Rules, Clippings, Winning Entry, Babson-Bernays Competition Records, 1978 (79-M253—86-M79), Schlesinger Library; Lefkovitz, "The Problem of Marriage in the Era of Women's Liberation," 258.

110. Dorothy Woodworth, "A Practical Program to Achieve Economic Justice for Homemakers," 1978, p. 2, Box 1: Folder 1: Babson-Bernays Competition Records.

111. Ibid., 2–3.

112. Ibid., 8.

113. "Homemakers Need the Equal Rights Amendment," 14 March 1972, Folder 11.8, Berry Papers; Phyllis Schlafly, "How ERA Would Change Federal Laws," *Phyllis Schlafly Report*, November 1981, Box 3: Folder F003: Equal Rights Amendment [1/3], Elizabeth Dole Files: Series I: Subject Files, Ronald Reagan Presidential Library.

114. Ellen Sim Dewey, "Letter to Ellie Smeal from Ellen Sim Dewey," 7 June 1977, Folder 46.38, NOW LDEF Records.

115. Self, *All in the Family*, 5–6.

116. Cowie, *Stayin' Alive*, 11–12, 229–230.

117. Lefkovitz, "The Problem of Marriage in the Era of Women's Liberation," 294.

118. Robert G. Kaiser, "Republican Party Molds Platform in Reagan's Image," *Washington Post,* 11 June 1980.

Chapter 3

1. Faith A. Seidenberg, "Statement Before the National Commission on Consumer Finance," 22 May 1972, PA730-0067B, Ford Foundation Archives, Sleepy Hollow, New York.

2. Betty Binder to Congressman Roybal, 15 October 1973, Folder 44. 33, NOW Records.

3. Louis Hyman, *Debtor Nation: The History of America in Red Ink* (Princeton, N.J.: Princeton University Press, 2011), 193.

4. Cott, *Public Vows*, 11–12.

5. Betty Berry, "Civil Disabilities in Marriage and Divorce," no date, 6, Folder 1.3, Berry Papers.

6. Margaret Gates, "Testimony of Margaret Gates Before the Subcommittee on Consumer Affairs of the House Committee on Banking and Currency," 13 November 1973, Grant File PA: 73-67, Ford Foundation Archives.

7. Lefkovitz, "The Problem of Marriage in the Era of Women's Liberation," 44.

8. Ibid., 138.

9. Mayeri, *Reasoning from Race*, 13.

10. Sharyn Campbell, "Letter from Sharyn Campbell to Marjorie Steinberg," 19 March 1975, Folder 45.38, NOW Records.

11. A notable exception to the tendency of scholars to overlook credit's place in the social welfare regime is Melinda Cooper, whose masterful book, *Family Values: Between Neoliberalism and the New Social Conservatism* (Cambridge, Mass.: MIT Press, 2017) recognizes the vast and "unique role" that "the government promotion of consumer credit has long played . . . in America's public-private welfare state." Cooper argues compellingly that "alongside social insurance," credit has served "as one of the key redistributive mechanisms developed under the New Deal" (143).

12. Hyman, *Debtor Nation*.

13. Genevieve LeBaron and Adrienne Roberts, "Confining Social Insecurity: Neoliberalism and the Rise of the 21st Century Debtors' Prison," *Politics and Gender* 8, no. 1 (March 2012): 30.

14. M. Margaret Conway, *Women and Public Policy: A Revolution in Progress*, 2nd ed. (Washington, D.C.: CQ Press, 1999), 101.

15. Hyman, *Debtor Nation*, 132.

16. Ibid., 221.

17. Premilla Nadasen, *Welfare Warriors: The Welfare Rights Movement in the United States* (New York: Routledge, 2005), 106.

18. Hyman, *Debtor Nation*, 3.

19. Morrigene Holcomb, "Credit Availability to Women: Issue Brief Number IB74006: Government and General Research Division, Library of Congress, CRS, Major Issues System," 1975, Box 609, Folder: Credit—General, Abzug Papers.

20. Office of Economic Opportunity, Community Action Program, *Green Power: Consumer Action for the Poor*, August 1969, Box 2032, National Welfare Rights Organization Papers, Manuscript Division, Moorland-Spingarn Research Center, Howard University, Washington, D.C. (hereafter cited as NWRO Papers).

21. Dee Dee Ahern, "Women's Growing Financial Awareness and Her Impact on the Credit World: Address Delivered to American Bankers Association Western Regional Conference, Bank Card Division, San Diego, March 6–8 1974," March 1974, Box 609, Folder: Credit—General, Abzug Papers.

22. *Glamour* editorial, "You Won't Get Credit for Being a Woman," November 1972, Folder 45.31, NOW Records.

23. Hyman, *Debtor Nation*, 191.

24. United States National Commission on Consumer Finance, *Consumer Credit in the United States; Report* (Washington D.C.: U.S. Government Printing Office, 1972).

25. "Transcript of Proceedings, National Commission on Consumer Finance, Commission Meeting" (ACE Federal Reporters, Inc., 18 April 1972), Box 32, RG 220: Records of the National Commission on Consumer Finance, 1970–1972, Minutes and Transcripts of Commissions and Meetings, January 1971–June 1972, National Archives [NARA], College Park, Md.; Robert L. Meade, "Minutes: Meeting of the National Commission on Consumer Finance" (Washington, D.C., 18 April 1972), Box 32: Inserted Inside Transcript of Proceedings, National Commission on Consumer Finance, Commission Meeting, D.C. 18 April 1972, ACE Federal Reporters Inc., RG 220: Records of the National Commission on Consumer Finance, 1970–1972, Minutes and Transcripts of Commissions and Meetings, January 1971–June 1972, NARA.

26. Ira M. Millstein, Chairman, National Commission on Consumer Finance, "Opening Statement: Hearings on Availability of Credit to Women," 22 May 1972, p. 1, PA730-0067B, Ford Foundation Archives.

27. "Transcript of Proceedings, National Commission on Consumer Finance, Commission Meeting," 18 April 1972, p. 10.

28. Ibid., 14.

29. Jorie Lueloff, "Testimony of Jorie Lueloff Friedman Before the National Commission on Consumer Finance," 22 May 1972, Box 35: Folder: Testimony from Hearings on Availability of Credit to Women, RG 220: Records of the National Commission on Consumer Finance, 1970–1972, Minutes and Transcripts of Commissions and Meetings, January 1971–June 1972, NARA. See also Hyman, *Debtor Nation,* 194.

30. Hyman, *Debtor Nation*, 196.

31. Citizens' Advisory Council on the Status of Women, "CACSW Recommendation on Credit," 7 October 1972, Folder 10.41, Catherine East Papers.

32. Hyman, *Debtor Nation*, 195.

33. Steven M. Rhode, "Statement of Steven M. Rhode, Center for National Policy Review, School of Law, Catholic University, Before the National Commission on Consumer Finance," 22 May 1972, Box 16: Folder: Griffiths Hearings—Veterans Benefits [Folder 2 of 3], Citizens' Advisory Council on the Status of Women, RG 0220, Entry A1#: 35080-C, NARA.

34. Ibid., 17–20.

35. Self, *All in the Family*,110.

36. Jane Chapman, "Women's Access to Credit," *Challenge* 17, no. 6 (January–February 1975): 42.

37. "Transcript of Proceedings: National Commission on Consumer Finance, Hearing on Availability of Credit to Women," National Commission on Consumer Finance (ACE Federal Reporters, Inc., 23 May 1972), p. 23.

38. Ibid., 126, 156.

39. Sharyn Campbell, "Statement of Sharyn Campbell on Behalf of the Women's Legal Defense Fund Before the National Commission on Consumer Finance Concerning the Availability of Credit to Women," 22 May 1972, Box 35: Folder: Testimony from Hearings on Availability of Credit to Women, p. 5, RG 220: Records of the National Commission on Consumer Finance, 1970–1972, Minutes and Transcripts of Commissions and Meetings, January 1971–June 1972, NARA; Hyman, *Debtor Nation*, 198–199.

40. "Transcript of Proceedings: National Commission on Consumer Finance, Hearing on Availability of Credit to Women," 23 May 1972, 31.

41. Lizabeth Cohen, *A Consumer's Republic: The Politics of Mass Consumption in Postwar America* (New York: Vintage Books, 2003), 381.

42. Ibid., 378.

43. United States National Commission on Consumer Finance, *Consumer Credit in the United States; Report*, 156–158.

44. Hyman, *Debtor Nation*, 192.

45. United States National Commission on Consumer Finance, *Consumer Credit in the United States; Report*, 160.

46. "Transcript of Proceedings, National Commission on Consumer Finance, Commission Meeting" (ACE Federal Reporters, Inc., 21 June 1972), Box 32, RG 220: Records of the National Commission on Consumer Finance, 1970–1972, Minutes and Transcripts of Commissions and Meetings, January 1971–June 1972, NARA.

47. United States National Commission on Consumer Finance, *Consumer Credit in the United States: Report*, 153.

48. "Women's Equity Action League, 1972 Resolutions," December 1972, Folder: 21.39, Women's Equity Action League Records (MC 500), Schlesinger Library (hereafter cited as WEAL Records); Center for Women's Policy Studies, "Letter to Susan Berresford (Ford Foundation) requesting extension of grant," 21 November 1973, Ford Foundation, Grant File PA: 73-67.

49. Martha Griffiths, Milton Schuller, and Charles F. Hayward, "Associated Credit Bureau's Panel on 'Sex Discrimination in Credit Granting,'" 10 May 1973, Box 59, Cassette Tape, Martha Griffiths Papers.

50. Ibid.

51. Hyman, *Debtor Nation*, 202–203.

52. Ibid., 196.

53. An extensive literature exists on the growth in welfare rolls and the welfare rights movement. For example, see Premilla Nadasen, *Welfare Warriors: The Welfare Rights Movement in the United States* (New York: Routledge, 2005); Jennifer Mittlestadt, *From Welfare to Workfare: The Unintended Consequences of Liberal Reform, 1945–1965* (Chapel Hill: University of North Carolina Press, 2005); Felicia Ann Kornbluh, *The Battle for Welfare Rights: Politics and Poverty in Modern America* (Philadelphia: University of Pennsylvania Press, 2007); and Chappell, *The War on Welfare: Family, Poverty, and Politics in Modern America*. Nadasen and Kornbluh have specifically written about welfare rights activists' credit campaign.

54. Katz, *In the Shadow of the Poorhouse*, 327; Chappell, *War on Welfare*, 146.

55. Congress, House, Committee on Banking and Currency, Subcommittee on Consumer Affairs, *Statement of the National Organization for Women Concerning H.R. 14856—The Equal Credit Opportunity Act Before the House Subcommittee on Consumer Affairs Submitted by Ann Scott, Vice President, Legislation*, 93rd Cong., 2nd Sess., 21 June 1974, p. 353, "Notes on NWRO Sears Boycott," no date, Box 2038, Folder: Sears—To Write, NWRO Papers.

56. Congress, Senate, Committee on Banking and Currency, Subcommittee on Financial Institutions, *Hearing on S. 2146 and S. 225: Statement of Dr. George Wiley, Accompanied by Mrs. Etta Horn, Chairman Ways and Means Committee, National Welfare Rights Organization*, 91st Cong., 2nd Sess., 14 January 1970, p. 57, copy from NWRO Papers, Box 2038, No Folder.

57. "Notes on NWRO Sears Boycott," no date, Box 2038, Folder: Sears—To Write, NWRO Papers.

58. Nadasen, *Welfare Warriors*, 38–43.

59. Rebecca A. London, "The Difference Between Divorced and Never-Married Mothers' Participation in the Aid to Families with Dependent Children Program," *Journal of Family Issues* 17, no. 2 (1 March 1996): 171; Robert M. Ball, "Letter to Betty Berry from Robert M. Ball, Commissioner of Social Security, Department of Health, Education, and Welfare, Social Security Administration, Baltimore Maryland," 2 December 1970, Folder 2.13, Berry Papers.

60. Harold Black and Robert H. Dugger, "Credit Union Structure, Growth and Regulatory Problems," *Journal of Finance* 36, no. 2 (May 1, 1981): 529–531.

61. "Nationwide Sears Credit Campaign," Box 2039, Folder: Sears, Manuscript Division, NWRO Papers.

62. Kornbluh, "To Fulfill Their 'Rightly Needs': Consumerism and the National Welfare Movement," *Racial History Review* 1997, 69 (Fall 1997), 84–85.

63. Letter from George Wiley to Cecil L. Wright, Chairman of the Board of J. C. Penney, 3 April 1969, Box 2038, Folder: Consumer-Credit, Manuscript Division, NWRO Papers.

64. "Some Sears Action Ideas," no date, Box 2038, Untitled Folder previously marked "Paul," NWRO Papers; "Welfare Mothers Plan More Protests," *Newark Evening News*, 9

April 1969 clipping from Box 2038, Folder: Newspaper Clippings 2, NWRO Papers; "Welfare Mothers Stage Shop-In," *Boston Globe,* 4 April 1969, clipping from Box 2038, Folder: Newspaper Clippings 2, NWRO Papers.

65. NWRO Sears Action List, Box 2038, Folder: Sears Miscellaneous, NWRO Papers; Proxy Vote Contracts, 18 May 1969, Box 2038, Folder: Sears Private Publications, Manuscript Division, NWRO Papers.

66. "NWRO Steps Up Campaign Against Sears Chain," *National Welfare Leaders Newsletter* 3, no. 2 (May 1969).

67. Ibid.

68. George Willey, "Letter from George Wiley to Cecil L. Wright," 3 April 1969, Box 2038, Folder: Consumer Credit, NWRO Papers.

69. "Draft Agreement with Montgomery Ward," Box 2038, untitled folder previously marked "Paul," NWRO Papers.

70. Kornbluh, "To Fulfill Their 'Rightly Needs,'" 85; Etta Horn, Memo: Sears Credit Campaign, 30 July 1969, Box 2038, Folder: Ways and Means, NWRO Papers.

71. Ashley DesShazor, "Letter from Ashely DeShazor Vice President for Credit, Montgomery Wards, to George Wiley," 15 September 1970, Box 2247, Folder: Montgomery Ward, NWRO Papers.

72. J. Biondi, "Letter from J. Biondi to NWRO," 11 September 1968, Box 2247, Folder: Ways and Means Committee, NWRO Papers.

73. Jo Ann Levine, "Poor—Good Credit Risks?: Representatives Give Testimony Race Seen as Credit Factor Bureau Identification Offered," *Christian Science Monitor,* 18 February 1970; F. B. Taylor, "Zayre's to Meet Demands of Welfare Rights Group," *Boston Globe,* 17 February 1970; Elizabeth M. Fowler, "Retailers Duck Credit Issue for Welfare Recipients," *New York Times,* 9 May 1970, sec. Business and Finance; "30 Protest at Sears on Welfare Credit," *New York Times,* 4 July 1969; "Welfare Recipients Will Boycott Sears to Demand Credit," *New York Times,* 27 March 1969; "Montgomery Ward Extends Credit to Welfare Clients," *New Pittsburgh Courier, City Edition,* 20 December 1969, sec. Business.

74. George Wiley, "Letter from George Wiley to Mrs. S. N. Levens," 16 April 1969, Box 2038, Folder: Correspondence with People About Sears, Manuscript Division, NWRO Papers.

75. Ibid.

76. This average monthly payment conceals tremendous regional variation. Mildred Rein, "Determinants of the Work-Welfare Choice in AFDC," *Social Service Review* 46, no. 4 (December 1, 1972): 546.

77. "Sears Credit Practices" 8 April 1968, Box 2038, Folder: Sears General Publications, NWRO Papers.

78. "NWRO Steps-Up Campaign Against Sears Chain," *National Welfare Leaders Newsletter* 3, no. 2 (May 1969): 3, NWRO Papers.

79. Ibid.

80. Kessler-Harris, *In Pursuit of Equity,* 13–15.

81. For an extended discussion of the way motherhood undergirded the activism of welfare recipients and informed their political vision, see Annelise Orleck, *Storming Caesars Palace: How Black Mothers Fought Their Own War on Poverty* (Boston: Beacon Press, 2005), 149.

82. Chappell, *The War on Welfare,*147.

83. Ibid., 13.

84. Sharyn Campbell, "General Information Sheet," no date, Box 45: Folder 33, NOW Records.

85. "WEAL Press Release Used in Women's Credit Month," Folder: 21.39: p. 23, WEAL Records.

86. Center for Women's Policy Studies, "Women and Credit: A Listing of Activities in the Public and Private Sector Relating to Women and Credit," no date, p. 13, Folder: Emily Card Box 1: Equal Credit Act 1973, Newcomb Collection, Center for Research on Women: Newcomb Archives: Emily Card Collection (hereafter cited as Emily Card Collection).

87. "Feminist Federal Credit Union: Women's Self-Help Financial Center," no date, Folder 45.3, NOW Records.

88. "Florida Feminist Credit Union Brochure," no date, Folder 44.37, NOW Records.

89. Virginia Lee Warren, "When a Bank Run by Women Opens, The Reason Is Not Always Feminism," *New York Times*, 17 September 1975, 6.

90. Friedan, *It Changed My Life*, 332.

91. Anne Enke, *Finding the Movement: Sexuality, Contested Space, and Feminist Activism* (Durham, N.C.: Duke University Press, 2007), 201–202.

92. "An Open Letter to Feminists Interested in Helping Organize and Participating in a 'Women's Self-Help Financial Center'—A Feminist Credit Union," 1973, Box 50: Folder: L/JEC Women's Hearings—Credit, Martha Griffiths Papers.

93. Beatrix Rebecca Hoffman, *Health Care for Some: Rights and Rationing in the United States Since 1930* (Chicago: University of Chicago Press, 2012), 143–166.

94. Ibid.

95. Joanne Parrent and Valerie Angers Klaetke, "Letter to Martha Griffiths from Joanne Parrent and Valerie Angers Klaetke" (Detroit, Mich., 16 August 1973), Box 50: Folder: L/JEC Women's Hearings—Credit, Martha Griffiths Papers.

96. Debra Law, "Letter from Debra Law to Susan Onaitas," 16 January 1976, Folder 45.3, NOW Records.

97. "Giving Women Credit," *Do It NOW*, September–October 1975, Schlesinger Library Periodicals.

98. Ibid. The history of the feminist credit union movement speaks to Stephanie Gilmore's contention that historians have made too much of the divide between the liberal feminists and women's liberationists. On a local level, NOW members worked with liberationists to advance their shared aims of getting women access to credit in the short term and using these loans to change perceptions of women and, ultimately, credit policy around the country.

99. Sylvia Beckey, *Women and Credit: Available Legal Remedies Against Discriminatory Practices* (Washington, D.C.: Congressional Research Service, 1974), 2.

100. "A Preliminary Report on Women and Credit, Prepared by the Durham, North Carolina NOW Chapter Task Force on Women and Credit," 15 October 1973, p. 1, Folder 211.41, NOW Records.

101. Ibid.

102. Griffiths, Schuller, and Hayward, "Associated Credit Bureau's Panel on 'Sex Discrimination in Credit Granting.'"

103. "Summary of Information on Senator Brock's Credit Bills," 14 April 1973, Folder: EC Box 1: ECOA working file [ca. 1973], Emily Card Collection.

104. Rick Perlstein, *The Invisible Bridge: The Fall of Nixon and the Rise of Reagan* (New York: Simon and Schuster, 2014), 318; Congress, Senate, Committee on Banking and Cur-

rency, Subcommittee on Financial Institutions, *Hearing on S. 2146 and S. 225: Statement of Dr. George Wiley, Accompanied by Mrs. Etta Horn, Chairman Ways and Means Committee, National Welfare Rights Organization*, 91st Cong., 2nd Sess., 14 January 1970, p. 73, copy from NWRO Papers, Box 2038).

105. William Proxmire, "Truth in Lending Act Amendments: Report of the Committee on Banking, Housing and Urban Affairs, United States Senate, To Accompany S. 2101 Together with Additional Views" (Senate, 93rd Cong., 1st Sess., July 28, 1973), p. 34, Box NAC 179: Folder: EC Box 2: Equal Credit Act (folder 2 of 2), Emily Card Collection.

106. Tim Wyngaard, "Lending Law Revision Major Victory," *Press-Scimitar*, 24 July 1973, Box 1: NAC 178: Folder: EC Box 1: Equal Credit Act Correspondence and Articles [c. 1973–1975], Emily Card Collection.

107. "Summary of Information on Senator Brock's Credit Bills."

108. Wyngaard, "Lending Law Revision Major Victory"; Proxmire, "Truth in Lending Act Amendments: Report of the Committee on Banking, Housing and Urban Affairs, United States Senate, To Accompany S. 2101 Together with Additional Views." (Quote from Proxmire.)

109. Emily Card, "Memo: To: Senator Brock: From: Emily; Re: S. 210, Title III, Floor Working Paper," 23 July 1973, Box NAC 200, Folder: Floor Preparation, July 23, Working File, Emily Card Collection.

110. "Summary of Information on Senator Brock's Credit Bills"; *Economic Problems of Women: Hearings Before the Joint Economic Committee, Congress of the United States, Ninety-Third Congress, First Session–Second Session* (Washington, D.C.: 1973), 446–465.

111. United States National Commission on Consumer Finance, *Consumer Credit in the United States: Report*, 233; Irwin N. Gertzog, *Women and Power on Capitol Hill: Reconstructing the Congressional Women's Caucus* (Boulder, Colo.: Lynne Rienner, 2004), 8.

112. Sharyn Campbell, "Letter from Sharyn Campbell to Task Force," 21 May 1974, Folder 45.24, NOW Records.

113. The few legislative histories of the ECOA largely skip over the congressional debates that occurred around it, suggesting a lack of contention in the legislative process; see, for example, Hyman, *Debtor Nation*, 213; M. Margaret Conway, "Discrimination and the Law: The Equal Credit Opportunity Act," in *Race, Sex, and Policy Problems*, ed. Marian Lief Palley and Michael B. Preston (Lexington, Mass.: Lexington Books, 1979): 77–78; Joyce Gelb and Marian Lief Palley, *Women and Public Policies: Reassessing Gender Politics, with a New Prologue and Epilogue* (Charlottesville: University Press of Virginia, 1996), Chapter 4.

114. John M. Fakes, "Letter to Mr. S. R. Jones, Jr., President First Pasadena State Bank, from John M. Fakes, Esq.," 3 July 1973, Box NAC 200, Folder: 1973, ABA Letters from States on Credit, Emily Card Collection.

115. J. H. Hines, "Letter to Charles R. McNeil, Executive Director, Government Relations, American Bankers Association, from J. H. Hines, Chairman of the Executive Committee, Deposit Guarantee, National Bank," 9 July 1973, Box NAC 200, Folder: 1973, ABA Letters from States on Credit, Emily Card Collection.

116. Sonia Pressman Fuentes, "National Commission on Consumer Finance, Statement of Ms. Sonia Pressman Fuentes," 22 May 1972, Box 35: Folder: Testimony from Hearings on Availability of Credit to Women, RG 220: Records of the National Commission on Consumer Finance, 1970–1972, Minutes and Transcripts of Commissions and Meetings, January 1971–June 1972, NARA.

117. Margaret Connor Begin, "Letter from Margaret Connor Begin to James Elsner, Credit Manager, G. Fox Company," 2 March 1974, Folder 44.35, NOW Records.

118. Bella Abzug, "Letter to Karen Curtis from Bella Abzug," 22 August 1972, Box 598: Subject File: Women: Correspondence, 1972, Abzug Papers.

119. Eleanor Knight, "Letter to Robert Tetrie from Eleanor Knight," 6 October 1972, Folder 44. 35, NOW Records.

120. JoAnn Hvizdos, "Letter to J. C. Penny Credit Manager from JoAnn Hvizdos," 29 April 1974, Folder 45. 19, NOW Records.

121. Y. D. Mathes, "Letter to Y. D. Mathes from Bella Abzug" (Washington D.C., 27 July 1972), Box 598: Subject File: Women, Correspondence, 1971–1972, Abzug Papers.

122. Transcript of Proceedings: National Commission on Consumer Finance, Hearing on Availability of Credit to Women, 22 May 1972, p. 87.

123. James Stegenga, "Letter to the Principal Executives of Sears, Roebuck and Co. From James A. Stegenga" (West Lafayette, Indiana, 18 January 1971), Folder 10.41, Catherine East Papers.

124. Card, "Memo: To: Senator Brock: From: Emily; Re: S. 210, Title III, Floor Working Paper," 23 July 1973.

125. Mayeri, *Reasoning from Race*, 3–4.

126. Gelb, *Women and Public Policies*, 75.

127. Ibid., 72; Sharyn Campbell, "Letter to Task Force Members," 21 May 1974, Folder 45.24, NOW Records.

128. Sharyn Campbell, "Letter to Esther Kaw," November 1974, Folder 51.13, NOW Records.

129. Ann Scott, "Statement of the National Organization for Women Concerning H.R. 14856—The Equal Credit Opportunity Act Before the House Subcommittee on Consumer Affairs," 21 June 1974, Folder 45.34, NOW Records.

130. Susan Thistle, *From Marriage to the Market: The Transformation of Women's Lives and Work* (Berkeley: University of California Press, 2006), 79.

131. Del Dobbins, "Memo to Sharyn Campbell, Credit Task Force; Esther Kaw, Affirmative Action; Ann Scott, Leg. Office; from Del Dobbins, Minority Women's Task Force," 12 December 1974, Folder 45.24, NOW Records.

132. Esther Kaw, "Letter from Esther Kaw to Sharyn Campbell," 18 December 1964, Folder 45.24, NOW Records.

133. Wright Patman, *Depository Institutions Amendments of 1974: Conference Report [to Accompany H.R. 1121]* (House of Representatives, 93rd Cong., 2nd Sess., 4 October 1974), 37.

134. Gelb, *Women and Public Policies*, 75–76.

135. "The Equal Credit Opportunity Act and Credit Rights in Housing," no date, Box 7 of 23 (April 2000): Folder: Untitled, Emily Card Collection.

136. Gelb, *Women and Public Policies*, 76; Marian Lief Palley and Michael B. Preston, eds., *Race, Sex, and Policy Problems* (Lexington, Mass.: Lexington Books, 1979), 83.

137. Susan Onaitis, "Testimony to Federal Reserve Board, Hearing on Proposed Regulations to Implement the Equal Credit Opportunity Act," 28 May 1975, Folder 45.25, NOW Records.

138. Linda Cohen and Karen DeCrow, "Statement of the National Organization of Women on Proposed Federal Reserve Board Regulations to Implement the Equal Credit Opportunity Act," 14 July 1975, Folder 201.12, NOW Records.

139. Karen DeCrow, "Letter to Susan Onaitis from Karen DeCrow," 19 September 1975, Folder 44.35, NOW Records.

140. Susan Onaitis, “Resignation Letter,” no date [October 1975], Folder 45.40, NOW Records.

141. “Statement of the National Organization of Women on Proposed Federal Reserve Board Regulations to Implement the Equal Credit Opportunity Act,” 14 July 1975, p. 11, Folder 201.12, NOW Records.

142. Ibid., 4.

143. Ibid., 26.

144. The new credit regulations also allowed creditors to ask if applicants would rely on alimony or child support to repay debts, but required them to inform applicants that they did not have to disclose such income if they would not rely on it to repay the loan. They also prohibited creditors from discounting part-time income automatically and from asking about birth control practices and plans (“Press Release: Federal Reserve: Proposed Regulations on ECOA,” 22 April 1975, Folder 10.41, Catherine East Papers).

145. Gerry Azzata, *Equal Credit Opportunity Act* (Boston: National Consumer Law Center, 1982), 5.

146. No author, date, or title, handwritten notes on credit that begin “The NOW Task Force on Women and Credit urges attention and action around the following . . .”, Box 609, Subject File: Women: Credit—Abzug—Notes, Memoranda, Abzug Papers.

147. See, for examples, National Women’s Political Caucus, “Women and Credit: A Position Paper,” no date [c. 1976], Folder 167.20, Records of the National Women’s Political Caucus (NWPC) (MC 522), Schlesinger Library, (hereafter cited as NWPC Records); Mary E. King and Cooki Lutkefedder, “Memorandum: To: Stu Eizenstat, Jack Watson, Kitty Shermer, Al Stern; From: Mary E. King, Cooki Lutkefedder; Subject: Policy Task Forces of Committee of 51.3%,” 13 August 1976, Box 30: Folder: Women, 12/74–9/76, Records of the 1976 Campaign Committee, Jimmy Carter Presidential Library; Emily Card, “Women’s History Week, Keynote Speech, Dr. Emily Card, West High, Torrence California,” 9 March 1982, Box 8: NAC 185: Folder: It’s Your Money (3), Emily Card Collection.

148. Soule and Olzak, “When Do Movements Matter?,” 475–476.

149. Chapman, “Women’s Access to Credit,” 45.

150. Yvonne Brathwaite Burke, “The Yvonne Brathwaite Burke Column: Credit—Availability to Women [Copley News Service],” 17 May 1976, Folder 396.46, Burke Papers.

151. Hyman, *Debtor Nation*, 244–247.

152. Genevieve LeBaron and Adrienne Roberts, “Confining Social Insecurity: Neoliberalism and the Rise of the 21st Century Debtors’ Prison,” *Politics and Gender* 8, no. 1 (March 2012): 25–49.

153. Arvonne Fraser, “Testimony of Arvonne S. Fraser, Legislative Chair and Past President, Women’s Equity Action League (WEAL), Before the Board of Governors, Federal Reserve System, May 28, 1975, Washington D.C., Concerning the Proposed Regulations to Implement the Equal Credit Opportunity Act,” 28 May 1975, pp. 1–3, Box 4: Location: 144.A.17.6F: Folder: 1974, ASF Speeches, Statements, Etc., Arvonne Fraser Papers.

Chapter 4

1. Betty Berry, “Education for Marriage, Divorce and the Family,” 16 November 1974, Folder 2.10, Berry Papers.

2. Ibid.

3. Shields, *Displaced Homemakers*, 25–26.

4. Hoffman, *Health Care for Some*, 143–166.

5. Hacker, *Divided Welfare State*, 189.

6. Ibid., 191–192.

7. Ibid., 195; Daniel T. Rodgers, *Atlantic Crossings: Social Politics in a Progressive Age* (Cambridge, Mass.: Belknap, 1998), 195.

8. Hacker, *Divided Welfare State*, 195; Colin Gordon, *Dead on Arrival: The Politics of Health Care in Twentieth-Century America* (Princeton, N.J.: Princeton University Press, 2003), 154.

9. Klein, *For All These Rights*, 119.

10. Hacker, *Divided Welfare State*, 200.

11. Ibid., 201.

12. Jennifer Klein, "The Business of Health Security: Employee Health Benefits, Commercial Insurers, and the Reconstruction of Welfare Capitalism, 1945–1960," *International Labor and Working-Class History*, no. 58 (October 1, 2000): 295; Klein, *For All These Rights*, 177–181.

13. Klein, "Business of Health Security," 300.

14. Klein, *For All These Rights*, 300–302.

15. Paul Starr, *Remedy and Reaction: The Peculiar American Struggle Over Health Care Reform* (New Haven, Conn.: Yale University Press, 2011), 28, 42.

16. Klein, "Business of Health Security," 303.

17. Klein, *For All These Rights*, 302.

18. Jacob Hacker, *The Road to Nowhere: The Genesis of President Clinton's Plan for Health Security*, Princeton Studies in American Politics (Princeton, N.J.: Princeton University Press, 1997), 11; Hoffman, *Health Care for Some*, 36, 62.

19. Hoffman, *Health Care for Some*, 120.

20. Hacker, *Divided Welfare State*, 179–180; Hacker, *Road to Nowhere*, 12. See also Starr, *Remedy and Reaction*, 2–3, 11.

21. Medicaid left a significant number of poor people uncovered both because it was a program that states had to opt in to and because coverage went mainly to poor mothers and their children who received AFDC. Poor single men derived few benefits from the program (Hoffman, *Health Care for Some*, 134–135). The share of uninsured Americans would only grow in the following decades. By 2009, just before the passage of the Affordable Care Act, 16.7 percent of Americans, some 50.7 million people, had no insurance (Starr, *Remedy and Reaction*, 5).

22. Gordon, *Dead on Arrival*, 80–82.

23. "Evidence of How Discrimination Against Women in Sale of Disability and Health Ins. Takes Place," no date, p. 304, Folder 125.6, NOW LDEF Records.

24. "Statement of the National Federation of Business and Professional Women's Clubs, Inc. on S. 372 the 'Fair Insurance Practices Act' to the Senate Committee on Commerce, Science and Transportation," 12 April 1983, Folder 362.11, NOW Records.

25. *Hearing on Nondiscrimination in Insurance (H.R. 100)*, Subcommittee on Consumer Protection and Finance, Committee on Interstate and Foreign Commercer, House of Representatives, 96th Cong., 1st Sess. (Washington, D.C.: 21, 28 August 1989), Testimony of Charles Hewitt, American Academy of Actuaries, p. 185, and Appendix Report of Barbara Lautzenshier, Vice President Phoenix Mutual, p. ii.

26. Frances Leonard, "Draft: Gray Paper on Health Insurance," 15 June 1985, Folder 15-7, Tish Sommers Papers.

27. "Evidence of How Discrimination Against Women in Sale of Disability and Health Ins. Takes Place," no date, pp. 3–4, Folder 125.6, NOW LDEF Records.

28. Gordon, *Dead on Arrival*, 124.

29. Alice Lake, "Divorcees: The New Poor," *McCall's*, September 1976, p. 2, Folder 1.2, Berry Papers; Alice Quinlan, "Statement of the Older Women's League to the 1982 Advisory Council on Social Security," 13 December 1982, pp. 4–5, Folder 15-33, Tish Sommers Papers.

30. Tish Sommers, "Draft: Statement of Tish Sommers, President, Older Women's League, San Francisco California," 18 March 1984, p. 36, Folder 15-34, Tish Sommers Papers.

31. Hoffman, *Health Care for Some*, 134; Quinlan, "Statement of the Older Women's League to the 1982 Advisory Council on Social Security," 4–5.

32. Quinlan, "Statement of the Older Women's League to the 1982 Advisory Council," 4–5.

33. Leonard, "Draft: Gray Paper on Health Insurance," 2.

34. Ibid., 15.

35. Hoffman, *Health Care for Some*, 139.

36. Starr, *Remedy and Reaction*, 47; Chappell, *War on Welfare*, 206–207.

37. Frances Leonard, "State Legislative Solutions to Loss of Health Coverage," February 1984, p. 1, Folder 15-6, Tish Sommers Papers; In re the Marriage of Brantner, 67 Cal. App. 3d 416, 418 (Court of Appeals, 4th Dist., Div. 2, Cal., 1977).

38. Marriage and Divorce Committee, NOW-NYC, "Divorce Survival Kit, Second Edition," October 1975, p. 6, Box 17: Folder: Marriage and Divorce Committee, 1974–1975 (Folder 9), NOW-NYC Papers.

39. Leonard, "Draft: Gray Paper on Health Insurance," 15.

40. Edward Klebe, "National Health Insurance Issue Brief Number IB73015," 14 August 1976, p. 1, Folder 122.17, Burke Papers.

41. *Economic Problems of Women: Hearings Before the Joint Economic Committee, Congress of the United States, Ninety-Third Congress, First Session–Second Session* (Washington, D.C.: U.S. Government Printing Office, 1973), hereafter cited as *Economic Problems of Women*, 165, 168.

42. Ibid.

43. Ibid., 158.

44. Naomi Naierman, Ruth Brannon, and Beverly Wahl, "WEAL: Sex Discrimination in Insurance, a Guide for Women," 1977, p. 19, Folder 77.36, WEAL Records.

45. Elizabeth Forsling Harris, "Letter to NOW Board Member from Elizabeth Forsling Harris," 18 April 1974, Folder 34.7, NOW Records; Matt Bai, "The Lives They Lived: Anne Wexler: Super Lobbyist," *New York Times Magazine*, 23 December 2009, 32; Nick Ravo, "Elizabeth F. Harris, First Publisher of Ms.," *New York Times*, 7 August 1999, http://www.nytimes.com/1999/08/07/nyregion/elizabeth-f-harris-77-the-first-publisher-of-ms.html.

46. Anne Wexler and Elizabeth Forsling Harris, "Memo: To: The Board of Directors of NOW; From: Elizabeth Forsling Harris and Anne Wexler; Subject: Insurance," 15 April 1973, Folder 34.7, NOW Records.

47. Ibid., 1.

48. Elizabeth Forsling Harris, "Letter to NOW Board Member from Elizabeth Forsling Harris," 18 April 1974, Folder 34.7, NOW Records.

49. Jack T. Hunn, "Smith-Sternau Organization, Inc. Memo: To: Ms. Elizabeth Forsling Harris and Ms. Anne Wexler; Re: Non-discriminatory Insurance Product Development for Groups of Women," 2 April 1973, Folder 34.7, NOW Records.

50. Thomas Sternau, "Letter to Elizabeth Forsling Harris from Thomas Sternau," 18 April 1974, Folder 34.7, NOW Records.

51. Jack T. Hunn, "Smith-Sternau Organization, Inc. Memo: To: Ms. Elizabeth Forsling Harris and Ms. Anne Wexler; Re: Non-Discriminatory Insurance Product Development for Groups of Women," 2 April 1973, p. 6, Folder 34.7, NOW Records; Anne Wexler and Elizabeth Forsling Harris, "Memo: To: The Board of Directors of NOW; From: Elizabeth Forsling Harris and Anne Wexler; Subject: Insurance," 15 April 1973, p. 1, Folder 34.7, NOW Records.

52. Wexler and Harris, "Memo: To: The Board of Directors of NOW; From: Elizabeth Forsling Harris and Anne Wexler; Subject: Insurance," 1. This would indeed have been a huge advance. As Jonathan Levy has shown, when the insurance industry developed in the nineteenth century to cover disability and injury, it left women out because insurance agents refused to understand women's work in the home as productive labor (Jonathan Levy, *Freaks of Fortune: The Emerging World of Capitalism and Risk in America* [Cambridge, Mass.: Harvard University Press, 2012], 87).

53. Gerry Dahlin, "Letter to Mary Lynn Myers from Gerry Dahlin," 28 June 1974, Folder 34.8, NOW Records.

54. "National Organization for Women Board of Directors Meeting, April 27–28, 1974, Princeton, N.J.," 27 April 1974, Folder 2.31, NOW Records.

55. The health insurance option that NOW ultimately offered (along with a life insurance product) was developed with the Consumers United Insurance Company, both the largest worker-owned-and-managed insurance company in the United States and the only insurance company to endorse the Economic Equity Act (Judy Goldsmith, "Letter to NOW Members from Judy Goldsmith," July 1985, Folder 85.15, NOW Records; "NOWMed Booklet," c. 1984, Folder 85.18, NOW Records; Flyer: NOWMed, 1984, Folder 85.15, NOW Records).

56. Task Force to Investigate Unfair Discrimination Against Women by the Insurance Industry, "Preliminary Report and Recommendations on Discriminatory Practices in the Insurance Industry, A Report by the Task Force to Investigate Unfair Discrimination Against Women by the Insurance Industry," 10 September 1976, Box 297: Folder: Health and Disability Insurance Discrimination, Jimmy Carter Presidential Library.

57. National Women's Law Center, "Leadership Conference on Civil Rights: Elimination of Sex Discrimination in Insurance," 23 January 1983, Box 103: Folder: 1983-4 EEA Insurance (H.R. 100), letters + fact sheets, Patricia Schroeder Papers.

58. Aetna, "Advertisement: Our Case for Sex Discrimination," *U.S. News and World Report*, 14 September 1981, Folder 126.4, NOW LDEF Records.

59. Ibid.

60. Health Insurance Association of America and American Council of Life Insurance, "Advertisement: A Bill Is Moving Through Congress That Will Force Single Men to Buy Maternity Benefits for Themselves in Their Health Insurance," *New York Times*, 8 June 1983, Folder 126.7, NOW LDEF Records.

61. Mary Jean Collins, "NOW, Inc. Memo: To: The Leadership List; From: Mary Jean Collins, Vice President—Action; Subject: Non-Discrimination in Insurance Alert [and Attachments]," 2 May 1983, Folder 362.10, NOW Records.

62. Anne K. Justice, ed., "The Insurance Connection with Stop ERA Forces: A Report," September 1974, Folder 193.4, NOW Records.

63. Ibid., 28.

64. "Analysis of Economic Equity Act (EEA) of 1981," 1981, Box 4: Folder F014:Women—1981 (4), Elizabeth Dole Files: Series IV: Women's Issues, Ronald Reagan Presidential Library.

65. No author [NWPC], "DRAFT FACTSHEET: The New H.R. 100, Action: Letters of Support to Your Members of Congress," 14 October 1983, Folder 164.14, NWPC Records.

66. Hacker, *Divided Welfare State,* 180.

67. No author [WEAL], "Insurance Industry 'Buys' the First Round in the Fight to End Economic Discrimination in Insurance," 18 April 1984, Folder 54.11, WEAL Records.

68. Tish Sommers, "Testimony on Displaced Homemakers (S.B. 825): Health and Welfare Committee, California Senate," 14 May 1975, p. 1, Folder 7-15, Tish Sommers Papers.

69. Sommers, "Draft: Statement of Tish Sommers, President, Older Women's League, San Francisco California," 35.

70. Hoffman, *Health Care for Some*, pp. 163–165.

71. Ibid., 163.

72. Ibid.; Martha Griffiths, "Griffiths Short Statements on H.R. 22, 'My National Health Insurance Bill' and the Equal Rights Amendment (One Page)," no date, Box 45: Folder: 92nd: Statements of MWG, Martha Griffiths Papers.

73. Hoffman, *Health Care for Some*, 148.

74. "March for International Women's Day," 1974, Box 23: Folder: International Women's Year (1975), 1973–1975 (Folder 11), NOW-NYC Papers.

75. Betty Berry, "Letter to Governor Nelson Rockefeller from Betty Berry," 15 March 1968, Folder 4.6, Berry Papers.

76. Betty Berry, "Letter to Senator Jacob K. Javits from Betty Berry," 1 June 1970, Folder 4.8, Berry Papers.

77. Task Force to Investigate Unfair Discrimination Against Women by the Insurance Industry, "Preliminary Report and Recommendations," 1.

78. Mary E. King and Cooki Lutkefedder, "Memorandum: To: Stu Eizenstat, Jack Watson, Kitty Shermer, Al Stern; From: Mary E. King, Cooki Lutkefedder; Subject: Policy Task Forces of Committee of 51.3%," 13 August 1976, p. 1, Box 30: Folder: Women, 12/74–9/76, Collection: Records of the 1976 Campaign Committee, Jimmy Carter Presidential Library.

79. Task Force to Investigate Unfair Discrimination Against Women by the Insurance Industry, "Preliminary Report and Recommendations," 16.

80. Marilyn deMara Clancy, "National Women's Political Caucus: National Health Insurance, Hearings Before Joseph Califano, Secretary of Health, Education and Welfare," 4 October 1977, Folder 164.8, NWPC Records, 2.

81. Naierman, Brannon, and Wahl, "WEAL: Sex Discrimination in Insurance, a Guide for Women," 30.

82. Ibid.

83. Ibid.

84. Sandra Morgen, *Into Our Own Hands: The Women's Health Movement in the United States, 1969–1990* (New Brunswick, N.J.: Rutgers University Press, 2002).

85. Wendy Kline, "The Making of *Our Bodies, Ourselves*: Rethinking Women's Health and Second Wave Feminism," in *Feminist Coalitions: Historical Perspectives on Second-Wave Feminism in the United States*, ed. Stephanie Gilmore (Urbana: University of Illinois Press, 2008), 64.

86. Hoffman, *Health Care for Some*, 157.

87. Morgen, *Into Our Own Hands*, 110.

88. Tish Sommers, "Testimony for Secretary's Advisory Committee on Rights and Responsibilities of Women, Dept. Health, Education, and Welfare, Task Force on Older Women of the National Organization for Women (NOW)," 4 December 1974, p. 2, Folder 48.22, NOW

Records. See also NOW Task Force on Older Women for HEW, Western Regional Office, "Well-Woman Center, Feasibility Study," no date, Box 12: Location 146.E.9.9B: Folder: Economics: Older Women: NOW Task Force on Older Women, 1974–1976, Arvonne Fraser Papers.

89. Tish Sommers and Ruth McElhinney, "Growing Older Female," no date [c. 1974], Folder: L/JEC: Women, Social Security, Martha Griffiths Papers.

90. Ibid.

91. Sommers, "Testimony for Secretary's Advisory Committee on Rights and Responsibilities of Women," 1–2.

92. NOW Task Force on Older Women for HEW, Western Regional Office, "Well-Woman Center, Feasibility Study."

93. "Displaced Homemakers Bill—Pilot Program: Well-Woman Clinics," no date, Folder 7-16, Tish Sommers Papers.

94. Ibid.

95. Ibid.

96. Tish Sommers, "Task Force [on Older Women] Statement for Letter to Congress (and Attached Displaced Homemakers Act)," 28 February 1975, Folder: 89.41, NOW Records.

97. "End-of-Year Report—1976, The Displaced Homemakers Center, Oakland, California," 1976, Folder 197.9, Burke Papers.

98. Angela Dodson, "Programs to Help Displaced Homemakers Cope," *New York Times*, 18 June 1986.

99. Starr, *Remedy and Reaction*, 60; Hoffman, *Health Care for Some*, 165.

100. Hoffman, *Health Care for Some*, 165; Starr, *Remedy and Reaction*, 76; Sarah Weddington, "Carter Health Care Plan Has Special Significance for Women," *White House News on Women*, no date, Box 44: Folder: Publications File: "White House News on Women"—Vol. I; Issue III, Collection: Sarah Weddington Files, Jimmy Carter Presidential Library.

101. Hacker, *Road to Nowhere*, 81.

102. Starr, *Remedy and Reaction*, 51.

103. "Equality in Family Relations, Report of the Task Force on Marriage, Divorce, and Family Relations, Goals of the Task Force," October 1972, Box 611, Subject File: Women: Divorce, Abzug Papers; Elizabeth Cox Spalding, "NOW Task Force on Marriage, Divorce and Family Relations," November 1973, Folder 47.45, NOW Records.

104. Betty Berry, "Draft: A NOW New York Position Paper on Marriage and Divorce," no date, p. 9, Folder 132.1642, Friedan Papers.

105. Berry, "Letter to Governor Rockefeller."

106. Statement of Elizabeth Morrison, Baltimore, Md., Vice President, Herget and Co., in U.S. Senate, Special Committee on Aging, *Americans at Risk: The Case of the Medically Uninsured* (Washington, D.C.: U.S. Government Printing Office, 1985), 10–11.

107. Betty Berry, "Testimony of Betty Berry, Editor and Publisher of the Marriage, Divorce, and the Family Newsletter and Consultant to the United Presbyterian Church on Divorce, Before the Senate Judiciary Committee," 4 February 1977, p. 2, Folder 4.15, Berry Papers.

108. Ibid.

109. Isabel Marcus, "Locked In and Locked Out: Reflections on the History of Divorce Law Reform in New York State," *Buffalo Law Review* 37 (1988–1989): 441.

110. Statement of Elizabeth Morrison in *Americans at Risk*, 10–11.

111. "Appendix: Testimonial Letters to the Maryland Legislature in Support of HB 1154, Continuation of Health Insurance, Letter from Chase Ridgley, Jr.," in *Americans at Risk*, 108.

112. Leonard, "State Legislative Solutions to Loss of Health Coverage."

113. Divorce activists may have hoped that knowing that conversion was a possibility, judges would include its cost in alimony awards, but they never made this argument.

114. Betty Berry, "Letter to John Hughes from Betty Berry," 8 April 1971, Folder 4.6, Berry Papers.

115. Betty Berry, "Letter to David Arens from Betty Berry," 13 March 1971, Folder 4.16, Berry Papers.

116. Marriage and Family Committee, NOW, "Memo: To Mary Phillips, Donna Loercher; From: The Marriage and Family Committee; For: The Newsletter," no date, Box 17: Folder: Marriage and Divorce Committee, 1970 (folder 3), NOW-NYC Papers; Davis, *Moving the Mountain*, 116; Echols, *Daring to Be Bad*, 198.

117. Berry, "Letter to David Arens"; Betty Berry, "State Legislative Program for Marriage and Divorce," 3 April 1971, Folder 2.18, Berry Papers.

118. Roger W. Tompkins, "Letter to Betty Berry from Roger W. Tompkins," 15 July 1971, Box 17: Folder: Marriage and Divorce Committee, 1971 (folder 4), NOW-NYC Papers.

119. Patricia McCormack, "Newsletter a Help in Divorce Throes," *Rocky Mountain News "NOW,"* 29 August 1976, p. 8, NOW Records.

120. Glenn Markus, "Health Benefits: Loss Due to Unemployment," Major Issues System (Library of Congress: Congressional Research Service, December 14, 1983), 6.

121. *Health Benefits: Loss Due to Unemployment, Hearings Before the Committee on Energy and Commerce and the Subcommittee on Health and the Environment, Ninety-Eighth Congress, First Session on H.R. 2552, A Bill to Amend the Social Security Act to Provide for a Program of Grants to States to Provide Health Care Benefits for the Unemployed, and for Other Purposes, H.R. 1823, A Bill to Provide for Continuation of Health Insurance for Workers Who Lose Such Insurance by Reason of Unemployment* (Washington, D.C.: U.S. Government Printing Office, 1983), 121–127.

122. Cowie, *Stayin' Alive*, 222–224.

123. Jane Sobie, "In Step with the National Military Wives Association," *Ladycom*, Clipping, no date, p. 76, Folder H4092: Military Spouse Background, G. William Whitehurst Records, Washington and Lee University Library, Lexington, Va.

124. Annette K. Smail, "Action Alert Memo: To: Organizers of All Local Chapters of MED (Medical Equality for Dependents) and Other Groups Campaigning to Restore Benefits for Former Wives of the Military, Re: Nation-Wide Coordination of Our Lobbying Efforts," June 1980, Folder 15-39, Tish Sommers Papers.

125. Ibid.

126. Lauraine Merlini, "MBA Briefs: Working Woman Award," August 1983, Box 124: Folder: Former Spouses Press, Patricia Schroeder Papers.

127. President's Commission on Pension Policy, *Public Hearing on Retirement Income and Coverage of Women and Minorities* (Washington, D.C.: President's Commission on Pension Policy, 1979), 32–34.

Chapter 5

1. Bella Abzug, "Speech by Congresswoman Bella Abzug to NOW Marriage and Divorce Conference, Hotel Commodore, New York," 19 January 1974, p. 5, Box 759 A: Folder: NOW Marriage and Divorce Conference Speech, Abzug Papers.

2. Shelley Lapkoff and Edith U. Fierst, *Working Paper: Working Women, Marriage, and Retirement* (Washington, D.C.: President's Commission on Pension Policy, 1980), ix, 30.

3. Linda J. Wait, *U.S. Women at Work* (Rand Publication Series: R-2824-RC, 1981), 20.

4. Self, *All in the Family*, 322.

5. Tish Sommers, "Social Security: A Feminist Critique" (Speech to Conference, Ann Arbor, Mich., Institute of Gerontology, 24 August 1975), p. 12, Box 537: Subject File: Social Security—General, Abzug Papers.

6. Ira Katznelson, *When Affirmative Action Was White: An Untold History of Racial Inequality in Twentieth-Century America* (New York: W. W. Norton, 2005), 45.

7. Kessler-Harris, *In Pursuit of Equity*, 128; Eleanor Cutri Smeal, "Testimony of Eleanor Cutri Smeal, President National Organization for Women, Before the Subcommittee on Retirement Income and Employment of the Select Committee on Aging, United States House of Representatives," 7 May 1979, Folder 47.3, NOW Records.

8. Quadagno, *Transformation of Old Age Security.*

9. Kessler-Harris, *In Pursuit of Equity*, 131–141.

10. "Equity in Social Security for Individuals and Families Act, H.R. 14119, H.R. 15710, Impact on Women," *Fraser Reports from Congressman Donald M. Fraser*, December 1976, p. 1, Folder 50.66, Burke Papers.

11. Virginia P. Reno, "Women Under Social Security," November 1974, p. 4, Folder 96.37, NOW Records.

12. President's Commission on the Status of Women, *Report of the Committee on Social Insurance and Taxes to the President's Commission on the Status of Women* (Washington, D.C.: Superintendent of Documents, U.S. Government Printing Office, 1963), 13.

13. Ibid., 13–14.

14. Ibid., 11.

15. Yvonne Brathwaite Burke, "Subcommittee on Retirement Income and Employment of the Select Committee on Aging, Hearing on Minority and Low Income Older Women and the Displaced Homemakers Act," 12 November 1975, p. 6, Folder 21.41, Burke Papers.

16. "Section 31: 20th Century Statistics," in U.S. Census Bureau, Statistical Abstracts of United States, 1999 (http://www.census.gov/prod/99pubs/99statab/sec31.pdf).

17. President's Commission on the Status of Women, *Report of the Committee on Social Insurance and Taxes to the President's Commission on the Status of Women*, 4.

18. Ibid., 31.

19. Ibid., 5.

20. Ibid, 5–6.

21. Ibid., 4, 31–32.

22. Ibid., 32–33.

23. Ibid, 37.

24. Catherine East, "Letter from Catherine East to Marguerite [no last name]," 10 May 1971, Box 617: Subject File—Women: Insurance—Health, Disability, Workers' Compensation and General, Abzug Papers.

25. Richard P. Edgar and Anni Landauer, "Dear Friends Letter from Richard P. Edgar and Anni Landauer, General Board of Christian Social Concerns of the Methodist Church," 13 October 1966, Folder 70: 1375, Esther Peterson Papers (MC 450), Schlesinger Library (hereafter cited as Esther Peterson Papers).

26. Martha Griffiths, "Letter to Gladys Kissel from Martha Griffiths," 20 April 1965, Box 26: Folder: 89th: Social Security for Women, Martha Griffiths Papers. For a letter with very similar wording, see also Martha Griffiths, "Letter to Alice Davis from Martha Griffiths," 26 February 1965, Box 26: Folder: 89th: Social Security for Women, Martha Griffiths Papers.

27. Kessler-Harris, *In Pursuit of Equity*, 163; Education and Public Welfare Division, Congressional Research Service, *Committee on Finance, United States Senate, Brief Summary of Major Provisions of and Detailed Comparison Showing Changes Made in Existing Law by H.R. 6675 As Passed by the House of Representatives* (Washington, D.C., 1965), 44.

28. Education and Public Welfare Division, Congressional Research Service, *Committee on Finance, United States Senate, Brief Summary of Major Provisions of and Detailed Comparison Showing Changes Made in Existing Law by H.R. 6675 As Passed by the House of Representatives*, 44–45.

29. Carolyn Shaw Bell, "Statement of Carolyn Shaw Bell, Katharine Coman Professor of Economics, Wellesley College, Wellesley, Mass.," in *Economic Problems of Women*, 3; Elaine Staniec, "Letter to Rep. Fraser from Elaine Staniec," 4 February 1977, Box 85: Location 151.H.2.10 (F): Folder: Social Security—1977, Don Fraser Papers, Minnesota Historical Society, St. Paul, Minn. (hereafter cited as Don Fraser Papers).

30. Edgar and Landauer, "Dear Friends Letter"; Women's Division of the Board of Missions of the Methodist Church, "Proposed Amendment to the Social Security Act Concerning Dependent Divorced Wives and Widows," January 1966, Folder 5.5, Berry Papers.

31. Edgar and Landauer, "Dear Friends Letter."

32. Martha Griffiths, "Letter from Martha Griffiths to Anni Landauer," 24 March 1966, Box 546: Subject File Social Security: Women–General, Abzug Papers.

33. Francis J. Crowely, "Memo: To: Honorable William L. St. Onge; From: Education and Public Welfare Division, Library of Congress (Francis J. Crowley); Subject: Time Requirements in the Social Security Act, an Inquiry You Received from Mrs. Anni Landauer," 12 December 1969, Folder 70: 1375, Esther Peterson Papers.

34. Gladys F. Kissel, "Letter to Martha Griffiths from Gladys F. Kissel" (Syracuse, N.Y.), 18 April 1965, Box 26: Folder: 89th: Social Security for Women, Martha Griffiths Papers.

35. Walter Carlson, "Advertising: Window Dressing by Chase," *New York Times*, 6 July 1965, sec. Business Financial; H. D. Quigg, "What's a Wife Worth?," *Washington Post, Times Herald*, 16 February 1965, sec. For and About Women; H. D. Quigg, "A Wife Earns $159 a Week," *Boston Globe*, 6 February 1965.

36. Alice Rossi, "NOW: Task Force on the Family," no date [penciled in 1967], Folder 47.42, NOW Records.

37. "Memo: To: Interested Parties; From: ACLU Women's Rights Project; Re: Social Security and Sex Discrimination," Box 546: Subject File Social Security: Women—General, p. 1, Abzug Papers.

38. Ibid., 1.

39. Ruth Bader Ginsburg, "Equality in Social Security," *Monitor*, May–June 1977, Folder 195.16, NOW Records.

40. Betty Berry, "Report to 1968 National NOW Conference, Atlanta GA. December 7, 1968 by NOW New York Subcommittee on Divorce, Alimony, and Child Support. Prepared by Betty Berry Chairman," 7 December 1968, p. 5, Box 17: Folder: Marriage and Family Committee, 1968–1969 (Folder 2), NOW-NYC Papers.

41. See, for example, "Marriage and the Family Action Resolutions Passed at the 4th Annual Conference of the National Organization for Women," March 1970, Folder 3.5, Spalding Papers.

42. "NOW 1974 Resolutions [pp. 5–7 in Folder]," [1974], Folder 1.3, Spalding Papers.

43. Self, *All in the Family*, in particular pp. 114–126, 375.

44. "Task Force on Older Women: Resolution Adopted at National Convention," 27 May 1974, Folder 7.14, Berry Papers.

45. Jessica, "Memo: From Jessica; To Bella; Re: Legislation in the Women's Area," 1971, Box 546: Subject File: Social Security: Women—General, Abzug Papers.

46. Ibid.

47. Ibid.

48. Caspar Weinberger, "Prepared Statement of Hon. Caspar Weinberger," in *Economic Problems of Women*, 410.

49. In fact, precedent existed for providing Social Security to people who had not earned wages. Non-paid members of religious orders received Social Security credits, and Congress had more than once retroactively provided wage credits to men who served in the military. Heidi I. Hartmann, "Strengthening Social Security for Women: A Report from the Working Conference on Women and Social Security" (Warrentown, Va., 19 July 1999), p. 8, Folder 372.3, NOW Records; Tish Sommers and Ruth McElhinney, "Growing Older Female," [c. 1974], p. 3, Folder: L/JEC: Women, Social Security, Martha Griffiths Papers.

50. Kessler-Harris, *In Pursuit of Equity*, 126.

51. Carolyn Hull-Ryde, "Memo: From Carolyn A. Hull-Ryde to Susan Bennett; Re: New Abzug Bill," no date, Box 638: Folder: Subject File: Women, Social Security—Homemakers—Legislation, Abzug Papers; Bella Abzug, *H.R. 252*, 1973, https://www.congress.gov/bill/93rd-congress/house-bill/252/titles.

52. Abzug, *H.R. 252*; Esther Peterson, "Speech to Wisconsin Commission on the Status of Women, Madison, Wisconsin," 27 July 1974, p. 7, Folder 152.3561, Esther Peterson Papers.

53. "Resolutions Passed by Marriage and Divorce Committee, 1967–1971, as Listed in the N.O.W. Resolutions Book (with 1973 Resolutions Added)," [1973], Folder 1.3, Spalding Papers.

54. Martha Griffiths and Barbara Jordan, "Joint Statement of Representative Barbara Jordan (D-Texas) and Representative Martha Griffiths (D-Michigan): Social Security for Homemakers," 6 February 1974, Folder 89.41, NOW Records.

55. Carolyn Hull-Ryde, "Memo: From Carolyn Hull-Ryde; To Sue Bennette Re: Comparison of Bills to Extend Social Security Coverage to Homemakers," no date, Box 638: Folder: Subject File: Women, Social Security—Homemakers—Legislation, Abzug Papers; "Homemaker Bills: Comparison of H.R. 3009 (Jordan, Burke) and an Identical Bill, H.R. 10750 (Heckler), with H.R. 11840 (Abzug)," 31 March 1976, Box 638: Subject File: Women, Social Security—Homemakers—Legislation, Abzug Papers.

56. Martha Griffiths and Barbara Jordan, "Joint Statement of Representative Barbara Jordan (D-Texas) and Representative Martha Griffiths (D-Michigan): Social Security for Homemakers," 6 February 1974, Folder: 89.41, NOW Records.

57. For an extended discussion of the consistent undervaluing of women's care work, see Eileen Boris and Jennifer Klein, *Caring for America: Home Health Workers in the Shadow of the Welfare State* (New York: Oxford University Press, 2012), 8–9. For first pointing out this problem with many of the Social Security for homemakers proposals to me I thank Arvonne Fraser (author interview with Arvonne Fraser, 8 October 2014).

58. Mignon Duffy, "Doing the Dirty Work: Gender, Race, and Reproductive Labor in Historical Perspective," *Gender and Society* 21, no. 3 (June 1, 2007): 313–336.

59. "Homemaker Bills: Comparison of H.R. 3009 (Jordan, Burke) and an Identical Bill, H.R. 10750 (Heckler), with H.R. 11840 (Abzug)."

60. Jack Strausle, "Letter to Martha Griffiths from Jack Strausle Jr." (Little Rock, Ark., 20 February 1974), Box 50: Folder: Ways and Means—Social Security, Homemakers, H.R. 12645 Against, Martha Griffiths Papers.

61. F. B. Mitchell, "Letter to Griffiths [Honorable Ladies] from F. B. Mitchell" (Silver Spring, Md., 23 February 1974), Box 50: Folder: Social Security—Homemakers (H.R. 12645), Martha Griffiths Papers.

62. Lefkovitz, "The Problem of Marriage in the Era of Women's Liberation," 271–278.

63. Robert O. Self, *American Babylon: Race and the Struggle for Postwar Oakland* (Princeton, N.J.: Princeton University Press, 2003), 282; Thomas Borstelmann, *The 1970s: A New Global History from Civil Rights to Economic Inequality* (Princeton, N.J.: Princeton University Press, 2012), 123–125, 155–156.

64. Betty Berry, "Letter to Ruth Bader Ginsburg from Betty Berry," 28 June 1971, Folder 4.4, Berry Papers.

65. Grace Ganz Blumberg, "Adult Derivative Benefits in Social Security," *Stanford Law Review* 32, no. 2 (January 1, 1980): 241.

66. Mitchell, "Letter to Griffiths [Honorable Ladies] from F. B. Mitchell," 1974.

67. Ibid.

68. Martha Griffiths, "H.R. 3289, In the House of Representatives," 2 February 1971, Box 36: Location 147.G.11.3 (B): no folder, Don Fraser Papers; Donald M. Fraser, "Fraser Urges Fairer Treatment for Working Women Under Social Security," 16 October 1968, Box 13: Location 146.E.9.10 (F): Folder: Economics: Social Security, Statistics and Facts on Women, 1968–1975, Arvonne Fraser Papers.

69. Arlene Kaplan Daniels, "W.E.A.L.: The Growth of a Feminist Organization" (Northwestern University, March 1977), Box 10: Location 146.E.9.7 (B): Folder: WEAL: Historical Background, 1975–1980, Arvonne Fraser Papers; Arvonne Fraser, "Insiders and Outsiders: Women in the Legislative and Political Arena," no date, Box 9: Location 144.A.18.3 (B): Folder: Writings: Insiders and Outsiders: Women in the Political Arena, 1982–1983 (2/2), Arvonne Fraser Papers.

70. Arvonne Fraser, "Insiders and Outsiders," 6–7.

71. Author interview with Arvonne Fraser, 8 October 2014.

72. Arvonne Fraser, "Insiders and Outsiders," 2–5.

73. Daniels, "W.E.A.L.: The Growth of a Feminist Organization."

74. Tish Sommers, "Task Force [On Older Women] Statement for Letter to Congress (and Attached Displaced Homemakers Act)," 28 February 1975, Folder: 89.41, NOW Records; Sommers, "Social Security: A Feminist Critique," 13.

75. Jane C. Sherburne, "Women and Social Security: Seizing the Moment for Change," *Georgetown Law Journal* 70 (1981–1982): 1595.

76. Arvonne Fraser, "Testimony of Arvonne S. Fraser, Legislative Chair, Women's Equity Action League (WEAL) Before the House Select Committee on Aging," 29 September 1975, Box 5: Location 144.A. 17.7 (B): Folder: Speeches, 1975–1976, Arvonne Fraser Papers.

77. Ibid., 3–4.

78. Arvonne Fraser, "Statement of Arvonne S. Fraser, President, Women's Equity Action League (WEAL), Washington, D.C., Before the Hearings on Problems Facing Women in Pov-

erty Held by the U.S. Civil Rights Commission in Chicago, Illinois, June 19, 1974," 19 June 1974, p. 2, Box 4: Location 144.A.17.6 (F): Folder: 1974, ASF Speeches, Statements, Etc., Arvonne Fraser Papers.

79. Arvonne Fraser, "Testimony of Arvonne S. Fraser, Legislative Chair and Past President, Women's Equity Action League (WEAL), Before the Board of Governors, Federal Reserve System, May 28, 1975, Washington D.C., Concerning the Proposed Regulations to Implement the Equal Credit Opportunity Act," 28 May 1975, Box 4: Location 144.A.17.6 (F): Folder: 1974, ASF Speeches, Statements, Etc., Arvonne Fraser Papers.

80. Arvonne Fraser, "Statement of Arvonne S. Fraser, Legislative Chair and Former President, Women's Equity Action League (WEAL) Before the Senate Special Committee on Aging," October 23, 1975, 4, Box 130: Folder: 21: Women's Issues, Collection: Records of the 1976 Campaign Committee, Jimmy Carter Presidential Library.

81. Ibid., 4–5.

82. United States Department of Health, Education, and Welfare, *Social Security and the Changing Roles of Men and Women* (Washington, D.C.: Dept. of Health, Education, and Welfare, 1979), 35.

83. Arvonne Fraser, "Statement of Arvonne S. Fraser Before the Senate Special Committee on Aging," pp. 7–8.

84. For example, take two couples earning $100 a year: In a couple with a husband earning $100 and a wife earning nothing, each spouse would receive a $75 benefit each year. In a couple where each spouse earned $50 a year, each spouse would only receive a $50 benefit (Arvonne Fraser, "Letter to Grace Ganz Blumberg from Arvonne Fraser," 2 August 1977, Box 85: Location 151.H.2.10 (F): Folder: Social Security—1977, Don Fraser Papers).

85. Donald Fraser, "Equity in Social Security for Individuals and Families Act, H.R. 14119, H.R. 15710, Impact on Women," 1.

86. Ibid., 2.

87. In his 1999 article on earnings sharing, Goodwin Liu argues that earnings sharing proposals are best understood as the adoption of community property rules by the federal government. He writes that earnings sharing's "operative principle is a particular normative interpretation of the marriage contract." Yet, he writes, earnings sharing does little to rectify the "invisibility of unpaid household labor" because it does not "assign independent economic value to non-wage work." Goodwin Liu, "Social Security and the Treatment of Marriage: Spousal Benefits, Earnings Sharing, and the Challenge of Reform," *Wisconsin Law Review* 1999, 1.

88. Robert M. Ball, "Letter to Betty Berry from Robert M. Ball, Commissioner of Social Security, Department of Health, Education, and Welfare, Social Security Administration, Baltimore Maryland," 2 December 1970, Folder 2.13, Berry Papers.

89. Bella S. Abzug, *H.R.4357–A Bill to Amend Title II of the Social Security Act to Permit the Payment of Benefits to a Married Couple on Their Combined Earnings Record*, 1975 (http://thomas.loc.gov/cgi-bin/bdquery/z?d094:HR04357:@@@P).

90. Arvonne Fraser, "Social Security Is a (Complicated) Women's Issue," no date, p. 19, Box 13: Location 146.E.9.10 (F): Folder: Economics: Social Security Correspondence, 1975, Arvonne Fraser Papers.

91. Arvonne Fraser, "Testimony Before the House Select Committee on Aging," 2.

92. Sommers, "Task Force [On Older Women] Statement for Letter to Congress (and Attached Displaced Homemakers Act)."

93. Sommers, "Social Security: A Feminist Critique," 13.

94. "Report of the Advisory Council on Social Security," 1975, p. 41, Box 13: Location 146.E.9.10 (F): Folder: Report of Advisory Council on Social Security (1975), Arvonne Fraser Papers.

95. Blumberg, "Adult Derivative Benefits in Social Security," 265.

96. "Report of the Advisory Council on Social Security," 36–38.

97. Blumberg, "Adult Derivative Benefits in Social Security," 266–269.

98. Committee on 51.3%, "Ad: Jimmy Carter Feels It's Time Your Government Did Something Positive to End Discrimination Against Women," 1976, Box 414: Folder: Women—51.3% Committee, Records of the 1976 Campaign Committee, Jimmy Carter Presidential Library.

99. "National Plan of Action: Adopted at National Women's Conference" (Houston, Texas, 18 November 1977), p. 15, Box 103: Location 151.H.4.8 (F): Folder: National Women's Conference, Don Fraser Papers; Suzanne Crowell, "Four Days in Houston," *Civil Rights Digest*, 1978, Box 103: Location 151.H.4.8 (F): Folder: National Women's Conference, Don Fraser Papers.

100. Kessler-Harris, *In Pursuit of Equity*, 168; Amy Leigh Campbell, *Raising the Bar: Ruth Bader Ginsburg and the ACLU Women's Rights Project* (USA: XLibris, 2003), 93–98, 123.

101. Ginsburg, "Equality in Social Security." Interestingly, only a year earlier, the Supreme Court had upheld the Social Security law's differential treatment of divorced and married women in *Mathews v. De Castro* (Mathews v. De Castro, 97 S.Ct. 431 [Supreme Court, United States, 1976]). In that case, the court ruled the law that allowed married women under sixty-two with dependent children in their care to start to draw Social Security dependent benefits whenever their husbands retired, but required divorced women with children drawing dependent benefits on a retired ex-husband's Social Security account to wait until they turned sixty-two was constitutional. Even as the court struck down gender distinctions in the law, it consistently upheld a variety of distinctions made on the basis of marital status.

102. John Snee and Mary Ross, "Social Security Amendments of 1977: Legislative History and Summary of Provisions," *Social Security Bulletin*, March 1978, 4.

103. Ibid., 2.

104. "Answers to Goldfarb," [no date], p. 1, Box 5: Location 144.A. 17.7 (B): no folder: Arvonne Fraser Papers.

105. Snee and Ross, "Social Security Amendments of 1977," 5–6.

106. For an extended discussion of the intersection of Second Wave feminists' demands for equality in the market and the rise of neoliberalism, see Nancy Fraser, "Feminism, Capitalism, and the Cunning of History," *New Left Review* 56 (March–April 2009): 97.

107. *President Carter's Social Security Proposals, Hearing: Thursday, July 21, 1977, House of Representatives Subcommittee on Social Security, Committee on Ways and Means*, 566.

108. Don Fraser, "Press Release: Fraser Says Social Security Dependency Plan Based on Misconceptions About Women's Role," 21 July 1977, Box 43: Location 152. K. 9. 14 (F): Folder: Fraser: Equity in Social Security for Individuals and Family Act, 1974–1978—correspondence, press release, papers, Don Fraser Papers.

109. *President Carter's Social Security Proposals, Hearing: Thursday, July 21, 1977, House of Representatives Subcommittee on Social Security, Committee on Ways and Means*, 579–584, 593, 607.

110. Snee and Ross, "Social Security Amendments of 1977," 15; United States Department of Health, Education, and Welfare, *Social Security and the Changing Roles of Men and Women*, 143.

111. Snee and Ross, "Social Security Amendments of 1977," 15.

112. Mark Hannaford, "Statement of Honorable Mark W. Hannaford Before the Subcommittee on Ways and Means," February 5, 1976, Box 704: Folder: Social Security, Abzug Papers.

113. Snee and Ross, "Social Security Amendments of 1977," 7; Margaret Heckler, *H.R.3059–Equity in Social Security Act*, 1977 (http://thomas.loc.gov/cgi-bin/bdquery/D?d095:2:./temp/~bdJeVa).

114. United States Department of Health, Education, and Welfare, *Social Security and the Changing Roles of Men and Women*, 5.

115. Ibid., 72, 118.

116. Nancy M. Gordon, "Statement of Nancy M. Gordon Before the Hearings of the President's Commission on Pension Policy on 'Retirement Income and Coverage of Women and Minorities,'" 30 November 1979, 5, Box 24: Folder: Older Women, Collection: Records of the Office of the Assistant to the President for Women's Affairs, Sarah Weddington, Jimmy Carter Presidential Library; United States Department of Health, Education, and Welfare, *Social Security and the Changing Roles of Men and Women*, 35.

117. No author [AP], "Today's Living: Women Back Pooling of Social Security," *Duluth News Tribune*, 27 June 1979, Folder 87.55, 1979–1980, NOW Records.

118. Cris Candela, "Letter to Mary Rose Oakar from Cris Candela, President, WEAL," 1 August 1979, Folder 168.8, NWPC Records.

119. Margaret Mason, "Memo: To: NOW Board Members, State Coordinators, and Chapter Presidents in States Where Social Security Symposia Are Being Held; From: Margaret Mason, Economic Rights Aide (and Attachments)," 23 October 1979, Folder 48.23, NOW Records.

120. Phyllis Schlafly, "Changing Social Security to Hurt the Homemaker," *The Phyllis Schlafly Report*, June 1979, 1, Folder 87.54, NOW Records.

Chapter 6

1. Jimmy Carter, "Remarks at the Opening Session of the White House Conference on Families," 5 June 1980, Collection: Office of Anne Wexler, Special Assistant to the President, Jane Hartley's Subject Files, Jimmy Carter Presidential Library.

2. Jimmy Carter, "Press Release: Office of the White House Press Secretary: Text of the President's Address to the White House Conference on Families" (Baltimore, Md., June 5, 1980), Box: 235: Folder: Small Business—President's Address to the White House Conference on Families, Collection: Office of Anne Wexler, Special Assistant to the President, Carolyn Landow's White House Conference on Small Business Files, Jimmy Carter Presidential Library.

3. Notes Labeled "Speech—CLS—April 22," no date, Folder 0A9103: Family Policy 1982 (2), Stephen Galebach Files, Ronald Reagan Presidential Library.

4. "A Timeline of the Evolution of Retirement in the United States" (Georgetown University Law Center, Workplace Flexibility, 2010): https://scholarship.law.georgetown.edu/cgi/viewcontent.cgi?referer=https://www.google.com/&httpsredir=1&article=1049&context=legal.

5. Tish Sommers and Laurie Shields, "Gray Paper No. 4: Issues for Action: Older Women and Pensions: Catch 22," no date, p. 13, Box 26: Folder: Issues—Women [1], Collection: First Lady's Office—Projects Office—Cade Subject Files, Jimmy Carter Presidential Library.

6. Jimmy Carter, "Carter-Mondale on the Issues: Remarks by Jimmy Carter on the American Family, Manchester, New Hampshire," 3 August 1976, Box 2: Folder: Briefing Book 4: Part 2, Planning and Organizing the National Advisory Committee, Collection: White House

Conference on Families (39065-A), NARA; J. Brooks Flippen, *Jimmy Carter, the Politics of Family, and the Rise of the Religious Right* (Athens: University of Georgia Press, 2011), 89.

7. Carter, "Remarks by Jimmy Carter on the American Family, Manchester, New Hampshire."

8. Flippen, *Jimmy Carter*, 103.

9. Self, *All in the Family*, 333.

10. Walter Mondale, "Testimony of Walter Mondale," *American Families: Trends and Pressures, 1973, Hearings Before the Subcommittee on Children and Youth of the Committee on Labor and Public Welfare, United States Senate, Ninety-Third Congress, First Session on Examinations on the Influence That Governmental Policies Have on American Families* (Washington, D.C.: U.S. Government Printing Office, 1973), p. 2.

11. A ProQuest Historical Newspapers search of all hits for "Mondale" and "American families" and "hearings" before 1974 turns up a total of nine articles.

12. Sidney Johnson, "Memorandum: To: Joseph A. Califano Jr., Secretary of Health, Education and Welfare; From: Sidney Johnson; Re: White House Conference on Families and HEW Family Initiatives," 26 January 1977, Box 5: Folder: Interdepartmental Communications 8/76–4/77, Collection: White House Conference on Families (39065-A), National Archives and Records Administration, College Park, Md.; Marilyn G. Haft, "Memorandum: To: Margaret Costanza and OPL Staff; From: Marilyn G. Haft; Via: Bob Nastanovich; Re: FYI-White House Conferences and White House Mini-Conferences," 10 May 1977, Box 117: Folder: White House Conference on Family Life, Collection: Office of the Public Liaison: Midge Costanza, Jimmy Carter Presidential Library.

13. Nicholas C. Chriss, "'LADIES, NOT LIBBERS': Antifeminist Rally Attracts 11,000," *Los Angeles Times* (1923–Current File), November 20, 1977, sec. Part I; Marlene Cimons, "Phyllis Schlafly Heads for Houston: Balks at Being Shut Out of Women's Conference," *Los Angeles Times* (1923–Current File), November 11, 1977, sec. Part 4; Ellen Goodman, "The Lessons of Houston," *Boston Globe* (1960–1982), November 25, 1977, 39; Nora Sayre, "Harmony and Dissonance in Houston," *Progressive*, February 1978, 14, Box 103: Location 151.H.4.8 (F): Folder: National Women's Conference, Don Fraser Papers; Marjorie J. Spruill, *Divided We Stand*, 8.

14. "National Plan of Action: Adopted at National Women's Conference" (Houston, Tex., 18 November 1977), Box 103: 151.H.4.8 (F) Folder: National Women's Conference, Don Fraser Papers.

15. Joan Gubbins, "Minority Report: International Women's Year Conference, Houston," November 1977, p. 1, Box 103: 151.H.4.8 (F) Folder: National Women's Conference, Don Fraser Papers.

16. Ibid., 1.

17. Ibid., 3–7 (quote from p. 3); Spruill, *Divided We Stand*, 249.

18. Flippen, *Jimmy Carter*, 149.

19. Spruill, *Divided We Stand*, 251.

20. Gubbins, "Minority Report," 7.

21. "Divorcee Quits Conference on Families," *Sun*, Baltimore, Md., 3 June 1978, A13.

22. Susan Dworkin, "Notes on Carter's Family Policy—How It Got That Way, What Happened to His White House Conference, and Some Warnings for the Future," *Ms.*, September 1978, 63, Box 15: Folder: Family, 1/74–12/78, Collection: Domestic Policy Staff, Ellen Goldstein Subject Files, Jimmy Carter Presidential Library.

23. Dworkin, "Notes on Carter's Family Policy," 63.

24. "Divorcee Quits Conference on Families."

25. Flippen, *Jimmy Carter*, 121–122.

26. Dworkin, "Notes on Carter's Family Policy."

27. Michael Putzel, "Green Sheet Clipping: White House Officials Have Picked a Former Democratic Congressman from Arkansas to Run the Oft-Delayed and Sometimes-Controversial White House Conference on Families," no date, Box 13: Folder: Families—White House Conference on, 9/7/1979, Collection: Domestic Policy Staff, Ellen Goldstein Subject Files, Jimmy Carter Presidential Library.

28. Betty Friedan, "Feminism Takes a New Turn," *New York Times*, 18 November 1979, *New York Times Magazine*.

29. NOW Legal Defense and Education Fund, "National Assembly on the Future of the Family Resource Book," 19 November 1979, p. 16, Folder 341.10, NOW LDEF Records.

30. Ibid.

31. Kathy Bonk, "Press Release: NOW-LDEF Presents: Assembly on Future of Family—November 19," 19 November 1979, Folder 341.4, NOW LDEF Records.

32. "Couples: After Some On-the-Job Training with Wife Betty, Jim Guy Tucker Heads Up the Conference on Families," *People Magazine*, 7 January 1980, Box 26: Folder: Families, White House Conference on, Collection: Presidential Papers—Staff Offices Ethnic Affairs, Aiello, Jimmy Carter Presidential Library.

33. Ibid.

34. No author, "NAC's Process: WHCF Open to All," *Report from the White House Conference on Families*, November 1979, Box 26: Folder: Families, White House Conference on, Collection: Presidential Papers—Staff Offices Ethnic Affairs, Aiello, Jimmy Carter Presidential Library.

35. "Green Sheet Clipping: Alabama Will Bypass the Conference on Families," *New York Times*, 12 February 1980, Box 14: Folder: Families—White House Conference on, 11/2/79–3/9/80, Collection: Domestic Policy Staff, Ellen Goldstein Subject Files, Jimmy Carter Presidential Library.

36. AP, "Alabamians Going to Family Confab," *Tuscaloosa News*, 25 April 1980.

37. Ibid.

38. Gordon Humphrey, "Senator Gordon Humphrey, Dear Concerned Neighbor Letter," no date, Box 13: Folder: Families—White House Conference on, 9/7/1979, Collection: Domestic Policy Staff, Ellen Goldstein Subject Files, Jimmy Carter Presidential Library.

39. Jim Guy Tucker, "Letter to Hon. Gordon Humphrey from Jim Guy Tucker," 30 April 1980, Box 365: Folder: White House Conference on Families, Collection: Office of Congressional Liaison, Jimmy Carter Presidential Library.

40. No author, "NAC's Process: WHCF Open to All."

41. Susan Faludi, *Backlash: The Undeclared War Against American Women* (New York: Random House, 1991), 256.

42. Helen Dewar, "Conference on the Family Is Rallying 'New Right' Activists," *Washington Post*, 18 January 1980, sec. A, Box 18: Folder: Families—White House Conference on Families, Collection: First Lady's Office—Projects Office—Cade Subject Files, Jimmy Carter Presidential Library.

43. Ibid.

44. Ibid.

45. Muriel Fox, "Note and Clippings About WHCF to Stephanie, Celia, Ellen, Barbara, Shula; Cc: Jane Wells-Schooley; From Muriel," no date [c. 1979], Folder 341. 8, NOW LDEF Records.

46. Dixie White (Recorder), "Societal Equality Committee, Meeting, Saturday, December 8, 1979," 8 December 1979, Folder 42.31, NOW Records.

47. Spruill, *Divided We Stand*, 301.

48. No author, "Recommendations by Baltimore Delegates," *White House Conference on Families Newsletter* 1, no. 8 (June 19, 1980).

49. Spruill, *Divided We Stand*, 302.

50. Mike Causey, "Pension Split for the Split," *Washington Post*, 6 May 1977, Folder 55.1, WEAL Records.

51. Ibid.; Patricia Schroeder, "Memo: To Congresswomen's Caucus; From: Pat Schroeder," 16 May 1977, Folder 55.1, WEAL Records. (Quote from Causey article.)

52. Ralph Nader, "How You Lose Money by Being a Woman," *McCall's*, January 1972, Folder 16.3, Catherine East Papers.

53. Ibid.; "Ferraro News: The Retirement Equity Act of 1984, HR 4280," no date [c. 1984], Box 131: Folder: Campaign, Women: Pension Bill, Geraldine Ferraro Papers.

54. Lapkoff and Fierst, *Working Paper: Working Women, Marriage, and Retirement*, 34.

55. BPR Staff Correspondent and the Bureau of National Affairs, "Clipping: Divorce: ABA Conference Discusses Impact of ERISA on Division of Property," *BPR*, no. 48 (18 August 1975), Folder 11.19, Catherine East Papers.

56. Ibid.

57. Jean Snyder, "Private Pension Reform Bill," no date [c. 1973], Folder 48.26: NOW Records.

58. Ibid.

59. Arvonne Fraser, "Women and Women's Rights, Election Year, 1974," 21 May 1974, p. 14, Box 30: Folder: Women, 5/74–11/74, Collection: Records of the 1976 Campaign Committee, Jimmy Carter Presidential Library.

60. James A. Wooten, *The Employee Retirement Income Security Act of 1974: A Political History* (Washington, D.C.: Employee Benefit Research Institute, 2004), 212–215.

61. No author [NWPC], "Pension Reform: A Position Paper Developed by the National Women's Political Caucus," 1974, Folder 167.19, NWPC Records.

62. Ibid.

63. Alan K. Ragan, "Balancing ERISA's Anti-Alienation Provisions Against Garnishment of a Convicted Criminal's Retirement Funds: Unscrambling Approaches to Protecting the Retirement Nest Egg," *University of Baltimore Law Review* 39, no. 1 (Fall 2009); Carin Ann Clauss et al., "United States Court of Appeals for the Ninth Circuit, Brief of the Secretary of Labor, Amicus Curiae, No. 78-2313, Noel Zeona Stone (Plaintiff-Appellee) v. Ward Herbert Stone (Defendant) and Seafarer's International Union, Pacific District–Pacific Maritime Association Pension Plan," 1978, Folder 28.18, Catherine East Papers.

64. Shirley Sandage, "Statement of the Older Women's League on Women's Pension Equity Before the House Select Committee on Aging." 14 June 1983, p. 15, Folder 13-40, Tish Sommers Papers.

65. Lapkoff and Fierst, *Working Paper: Working Women, Marriage, and Retirement.*

66. No author, "National Military Wives Association, Inc. [no Title, but Some Sort of Memo on Their Purpose, Etc.]," no date [c. 1981–1982], Folder 54.30, WEAL Records; Congressional Caucus for Women's Issues, "Former Military Spouse Benefits: A Briefing Paper," April 1988, Box 128: No Folder: (Loose Binder Papers in box), Patricia Schroeder Papers.

67. No author, "Congresswomen's Caucus Meeting with Social Security Commissioner Stanford Ross," 25 July 1979, Box 199: Folder: July 1979 (2), Patricia Schroeder Papers.

68. *President's Commission on Pension Policy: Public Hearing on Retirement Income and Coverage of Women and Minorities* (Washington, D.C., 1979), pp. 32–34.

69. Ibid., 34.

70. Sara Deane, "Testimony Before Employment and Compensation Subcommittee, Post Office and Civil Service Committee, First Hearing, Schroeder-Spellman Bill, April 19, 1977, 9:30 AM," 19 April 1977, p. 1, Folder 55.1, WEAL Records.

71. Ibid., 4.

72. See, for example, "Fact Sheet on H.R. 3951," no date [c. 1977], Folder 46.38, NOW Records; G. William Whitehurst, "Testimony of the Hon. G. William Whitehurst Before the Subcommittee on Military Personnel of the Committee on Armed Services," 26 October 1977, GWW Committee Meeting Files Folder HR 4702, G. William Whitehurst Records, Washington and Lee University Library, Lexington, Va.; Schroeder, "Memo: To Congresswomen's Caucus; From: Pat Schroeder."

73. "Fact Sheet on H.R. 3951."

74. Causey, "Pension Split for the Split."

75. *Hearing on H.R. 2817, H.R. 3677, and H.R. 6270: Legislation Related to Benefits for Former Spouse of a Military Retiree,* Military Compensation Subcommittee of the Committee on Armed Services, House of Representatives, 96th Cong., 2nd Sess., (Washington, D.C.: 28 May 1980), 68.

76. Ibid., 85.

77. Ibid.

78. Patricia Schroeder, "Dear Friend Letter, Re: Former Spouse Legislation in Foreign Service Act of 1980," [no date], from the personal files of Diana Janczewski.

79. "The Family Protection Act: Symbol and Substance," *Heritage Foundation Education Update*, September 1981, Box 4: Folder F003: Family Protection Act of 1982 (3) [Packet (2/2)], Elizabeth Dole Files: Series I: Subject Files, Ronald Reagan Presidential Library.

80. Self, *All in the Family*, 379; Senator Paul D. Laxalt, "Family Protection Act," Pub. L. No. S.1808 (1979)|; Representative George V. Hansen, "Family Protection Act," Pub. L. No. H.R. 311 (1981).

81. Self, *All in the Family*, 379; Laxalt, "Family Protection Act"; Hansen, "Family Protection Act."

82. Hacker, *Divided Welfare State*, 150.

83. Ibid., 153.

84. Donna Batten, ed., "Keogh Plan," in *Gale Encyclopedia of American Law*, 3rd ed., vol. 6 (Detroit: Gale, 2011), 152–153; Hacker, *Divided Welfare State,* 150.

85. "Press Release: Rep. Bertram L. Podell Introduces Housewives' Pension Fund," 10 August 1970, Folder 7.4, Berry Papers.

86. Ibid.; "Bill to Help Housewives Clean Up," *New York Daily News*, 4 December 1971, Box 17: Folder: Marriage and Divorce Committee, 1971 (folder 4), NOW-NYC Papers.

87. Bertram Podell, "Statement of the Honorable Bertram L. Podell, A U.S. Representative in Congress from the 13th Congressional District of the State of New York," in *Economic Problems of Women*, 445.

88. "Bill to Help Housewives Clean Up."

89. Nader, "How You Lose Money by Being a Woman."

90. Betty Berry, "Letter to Catherine East from Betty Berry," 4 January 1975, Folder 19.1, Catherine East Papers.

91. Rachel Liss, "Letter to Chairman Al Ullman from Rachel Liss et al." (Cerritos, California, 21 January 1976), Box 637: Subject File: Women: Social Security—Homemakers—Correspondence, Abzug Papers.

92. Ibid.

93. William Roth, "Retirement Security for Housewives," *Congressional Record, Proceedings and Debates of the 94th Congress, Second Session, Senate*, 8 April 1976, Box 15: Folder: Committee on Women's Pension Issues, CACASW, RG 0220, Entry A1#: 35080-C, NARA.

94. William Roth, "Senate, Wednesday December 3, 1975, Legislative Day of Tuesday, December 2, 1975: Individual Retirement Accounts for Spouses—S. 2732," 3 December 1975, Folder 7.4, Berry Papers.

95. Mildred Jeffrey, "National Women's Political Caucus Statement by Mildred Jeffrey, Chair, National Women's Political Caucus on S. 94—Homemaker Retirement Bill Before Pension Subcommittee of the Senate Finance Committee," 3 April 1979, Folder 167.17, NWPC Records.

96. Helen Benson, "Women and Private Pension Plans," 20 March 1980, pp. 32–33, Carton 8: Folder 90, Wider Opportunities for Women Papers (90-M59), Schlesinger Library.

97. Wendell Anderson, "Dear Colleague Letter from Senator Wendell Anderson," 9 March 1978, Folder: 89.41, NOW Records.

98. Julian E. Zelizer, *Taxing America: Wilbur D. Mills, Congress, and the State, 1945–1975* (New York: Cambridge University Press, 1998), 351.

99. President's Commission on Pension Policy, *Meeting of the Commission*, 3 May 1980, pp. 54–55, Box 4, President's Commission on Pension Policy (39043-A), NARA.

100. Ibid., 55.

101. President's Commission on Pension Policy, *An Interim Report: President's Commission on Pension Policy* (Washington, D.C.: President's Commission on Pension Policy, 1980), 32–37.

Chapter 7

1. Center for American Women and Politics, "The Gender Gap: Voting Choices in Presidential Election" (Eagleton Institute of Politics, Rutgers University, New Brunswick, N.J., 2012), http://www.cawp.rutgers.edu/fast_facts/voters/documents/GGPresVote.pdf.

2. Maryann Barakso, *Governing NOW: Grassroots Activism in the National Organization for Women* (Ithaca, N.Y.: Cornell University Press, 2004), 76; Jane Perlez, "Plan to Omit Rights Amendment from Platform Brings Objections," *New York Times*, 17 May 1984 (http://www.nytimes.com/1984/05/17/us/plan-to-omit-rights-amendment-from-platform-brings-objections.html).

3. For examples of works that suggest the Reagan administration served as the end of the era of possibility for the Second Wave feminist agenda, see Self, *All in the Family*; Natasha Zaretsky, *No Direction Home: The American Family and the Fear of National Decline, 1968–1980* (Chapel Hill: University of North Carolina Press, 2007); Sara Evans, *Tidal Wave: How Women Changed America at Century's End* (New York: Free Press, 2003); Christine Stansell, *The Feminist Promise: 1792 to the Present* (New York: Modern Library, 2010); and Levenstein, "'Don't Agonize, Organize!'" 114. A notable exception to the narrative of feminist retreat in the 1980s is Katherine Turk's *Equality on Trial*, which shows that comparable worth campaigns continued to thrive in the courts in the early part of the decade (*Equality on Trial: Gender and Rights in the Modern American Workplace* [Philadelphia: University of Pennsylvania Press, 2016], 104–105). In addition, Marisa Chappell's 2012 article, "Reagan's 'Gender

Gap' Strategy and the Limitation of Free-Market Feminism," *Journal of Policy History* 24, no. 1 (2012): 115–134, begins the important work of examining the politics of the gender gap.

4. Barakso, *Governing NOW*, 90.

5. Cowie, *Stayin' Alive*, 303–307.

6. Barakso, *Governing NOW*, 73–77.

7. Soule and Olzak, "When Do Movements Matter?," 476. The two states to formally rescind their ratifications of the ERA during the Carter presidency were Idaho and Kentucky. Nebraska and Tennessee had already rescinded their ratifications in 1973 and 1974.

8. Davis, *Moving the Mountain*, 193–194; Shields, *Displaced Homemakers*, 121.

9. Barakso, *Governing NOW*, 76.

10. Ibid., 77.

11. Nelson H. Cruikshank, "Memorandum for Members of the Senior Staff from Nelson H. Cruikshank and Attached Talking Points Concerning Improvements in Social Security in the Carter Administration," 17 August 1979, Box 69: Folder: Welfare Reform, Collection: Office of Anne Wexler, Special Assistant to the President: Anne Wexler's Subject Files, Jimmy Carter Presidential Library.

12. Sarah Weddington, "The Record of President Jimmy Carter on Women's Issues," October 1979, Box 26: Folder: Issues—Women [1], Collection: First Lady's Office—Projects Office—Cade Subject Files, Jimmy Carter Presidential Library.

13. Self, *All in the Family*, 359.

14. Flippen, *Jimmy Carter*, 283.

15. Self, *All in the Family*, 320.

16. John B. Anderson, "Speech: Justice for American Women," no date [c. 1980], pp. 2, 4, Folder 26.12, Catherine East Papers.

17. Ibid., 5.

18. Catherine East, "Memo: To: Cliff Brown; From: Catherine East; Re: Resignation," 29 September 1980, Folder 25.14, Catherine East Papers.

19. Ibid.

20. "Equal Opportunity for Women Through a New Era of Leadership and Economic Growth," no date [c. 1980], p. 4, Box 23: Folder F014: Women—Issues—1981 (6), Elizabeth Dole Files: Series I: Subject Files, Ronald Reagan Presidential Library.

21. Ibid., 4–5.

22. "Official Minutes: Women's Policy Board Meeting," 18 September 1980, p. 9, Box 23: Folder F014: Women—Issues—1981 (8), Elizabeth Dole Files: Series IV: Women's Issues, Ronald Reagan Presidential Library; Catherine E. Rymph, *Republican Women: Feminism and Conservatism from Suffrage Through the Rise of the New Right* (Chapel Hill: University of North Carolina Press, 2006), 229; "Report of the Family Policy Advisory Board," 20 November 1980, Box 23: Folder F014: Women—Issues—1981 (5), Elizabeth Dole Files: Series IV: Women's Issues, Ronald Reagan Presidential Library.

23. Mitra Toosi, "A Century of Change: The U.S. Labor Force, 1950–2050," *Monthly Labor Review*, May 2002, 18 (http://www.bls.gov/opub/mlr/2002/05/art2full.pdf).

24. Ann Fairbanks, "The Social Security System and Women," 26 October 1980, 1–2, Box 23: Folder F014: Women—Issues—1981 (6), Elizabeth Dole Files: Series IV: Women's Issues, Ronald Reagan Presidential Library.

25. Ibid., 4.

26. "Report of the Family Policy Advisory Board," 1.

27. Mary Frances Berry, *Why ERA Failed: Politics, Women's Rights, and the Amending Process of the Constitution* (Bloomington: Indiana University Press, 1986), 70.

28. Patricia A. Seith, "Congressional Power to Effect Sex Equality," *Harvard Journal of Law and Gender* 36, no. 1 (Winter 2013): 17; Irwin N. Gertzog, *Women and Power on Capitol Hill: Reconstructing the Congressional Women's Caucus* (Boulder, Colo.: Lynne Rienner, 2004), 7.

29. Seith, "Congressional Power to Effect Sex Equality," 36.

30. Ibid., 4–5.

31. Ibid., 78–79.

32. Marsha L. and Judy A., "Memo: To: LDEF Staff; From: Marsha L. and Judy A.; Re: Establishment of Family Law Project," 20 December 1983, Folder 125.3, NOW LDEF Records.

33. Ibid.

34. "Family Law Proposal," no date, Folder 125.3, NOW LDEF Records.

35. Chappell, "Reagan's 'Gender Gap' Strategy and the Limitations of Free-Market Feminism," 115.

36. Ibid., 129.

37. Ronald H. Hinckley, "Memorandum for Ed Harper and Emily Rock; From: Ronald H. Hinckley; Subject: 'Gender Gap'; Date: November 5, 1982," 5 November 1982, p. 5, Box 28: Folder F014: Women—Gender Gap [1 of 2], Elizabeth Dole Files: Series IV: Women's Issues, Ronald Reagan Presidential Library.

38. Ibid., 6.

39. Ibid.

40. Richard S. Beal, "Memo: Supplement to Strategic Evaluation Memorandum #10; To: Edwin Meese, James Baker, Michael Deaver, Elizabeth Dole; From: Richard S. Beal; Subject: Women Constituency Support," 6 May 1982, p. 3, Box 38: Folder OA 9461: Women's Issues (5), Edwin Meese Files, Ronald Reagan Presidential Library.

41. Hinckley, "Memorandum for Ed Harper and Emily Rock," 6.

42. Ibid., 8.

43. Char Mollinson, "WEAL Fund May 1981, Dear Friend Letter," May 1981, Folder 26.34, WEAL Records.

44. Ibid.

45. Ann Smith, "Congresswomen's Caucus Memo: To: Members; From: Ann Smith; Re: Survey of Current," 20 July 1981, Box 190: Folder: No Folder, Loose Paper, University of Colorado Boulder, Patricia Schroeder Papers; "Social Security Fund Transfer Adopted by Conferees; Minimum Benefit Restored," *Wall Street Journal*, 15 December 1981, sec. 1.

46. "The Reagan Administration's Social Security Proposals: A Bleak Picture for Women," no date, p. 1, Folder 55.40, WEAL Records.

47. "WEAL Facts: Social Security Is a Women's Issue," no date, p. 2, Folder 96.40, NOW Records; "The Reagan Administration's Social Security Proposals: A Bleak Picture for Women," 3.

48. "Executive Summary: Report on Earnings Sharing Implementation Study," no date, Folder 96.40, NOW Records; "Notes and Brief Reports: Long-Range Projection of Average Benefits Under OASDI," *Social Security Bulletin* 45, no. 1 (January 1982): 19.

49. "Citizens' Council on Earnings Sharing Agenda, January 30, 1984 and Attachments," 30 January 1984, Folder 18-1, Tish Sommers Papers.

50. Ibid.; NWPC, "National Women's Political Caucus: Convention 1983, Resolutions Approved, July 10, 1983," July 10, 1983, Folder 70.16: Resolutions, 1982–1983, NWPC Records;

Maxine Forman, "Letter to the Editor, Wall Street Journal, From Maxine Forman, Directory, Policy Analysis, WEAL," 26 January 1984, Folder 18-1, Tish Sommers Papers.

51. "Draft: Specific Actions Suggested to Build Support for the Reagan Administration Among Women Voters," no date, 3, Box 25: Folder F014: Women's Issues—July–August, 1982 (9): Elizabeth Dole Files: Series IV: Women's Issues, Ronald Reagan Presidential Library; Mary Jean Collins, "Testimony of Mary Jean Collins: Social Security Inequities Hearing of September 22, 1983, U.S. House of Representatives, Special Committee on Aging," 22 September 1983, p. 90, Folder 96.30, NOW Records.

52. Judith Finn, "Statement by Judith Finn: Hearing on the Equal Rights Amendment and Social Security, Committee on the Judiciary, U.S. Senate," 20 March 1984, p. 6, Folder 191.32, NOW Records.

53. Ibid., 9.

54. Ronald Reagan, "Address Before Joint Session of the Congress on the State of the Union," 25 January 1983 (http://www.presidency.ucsb.edu/ws/?pid=41698).

55. John A. Svahn and Mary Ross, "Social Security Amendments of 1983: Legislative History and Summary of Provisions," *Social Security Bulletin* 46, no. 7 (July 1983): 3.

56. William French Smith, "Memorandum to the Members of the Cabinet Council on Legal Policy from William French Smith, Attorney General," 7 September 1983, Box 62: Folder: Women's Issues—Legal Equity (2), Michael Deaver Files: Series IV: Subject Files, Ronald Reagan Presidential Library.

57. Tish Sommers and Arthur Flemming, "Draft Letter by Tish Sommers and Arthur Flemming, Re: Earnings Sharing, Date Stamped, July 21, 1983," 21 July 1983, Folder 17-52, Tish Sommers Papers.

58. Ibid.

59. "Draft: Older Women's League—Philosophy of Earnings Sharing," 10 May 1983, Folder 16-22, Tish Sommers Papers.

60. Citizens' Council on Earnings Sharing, "General Principles," 22 September 1983, Folder 18-1, Tish Sommers Papers.

61. Maxine Forman [contact], "WEAL Press Release: Social Security Shortcoming Are Real, Not Just 'Perceived,'" 21 February 1985, Folder 17-54, Tish Sommers Papers.

62. WEAL, "Earnings Sharing: Equity and Adequacy for Women Under Social Security," no date [c. 1985], p. 4, Folder 78.25, WEAL Records.

63. Mary Rose Oakar, "Mary Rose Oakar Press Release: HHS Earnings Sharing Report a Disappointment," 21 February 1985, Folder 17-54, Tish Sommers Papers.

64. Arvonne Fraser, "Why Earnings Sharing?" 9 January 1985, Folder 14-65, Tish Sommers Papers.

65. Seith, "Congressional Power to Effect Sex Equality," 79.

66. Chappell, "Reagan's 'Gender Gap' Strategy and the Limitations of Free-Market Feminism," 129.

67. Judith Avner and Anne E. Simon, "NOW LDEF: Technical Assistance Memorandum: The Retroactive Application of the U.S. Supreme Court Decision in McCarty v. McCarty," 1981, p. 2, Box 33: Folder McCarty Materials—NOW LDEF, National Center on Women and Family Law Records, 1977–1996 (96-M105), Schlesinger Library.

68. McCarty v. McCarty, 453 U.S. 210 (Supreme Court, 1981).

69. Avner and Simon, "NOW LDEF: Technical Assistance Memorandum: The Retroactive Application of the U.S. Supreme Court Decision in McCarty v. McCarty," p. 2.

70. Brief of NOW LDEF et al. Amicus Curiae, p. 12, McCarty v. McCarty, 453 U.S. 210 (1981); Brief of Certain Members of Congress (John L. Burton et al.) Amicus Curiae, p. 53, McCarty v. McCarty, 453 U.S. 210 (1981).

71. McCarty v. McCarty, 453 U.S. 210 (Supreme Court, 1981). The *McCarty* decision was very similar to the decision the Supreme Court had made two years earlier in *Hisquierdo v. Hisquierdo* (439 U.S. 572, Supreme Court, 1979), a case that raised the same question as *McCarty* but for Railroad Retirement Benefits.

72. McCarty v. McCarty, 453 U.S. 210, 234 (Supreme Court, 1981).

73. No author, "A Look at Our Past," *Ex-P.O.S.E. Newsletter*, July/August 1986, from personal files of Diana Janczewski.

74. "National Military Wives Association, Inc. [no Title, Memo on Their Purpose, Etc.]," no date [c. 1981–1982], Folder 54.30, WEAL Records.

75. Fay Zeman, "A Profile of the Divorced Military Family (Second Edition): This Is a Compilation of Facts Done by a Professional Statistician. I Believe You Will Find It Interesting and Useful. It Is Well Done," March 1982, p. 2, Box 129: Folder: Linda, Patricia Schroeder Papers.

76. Ibid., 3–4.

77. Ibid.

78. Self, *All in the Family*, 110.

79. "National Military Wives Association, Inc. [no Title], 2–4."

80. Patricia Schroeder, "Extension of Remarks, Rep. Patricia Schroeder, Colorado, May 23, 1984: National Military Spouse Day," 23 May 1983, Box 127: National Military Spouse Day!, Patricia Schroeder Papers.

81. "National Military Wives Association, Inc. [no Title]."

82. Myrna L. Olson, Lynne W. Osborne, and Mary Ellen Rose, "Divorce and the Service Wife," February 1981, p. 4, Folder 54.30: Women and the Military. National Military Wives Association [printed] 1981–1982, WEAL Records.

83. Edith Bartley, "Letter to Pat Schroeder from Edith Bartley," no date [c. 1983–1984], Box 124: Folder: Sample TTS resources: Fun Facts to Know and Tell, Patricia Schroeder Papers.

84. "National Military Wives Association, Inc. [no Title]," 8.

85. Mary T. Scully, "To Ex-POSE A National Disgrace—The Beached Service Wife: Promises, Promises from the Military; Finally Some Action on the Hill," *Virginia Country*, no date, p. 2, from personal files of Diana Janczewski.

86. "Dear Fellow Catholic Letter," April 1982, Folder H4092: Military Spouse Background, G. William Whitehurst Records.

87. "Congress Views Pension Sharing for Ex-Wives," *Women and Pensions*, 1982, Folder 125.3, NOW LDEF Records; *Hearing on H.R. 2817, H.R. 3677, and H.R. 6270: Legislation Related to Benefits for Former Spouse of a Military Retiree Before the Military Compensation Subcommittee of the Committee on Armed Services, House of Representatives, Ninety-Sixth Congress, Second Session* (Washington, D.C.: U.S. Government Printing Office, 1980).

88. Patricia Schroeder, "Testimony Before the House Armed Services Subcommittee on Military Compensation," p. 2, Box 124: Folder: Ex-Military Spouses, Articles, Law Reviews, Patricia Schroeder Papers.

89. Lawrence Kudlow, "Memorandum for Martin Anderson; From: Lawrence A. Kudlow; Subject: OMB Comments on the Economic Equity Act (S. 888)," 14 April 1981, Box 23: Folder F014: Women—1981 (4), Elizabeth Dole Files: Series IV: Women's Issues, Ronald Reagan Presidential Library.

90. *Hearing on H.R. 2817, H.R. 3677, and H.R. 6270: Legislation Related to Benefits for Former Spouse of a Military Retiree Before the Military Compensation Subcommittee of the Committee on Armed Services, House of Representatives, Ninety-Sixth Congress, Second Session*, p. 68.

91. "Dear Fellow Catholic Letter," 2.

92. Merlini, "MBA Briefs: Working Woman Award."

93. "WEAL Facts: Benefits for Former Spouses of Retired Military Personnel," no date, Folder 78.35, WEAL Records. The laws also said no more than 50 percent of military retirement pay could be granted to a former spouse.

94. Jill Elaine Hasday, *Family Law Reimagined* (Cambridge, Mass.: Harvard University Press, 2014), 24.

95. Merlini, "MBA Briefs: Working Woman Award."

96. Ann Banks, "Saturday Night at the Officers' Club," *The Single Parent*, March 1980, 15–17, from personal files of Diana Janczewski.

97. Frances Tracy Dobbs, "Memo: To: The Members of Congress; From: Frances Tracy Dobbs; Re: Why Already-Divorced Foreign Service Spouses Are Entitled to Remain on Federal Employees Health Benefits Plan" (McLean, Va., 4 September 1983), pp. 2–3, Box 129: Folder: Ferraro: Subject, Women (5 of 7), Geraldine Ferraro Papers.

98. Patricia Schroeder, "Opening Statement of Rep. Patricia Schroeder, Chairwoman, Civil Service Subcommittee, at Hearings on Foreign Service Act of 1979," 24 July 1979, Box 128: Folder: Schroeder on Former Civil Service Spouses, Patricia Schroeder Papers.

99. Dobbs, "Memo: To: The Members of Congress; From: Frances Tracy Dobbs; Re: Why Already-Divorced Foreign Service Spouses Are Entitled to Remain on Federal Employees Health Benefits Plan."

100. Ibid., p. 1.

101. William Raspberry, "Clipping: A Better Deal for Ex-Spouses," *Washington Post*, 13 July 1983, Box 127: Folder: Civil Service Ex-Spouses, Patricia Schroeder Papers.

102. Linda Ittner, "Memo: To: Sally Narey and Mary Ann Suratt; From: Linda Ittner," 26 May 1983, Box 127: Folder: Civil Service Ex-Spouses, Patricia Schroeder Papers.

103. Gwen [no last name], "Fact Sheet: HR. 2715—Uniformed Services Former Spouses Health Care Act of 1983 [attached to Memo to Maureen]," 22 September 1983, Box 129: Folder: Military Ex-Spouse Medical Benefits, Patricia Schroeder Papers.

104. "WEAL Facts: Benefits for Former Spouses of Retired Military Personnel."

105. Patricia Schroeder, "H.R. 2300: Civil Service Spouse Retirement Equity Act, Introduced by Rep. Pat Schroeder (D. Colo.)," no date, Box 129: Folder: Former Spouse Prints, Civil Service, Patricia Schroeder Papers; "A History of Federal Legislation Relating to Retirement Benefits for Divorced Spouses," no date, Box 127: Folder: Civil Service Ex-Spouses, Patricia Schroeder Papers.

106. Patricia Schroeder, "Statement of Rep. Patricia Schroeder Before the Subcommittee on Legislation of the Permanent Select Committee on Intelligence on H.R. 5805," 12 September 1984, Box 129: Folder: HR 2300/Civil Service Spouses, Patricia Schroeder Papers.

107. Robert K. Dornan, "Prepared Statement of Congressman Robert K. Dornan of California Before the House Armed Services Subcommittee on Military Personnel and Compensation," 4 April 1990, p. 6, Box 128, Folder: 4/4/90, Patricia Schroeder Papers.

108. NOW LDEF et al., "Suggestions Amici Curiae in Support of Motion of Rehearing, Supreme Court of Missouri, Kuchta v. Kuchta (No. 62439) Appeal from the Circuit Court of

Platte County, Honorable John M. Yeaman, Judge," no date, Box 16: Kuchta v. Kuchta, Mo. Pension Case, National Center on Women and Family Law Records.

109. John E. Bardgett, "The Supreme Court of Missouri En Banc, E. Arlene Kuchta, Appellant, vs. Eustis Kuchta, Respondent, Appeal from the Circuit Court of Platte County, Honorable John M. Yeaman, Judge, No. 62439," September 8, 1981, Box 16: Kuchta v. Kuchta, Mo. Pension Case, National Center on Women and Family Law Records.

110. Shirley Sandage, "Statement of the Older Women's League on Women's Pension Equity Before the House Select Committee on Aging," 14 June 1983, Folder 13-40, Tish Sommers Papers.

111. Diana Lozano, "Memorandum for Elizabeth H. Dole; From: Diana Lozano; Subject: Economic Equity Act: Pension Reform [and Attached Materials from PRC]," 11 November 1982, p. 1, Box 25: Folder F014: Women's Issues—October–December, 1982 (10), Elizabeth Dole Files: Series IV: Women's Issues, Ronald Reagan Presidential Library; Congressional Caucus for Women, "Congressional Caucus for Women Fact Sheets," 1.

112. Robert Cepale, "Letter to Jeffrey Horn from Robert Cepale," 30 January 1983, Box 130: Folder: Ferraro: Subject, Women, Pensions (4 of 9), Geraldine Ferraro Papers.

113. Geraldine Ferraro, "Letter to Robert Cepale from Geraldine Ferraro," 13 February 1984, Box 130: Folder: Ferraro, Subject, Women, Pensions (4 of 9), Geraldine Ferraro Papers.

114. Robert Cepale, "Letter to Geraldine Ferraro from Robert Cepale," 30 January 1984, Box 130, Folder: Ferraro: Subject, Women, Pensions (4 of 9), Geraldine Ferraro Papers.

115. Jean Haseltine, "Letter to Geraldine Ferraro from Jean Haseltine" (Laguna Hills, Calif., 7 May 1982), Box 129: Folder: Ferraro: Subject, Women (1 of 7), Geraldine Ferraro Papers.

116. Lozano, "Memorandum for Elizabeth H. Dole; From: Diana Lozano; Subject: Economic Equity Act: Pension Reform [and Attached Materials from PRC]."

117. Michael Uhlmann, "Memo: For: Edwin L. Harper; From: Michael M. Uhlmann; Subject: Status Report on Women's Issues," 17 January 1983, Box 44: Folder: OA9951: Women's Issues (at 132), Edwin Meese Files, Ronald Reagan Presidential Library.

118. "Private Pension Reforms," no date [c. 1983], Box 63: Folder: Women's Issues Meeting 07/13/1983 MKO, Michael Deaver Files: Series IV: Subject Files, Ronald Reagan Presidential Library; Craig L. Fuller et al., "Memorandum for the President; From: Craig L. Fuller; Subject: Review of Administration Efforts on Behalf of Women and Attached Materials from Review," 6 September 1983, Box 62: Folder: Women's Issues—Legal Equity (1), Michael Deaver Files: Series IV: Subject Files, Ronald Reagan Presidential Library.

119. Judith Avner, "Testimony of NOW Legal Defense and Education Fund Before the Senate Finance Committee on the Retirement Equity Act of 1983 (S.19) and the Economic Equity Act of 1983 (S. 888)," 21 June 1983, p. 6, Folder 126.6, NOW LDEF Records.

120. Ferraro, "Press Release on Pass of HR 4280, The Retirement Equity Act of 1984," 9 August 1984, Box 131: Folder: Campaign, Women: Pension Bill, Geraldine Ferraro Papers.

121. Marsha Ackerman, "Press Release: Economic Equity Act Includes Ferraro Pension, IRA Reform Bills," 14 March 1983, Box 76: Folder: Economic Equity Act Fact Sheet, Geraldine Ferraro Papers.

122. Ibid.

123. Elizabeth Dole, "Memorandum for the President; From: Elizabeth H. Dole; Subject: Office of Public Liaison Briefing on the Family Protection Act," 19 October 1981, Box 4: Folder F003: Family Protection Act (1), Elizabeth Dole Files: Series I: Subject Files, Ronald Reagan Presidential Library.

124. Catherine England, "The Economic Equity Act (H.R. 2090-S. 888)," Heritage Foundation Report, 1983, https://www.heritage.org/report/the-economic-equity-act-hr2090-s888.

125. "Summary of Provisions in Economic Equity Act (HR 2090 and S888)," no date, Box 62: Folder: Women's Issues (1), Michael Deaver Files: Series IV: Subject Files, Ronald Reagan Presidential Library.

126. Office of Policy Development, "Decision Memo: Women's Issues—Independent Retirement Accounts: Limit on Spousal Contributions," 18 May 1983, Box 62: Folder: Women's Issues (4), Michael Deaver Files: Series IV: Subject Files, Ronald Reagan Presidential Library.

127. Jack A. Savhn, "Memorandum for the President; From: Jack A Savhn; Subject: The Economic Equity Act of 1983," 24 October 1983, Box 63: Folder: OA 11841: Women's Issues (4), Edwin Meese Files, Ronald Reagan Presidential Library.

128. M. Izat, "Letter to Geraldine Ferraro from M. Izat" (Massena, N.Y., 5 August 1984), Box 131: Folder: Ferraro, Subject: Women, Pensions (7 of 9), Geraldine Ferraro Papers; Joan Hinrichs, "Letter to Geraldine Ferraro from Joan Hinrichs" (Basking Ridge, N.J., 25 July 1984), Box 131: Folder: Ferraro, Subject: Women, Pensions (9 of 9), Geraldine Ferraro Papers.

129. Hinrichs, "Letter to Geraldine Ferraro from Joan Hinrichs."

130. Edwin Meese III, "Memorandum for William Bennet, From Edwin Meese III, Subject: Family Working Group," 4 March 1986, Box Folder 0A16922: Ed Meese / Charter [Family Working Group], Gary Bauer Files, Ronald Reagan Presidential Library.

131. Gary Bauer, "Memorandum for the Domestic Policy Council; From: Gary L. Bauer; Subject: Domestic Policy Council Meeting on the Family Report," 6 June 1988, Box 7: Folder OA18380: Domestic Policy Council (DPC), 06/09/1988: The Family, Nancy Risque, Cabinet Secretary Files, Ronald Reagan Presidential Library; no author, "5/5/88 Document Starting with 'Introduction,'" 5 May 1988, Box 36: Folder: OA18785: 320: Working Group on the Family (1988) (1), Ralph C. Bledsoe Files, 1985–1988, Domestic Policy Council, Series I, Subject File, 1985–1988, Ronald Reagan Presidential Library.

132. In 1996, under President Clinton, Congress finally amended the law to allow couples to contribute equal amounts to an IRA on behalf of a breadwinner and dependent spouse (https://www.irs.gov/pub/irs-prior/p590—1997.pdf). M. Peter McPherson, "Letter to Gary Bauer from M. Peter McPherson, Deputy Secretary of the Treasury," 20 June 1988, Box 6: Folder: OA18785: 320: Working Group on the Family (1988) (6), Ralph C. Bledsoe Files, 1985–1988, Domestic Policy Council, Series I, Subject File, 1985–1988, Ronald Reagan Presidential Library.

133. Morgen, *Into Our Own Hands*, 185.

134. OWL, "OWL: Fact Sheet," no date [c. 1985], Folder 14-41, Tish Sommers Papers.

135. OWL, "Mother's Day Ads," no date, Folder 16-20, Tish Sommers Papers.

136. No author [OWL], "Selected Chronology on Health Insurance Continuation for Spouses," no date [c. 1986], Folder 54.12, WEAL Records.

137. OWL, "Older Women's League: National OWL Agenda," Folder 14-40, Tish Sommers Papers.

138. Leonard, "Draft: Gray Paper on Health Insurance," 18.

139. Alice Kitchen, "News Release [on WEAL Stationary]," 31 March 1983, Folder 11.18, WEAL Records; Alice Kitchen, "Memo: To: Char Mollison, Ex. Director WEAL; From: Alice Kitchen, Missouri WEAL; RE: Missouri Bill Signing Ceremony," no date [c. 1985], Folder 11.20, WEAL Records.

140. Frances Leonard, "Memo: To: Tish and Shirley; From: Fran; Re: Kansas Trip," 9 April 1984, Folder 15-6, Tish Sommers Papers.

141. Kitchen, "News Release [on WEAL Stationary]"; Kitchen, "Memo: To: Char Mollison, Ex. Director WEAL; From: Alice Kitchen, Missouri WEAL; RE: Missouri Bill Signing Ceremony."

142. *Health Benefits: Loss Due to Unemployment, Hearings Before the Committee on Energy and Commerce and the Subcommittee on Health and the Environment, Ninety-Eighth Congress, First Session* (Washington, D.C.: U.S. Government Printing Office, 1983), 15.

143. Ibid., 94.

144. Ibid.

145. Ibid., 128–138.

146. Shields, *Displaced Homemakers*, 47.

147. Seith, "Congressional Power to Effect Sex Equality," 78.

148. Ibid., 77–85.

149. Hacker, *The Road to Nowhere*, 85; Starr, *Remedy and Reaction*, 20.

150. Even ex-military wives found themselves relying on conversion legislation. In 1985 they successfully won for wives who had only been married for fifteen years of military service the ability to purchase "transitional medical care" from the Department of Defense (Congressional Caucus for Women's Issues, "Former Military Spouse Benefits: A Briefing Paper.")

151. Victoria Jaycox [contact] and Alice Quinlan [contact], "Older Women's League Supports Kennedy-Stark Health Initiative Program," 20 June 1985, Folder 15-6, Tish Sommers Papers.

152. Ibid.

153. Seith, "Congressional Power to Effect Sex Equality," 74.

154. "New Health Insurance Law to Benefit Mid Life Women," *WEAL Washington Report*, June–July 1986, Folder 17.54, WEAL Records.

155. Ibid.; Susan Bales [contact], "News Release: Major Legislative Victory for Midlife and Older Women Signed into Law: Budget Reconciliation Allows Widows, Divorced Spouses, Families of Unemployed to Continue Group Health Insurance," 8 April 1986, Folder 54.12, WEAL Records.

156. "Future Efforts in the Area of Insurance Equity," no date, Folder 54.12, WEAL Records; Janet I. Jenson, "OWL Memo To: Attorneys and Others Who Requested Information on Public Law 992-272 (COBRA)—Group Health Insurance Continuation; From: Janet I. Jenson, Attorney, Older Women's League; Re: 'Practice Tips' for Application of the New Federal Law on Group Health Insurance Continuation, Title X of Public Law 99-272 (COBRA)," no date [c. 1986], Folder 53.40, WEAL Records.

157. In her article "Allocating Family Assets at Divorce," feminist law professor Judith Areen, argued just this (Areen, "Allocating Family Assets at Divorce," 25 August 1979, p. 36, Folder 112.5, NOW LDEF Records).

158. In 1975 the Supreme Court heard a challenge to the Social Security system's requirement that a marriage have lasted at least nine months in order for widows and their children to claim benefits brought by the widow and stepchild of a Social Security beneficiary. The court upheld the legitimacy of duration-of-marriage requirements. The court noted that in the case of the nine-month rule, Congress waived the duration-of-marriage requirement in the case of widows who were also the mother of the late husband's children either biologically or through adoption. In the court's mind this exception further legitimized the duration-of-marriage requirements. It wrote, "The common denominator of these disjunctive requirements appears to us to be the assumption of the responsibilities normally associated with marriage" (Weinberger v. Salfi, 422 U.S. 749, Supreme Court, 1975).

Chapter 8

1. Roger Jespen, "Letter to Ronald Reagan from Roger Jepsen," 23 December 1981, Box 9: Folder: Family Protection Act (4 of 5), Moreton Blackwell Files, Series I, Ronald Reagan Presidential Library.

2. "Family Protection Act Q's and A's," no date [c. 1981], Box 9: Folder: Family Protection Act (5 of 5), Moreton Blackwell Files, Series I, Ronald Reagan Presidential Library.

3. Campbell, *Raising the Bar.*

4. Katherine Turk, *Equality on Trial*, 104–105.

5. Roger Jespen, "Letter to Ronald Reagan."

6. Self, *All in the Family*, 379–380; Seith, "Congressional Power to Effect Sex Equality," 40.

7. Self, *All in the Family*; Seith, "Congressional Power to Effect Sex Equality"; Lefkovitz, "The Problem of Marriage in the Era of Women's Liberation"; Marisa Chappell, *War on Welfare.*

8. Seith, "Congressional Power to Effect Sex Equality"; Geraldine Ferraro, "Rep. Geraldine A. Ferraro—One-Minute—Economic Equity Act," 25 January 1983, Box 48: Folder: Ferraro Speeches: January 25, 1983, Economic Equity Act, Geraldine Ferraro Papers; Pat Reuss, "WEAL Informed Memo: To: WEAL INFORMED Subscribers; From: Pat Reuss, WEAL Legislative Director; Re: The 1983 Economic Equity Act, S. 888 and H.R. 2090," 8 April 1983, Folder 56.19, WEAL Records.

9. Ruth Bader Ginsburg and Brenda Feigen-Fasteau, *Sex Bias in the U.S. Code: A Report of the U.S. Commission on Civil Rights* (Washington, D.C.: U.S. Government Printing Office, 1977), 206.

10. "Family Protection Act: Dear to New Right But Unlikely to Get Out of Committees," *Congressional Quarterly, Weekly Report: Health/Education/Welfare*, 3 October 1981, Box 9: Folder: Family Protection Act (5 of 5), Moreton Blackwell Files, Series I, Ronald Reagan Presidential Library.

11. "Family Protection Act Q's and A's."

12. Self, *All in the Family*, 378; Hansen, "Family Protection Act," 1981.

13. "Family Protection Act: Dear to New Right But Unlikely to Get Out of Committees."

14. Wendy Borcherdt, "Memo: To Elizabeth Dole, Diana Lozanao, Mary Elizabeth Quint; From: Wendy Borcherdt; Subject: Speech by Kathy Wilson to the Federally Employed Women [and Attached Speech]," 14 August 1982, Box 23: Folder F014: Women's Issues—July–August, 1982 (4), Elizabeth Dole Files: Series IV: Women's Issues, Ronald Reagan Presidential Library.

15. Margalit Fox, "Kathy Wilson, 54, Women's Rights Advocate Dies," 9 September 2005, *New York Times*, C15.

16. NWPC, "National Women's Political Caucus Resolutions, Passed July 12, 1981, Albuquerque, New Mexico, at the Fifth Biennial Convention," 12 July 1981, Folder 70.15, NWPC Records.

17. "Minutes of Coordinating Council on Women," 16 December 1982, Box 26: Folder F014 [Women] Coordinating Council on Women, 1982 [9 of 10], Elizabeth Dole Files: Series IV: Women's Issues, Ronald Reagan Presidential Library; Borcherdt, "Memo: To Elizabeth Dole, Diana Lozanao, Mary Elizabeth Quint; From: Wendy Borcherdt; Subject: Speech by Kathy Wilson to the Federally Employed Women [and Attached Speech]."

18. Irwin N. Gertzog, *Women and Power on Capitol Hill: Reconstructing the Congressional Women's Caucus* (Boulder, Colo.: Lynne Rienner, 2004), 30.

19. Olympia J. Snowe, "Letter to Elizabeth Dole from Representative Olympia Snowe," 21 December 1982, Box 2x: Folder F014, Women's Issues, 1983 (6), Elizabeth Dole Files: Series IV: Women's Issues, Ronald Reagan Presidential Library.

20. "Family Protection Act: Dear to New Right But Unlikely to Get Out of Committees"; Elizabeth Dole, "Memorandum for the President; From: Elizabeth H. Dole; Subject: Office of Public Liaison Briefing on the Family Protection Act," 19 October 1981, Box 4: Folder F003: Family Protection Act (1), Elizabeth Dole Files: Series I: Subject Files, Ronald Reagan Presidential Library; Jespen, "Letter to Ronald Reagan from Roger Jepsen."

21. "Briefing Book Beginning with Cover Note: 'Info in This Notebook Appears to Be Background Material to Cabinet Meeting of May 24, 1983,'" 1 August 1983, Box 62: Folder: Women's Issues (2), Michael Deaver Files: Series IV: Subject Files, Ronald Reagan Presidential Library.

22. Seith, "Congressional Power to Effect Sex Equality," 72.

23. Office of Policy Development, "Decision Memo: Women's Issues—Independent Retirement Accounts: Limit on Spousal Contributions," 18 May 1983, Box 62: Folder: Women's Issues (4), Michael Deaver Files: Series IV: Subject Files, Ronald Reagan Presidential Library.

24. "Briefing Book Beginning with Cover Note: 'Info in This Notebook Appears to Be Background Material to Cabinet Meeting of May 24, 1983'"; Jack A. Savhn, "Memorandum for the President; From: Jack A. Savhn; Subject: The Economic Equity Act of 1983," 24 October 1983, Box 63: Folder: OA 11841, Women's Issues (4), Edwin Meese Files, Ronald Reagan Presidential Library.

25. Lawrence A. Kudlow, "Memorandum for Martin Anderson; From: Lawrence A. Kudlow; Subject: OMB Comments on the Economic Equity Act (S. 888)," 14 April 1981, p. 1, Box 23: Folder F014: Women—1981 (4), Elizabeth Dole Files: Series IV: Women's Issues, Ronald Reagan Presidential Library.

26. Michael Uhlmann, "Memorandum for Edwin L. Harper; From: Michael M. Uhlmann; Subject: Economic Equity Act (For Women) Reference # 07251PD," 21 June 1982, Box 29: Folder F014: Women's Strategy: Jan–June 1982 [2 of 6], Elizabeth Dole Files: Series IV: Women's Issues, Ronald Reagan Presidential Library.

27. For examples of these kinds of arguments, see Jacob S. Hacker, *Winner-Take-All Politics: How Washington Made the Rich Richer—and Turned Its Back on the Middle Class* (New York: Simon and Schuster, 2010), 187; Self, *All in the Family*, 369, 378; Chappell, *War on Welfare*, 201–202.

28. Borcherdt, "Memo: To Elizabeth Dole, Diana Lozanao, Mary Elizabeth Quint; From: Wendy Borcherdt; Subject: Speech by Kathy Wilson to the Federally Employed Women [and Attached Speech]."

29. George C. Edwards, *At the Margins: Presidential Leadership of Congress* (New Haven, Conn.: Yale University Press, 1989), 36, 72.

30. Alice Lake, "Divorcees: The New Poor," *McCall's*, September 1976, p. 3, Folder 1.2, Berry Papers.

31. Seith, "Congressional Power to Effect Sex Equality,"72.

32. Marsha L. and Judy A., "Memo: To: LDEF Staff; From: Marsha L. and Judy A.; Re: Establishment of Family Law Project."

33. Many other state courts across the country soon issued similar rulings. For details, see William M. Howard, "Spouse's Professional Degree or License as Marital Property for Purposes of Alimony, Support, or Property Settlement," 3 A.L.R. 6th 447 (2005).

34. *NOW LDEF Annual Report*, 1982, 11, Folder 348.12, NOW LDEF Records.

35. Virginia G. Watkin, Judith Avner, et al., "Motion for Leave to File Brief Amici Curiae of NOW LDEF, WEAL, NCOWFL, ACLU of National Capital Area, the Organization of Women for Legal Awareness, Inc., and the Pensions Rights Center in District of Columbia Court of Appeals No. 81-1604 Matthew McCree, Appellant v. Leona McCree, Appellee," 22 October 1982, Box 33: Folder: McCree, National Center on Women and Family Law Records (96-M105), Schlesinger Library; Virginia G. Watkin, Judith Avner, et al., "Brief Amici Curiae of NOW LDEF, WEAL, NCOWFL, ACLU of National Capital Area, the Organization of Women for Legal Awareness, Inc., and the Pensions Rights Center in District of Columbia Court of Appeals No. 81-1604 Matthew McCree, Appellant v. Leona McCree, Appellee," 22 October 1982, Box 33: Folder: McCree, National Center on Women and Family Law Records; Edith U. Fierst, "Motion for Leave to File Brief Amici Curiae of the Association of American Foreign Service Women and the Honorable Patricia Schroeder in J. Edgar William v. Loretta Williams (District of Columbia Court of Appeals, No. 82-1257)," no date, Box 129: Folder: Linda, Patricia Schroeder Papers.

36. See, for example, McCree v. McCree, 464 A.2d 922 (District of Columbia Court of Appeals, 1982); Williams v. Williams, 472 A.2d 896 (District of Columbia Court of Appeals, 1983).

37. Stephanie Clohesy, "Letter to Deborah Tuck, Director, the Needmore Fund, from Stephanie J. Clohesy, Executive Director, NOW-LDEF," 31 May 1984, Folder 125.3, NOW LDEF Records.

38. "Proposal for the NOW LDEF Family Law Project," no date [c. 1984], Folder 125.3, NOW LDEF Records.

39. Ibid. The NOW LDEF proposal cited a Lenore Weitzman survey of 44 family court judges and 167 family lawyers in California that found that the majority of judges thought half of all divorcing women in California received alimony in 1977. The majority of lawyers estimated two-thirds. The actual number was 16.7 percent.

40. Ibid.

41. No author [CT State Conference, NOW], "Projects Suggested at the Conference for Marriage and Divorce Task Force," September 1973, Folder 3.8, Spalding Papers.

42. *NOW LDEF Annual Report*, 1979, 2, Folder 348.10, NOW LDEF Records; "Script: National Judicial Education Program Presentation, 'The Economic Consequences of Divorce: Child Support and the Feminization of Poverty,' Panel at NJ Statewide Conference on Child Support Enforcement," 9 May 1982, Folder 309.5, NOW LDEF Records; Lynn Hecht Schafran, "Bias in Support and Custody: Old Stereotypes and New" (California Center for Judicial Education and Research, Family Law Institute, San Diego, Calif., 14 March 1987), Folder 309.6, NOW LDEF Records.

43. Marsha L. and Judy A., "Memo: To: LDEF Staff; From: Marsha L. and Judy A.; Re: Establishment of Family Law Project."

44. *NOW LDEF Annual Report*, 1983–1984, Folder 348.12, NOW LDEF Records.

45. Ibid.: In Re Marriage of Degener, 119 Ill. Ap. 3d 1079 (Appellate Court of Illinois, 2nd District, 1983).

46. *NOW LDEF Annual Report: Changing Lives: Report 2000*, 1985, 3, Folder 348.12, NOW LDEF Records.

47. "NOW Insurance Project: Plan of Action—A Proposal," no date [c. 1982], p. 1, Folder 126.5, NOW LDEF Records.

48. Judy Murphy (contact) and Lillian Ciarrochi (contact), "Press Release: NOW Charges That ERA Opponents Uphold Insurance Interests Over Equal Rights for Women," 14 June 1982, Folder 158.44, NOW Records.

49. Campbell, *Raising the Bar*, 126, 129. This conclusion was upheld again in 1983 when the court ruled on a similar issue in *Norris v. Arizona.*

50. National Organization for Women v. Mutual of Omaha, 531 A.2d 274 (Court of Appeals, District of Columbia, 1987); National Organization for Women et al. v. Metropolitan Life Insurance Company, 131 A.D. 2d 356 (Supreme Court, Appellate Division, First Department, New York, 1987).

51. Kudlow, "Memorandum for Martin Anderson; From: Lawrence A. Kudlow; Subject: OMB Comments on the Economic Equity Act (S. 888)."

52. No author, "Law and the Family: Draft Report for the Family Working Group," 14 August 1986, pp. 6, 8, Box 9: Folder OA 18682: [Status Report on Parental Working Group] (2), Nancy Risque, Cabinet Secretary Files, Ronald Reagan Presidential Library.

53. Dorothy Jonas, "Report from the Chair (Article Appearing in the California Commission on the Status of Women Newsletter)," January 1986, Folder 327.14, NOW Records.

54. Dorothy Jonas, "Memo: To: Members of the NOW Task Force on the Rights of Women in Marriage; Subject: Meeting on June 6, 1987," 8 April 1987, Folder 327.14, NOW Records.

55. Ibid.

56. Ibid.

57. "Members, NOW National Task Force on the Rights of Women in Marriage," c. 1988, Folder 327.9, NOW Records.

58. Weitzman, *Divorce Revolution.*

59. Marygold Melli and Sherwood Zink, "Alternatives to Judicial Child Support Enforcement: A Proposal for a Child Support Tax, Presented at International Society on Family Law," 29 April 1982, Box 19, Folder 2, ULC Main Office Papers.

60. June Miller Weisberger, "The Uniform Marital Property Act: An Outline," 1 February 1983, Folder 28.20, Catherine East Papers.

61. National Conference of Commissioners on Uniform State Laws, "Uniform Marital Property Act," 8 August 1994 (http://www.uniformlaws.org/shared/docs/marital%20property/umpa_final_83.pdf).

62. Ibid.

63. Dorothy Jonas, "Memo: To: Task Force Members and Participants at the June 4–5 Meeting," 8 June 1988, Folder 327.14, NOW Records.

64. Ibid.

65. "Key Child Support Issues in Proposed Family Support Act Regulations" c. 1989, Folder 50.29, WEAL Records.

66. "Sample Letter, Re: Saving Displaced Homemaker Network Funding," no date (c.1983), Folder 51.31, WEAL Records.

67. "Letter to NOW LDEF, Sender Name Redacted" (Princeton, N.J., 20 June 1986), Folder 431.5, NOW LDEF Records.

68. "Letter to NOW LDEF, Sender Name Redacted" (St. Louis, Mo., 21 March 1986), Folder 431.8, NOW LDEF Records.

69. "National Board Meeting Minutes, October 31–November 1, 1987," Folder 6.35, Schlesinger Library, NOW Records.

70. Ibid.

Chapter 9

1. "Saving the Next Generation," *New York Times*, 30 June 1985, Section 4, 22.

2. Ibid.

3. James L. Hymes Jr., *Early Childhood Education: Twenty Years in Review, A Look at 1971–1990* (Washington, D.C.: National Association for the Education of Young Children, 1991), 293.

4. Ibid.; Center for Disease Control and Prevention, National Center for Health Statistics, "Nonmarital Childbearing in the United States, 1940–99," *National Vital Statistics Report* 48, no. 16 (revised) (28 October 2000), https://www.cdc.gov/nchs/data/nvsr/nvsr48/nvs48_16.pdf.

5. Arvonne Fraser, "Where Do We Go from Here? Women and Public Policy [Speech at the Women's National Democratic Club]," 15 June 1987, Box 6: Location 144.A. 17.8 (F): Folder: Alpha, Arvonne S. Fraser, Speeches, 1980–1987, Arvonne Fraser Papers.

6. Betsey Stevenson and Justin Wolfers, "Marriage and Divorce: Changes and Their Driving Forces," *Journal of Economic Perspectives* 21, no. 2 (April 1, 2007): 29.

7. "Labor Force Participation Rate of Mothers by Age of Own Child, March 1976–2012," Current Population Survey, U.S. Bureau of Labor Statistics, 25 January 2015, http://www.dol.gov/wb/stats/LForce_rate_mothers_child_76_12_txt.htm.

8. Diana Pearce, "The More Things Change . . . A Status Report on Displaced Homemakers and Single Parents in the 1980s" (Washington, D.C.: National Displaced Homemakers Network, May 1990), 8.

9. Michele Dauber, *The Sympathetic State: Disaster Relief and the Origins of the American Welfare State* (Chicago: University of Chicago Press, 2013), 13.

10. Ibid., 228.

11. Arvonne Fraser, "Where Do We Go from Here? Women and Public Policy."

12. Friedan, *It Changed My Life*, 409.

13. Susan Ferraro, "The Prime of Pat Schroeder," 1 July 1990, *New York Times Magazine*, Section 6, 12.

14. H.R. 2020—Parental and Disability Leave Act of 1985 (https://www.congress.gov/bill/99th-congress/house-bill/2020).

15. Ibid.

16. Lisa Vogel, *Mothers on the Job: Maternity Policy in the U.S. Workplace* (New Brunswick, N.J.: Rutgers University Press, 1993), 71.

17. Ibid., 2–3; Carol Kleinman, "Court Victory in War on Sex Bias Was Not Without Serious Casualties," *Chicago Tribune*, 22 June 1987.

18. Anya Bernstein, *The Moderation Dilemma: Legislative Coalitions and the Politics of the Family and Medical Leave Act* (Pittsburgh, Pa.: University of Pittsburgh Press, 2001), 44.

19. Patricia Shiu and Stephanie Wildman, "Pregnancy Discrimination and Social Change: Evolving Consciousness About a Worker's Right to Job-Protected, Paid Leave," *Yale Journal of Law and Feminism* 21, no. 6 (2009): 119–159.

20. Vogel, *Mothers on the Job*, 80–83.

21. Shiu and Wildman, "Pregnancy Discrimination and Social Change."

22. Vogel, *Mothers on the Job*, 84.

23. Ibid., 83–84.

24. Ibid., 88; *The Family and Medical Leave Act of 1987: Joint Hearings Before the Subcommittee on Labor-Management Relations and the Subcommittee on Labor Standards of the*

Committee on Education and Labor, House of Representatives, One Hundredth Congress, First Session, Hearings Held in Washington, D.C., February 25 and March 5, 1987 (Washington, D.C.: U.S. Government Printing Office, 1987).

25. *Family and Medical Leave Act of 1987: Joint Hearings.*

26. Ibid.

27. "National Board Meeting Minutes, January 13–15, 1989, Cincinnati, Ohio," January 1989, Folder 6.40, NOW Records.

28. Ibid.

29. Michael Wines, "Bush Vetoes Bill Making Employers Give Family Leave," *New York Times*, 23 September 1992, Section A, 1.

30. Ruth Milkman and Eileen Applebaum, *Unfinished Business: Paid Family Leave in California and the Future of U.S. Work-Family Policy* (Ithaca, N.Y.: Cornell University Press, 2013), 22.

31. Seith, "Congressional Power to Effect Sex Equality," 44.

32. Ibid., 80.

33. Quoted in ibid., 45.

34. NOW, "Resolution Comprehensive Childcare Action Program," 1988, Folder 6.39, NOW Records.

35. Ibid.

36. Hymes, *Early Childhood Education*, 349.

37. Ibid., 349–351; NOW, "Resolution Comprehensive Childcare Action Program."

38. "National Board Meeting, Houston Texas, January 31–31, 1988, Approved Minutes," January 1988, Folder 6.35, NOW Records.

39. Bernstein, *The Moderation Dilemma*, 103.

40. Hymes, *Early Childhood Education*, 352.

41. Quoted in ibid.

42. Ibid., 350.

43. Ibid., 350, 373–374.

44. Ibid., 405.

45. Barbara A. Butrica et al., "The Disappearing Defined Benefit Pension and Its Potential Impact on the Retirement Incomes of Baby Boomers," *Social Security Bulletin* 69, no. 3 (2009), https://www.ssa.gov/policy/docs/ssb/v69n3/v69n3p1.html.

46. United States General Accounting Office, "Report to the Chairman, Committee on Labor and Human Resources, U.S. Senate: Private Health Insurance, Continued Erosion of Coverage Linked to Cost Pressures," 24 July 1997: https://www.gao.gov/archive/1997/he97122.pdf.

47. Pearce, "The More Things Change . . . ," 9.

48. Ibid., 69–70.

49. "Fact Sheet on the Minimum Benefits for All Workers Act of 1987 (S. 1265/H.R. 2508)," no date [c. 1987], p.1, Folder 53.41, WEAL Records.

50. Lisa Loeb [contact], "Press Release: National Women's Organizations Applaud Leadership of Sen. Kennedy and Rep. Waxman in Providing Health Insurance to the Uninsured," 12 May 1989, Folder 53.31, WEAL Records.

51. No author, but seems to have been drafted by OWL for other women's organizations, "March 1, 1989 Draft Letter to Senator Kennedy [Rep. Waxman / Rep. Stark]," 1 March 1989, Folder 52.32: Health Insurance: Basic Health Benefits Act [letters, notes, fact sheets, etc.] 1989, WEAL Records.

52. Ibid.

53. No author, "Three Pages of Notes on Kennedy Bill (Coverage Targets, Concerns, Etc.)," January 1989, Folder 53.31: Health Insurance: Basic Health Benefits Act [letters, notes, fact sheets, etc.] 1989, WEAL Records.

54. Rachel Benson Gold, "Memo: To: Women and Health Insurance Task Force; From: Rachel Benson Gold; Subject: Committee Revision of S. 1265," 18 February 1988, Folder 53.42, WEAL Records; no author, "Revised Summary of the Minimum Health Benefits for All Workers Act," 17 February 1988, Folder 53.41, WEAL Records.

55. Gold, "Memo: To: Women and Health Insurance Task Force; From: Rachel Benson Gold; Subject: Committee Revision of S. 1265."

56. Ibid.

57. *The Family and Medical Leave Act of 1987: Joint Hearings.*

58. Quoted in Hymes, *Early Childhood Education*, 353.

59. Weathers, "Is Liberation Really Good for Women?," 64.

60. Ibid.

61. Michael Kelly, "Settling In: The President's Day; Clinton Cancels Baird Nomination for Justice Dept.," *New York Times*, 22 January 1993; David Johnson, "Clinton's Choice for Justice Dept. Hired Illegal Aliens for Household," *New York Times*, 14 January 1993, Section A, 1; Richard L. Berke, "Judge Withdraws from Clinton List for Justice Post," *New York Times*, 6 February 1993, Section A, 1.

62. Sarah Jane Glynn, "The Family and Medical Leave Act at 20: Still Necessary, Still Not Enough," *Atlantic*, 5 February 2013.

63. Bernstein, *Moderation Dilemma*, 115.

64. "National Organization for Women National Board Meeting Minutes, TN, February 5–7, 1993," 5 February 1993, Folder 6.56, NOW Records.

65. National Organization for Women, "A Guaranteed Adequate Income for All: Merging the Feminist Movement with the Poor Women's Movement (Draft, for Discussion Only)," 30 April 1993, Folder 373.8, NOW Records.

66. Ibid.

67. Starr, *Remedy and Reaction*, 81.

68. Adrianne Appel, "Coalition Urges Abortion Funds in Clinton Plan," *Chicago Tribune*, 17 October 1993.

69. Joan A. Kuriansky and Anne Kasper, "Memo: To: CWH Members; From: Joan A. Kuriansky, Chair, Campaign for Women's Health and Anne Kasper, Coordinator, Campaign for Women's Health; Re: CWH Model Benefit Package for Women," 6 April 1993, Folder 98.7, NWPC Records.

70. Kate Griffin, "Older Women's League Speaks on Health Care," *Chicago Tribune*, 24 April 1994.

71. No author, "Congressional Caucus for Women's Issues: Statement of Principles on Health Care Reform by the Congressional Caucus for Women's Issues," 14 September 1993, Box 195: Folder: Health Care Reform and Women's Health, Patricia Schroeder Papers.

72. "What's at Stake for Women in Healthcare Reform?" attached to memo, "Memo: To: NOW Activists; From: Patricia, Kim, Rosemary, and Karen; Re: NOW's Principles on Health Care Reform (and attachments)," March 1994, Folder 90.18, NOW Records.

73. Chappell, *War on Welfare*, 1.

74. National Organization for Women, "A Guaranteed Adequate Income for All."

75. Ann Clark and Martha Davis, "Roundtable for Advocates and Activists—Challenging the Welfare War on Women," 11 June 1992, Folder 373.8, NOW Records.

76. Ibid., 9.

77. Peter Edelman, "The Worst Thing Bill Clinton Has Done," *Atlantic*, March 1997, 46.

78. No author [NOW], "NOW's Answer to Welfare Reform: Guaranteed Annual Income," no date [1994], Folder 97.27, 1994–1995, NOW Records.

79. No author [NOW], "Welfare Reform Talking Points," 6 January 1994, Folder 97.27, NOW Records.

80. Tom Delay, Jim Talent, and Jan Meyers, "Welfare Busters Dear Colleague Letter," 22 July 1994, Box 187: Folder: Welfare Dear Colleagues, Patricia Schroeder Papers.

81. Gloria Woods, "Welfare Reform: 'Ending Poverty As We Know It,'" March 13, 1994, Folder 97.27, 1994–1995, NOW Records.

82. Chappell, *War on Welfare.*, 245.

83. Gene Falk, *The Temporary Assistance for Needy Families (TANF) Block Grant: A Primer on TANF Financing and Federal Requirements* (Congressional Research Service: 27 January 2014), 19.

84. Michael Wiseman, "Welfare Reform in the United States: A Background Paper," *Housing Policy Debate* 7, no. 4 (1996), 595.

85. Kimberly Freeman, "Jobs with Justice: Welfare Reform As We Know It: First-Hand Accounts from the Frontiers," 1997, Folder 28.4, 1997, Records of 9 to 5, Schlesinger Library.

86. NOW LDEF, "A Women's Rights Perspective on Welfare Reform: A Proposal to the Soros Foundation," c. 1997 (based on fax number), Folder 374.2, NOW Records.

87. Ibid.

88. No author [NOW], "Welfare Reform Talking Points," 6 January 1994, Folder 97.27, NOW Records.

89. NOW LDEF, "A Women's Rights Perspective on Welfare Reform."

90. Starr, *Remedy and Reaction*, 141.

91. Gordon, *Dead on Arrival*, 131; Starr, *Remedy and Reaction*, 141–142.

92. National Organization for Women, "A Guaranteed Adequate Income for All."

Conclusion

1. Elizabeth C. Spalding, Coordinator, National Task Force on Marriage and Divorce, "The Galaxy of Attitudes Towards Women, As Reflected by Certain Laws," p. 1, 24 August 1974, Folder 169.43, NOW Records.

2. Jonathan Oberlander, *The Political Life of Medicare* (Chicago: University of Chicago Press, 2003), 41.

3. Betsey Stevenson and Justin Wolfers, "Marriage and Divorce: Changes and Their Driving Forces," *Journal of Economic Perspectives* 21, no. 2 (April 1, 2007): 29–30; June Carbone and Naomi Cahn, *Marriage Markets: How Inequality Is Remaking the American Family* (Oxford: Oxford University Press, 2014), 16.

4. May, *Homeward Bound*, 6–9, 24, 150–151.

5. "Labor Force Participation Rate of Mothers by Age of Own Child, March 1976–2012," Current Population Survey, U.S. Bureau of Labor Statistics, 25 January 2015 (http://www.dol.gov/wb/stats/LForce_rate_mothers_child_76_12_txt.htm).

6. Heidi I. Hartmann, "Keep the Heart in Social Security, Statement by Heidi Hartman, Ph.D., Chair, National Council of Women's Organizations, Task Force on Women and Social Security, and President and Director, Institute for Women's Policy Research, Before the Forum on Social Security and Elderly Women, The Senate Democratic Task Force on Social Security," 13 September 1999, p. 3, Folder 372.3, NOW Records.

7. Patricia Ireland, "Statement of NOW President Patricia Ireland on Social Security," 3 December 1998, p. 1, Folder 372.3, NOW Records.

8. Susan K. Hoffman, Sharon J. Phillips, and Linda J. Wharton, "Brief Amici Curiae, Women's Law Project, NOW LDEF, Pennsylvania NOW, Senior Citizen Judicare Project, Community Women's Education Project, Supportive Older Women's Network, National Center on Women and Family Law, Inc., National Women's Law Center, Northwest Women's Law Center, Women's Law Center, Connecticut Women's Education and Legal Fund, and Older Women's League, in Support of Appellant in Charles L. Berrington (Appellee) v. Claire L. Berrington (Appellant) (No. 0020 W.D. Appeal Docket, 19992), Supreme Court of Pennsylvania Western District," 1992, Box 20: Folder: Berrington, National Center on Women and Family Law Records (96-M-105), Schlesinger Library.

9. Mark K. Altschuler, "Bright Line and Coverture in Divorce Pension Valuations and Distribution," *American Journal of Family Law* 23, no. 3 (Fall 2009): 117–124.

10. Hoffman, Phillips, and Wharton, "Brief Amici Curiae, . . . in Support of Appellant in Charles L. Berrington (Appellee) v. Claire L. Berrington (Appellant)"; Altschuler, "Bright Line and Coverture," 117.

11. Three state legislatures (North Carolina, Pennsylvania, and Virginia) passed statutes mandating the use of the coverture fraction (Altschuler, "Bright Line and Coverture," 122–123).

12. Lefkovitz, "The Problem of Marriage in the Era of Women's Liberation"; Linda K Kerber, *No Constitutional Right to Be Ladies: Women and the Obligations of Citizenship* (New York: Hill and Wang, 1998), 307; Cott, *Public Vows*, 211–212.

13. Priscilla Yamin, *American Marriage: A Political Institution* (Philadelphia: University of Pennsylvania Press, 2012), 154.

14. I am indebted to Allison Tait for making this point to me.

15. Louise Story, "Many Women at Elite Colleges Set Career Path to Motherhood," *New York Times*, 20 September 2005, Section A, 1.

16. Terry Martin Hekker, "Paradise Lost (Domestic Division)," *New York Times*, 1 January 2006, Section 9, 9.

17. Ibid.

18. The Supreme Court declared that Congress could distinguish between married and divorced women in the case *Mathews v. DeCastro*, in which it upheld a rule that gave Social Security benefits to the wife with a minor or dependent child in her care whenever her husband retired (or became disabled) regardless of her age but did not do the same for divorced women with children in their care (Mathews v. DeCastro, 429 U.S. 181, Supreme Court, United States, 1976).

19. Starr, *Remedy and Reaction*, 225, 287–292.

20. Hartmann, "Keep the Heart in Social Security," 3.

21. Rose M. Kreider and Renee Ellis, "Current Population Reports; Number, Timing, and Duration of Marriages and Divorces: 2009" (United States Census Bureau, May 2011, http://www.census.gov/prod/2011pubs/p70-125.pdf).

22. Kim Parker and Renee Stepler, "As U.S. Marriage Rate Hovers at 50%, Education Gap in Marital Status Widens," PEW Research Center: Fact Tank, 14 September 2017 (http://www.pewresearch.org/fact-tank/2017/09/14/as-u-s-marriage-rate-hovers-at-50-education-gap-in-marital-status-widens/).

23. Catharine A. MacKinnon, *Women's Lives, Men's Laws* (Cambridge, Mass.: Belknap, 2005), 38.

INDEX

Figures are indicated by page numbers followed by "fig."

ACKNOWLEDGMENTS

A decade-long project requires a lot of support. First, I thank my advisors. I had the rare opportunity to study with the woman whose book inspired me to go to graduate school in the first place: Alice Kessler-Harris. Alice's exacting standards and strong beliefs sharpened this project from the first. Ira Katznelson profoundly shaped the questions I asked, the kind of book I wanted to write, and continues to shape the kind of colleague I want to be. Thank you as well to Betsy Blackmar, Eric Foner, Premilla Nadasen, Ariela Dubler, Dirk Hartog, Jennifer Klein, and Beverly Gage, who all provided crucial guidance over the years.

Many scholars generously reviewed and gave feedback on this work. Thank you to Jennifer Brier, Debbie Dinner, Sarah Dubow, Beatrix Hoffman, Jennifer Mittlestadt, Patricia Seith, Serena Mayeri, and Karen Tani. Thank you, too, to the Penn Law Legal History Consortium, the 2013 members of the Hurst Summer Institute in Legal History, members of the Princeton Graduate Colloquium in Gender and Sexuality Studies, and the members of the Columbia Dissertation Support Group. Thank you to my dear graduate school friends, by now truly scholars in their own right, who gave layers upon layers of feedback and support over the years: Carolyn Arena, Anna Danziger-Halperin, Andre Deckrow, Ted Fertik, Emily Hainze, Maria John, Nick Juravich, Jessica Lee, Tim Shenk, and Asheesh Siddique. Once I left the academy, John Kuhn cheered this book project on alongside my professional pursuits; it meant the world to me. Then, he stepped in and gave the whole manuscript the ruthless cut it needed.

This project would not have been possible without funding from the American Council of Learned Societies and the Mellon Foundation, the William Nelson Cromwell Foundation, and the Schlesinger Library at the Radcliffe Institute, as well as research grants from the University of Southern California and Tulane University.

Like all historians, I'm indebted to the archivists who make our job possible. I thank the archivists at every collection in these footnotes from Howard University, to the National Archives, to the University of California, San Diego. Special thanks to all of the librarians at the Schlesinger Library who have created an archive that is a genuinely nice place to visit and to David Hays at the University of Colorado, Boulder, who took me out to lunch every day, made the connections that allowed me to interview Congresswoman Patricia Schroeder, and tracked down the parachute cartoon so it could be published here. Ryan Reft is not an archivist, but, lucky for me, he takes thorough photographs when in the archives. After a chance meeting at the American Historical Associations annual meeting, I came home to find a kind email with photographs he had taken on an archival trip of his own that he believed would be useful to my work. They were!

Some very generous women allowed me to interview them for this project: the women who founded Ex-Partners of Servicemembers for Equality and their lawyers, particularly Diana Janczewki, who sent me a packet of papers she had kept from her time with the organization; Herma Hill Kay; Arvonne Fraser; Barbara Dudley; and Congresswoman Pat Schroeder.

Traveling to archives across the country was only possible because so many people opened up their homes to me, providing beds and excellent company. For this I thank the entire Stern family in New Orleans, Deborah Hertz and Martin Bunzl in San Diego, Maggie Macdonald in Boulder, Eugene Garver in Austin, Nora Toiv in Washington, D.C., Rebecca Livengood in Cambridge and Philadelphia, Noah Dobin-Bernstein and Gabriella Villanueva in Chicago, Toby Miroff and Stephen Iino as well as Robin Swartout and Andrew Beaty in New York, and, of course, Richard Kazis and Jill Medvedow in Brookline, who gave me a home for an entire semester and much more.

I am so lucky to have had Robert Lockhart and Margot Canaday in this manuscript's corner from before I even finished graduate school. Having committed, kind, and smart editors who reached out early in this project's life and stuck with it has made all the difference in its actually becoming a book. In the four years since I finished grad school and got a job outside the academy this has been a demanding side project, one I easily could have walked away from if I had not had their unwavering support. Kathryn Krug provided an exceptional copy edit at the very end of this project.

I have been fortunate to find meaningful and intellectually satisfying work after graduate school. My coworkers at 32BJ SEIU and now the Roosevelt Institute have made me a sharper and more empathetic thinker and writer. Their mark, too, is on this book. I also would be remiss if I didn't thank my colleagues on SEIU's 2008 health care campaign—especially Bruce Colburn, I promised I'd acknowledge him here a decade ago. They showed me what a moral commitment to one's work paired with a fierce determination to make change should look like.

Finally, thank you to my family: Paul Kahn, Cathy Iino, Hannah Kahn, Jill Medvedow, Richard Kazis, and Sophie Kazis—a truly unique combination of amazing cheerleaders and exacting thinkers. I finished the dissertation that became this book a month before marrying Noah Kazis, submitted the first draft of this manuscript while in labor with Eliza Kazis, and completed the final round of edits during nap time (thanks, Eliza!). This work on the vulnerabilities created by marriage and caregiving, inevitably, shapes how I approach our family life, but Noah ensures that I never let the risks get so scary that I don't act. My life is so much richer for it.